The Untold Story of China's First Great Victory over the West

Tonio Andrade

PRINCETON UNIVERSITY PRESS
PRINCETON AND OXFORD

Published by Princeton University Press, 41 William Street, Princeton, New Jersey 08540

In the United Kingdom: Princeton University Press, 6 Oxford Street, Woodstock, Oxfordshire OX20 1TW

press.princeton.edu

Jacket art: *The Castle of Batavia, Seen from Kali Besar West*, by Andries Beeckman, 1656–1657, oil on canvas, 108 × 151.5 cm. Courtesy of the Collection Rijksmuseum, Amsterdam

Paperback ISBN 978-0-691-15957-7

Library of Congress Cataloging-in-Publication Data

Andrade, Tonio.
Lost colony : The Untold Story of China's First Great Victory over the West / Tonio Andrade.
p. cm.
Includes bibliographical references and index.
ISBN 978-0-691-14455-9 (hardcover : alk. paper) 1. Taiwan—History—Dutch rule, 1624–1661. 2. Zheng, Chenggong, 1624–1662. 3. History, Modern—17th century. I. Title.
DS799.67.A528 2011
951.24'902—dc22
2011009980

British Library Cataloging-in-Publication Data is available

Subvention graciously provided by Emory University's College of Arts and Sciences and Laney Graduate School

This book has been composed in Ehrhardt MT and Grotesque MT

Printed on acid-free paper. ∞

Printed in the United States of America

10 9 8 7 6 5 4 3 2 1

For Amalia, who loves a good story

Contents

List of Illustrations

Dramatis Personae

Listed in rough order of appearance. Chinese names are given with family name first.

Frederick Coyet—Governor of Taiwan, 1656–1662. Defeated by Koxinga. Treated as scapegoat by colleagues and countrymen.

Koxinga—Aka Zheng Chenggong, The Yanping Prince, Great Rebel-Quelling General, Bearer of the Imperial Surname. Warlord who devoted his adult life to the fight to restore the Ming Dynasty to China. Conqueror of Taiwan.

Zheng Zhilong—Koxinga's father, good-looking pirate who became fabulously wealthy.

Li Dan—Zhilong's wealthy old mentor and a master of Min trade. Possibly gay.

Zou Weilian—Upright Ming official who hated the Dutch and tried to make Zhilong break ties with them. Zhilong ousted him from power.

Hans Putmans—Dutch governor of Taiwan, 1629–1636. Fought for Zhilong and then against him, being defeated in 1633.

THE PIRATES

Li Kuiqi—Pirate leader under Zheng Zhilong who, when Zhilong went legit, went back to sea and led Zhilong's former comrades against him. The Dutch agreed to help Zhilong fight against him.

Zhong Bin—Pirate leader under Li Kuiqi who betrayed his master and helped the Dutch defeat Li Kuiqi on Zhilong's behalf.

Liu Xiang—Pirate chief who nearly defeated Zheng Zhilong.

THE MING EMPERORS

Longwu—Ming pretender-emperor who set up a court in the Land of Min to resist the Manchus. Liked Koxinga very much. Killed by the Qing in 1646.

Yongli—Ming pretender-emperor who ran a court in China's far southwest. Was captured and executed by the Qing in 1662.

Qian Qianyi—Koxinga's teacher and one of most famous poets of late Ming. When the Manchus entered Nanjing in 1645, he defected to them, a decision that haunted him for the rest of his life.

THE ZHENG FAMILY

Zheng Hongkui—Aka The Jianguo Duke. Koxinga's favorite uncle. Discoverer of the Spirit Cannons.

Zheng Lian—Uncle whom Koxinga executed to take over Xiamen.

Zheng Zhiwan—Cousin whom Koxinga executed after the cousin failed to defend Xiamen.

Zheng Tai—Koxinga's half brother. Refused to send rice to provision Koxinga's forces in Taiwan.

Huang Wu—After Koxinga demoted him, Wu defected to the Qing and provided inside information about Koxinga's operations and advice to weaken it.

Su Mao—One of Koxinga's top commanders. Lost a battle in 1656 and Koxinga had him executed. This act prompted Su Mao's cousin to plot with Huang Wu to defect to the Qing.

Yang Ying—Koxinga's chronicler.

Shunzhi—Young Qing emperor of China. Tried to woo Koxinga to his side.

Victorio Riccio—Italian missionary who lived for years under Koxinga's rule in and near Xiamen City. Chosen by Koxinga to lead a delegation to demand tribute from the Spanish Philippines in 1662.

Gan Hui—One of Koxinga's top commanders. Advised Koxinga to press attack against Nanjing in 1659. Captured and executed by the Qing in the disastrous battle that followed.

Zhang Huangyan—Devoted Ming loyalist and eloquent writer. Advised Koxinga during the drive up the Yangtze in 1659. Opposed Koxinga's decision to go to Taiwan.

He Bin—Chinese translator for the Dutch on Taiwan. Fled the colony after a scandal and brought Koxinga a map of Taiwan.

Yang Chaodong—Sychophantic underling of Koxinga. Spoke in favor of the plan to invade Taiwan while the other commanders were against it. Later became prefectural governor of Taiwan.

Ma Xin—Chinese general in command of forces that surrounded the Dutch stronghold Zeelandia Castle.

Thomas Pedel—Overconfident Dutch military commander. Consumed with anger about wounded son, died leading foolish musket attack against Chinese forces.

Chen Ze—Brilliant commander on Koxinga's side. Defeated Thomas Pedel with clever ruse. Defeated Dutch bay attack with clever ruse. Was defeated by Taiwanese aborigines in clever ruse.

Jacob Valentine—Dutch magistrate and second-in-command to Frederick Coyet. Surrendered Fort Provintia on Taiwanese mainland to Koxinga and was taken prisoner.

Philip Meij—Dutch surveyor captured by Koxinga early in the war. Wrote vivid account of captivity.

Antonio Hambroek—Missionary on Taiwan who was executed by Koxinga. Later he became the subject of a famous Dutch play.

Jan van der Laan—Dutch admiral who led a fleet to Taiwan in 1660, when there were rumors that Koxinga would invade. Finding no evidence of an invasion, he left. Coyet hated him. He hated Coyet.

Nicholas Verburg—Governor of Taiwan from 1649–1653 and subsequently member of High Council in Batavia. Coyet hated him. He hated Coyet.

Jacob Cauw—Commander of reinforcement fleet sent to Taiwan in the summer of 1661. Coyet hated him. He hated Coyet.

David Harthouwer—Dutch official who desperately wanted to leave Taiwan. Coyet didn't let him.

Prince of the Middag—Mysterious leader of an aboriginal kingdom in central Taiwan who defeated one of Koxinga's most powerful regiments in the summer of 1661.

Melchior Hurt and Jacob Clewerck—Minor Dutch officials who became unwitting ambassadors, swept up on a long and harrowing tour of southern China.

Geng Jimao—Viceroy of Fujian and one of most important figures in early Qing. Wanted to conclude an alliance with the Dutch.

Li Shuaitai—Governor-General of Fujian Provice. Worked with Geng Jimao to defeat Koxinga, cooperating with the Dutch.

Jacob Casembroot—High official in Taiwan. Feuded with Harthouwer and Coyet.

Hans Radis—German sergeant who defected from Dutch to Koxinga with vital military advice. Liked rice wine.

PREAMBLE

An Execution

Today, fifty-year-old Frederick Coyet was to be executed for treason, a verdict he found deeply unjust. They made him kneel in the dirt in front of the gallows, facing the Batavia River. How easy it would be for a free man to simply sail away. Pay two stuivers and a Chinese water taxi would row you out to the junks and East Indiamen swaying in the Java Sea. Or you could float the other way, along canals as magnificent as those of Amsterdam, except in Holland there were no crocodiles. Cayman Canal, Tiger Canal, Rhinoceros Canal—they were lined with palm trees and flowering tamarinds, whose scent nearly masked the rotten smell of the water, the shit-stench of the nightsoil collectors.

It had been years since he'd been free to explore Batavia, Queen of the East, capital of the Dutch Indies. He'd been imprisoned in his own house, able to appreciate the city's cosmopolitan splendor only through the windows. Outside walked Dutchmen with their rapiers and broad-brimmed hats, Javanese women in sarongs and vests, Malay merchants in turbans, Chinese men in flowing silk robes, whose perfumed hair was so long that newly arrived sailors mistook them for women. Sometimes a Chinese procession took over the streets, with clanging gongs and nasal horns, fitful dancing, and colorful idols that made pious Dutchmen nervous. Even African slaves seemed freer than him, walking about in their puffy pantaloons.[1]

This morning, people were heading to the execution grounds, because Coyet wasn't your usual sort of victim. He was no brawling sailor

Figure 1. A view of Batavia Castle, c. 1656. To the right, in the background, just beyond the horses in procession, can be seen the Hall of Justice, in front of which Coyet's execution took place. Andries Beeckman, c. 1656, oil on canvas, 108 × 151.5 cm. Courtesy of the Collection Rijksmuseum, Amsterdam.

or deserting soldier. He'd once been at the top, one of those privileged few who rode on horseback or in carriages or in palanquins with silk curtains, who, when they deigned to alight, had servants to shade them from the tropical sun. The largest parasols were reserved for the High Councilors of the Indies, who administered the empire from the stone castle that loomed near the gallows (figure 1). Coyet had once been a High Councilor, ex officio, and if he'd continued his rise he might have become Governor-General, ruler of the Dutch Indies, who ran a court so grand it rivaled the courts of European kings.

But he'd been unlucky. His last position was governor of Taiwan, the largest colony in the Dutch Indies and one of its wealthiest. It should have been a stepping stone to further advance, but it had been attacked by the Chinese warlord Koxinga. Coyet did his best to hold out, defending the colony for nine months against steep odds, but eventually he had to surrender, and when he arrived in Batavia, his colleagues didn't even let him make a report. They seized his belongings and stripped away his rank and privileges. His wife was forced to give up her pew and find a less distinguished church. They made him their scapegoat, treating him as though he had surrendered on purpose.

He was no patsy. He resisted at every step. At first he tried appealing to his colleagues' sense of justice, hoping that God, Ruler of All and Knower of Souls, might steer their hearts to clear his name, so he would, as he wrote, "again have the opportunity and pleasure of giving my faithful service for many more years."[2] But God didn't steer their hearts. They behaved badly. They tried to make him move out of his house and then, when he wouldn't, confined him to just one room. They forbade him to send letters home. They tried to keep him from reading the diaries and documents he'd kept so meticulously, even as they used those records to build their case, twisting the truth, portraying everything in the worst way. He wasn't trained as a lawyer like them, but he was stubborn and thorough. He fought on procedural grounds, refusing to sign papers and send affidavits, lodging statements of protest, filing countersuits. He kept the proceedings tied up for years.

They won in the end. Now he had to listen as the crier read out his sentence.[3] As governor of Formosa, the man intoned, Coyet knew beforehand that Koxinga would invade but failed to put the colony's soldiers and citizens into a state of manly preparation. He left forts defenseless, foodless, and with stinking wells. He let Koxinga sail through the sea channels and land his troops. He surrendered one expensive fort without a fight and abandoned the colony's wealthiest city, allowing the pirate to steal its rice and meat and wine. Then he hid like a coward behind the massive walls of Taiwan's main stronghold, Zeelandia Castle, without even trying to drive Koxinga away. Finally, he surrendered that castle before Koxinga even blasted a hole in the walls, letting him take everything: warehouses full of silk and sugar and silver. He could have sent those treasures away, but he didn't. All of which, the crier concluded, caused harm to the Dutch East India Company and to the Holy Church that had been planted on Taiwan, not to mention the men and women Koxinga tortured and beheaded and crucified.

The executioner raised his huge sword. The blow swished above Coyet's head. The penalty for treason was death, but the Council of Justice had decided to show mercy. It was a symbolic execution. Coyet's real punishment was the loss of his fortune and life-imprisonment on an isolated island. A couple weeks later, he was gone.

Authorities in Batavia were relieved, but if they thought banishment would silence him, they were wrong.

THE COYET QUESTION

On his humid island, Coyet kept thinking and writing, while relatives in Europe strove to free him. His younger brother was a famous diplomat, and he managed to persuade William of Orange, regent of the Netherlands, to intervene in the case. Coyet was released, and when he arrived in Amsterdam he immediately published a book called *The Neglected Formosa*, which argued that the loss of Taiwan wasn't his fault but the fault of the men who imprisoned him.[4] He made his case eloquently and methodically. If the High Councilors had sent the ships and troops he'd asked for, if they'd paid for improvements in the fortresses as he'd advised, if they'd devoted less attention to furthering their own careers and more attention to preserving the empire, then Koxinga would have been defeated and Taiwan would still be a Dutch possession.

His book has been widely read, and his derisive descriptions of his superiors are still parroted by historians, but what most strikes scholars today, three hundred and fifty years later, is an assumption he shares with his tormenters: that the Dutch could have defeated Koxinga at all.[5]

Koxinga commanded one of the most powerful armies in Asia, a hundred and fifty thousand troops who had come close to taking over China itself. That army had shrunk by the time he attacked Taiwan, but it still contained an order of magnitude more soldiers than the Dutch had in all the Indies, and he was able to concentrate those forces on Taiwan whereas the Dutch were spread across tens of thousands of miles of ocean, from the Island of Deshima in Japan to the coasts of Africa. At most, Batavia might have mustered an additional two thousand men to help Coyet. Would they really have been able to hold off tens of thousands of battle-hardened Chinese troops? Equally important, Taiwan lay just a hundred miles from Koxinga's base in mainland China, whereas Batavia was two thousand miles away and Amsterdam sixteen thousand miles away. Koxinga would seem to have had an insuperable advantage supplying his troops.

The question isn't an idle one. It's a piece of a bigger puzzle, one that's exercised great minds from Max Weber to Jared Diamond: Why did the countries of western Europe, which lay on the fringes of the Old World and were backward by Asian standards, suddenly surge to global importance starting in the 1500s?

There's relative agreement now about how Europeans surged over the New World. It was guns, germs, and steel.[6] But Moroccans, Ottomans, Gujaratis, Burmese, Malays, Japanese, Chinese, and countless other peoples had guns, germs, and steel, too, so what else lies behind the rise of Europe? What explains the global empires they founded—first the Portuguese and Spanish, then the Dutch and British—empires that expanded not just over the Americas but encircled the entire world?

Historians used to answer this question by saying that Europeans had a superior civilization: they had more advanced political organization, economic structures, science, and technology. But the growth of Asian history over the past decades has challenged this view. Any time someone argues that Europe had an advantage in a given area—say property rights, or per capita income, or labor productivity, or cannon manufacture—along comes an Asian historian pointing out that that claim is false. The case for European exceptionalism has unraveled like a ball of string and is now so tangled that there seems little chance to wind it up again.

Historians whose purview is the entirety of human history—the so-called global historians—have responded by reconceiving the history of the world, coming up with a Revisionist Model of world history.[7] They believe that the most developed societies of Asia were progressing along paths quite similar to western Europe and that the divergence between Europe and Asia came late. It wasn't 1492, when Columbus sailed, or 1497, when da Gama rounded Africa. It wasn't 1600 or 1602, when the English and Dutch East India Companies were founded. It wasn't even 1757, when the Englishman Clive defeated a huge Indian army at the famous Battle of Plassey, inaugurating the British Empire in India. No, the revisionists say, there was relative parity, both economically and technologically, between western Europe and many parts of Asia until the late eighteenth century, when industrialization and its concomitant economic revolutions changed the game.[8]

It's a radical proposition. The traditional narrative portrayed Europe as a beacon of enlightenment in a benighted world. In contrast, the revisionists see the rise of the west as part of a broader pattern of Eurasian development, a deep history of shared innovations in which Asian societies were prime movers.

The Revisionist Model isn't popular with everyone. A group of scholars have attacked the revisionists, frustrated that they're trying to overturn centuries of work by great thinkers from Adam Smith to Fernand Braudel. Some have accused the revisionists of distorting data and twisting logic, believing that they're motivated not by a scholar's love of evidence but by political correctness, an ideological zeal to dethrone the west and denounce Eurocentrism.[9]

The revisionists reply that the old view of world history *is* Eurocentric because it was formed when we knew next to nothing about Asia. They believe new data must be reflected in new theories. Each side buttresses its arguments with pulse-quickening statistics: wage levels of unskilled building workers in Gdansk, per capita grain consumption in seventeenth-century Strasbourg, animal-borne freight-hauling capacity in north India. Yet the debate seems far from resolution.

A key point of disagreement is the question of European colonialism before the industrial age. If the revisionists are right that the Great Divergence occurred around 1800, then how do we explain the preceding three centuries of conquest? Defenders of the old model believe that European colonialism is itself evidence of advancement, but the revisionists retort that European power was more fragile than had been assumed. This was, they say, especially true in Asia, where Europeans controlled few land colonies, and where they were deeply dependent on Asians for capital, protection, and trading opportunities. In addition, the revisionists argue, Europeans could expand into Asian seas only because Asians let them. Europe benefited from a maritime power vacuum. They had the good fortune to sail into a gaping breach.

I myself was a revisionist. My first book examined the birth and growth of the Dutch colony on Taiwan starting in 1624.[10] I argued that the Dutch were able to colonize the island not because of any superior technology or economic organization, but because the governments of China, Japan, and Korea wanted nothing to do with it. I wrote that the situation changed in the 1650s with the rise of Koxinga. His goal was to capture Beijing and restore the Ming Dynasty, but when he found he couldn't, he decided to invade Taiwan instead. In a short chapter on his conquest, I said that he had little trouble defeating the Dutch. I believed that his power was so overwhelming that the Dutch could never have defeated him. Thus I offered strong support for the Revisionist Model, and for the idea that political will, not technological prowess, was the most important factor underlying European expansion.[11]

I believed all of this at the time, and I still believe much of it, but after the book was published, I was asked to write an article on Koxinga's invasion of Taiwan. I agreed, thinking the task would be simple, that I'd just uncover some new sources to fill out the story I'd outlined in my first book. But when I dove into the documents, I found two things that surprised me.

First, the sources were incredibly rich. They were full of vivid characters: Koxinga himself, pale and scarred and handsome, deadly with a samurai sword and a bow and arrow, disconcerting in conversation, with his flitting eyes and pointed teeth and a tendency to yell wildly and chop off heads at a whim. But also the grim and heroic general Gan Hui, the ridiculously overconfident Dutch commander Thomas Pedel, the sycophantic and maudlin Dutchman Jacob Valentine whose tears smudged the ink on his letters, the eloquent and unlucky Chinese freedom fighter Zhang Huangyan, a brave and foolish Chinese farmer, two enterprising African boys, an ostentatious German alcoholic, a resentful Dutch admiral with a speech defect, and of course Coyet himself, meticulous and proud. The documents were full of dialogue and descriptions, drama and intrigue, and there were Chinese sources with a wealth of detail about Koxinga's military, including battle arrays, types of ships, strategies, and the like, sources that are largely unknown in western scholarship.

But the second and most important thing I found is that I had been wrong. Coyet, with his twelve hundred troops, might well have won the war. In a clear challenge to the Revisionist Model I'd believed in, Dutch technology turned out to have areas of decisive superiority. This finding surprised me. It also corroborates one of the most compelling models for understanding the rise of the west, a variant of the old orthodox model of world history called the Military Revolution Theory.

According to the Military Revolution Theory, pre-industrial Europeans did have a key advantage over people in the rest of the world: their warfare. Europeans, the argument goes, fought a lot with each other. Over time, they got better at it. Constant wars created a cauldron of innovation, so Europe developed the most powerful guns, the best-drilled units, the mightiest ships, and the most effective forts in the world.

Both the revisionists and their critics refer to the Military Revolution, but they take different lessons from it. The revisionists admit that Europeans had a slight military edge over other Eurasians but downplay the technological aspects of that edge and deny that it reflects any general European superiority. The counter-revisionists argue that Europeans' military advantage reflects a general lead European societies had vis-à-vis Asians, economically, politically, administratively, scientifically, and technologically.[12]

Making the matter more complex is the fact that military historians themselves debate the extent of Europeans' military advantage, a debate personified in a friendly disagreement between two Brits. On one side is Geoffrey Parker, a careful researcher who has worked in hundreds of archives and libraries around the world. His seminal work on the Military Revolution makes a persuasive and nuanced case for the superiority of European arms on the global stage. Europe's technological and organizational advantages in warfare, he argues, can help explain how Europe came to control thirty-five percent of the world's land before industrialization. On the other side is his friend Jeremy Black, a prodigious scholar who has written more books than he's had birthdays, and who argues that the technological gap between Europe and the rest of the world was small and easily made up. He, too, makes a persuasive case.[13]

The debate has been hard to resolve because we know little about non-European warfare. Historians have focused on European wars, whose study makes up by two or three orders of magnitude the majority of books and articles in the field of military history.

Recently, however, a group of younger scholars has focused on Chinese military history. Their conclusions are shaking the field because they argue convincingly that the Military Revolution began not in Europe but in China.

THE CHINESE MILITARY REVOLUTION

"The founding of the Ming dynasty in 1368," writes historian Sun Laichen, "started the 'military revolution' not only in Chinese but also world history in the early modern period."[14] Sun goes on to argue that "the 'military revolution' in China modernized [China's] military forces and made it a military superpower and the first 'gunpowder' empire in the early modern world."[15] It was the founder of the Ming Dynasty (1368–1644) who inaugurated the revolution. As he levied his cannons against neighbors, those neighbors quickly copied them. Gunpowder states emerged on China's borders, expanding at the expense of neighbors farther away.[16] The new technologies exploded outward from their Chinese epicenter, with global historical consequences. Other historians have corroborated Sun's findings.[17]

It's a striking change of perspective. We have to keep in mind that the standard model for understanding the rise of the west emerged when many westerners believed that gunpowder was independently invented in Europe.[18] Indeed, until the 1970s, historians in the west believed that the gun itself was a European invention and that China, although it invented gunpowder, didn't think to put it into metal tubes and use it to hurl projectiles.[19] Now we know that the first true guns emerged in China as early as the mid-1100s.[20] They became a mainstay of Chinese armies in the violent wars that preceded the establishment of the Ming Dynasty in 1368.

The members of the Chinese Military Revolution School admit that European guns became superior to Chinese guns after 1500 and that Chinese copied the new designs. Yet whereas counter-revisionists argue that China's adoption of European guns is evidence of Europe's relative modernization, the Chinese Military Revolution School takes the opposite lesson. Chinese, they argue, were able to adopt European guns so rapidly because the Military Revolution had begun in China. Historian Kenneth Swope writes, "When Europeans brought their arms to Asia, they did not introduce the technology, but rather they supplemented and expanded the options already available to war-makers."[21]

The Ming had always taken firearms seriously, establishing a special administrative unit to produce them and train gunners. When Portuguese guns arrived in the sixteenth century, the Ming quickly set up a new bureau to study them. When even more powerful western cannons arrived in the seventeenth century, Ming officials adopted them as well, going so far as to dredge them up from Dutch and English shipwrecks and reverse-engineer them.[22]

Thus, the Military Revolution must be viewed as a Eurasia-wide phenomenon. It began in China and spread through the world, eventually reaching the fractious and warlike states of Europe, who took up the new technologies rapidly and then brought them back, honed through a couple centuries of violent warfare, to be just-as-eagerly taken up in Japan, Korea, and China. This perspective, based on painstaking research, supports the revisionist position: developed parts of Asia were progressing along lines quite similar to those in Europe.

Still, the Chinese Military Revolution historians can't judge the relative efficacy of European versus Chinese arms because they focus on intra-Asian warfare, just as most military historians have focused on intra-European warfare. There are specific claims about European arms that must be examined carefully: Europe's purported advantage in drill, in fortification, and in ship design. To gauge the military balance between Europe and Asia, we must look at wars between Europeans and Asians, something that has, surprisingly, been done very little.

One of the most important wars was the struggle between Koxinga and the Dutch East India Company.

EUROPE'S FIRST WAR WITH CHINA

The Sino-Dutch War, 1661–1668, was Europe's first war with China and the most significant armed conflict between European and Chinese forces before the Opium War two hundred years later.[23] The Opium War, of course, was fought with powerful industrial steamships, and China lost badly. The Sino-Dutch War was fought with the most advanced cannons, muskets, and ships, and the Chinese won.

The revisionists and counter-revisionists refer to this war explicitly, but both take different lessons. Revisionists argue that Koxinga's victory over the Dutch shows the limits of Europeans' coercive power in Asia.[24] The counter-revisionists fire back that Koxinga achieved victory only by adopting European military technology, and so the war actually supports the old model.

Who's right? My full argument will unfold gradually throughout this book, but I'll adumbrate my findings here. It wasn't so much Dutch cannons and muskets that proved superior. As Coyet himself realized, Chinese cannons were just as good as his, a point that Chinese-language scholarship has corroborated. One scholar from Taiwan, for example, notes that an analysis of Koxinga's cannons and their use leaves one "astonished at his army's modernization."[25] Similarly, Dutch musket companies, with their deadly volley fire technique, which was invented in Holland and allowed musketeers to achieve a constant rain of fire, proved useless against Koxinga's troops. In fact, the Chinese had developed volley fire more than two centuries before.[26] Koxinga's soldiers were so well trained, well disciplined, and well led that the Dutch forces usually broke formation and ran.

No, what gave the Dutch their edge were two things: the renaissance fortress and the broadside sailing ship. The renaissance fortress is at the heart of the Military Revolution Model, and the one the Dutch built in Taiwan stymied Koxinga (figure 2). Although he'd conducted scores of sieges in his time, attacking places much larger and with walls much more massive, he simply couldn't find a way on his own to deal with the Dutch fort's capacity for crossfire. It wasn't until he got help from a defector from the Dutch side—the grandiose German alcoholic I mentioned earlier—that he finally managed to overcome it.

The argument about Dutch ships is a bit more involved. Suffice to say that Dutch ships, as the Military Revolution Model predicts, easily overwhelmed Chinese warships in deepwater combat. Chinese sources make this clear, and both Chinese and Dutch descriptions of

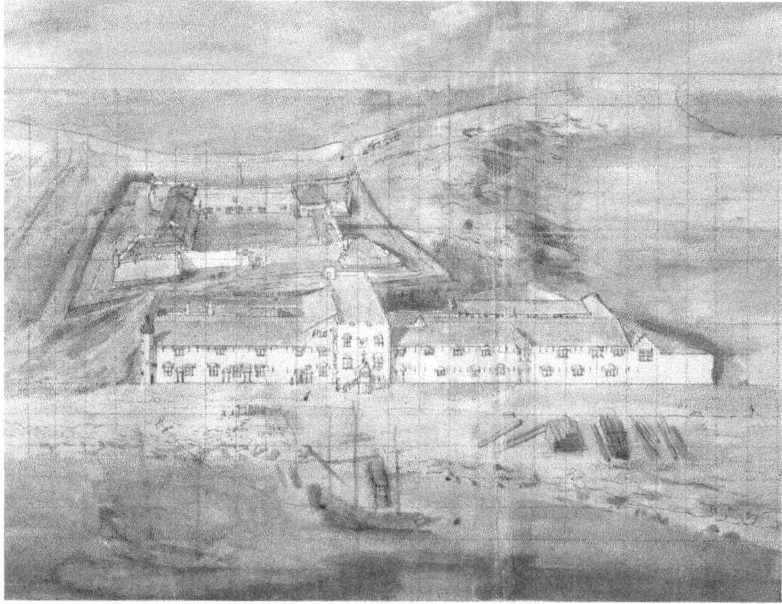

Figure 2. Zeelandia Castle, c. 1635. This drawing shows Zeelandia Castle in an early form. It was a classic square renaissance fortress, with four protruding bastions. Below it are warehouses and residences, the most prominent of which is the Governor's Mansion, which stands in the middle. These structures were later enclosed by more walls, which became known as the Lower Castle, whereas the original fort became known as the Upper Castle. The artist of this image was likely the famous mapmaker Johannes Vingboons, who was working from an original by David de Solemne. Image used by permission of The National Archives of the Netherlands, The Hague, VELH Verzameling Buitenlandse Kaarten Leupe: Eerste Supplement, finding aid number 4.VELH, inventory number 619.118.

sea battles show that Chinese captains had to find unusual ways to counter Dutch naval superiority. But Dutch ships also seem to have had another advantage: a surpassing ability to sail into prevailing winds. This is a venerable argument about European nautical superiority, and some might well dispute it.[27] But as we'll see, the Dutch ability to sail into the wind nearly turned the tide of the war, shocking Koxinga and throwing his officers into panic at a crucial period.

These points and other data from the war corroborate the Military Revolution Model and point us to a middle ground between the revisionists and their critics. The counter-revisionists are correct that the Dutch had a technological advantage over the Chinese in warfare, but the revisionists are right that it was a slight one, easily made up. The weapons Koxinga used were more advanced than those used even a hundred years before, so we must be wary of old narratives that portray Asian societies as stagnant and European societies as dynamic, a portrayal that in any case the huge outpouring of data from Asian history over the past four decades has made clear is false.

In many ways, Asian and European societies were developing along similar lines, toward specialization, commercialization, more effective agricultural techniques, and more deadly arms. But the revisionists should also admit that in certain areas at least, European societies were developing more quickly. Perhaps we have not a sudden Great Divergence occurring around 1800 but rather a small and accelerating divergence beginning in the sixteenth century. In many areas, this small divergence would have been imperceptible or absent. But as the decades passed, the divergence accelerated, and during the period of industrialization—the great take-off—the acceleration became so rapid that it appears in retrospect to be a sudden rupture.

These points about the revisionist debate are important, but this book is more than an extended argument. It's also a narrative history of this important but poorly understood conflict. The Sino-Dutch War is frequently mentioned in historical literature and in textbooks, but there's never been a major study of it in any language that makes use of the many sources—Chinese and European—that are available.[28] Historians will doubtless uncover new documents and find errors and omissions here, but I hope this book will lead to greater understanding of this fascinating episode of global history.

I've certainly found it fascinating to write. One thing that absorbed me as I read the sources is how the weather—the planet—became a major character. Time and time again, the war turned on a storm. Even before the war started, a typhoon destroyed a Dutch fortress on Taiwan and altered the sandy island on which it had been perched so much that the Dutch couldn't even rebuild it. This left Coyet particularly vulnerable to Koxinga's invasion. Another storm drove away the relief fleet that Coyet had managed to summon against the winds, dashing one of its vessels to the ground and, more importantly, taking from Coyet the element of surprise. Tide surges, unexpected currents, freak winds—over and over again nature changed the course of the war. I came to believe that nature was more important than any other factor in the war.

I say "nature," because to me all this is an expression of the stochasticity of a beautiful but indifferent universe. As a botanist friend of mine says, "What do the stars care about some slime mold at the edge of one galaxy?"[29] But of course the Dutch and Chinese saw it differently. Both felt that there was a higher power intervening in earthly affairs. The Dutch called it God, the Chinese called it Heaven, and although their cosmologies and theologies differed, they saw in storms and tides, famines and floods a divine purpose. That each side thought Heaven favored their own people—or should favor their own people—is just the way we're built, it seems.

The fact that I kept finding myself writing about nature comes mostly from the sources—or I believe so anyway—but it resonated with me because I'm trying to make sense of my own time, when climate catastrophe looms, when nature is about to start bucking like never before in our history. It bucked pretty hard in the mid-seventeenth century, too. Right around the time the action in this book takes place, the global climate cooled abruptly. The cooling might not have caused major problems by itself, but it was accompanied by severe climatic instability, just as global warming will be. There were floods and droughts, locusts and famines, riots and rebellions. Bandits raged and governments fell like never before and never since. In fact, if it hadn't been for this seventeenth-century global climate crisis, the Sino-Dutch War might never have happened. Koxinga might have ended up a Confucian scholar, passing examinations and writing poetry. The Dutch might have kept Taiwan for generations longer.

So did Koxinga win because he just happened to be better favored by the weather? No. Although luck played a role, Koxinga won because of leadership. His troops were better trained, better disciplined, and most important, better led than the Dutch. Bolstered by a rich military tradition, a Chinese "way of war," Koxinga and his generals outfought Dutch commanders at every turn. There's still an idea, prevalent in both the west and China, that the Chinese were a people for whom war was considered unimportant. We're learning now how false that idea is. In fact, a historian of China has recently argued that "until 1800 China had a military tradition unequaled by any other polity in the world."[30]

The Sino-Dutch War can thus teach us valuable lessons about military history. It was fought at a time when the technological balance between China and the west was fairly even, a time more similar to today that the periods of other Sino-Western wars—the Opium War, the Boxer Rebellion, the Korean War—all of which were fought across a steep technological gradient. Military historians have posited the existence of a "western way of war," a "peculiar practice of Western warfare . . . that has made Europeans the most deadly soldiers in the history of civilization."[31] But partisans of this sort of argument are generally ignorant of Chinese military tradition. In the Sino-Dutch War, Chinese strategies, tactics, and leadership were superior, and all were tied to a set of operational precepts drawn from China's deep history, a history that is as full of wars as Europe's own. The Chinese sources I read are woven through with strands of wisdom from classics like *The Art of War* and *The Romance of the Three Kingdoms.* Indeed, Chinese historians have argued that Koxinga's victory over the Dutch was due to his mastery of this traditional military wisdom.[32]

I often feel in my scholarship like I'm walking a tightrope, trying to balance between Eurocentrism and an overly Asiacentric counterposition, between revisionism and the standard model. When I feel I'm starting to teeter, waving my arms to stay balanced, I find it's best to dive into the sources. European documents make clear how the Dutch were outfoxed by Chinese commanders. Chinese sources admit freely that the "red-haired barbarians" had weapons and ships superior to their own. Both sides were deeply aware that nature—Almighty God or the Will of Heaven—was the supreme determinant of human affairs.

So let's go back to the early seventeenth century, before the war started, when Coyet's predecessors were laying the foundations of the Dutch Empire in the Indies. What they found when they tried to establish a presence in the rich China trade is that they needed help from Chinese citizens. One of the citizens they met was Koxinga's father, a pirate named Zheng Zhilong. Zhilong helped the Dutch make their new colony of Taiwan into "one of the most beautiful pearls in the crown" of the Dutch empire.[33] The Dutch helped Zhilong become the most powerful pirate in the world, a position he used to become fabulously wealthy, drawing an income larger than that of the Dutch East India Company itself. Since much of his wealth and power eventually passed to his son, it's no exaggeration to say that the company helped create the man who would defeat it.

ONE

Destinies Entwined

The first glimpse we get of Koxinga's father, Zheng Zhilong, is as a young boy, and, characteristically, he's misbehaving. The story goes that he and his brothers were running wild in the streets of their hometown, Quanzhou City, where their father worked for the prefectural governor as a minor functionary. It must have been May or June, when the lychees ripen, their watery white flesh sweet and floral-tinged. The boys saw a cluster of the fruit hanging from a branch jutting over a wall and began throwing rocks to knock it down. One stone flew over the wall and hit the governor in the head. The boys ran and were caught and hauled up before the governor, but Zhilong was good looking and charismatic. The governor took one look at him, smiled, and said, "This is the face of one destined for wealth and nobility."[1] He let him go.

The story may not be true, but like the best anecdotes in Chinese history it encapsulates a character. The real Zhilong was like the boy in the story: he ran wild, grasped at hanging fruit, got in trouble, and came out the better for it. His rise was so fast, so spectacular, and so unlikely, that it seemed destiny must be involved.

That destiny was entwined with the Dutch, or at least that's how a Chinese official who hated the Dutch later described it: "Entwined destinies," he would write, "are difficult to break."[2] As we'll see, the bonds proved too strong for this official. He ended up broken himself.

To understand how Zhilong's fate became linked to the Dutch, we have to start with his boyhood home, the Land of Min, a province of China known to westerners as Fujian. It was a land of many mountains and few fields. Poor and isolated, it bred adventurers who sought their fortunes at sea: fishermen, traders, and pirates. "The people of Min," Zhilong's earliest biographer wrote, "fear poverty but not death, so the rich ones make their living by contact with foreigners, while the poor ones make their living by pillage. Zhilong did both."[3]

It's not clear what exactly drove Zhilong to the sea. One source says he slipped a hand under his stepmother's skirt.[4] Other sources don't specify his offense, but just say his father chased him through the streets with a stick and Zhilong jumped on a ship.[5]

There were many ships to choose from. The people of Min were China's greatest seafarers. We're used to hearing about European trading routes, but in the far east, the Min carried more in volume and value than any Europeans—more, indeed, than any other nation. Huge Min junks sailed northward to Japan and southward to Vietnam, Siam, Java, Sumatra, and the Straits of Malacca (figures 3 and 4).[6] Everywhere they went, they built their houses and temples, and many chose to remain abroad. During the era of European colonialism, from 1500 to 1945, there were far more Min living abroad in Asia than there were Europeans. In fact, Min outnumbered Europeans even in European colonies. One of Zhilong's uncles—his mother's brother—lived in the Portuguese colony of Macau, a week's sail to the south. Zhilong went to join him.

Macau was an exotic place, a piece of Portugal on the Chinese coast, with plazas and priests and tolling bells. An immense cathedral dominated the hill in the middle of town, and Japanese artisans were engraving its stone façade, carving out ships, lions, figures in long robes, winged people playing horns. In one panel a woman floats above a many-headed serpent next to a caption that reads, in Chinese, "Holy Mother stomps the dragon head."[7] Zhilong must have found something he liked in this Holy Mother, who resembled the Min goddess Mazu, protector of sailors, because he chose to be baptized. To what extent he remained a Catholic is debatable. Some Portuguese noted years later that he "was so impious, or so ignorant, that he equally burnt incense to Jesus Christ and to his idols."[8] But other sources suggest that he held official masses until the end of his life.[9]

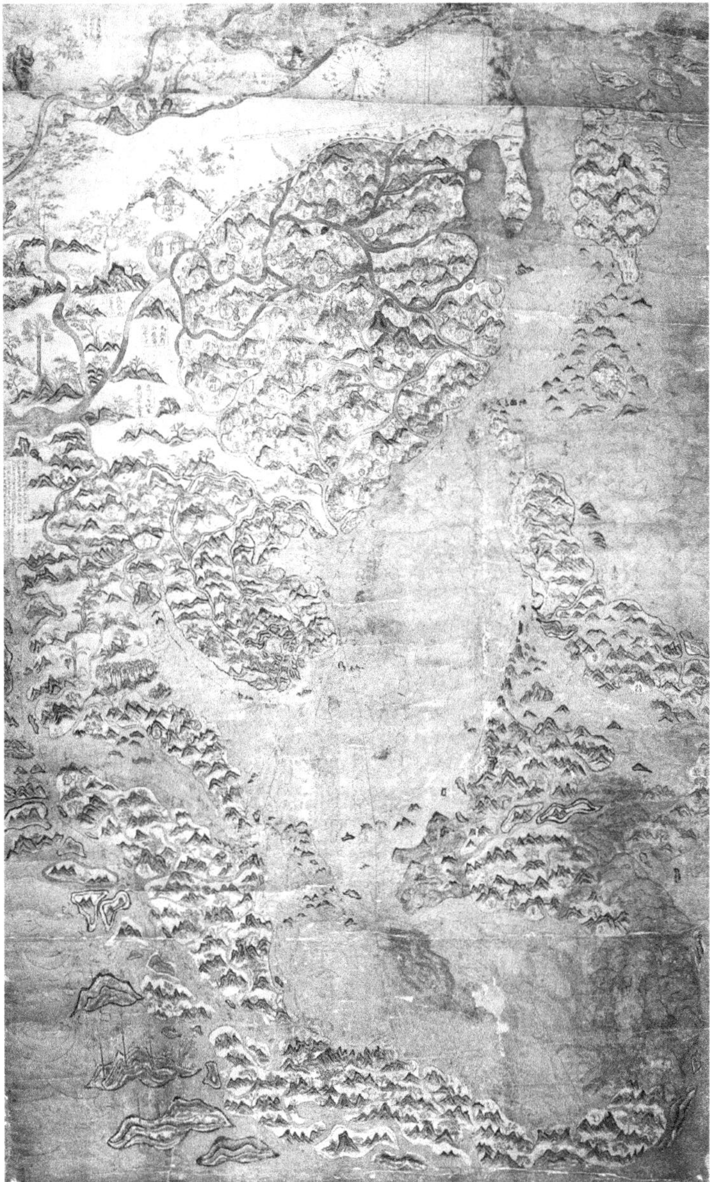

Figure 3. Rare map of Min trade routes, probably dating from the 1620s. This fascinating Chinese map seems to have been produced in Quanzhou City, where Zheng Zhilong lived as a boy. It shows the extensive Min trading routes that stretched out from Quanzhou to Japan, Manila, Vietnam, Siam, and the Indonesian Archipelago, all the way to the Strait of Melaka. Indeed, the map implies that navigators might sometimes have gone beyond Melaka. On the left a panel of text provides directions across the Indian Ocean, to Aden, Oman, and Hormuz. If historians are correct that the map was made in the late 1620s, there's a chance it was created by the Zheng family itself, perhaps under Zhilong's supervision. Used by permission of The Bodleian Libraries, University of Oxford, MS Selden supra 105.

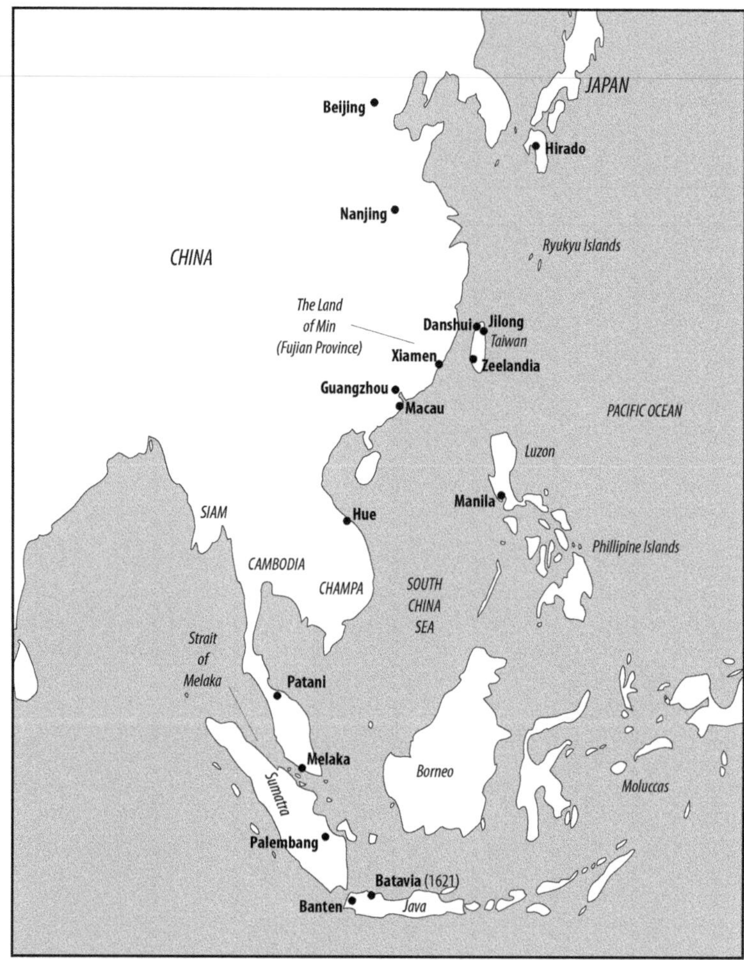

Figure 4. Main Min trading routes, 1600s. This map shows some of the main trading ports of Min mariners, but it's important to note that there are many ports they frequented that are not on this map. The Min found their way even to the most unfrequented backwaters, and they didn't confine themselves to coastal areas. Whenever the Dutch explored new areas they were likely to find that Min people had preceded them there. In fact, the Dutch often cooperated with the Min, who played important roles as guides, mediators, and interpreters.

His uncle asked him to take cargo to Japan, which is how he found himself stepping ashore in Hirado, a small port stuffed with ships from all over: Portuguese, Spanish, English, Dutch, and Chinese.[10] This was before the Japanese were forbidden to sail abroad, before the English left, before the Spanish and Portuguese were expelled, and before the Dutch and Chinese were confined to a small island in Nagasaki.

In Hirado, he caught the eye of a rich old Min man named Li Dan. There may have been a sexual dimension to their relationship. Zhilong's earliest extant biography notes: "As a young man, Zhilong was pleasing to the eye, and Li Dan took him as his male lover."[11] The biographer was a contemporary of Zhilong, but we know little about him and can't judge the truth of his claim. Homosexuality was openly practiced in the Land of Min, particularly among seafarers from Zhilong's region. A later source discusses the practice of "gentlemanly concubinage," noting with disapproval that many gentleman kept handsome servant boys, a custom called "contracting a little brother." "Even sons and younger brothers of good families," the author writes, "were seduced by bandits, who lured them into losing their virginity. Prosperous families made their living by selling on the seas, and they weren't willing to submit their own sons to such dangers, so they chose to contract little brothers of ability and send them out to dangerous places. In this way they reaped the rewards while others bore the risks. The poor could use this practice to get rich."[12] Was Zhilong serving as Li Dan's contractual little brother, using the connection to make his fortune?

If so, he wasn't exclusive. He also met and married a Japanese woman named Tagawa Matsu.[13] The fruit of their union was Koxinga, but Zhilong didn't wait to meet him. He left his pregnant wife and followed Li Dan to a meeting with the Dutch.

Li Dan had close ties to Europeans. He'd been friends with the English until they discovered he'd been embezzling from them. Now the Dutch needed help, as Zhilong found when he and his mentor joined them in the windswept Penghu Islands, a rocky archipelago that crouches low in the middle of the Taiwan Straits (figure 5), eighty miles from the Chinese coast and thirty miles from Taiwan. The Dutch had built a fortress there, on a deep bay near a Chinese temple, working Chinese prisoners to death in the hot sun, and they hoped to use it as a base to penetrate the China trade. Yet thousands of Ming troops had massed near the construction site. There'd already been skirmishes, but the Chinese commander didn't want to make the red-haired barbarians too desperate, so he agreed to let Li Dan and his handsome protégé mediate.[14]

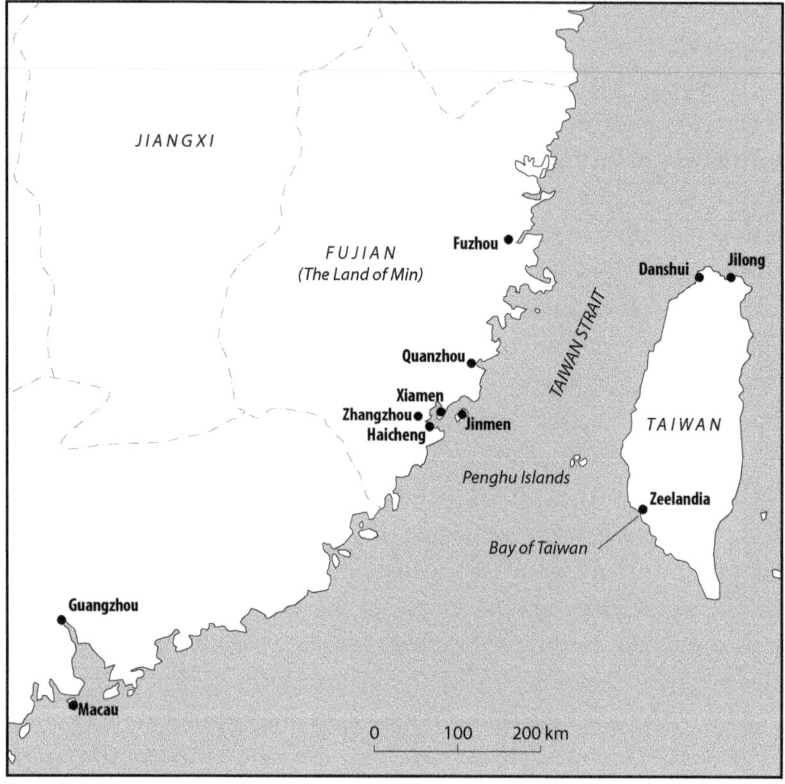

Figure 5. Taiwan Straits.

They persuaded the Dutch to leave. Since the Chinese government didn't claim Taiwan, the Dutch dismantled their fortress, sailed to Taiwan, and, on a long, narrow tongue of land just off the southern shore, constructed a new fortress, which they called Zeelandia Castle (figure 6).

The Dutch needed translators, so they offered Zhilong a job, talking with him in Portuguese. He lived with them for a time, witnessing the beginnings of their colony: how they built their first warehouses below the fort, not far from a Min village; how they founded another settlement just across the bay, on the Taiwanese mainland; how they encouraged Min settlers to take up residence near that settlement; how they contended with the headhunters who lived just inland in fortified villages; how they competed with wary Japanese traders.

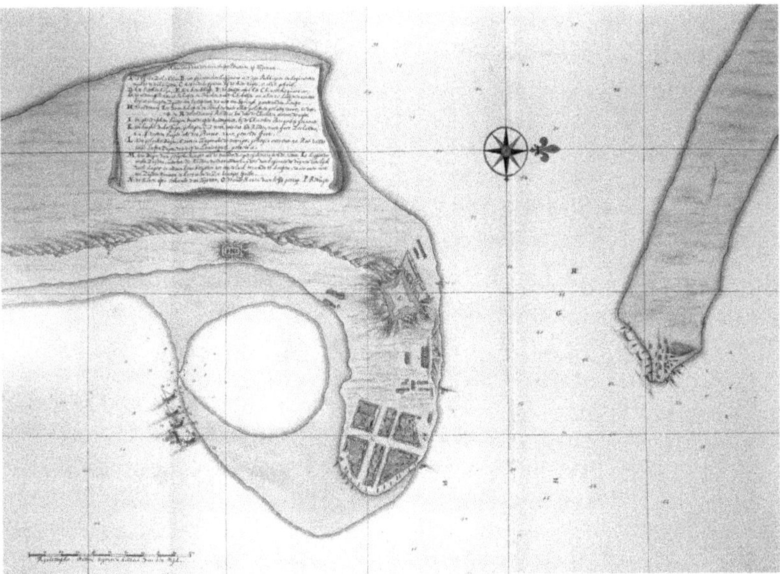

Figure 6. Early map of Zeelandia Castle and City, c. 1635. Zeelandia Castle, labeled here with a sideways A, was built to command the main entrance into the Bay of Taiwan. Ships entered from the west, i.e., from the top of this map. Zeelandia City, which lies below the castle, was originally a small trading settlement frequented by Min and Japanese mariners. The Dutch encouraged immigration, even inviting Min pirates to settle there. To the right, or north, is Baxemboy Island, which lies on the other side of the Channel, at the tip of which is a fishing village, marked with an I. Used by permission of the Austrian National Library, Vienna, Austria, Atlas Blau van der Hem, VOL XLI, sheet 2, 2.

He was especially interested in how they dealt with the Min pirates who used Taiwan as a base. They didn't drive them away or capture them as slaves but invited them to live in the town near Zeelandia Castle and employed them as privateers, encouraging them to attack vessels sailing to Macau or Manila.[15]

To profit from pirates wasn't a stretch, because the Dutch were pirates too. In fact, the United Netherlands, a new country, owed its existence in part to the Sea Beggars, privateers who fought for independence from Spain. In 1602, the Dutch government founded the United East India Company not just to make money but to attack the Spanish and Portuguese. The government allowed the company to levy troops to fight under the red, white, and blue flag (the red used to be orange, in honor of the House of Orange) and to arm itself with the superb muskets and cannons that formed a major part of the Dutch economy.[16] The government lent it ships and cannons and even gave it the right to declare war and make peace in the name of the fatherland. The booty seized in its raids was counted as profit.[17]

So the Dutch were merely following their charter when they made deals with Min pirates, who proved willing partners. Even Li Dan himself asked to pillage under the orange white and blue, although his request was denied because at that point the Dutch were trying not to alienate officials in China.[18] Shortly after Li Dan died in 1625, however, they began handing out flags liberally. Their handsome translator wanted in on the action. He quit his job and turned to piracy.[19]

Zhilong had probably been a pirate all along. In fact, some Chinese sources say he was a founding member of a Taiwan-based pirate band. Its members had originally met in Japan and taken an oath of loyalty before Heaven: "Though we were born on different days, let us die together."[20] It's possible that Zhilong served as the pirates' inside man, reporting on Dutch activities. It's not far-fetched. Around this time, another Chinese translator was secretly working with pirates, and the Dutch only found out later.[21]

The Dutch weren't upset that Zhilong quit his translator job. On the contrary, they encouraged him in his new career, and when he ran into trouble, they helped him out. In early 1626, his ship limped to the anchorage with a broken mast and a leaking hull. He was allowed to sail past the cannons and dock for repairs while Dutch officials counted out their share of the booty. "We received for our half," wrote the Dutch governor, "as we had agreed with him, about nine-hundred sixty pieces of eight."[22] This was good money—perhaps on the order of a hundred and fifty thousand U.S. dollars today—but it was nothing compared to what they received on another occasion, when Zhilong delivered nine captured junks and their cargos, a windfall whose total value was more than twenty thousand Chinese taels.[23] That would be worth on the order of five million dollars.

The Dutch felt that Zhilong had been a mediocre translator, but he proved a great pirate.[24] By 1627, he was leading four hundred junks and tens of thousands of men.[25] They ravaged the Chinese coast, capturing merchants' ships, raiding cities, even defeating Ming forces.

Chinese officials got nervous. The Governor-General of the provinces of Guangdong and Guangxi, south of the Land of Min, wrote to Beijing:

> This pirate Zhilong is extraordinarily cunning, practiced in the art of sea warfare. His followers are . . . more than thirty thousand in total. His cannons are made by foreign barbarians, and his warships are huge and tall and meticulously made. When they enter the water they never sink, and when they encounter a reef they never breach. His cannons are so accurate and powerful that they can strike at a distance of ten li and immediately annihilate anything they strike.[26]

In contrast, the official wrote, the government's own ships were few, small, and brittle, and their cannons were too rusty to hold Zhilong off.

What especially worried them was his connection to the Dutch: "Zheng Zhilong's power is based on barbarian ships and barbarian cannons."[27] Some even found evidence that he was employing Europeans and Japanese.[28]

Of course, they knew that his success wasn't just due to Dutch help. He was a canny tactician, who frequently outfoxed them. On one occasion he disguised his men as local militia forces to sneak around behind governmental troops and won a decisive victory.[29] Another time he used a decoy squadron to lure a Ming fleet into an ambush, destroying or capturing most of the Chinese vessels.[30]

He was also adept at public relations, so although his livelihood was based on plunder and protection payments, he culvitated an image as a seaborne Robin Hood, taking from the rich and giving to the poor.[31] His following surged, and there's evidence that he tried to prevent his men from pillaging the countryside. "By keeping his men from raping and robbing and burning and looting," wrote a Chinese minister of military affairs, "he made for himself the reputation of a person of benevolence and righteousness, so more and more joined him each day."[32] Recruits were also driven to him by famine in China. One Chinese source suggests that many thousands joined him in one ten-day period alone because they were fleeing starvation.[33]

Most shocking was the rapidity of his rise. As one official wrote, "When Zhilong started raising his men, he had just a few dozen ships, and at that time the relevant authorities didn't think anything of it, but soon he had more than a hundred ships, and then, less than a year after that, seven hundred, and today there are a thousand. How can so many of our people be so willing to join a bandit like this? . . . They flow to him like water."[34]

Ming officials began to realize they couldn't counter his power, so they considered other options. It was an ancient practice for the government to recruit virtuous rebels. The theory was that a good emperor and righteous officials could turn rebels to the side of the good. Usually it was used as a last resort, when a dynasty was weak.

Letters arrived in Beijing suggesting this course. A commander in Zhilong's hometown of Quanzhou wrote, "Zhilong's power is great, but he doesn't pursue his Chinese enemies, doesn't kill, doesn't burn, and doesn't loot. It seems he has a desire to show penitence. Annihilating him would be hard, and we've suffered severe military setbacks, but it's still possible to turn him to our side. Why don't we send someone with an edict of recruitment, so that he can expiate his crime by meritorious service?"[35] Zhilong encouraged these letters, or at least that's what people working in the central government thought: "Zhilong always had the idea of recruitment firmly in mind, and the local gentry who suffered from the pirates were writing scads of memorials about summoning and appeasing him, writing on his behalf to ask for recruitment."[36]

By this point Beijing had few alternatives. Its navy was useless. The coast was in tumult. There was famine in the Land of Min, and more and more locals joined the pirates. "There was no way," a Chinese official mused, "that this situation wouldn't end in recruitment."[37]

ZHILONG GOES LEGIT

So early in the year 1628, Zhilong kowtowed to Ming officials and received an official rank and title. He promised to atone for his crimes through service to the emperor.

His power abruptly waned. His followers needed money and there was no more plunder. He gave some of them land or bureaucratic posts, but most went back to sea. One of his subordinates became their leader. His name was Li Kuiqi, and soon he was as powerful as Zhilong had been, with thousands of men and four hundred junks.[38] He invaded Zhilong's coastal base and forced him and his family to flee.

Zhilong turned to the Dutch for help. Taiwan had a new governor named Hans Putmans. He was similar to Zhilong—a man of action who'd been born breathing salt air. He hailed from Middelburg, a North Sea port dark with rain and Calvinism, and had a talent for rising quickly through the ranks and outliving wives. He was on his second wife when he became governor of Taiwan in 1629 and started on his third halfway through his term. Putmans was worried about his colony. He needed more Chinese merchants to come there, more junks, more silk, more porcelain. Zhilong told him that if the Dutch could help put down the Chinese pirates, they'd become famous throughout China and officials would grant them trade.[39] He liked the idea of fighting on Zhilong's behalf. "This way," he wrote, "we'll have a true and sure man. No one will serve us better than him."[40]

So in February 1630, Putmans led a fleet to China. He made an alliance with one of Kuiqi's pirate commanders, a man named Zhong Bin.[41] (Zhong Bin was fed up with Kuiqi because the latter had screamed at him: "Stop bothering me or I'll cut off your head!"[42]) While Putmans fired on Kuiqi's fleet, Zhong Bin sailed around behind it. It was a classic pincer attack, beautifully executed by this Sino-Dutch force. "We shot powerfully from in front," wrote Putmans, "while Zhong Bin shot powerfully from behind. Kuiqi's junks weren't able to fire a single shot."[43]

After the victory, Zhilong arranged a celebration. Putmans was invited ashore in Zhilong's base and led to a Chinese temple. The former pirate gave him a gold medal with an engraving of the battle. A Ming official presented him with more medals and gilded roses and silver pieces of eight.

Putmans tried to talk to the official about free trade, but the man abruptly left because Putmans's ally Zhong Bin hadn't shown up to claim his medals. The nervous official had gone to confer with his superiors. Putmans received no guarantees about trade.[44]

Putmans was angry. He demanded that Zhilong live up to his promises and open trade, but Zhilong was in a delicate situation. A new Chinese governor had arrived in the Land of Min. He didn't like Zhilong, didn't like the Dutch, and didn't like the idea of barbarians getting medals in Chinese cities.

THE DRUMS OF WAR

This new governor was Zou Weilian, the man who wrote the lines about entwined destinies being hard to break. He was a different sort of man from Putmans and Zhilong. While Zhilong had been running wild in the streets, Zou had been memorizing Mencius. He passed each step of the civil service examinations, from the local level to the prefectural level to the provincial level and finally the national level. Only three hundred or so men made it that far once every three years from a population of around three hundred million. He was literally one in a million. Afterward he rose from post to post. In 1632, the emperor sent him to Min to do something about the Dutch and the pirates.

Zou felt that to get rid of the pirates you had to get rid of the Dutch. He wasn't alone in this view. A Chinese minister of military affairs, for example, traced the pirate troubles to the Dutch. "Ever since the red-haired barbarians occupied Penghu," he wrote, "rogue Chinese have followed them. All of the major pirates . . . were like this. That's one of the most important reasons for the rise of the pirates.. . . They find help from the red-haired barbarians."[45]

Zou had probably never met a Dutchman, but he knew he didn't like them: "The red-haired barbarians," he wrote, "whose homeland lies forty thousand *li* away from us, where dawn and dusk, night and day, are all the opposite of here, . . . have deep-set eyes and long noses, red hair and scarlet beards, and their character is cruel like bandits. They like to kill their enemies, and all the other barbarians fear them."[46]

He felt that his predecessors had been too soft on the Dutch, too willing to allow them to visit the Land of Min. They'd even allowed the Dutch "chieftain"—that would be Putmans—to ride a chariot inside the walls of a Chinese city. This kind of mixing was dangerous. "I've observed," he wrote, "that since ancient times, when Chinese and barbarians mix together, all kinds of troubles result."[47] To allow the Dutch to keep up such familiarity, he felt, "would be like letting a malignant tumor grow."[48]

Yet Zhilong seemed to be encouraging the Dutch, even though he'd been told to keep them away.[49] Zou surmised that this was because Zhilong had been dependent on the Dutch and was still grateful for their help.

"Entwined destinies," he wrote, "are difficult to break," but he was determined to try, because the current situation was "making the barbarians more and more arrogant and fearless."[50]

He was right about one thing: Putmans was getting belligerent. But what Zou didn't expect—and what Zhilong didn't expect either—is that Putmans was turning against Zhilong.

Few Chinese junks were coming to Taiwan, and whenever the Dutch sailed to China, people avoided them. Putmans didn't understand that Zhilong was facing pressure from Zou Weilian and others. To him, it just seemed like all of Zhilong's promises "disappeared into smoke."[51] As his frustration mounted, he began hating Chinese in general. "It is truly a sad state of affairs," he wrote, "that the wonderful trade of China can be accessed only through such a deceitful, treacherous, untrustworthy, craven, and lying nation as the Chinese."[52]

He developed a plan to defeat Zhilong: "The Chinese pirates," he wrote, "can amply show us how the empire of China can be pressured, because, as Zhilong, Kuiqi, and Zhong Bin have shown, the one pirate barely comes to power before the next overturns him and becomes the chief, gaining such power that the officials of China try all kinds of ways to control them, offering them the position of Admiralty of the Seas. . . . What would prevent us from likewise acquiring a force of Chinese, so long as we let them enjoy part of the booty?"[53]

He calculated that the average income of a Min seaman was only three or four taels per year, and often considerably less.[54] This was about a tenth of what the company paid its own sailors.[55] It would be cheap to build a huge Chinese pirate force.

So in the summer of 1633 he led a fleet to China, cannons clean, muskets oiled, flags waving in the bright sun.[56] He sent letters to the pirates, who began joining him, one or two junks at a time. It would be the first conflagration between the Dutch and the Zheng family.

Pirate War

The fleet Putmans led wouldn't have been possible without Chinese technology. The Chinese invented gunpowder and cannons and guns. They invented the compass. They invented the paper for Putmans's colorful sea charts. These tools had diffused westward, adopted by Europeans centuries after they were discovered in China, which had long been the technological powerhouse of the world. But how would Putmans's ships fare against the much larger fleet of Zheng Zhilong? Were his ships more powerful?

The revisionist school of world history is reticent when it comes to judging Europeans' technological, scientific, or economic prowess vis-à-vis Asians', preferring instead to focus on global parallels. Indeed, it's common in world history classes to learn that Chinese naval technology surpassed or equaled that of Europe, and that history might have been reversed, with the Chinese, not the Europeans, colonizing the world. To make this case, teachers adduce the voyages of the Chinese admiral Zheng He.

There's no doubt that these voyages were monumental. Zheng He's ships dwarfed those that Putmans now led. They were fleets unlike any before or since, floating cities carrying twenty-eight thousand people. There were probably more men on those fleets than lived in London at the time.[1] They reconnoitered Australia. They sailed to India. They sailed to Africa. They stopped in most of the major ports along their way, intimidating the kings and rajas and emirs who saw them. After three decades, the expeditions stopped, primarily because the government decided they were a waste of money. Every world history textbook has a unit on Zheng He, and the lesson is usually the same: China had the technology to rule the seas. It just decided not to.

But of course it's not so simple. According to the Military Revolution Theory, the European broadside sailing ship—a sturdy vessel that mounted rows of cannons facing to the side—provided a decided advantage over Asian warships. Geoffrey Parker, the doyen of the Military Revolution School, presents a nuanced argument, suggesting that although European vessels had the advantage, Asians were able to adapt European technologies for themselves and were sometimes able to counter Europeans on the seas.[2] Others deny that there was much of an advantage at all for Europeans, going so far as to say that European naval superiority over Asians was negligible until the Industrial Revolution.[3] Others argue that technology wasn't a major factor behind European seaborne empires, arguing that it was European states' *willingness* to use naval power in the service of trade that was the most important factor, a willingness that was unusual in world history, and that Europeans' maritime incursions in Asia succeeded because there was little opposition.[4]

Yet all this debate is conducted in a vacuum. Although there's an enormous literature about naval wars within Europe or between European powers, there are few studies of naval warfare between Europeans and non-Europeans in the age of sail, particularly for the period before 1750.[5] This is especially true for European conflicts with the Chinese, who would seem to be the ideal comparison case, having once been a sea power whose navies controlled Asian seas, and a global leader in technology for millennia.

The conflict about to erupt between Hans Putmans and Zheng Zhilong included one of the largest naval encounters between Chinese and European forces before the Opium War two hundred years later, larger even than any of the battles in the war Zhilong's son fought against the Dutch three decades later. The conflict is also described by sources from both sides, Dutch and Chinese. It offers a unique opportunity for us to begin answering the question of European naval power.

World historians are shy about judging Europeans' technological superiority, but seventeenth-century Chinese writers weren't. "Dutch ships are like mountains," one Ming official quipped, "whereas ours are like anthills."[6] Dutch ships, being so tall, were difficult to attack and nearly impossible to board. They also seemed unusually solid. A marvelous Chinese book that the Zheng family itself published notes that "The red-hairs build their ships tall as mountains and sturdy as an iron bucket, so solid that they can't be destroyed. . . . Ultimately, there's no way to stand up to them. With great ease they traverse the oceans without worry of being defeated or damaged."[7] (See figure 7.)

Such solid ships could carry heavy artillery. The official history of the Ming Dynasty, a work completed with great care by official scholars, noted that

> the Dutch base their power on their huge ships and cannons. The ships are three hundred feet long, sixty feet wide, and more than two feet thick. They have five masts, and behind them they have a three-story tower. On the sides are small ports where they place brass cannons. And underneath the masts they have huge twenty-foot-long iron cannons, which, when fired, can blast holes into and destroy stone walls, their thunder resounding for ten miles (several dozen li).[8]

There are many descriptions in Chinese sources about the superiority of Dutch ships, but I'll quote just one more. Zou Weilian, the governor of Fujian who hated the Dutch, noted, in terms quite similar to the description in the *Ming History*, that

> the red-haired barbarians have ships that are five hundred feet long and seventy feet wide. They're called decked-ships because within them they have three layers, all of which have huge cannons facing outwards that can pierce and split stone walls, their thunder sounding for ten miles.... The Hollanders' ability to ravage the seas is based on this technology. Our own ships, when confronting Dutch ships, are smashed into powder.[9]

How did the red-hairs learn to build their fearsome "decked ships"? A Chinese story provided an answer. Once upon a time, the great admiral Zheng He anchored his fleet in Holland. At that time, the poor Dutch, with their hawk noses and cat eyes, had no ships. They asked how his miraculous vessels worked. He didn't answer, knowing that if these barbarians ever got ships, they might cross the seas and ravage China. But the Dutch were persistent, so he got out an old, ruined writing brush and a piece of paper and drew a large oval. In the middle he scrawled three horizontal lines. Then he splayed the brush open, splotched it down several times, and handed them the paper. He thought these scribblings would confound them, but he was wrong. They used the drawing to design their own ships. The three lines became three decks, so their ships ended up being taller and sturdier than Chinese ships, each deck housing huge cannons. The splotches became a spiderweb of rigging to control a dozen sails, whereas Chinese ships had simple lines for simple sails. That's why, according to this story, when Dutch ships arrived in China, they turned out to be many times stronger than Chinese ships.[10]

Of course, the story isn't true. Zheng He never visited Europe, and the Dutch have been sailing since Holland was raised from the sea. Yet the story reveals the extent to which Chinese feared and admired European vessels.

It's important to point out that Chinese observers didn't think the Dutch advantages held for all conditions. "Their huge ships," the *Ming History* notes, "are difficult to turn, and when they encounter shallow sandy areas, they cannot move. And the Dutch people are not good at fighting, so frequently they are defeated in war.[11]

Putmans wouldn't have agreed with that last bit. In fact, he felt that he and his fleet could force the entire Empire of China "to dance to our tune."[12]

What he didn't know was that Zhilong was building a new fleet of his own. Just as Europeans had adapted Chinese technology, so Zhilong was adopting Dutch technology. He'd done so for years by this point, of course. But in the summer of 1633, he was taking it to a new level.

At the core of his new fleet were thirty huge vessels built according to European designs.[13] Each had two reinforced cannon decks and could mount thirty or thirty-six large guns—as many as a Dutch

Figure 7. Picture of western decked ship, 1646. This woodblock print of a western ship is from a strategy manual published by the Zheng family in 1646. The text on the right reads "Frankish Decked Ship." The text on the left calls attention to the complex rigging, which it describes as tangled and resembling a spider's web. Although the ship depicted here is an Iberian vessel, probably Portuguese, the manual's text discusses the Dutch as well, who are described as "more malevolent" than the Iberians. "They are

the terror of the seas. They frequently sail their huge ships into our bays and plunder and pillage. If a merchant ship should encounter [their ships], its crew and capital are as good as lost. They are deeply detestable." From Zheng Dayu, *Jing guo xiong lüe*, "Wu bei kao," juan 18, quote from folio 19v. Used by permission of Harvard Yenching Library.

Figure 8. Sketch of a Chinese warjunk, c. 1637. This rare sketch depicts a Chinese warjunk that Englishman Peter Mundy encountered near Guangzhou in 1637. He noted that although it had two decks of cannon ports, much like a European vessel, it could carry only light ordinance, and he judged the junk itself to be not terribly sturdy. Zheng Zhilong's warjunks—or those that Putmans destroyed in any case—were considerably larger and sturdier, able to mount rows of heavy cannons. Used by permission of The Bodleian Libraries, University of Oxford, MS. Rawlinson A. 315, plate no. 29 (Peter Mundy's Travels).

warship—whereas most Chinese junks held six or eight smaller cannons (figure 8). These new warjunks even had European-style gun ports, with carriages and mounts that included ringbolts and breeching lines so that they could be pulled back and loaded. These were important innovations. If Geoffrey Parker is right, it was the lack of such features that caused the Spanish to lose the Battle of the Spanish Armada in 1588.[14] In any case, Putmans was impressed. "Never before in this land," he would later write, "so far as anyone can remember, has anyone seen a fleet like this, with such beautiful, huge, well-armed junks."[15]

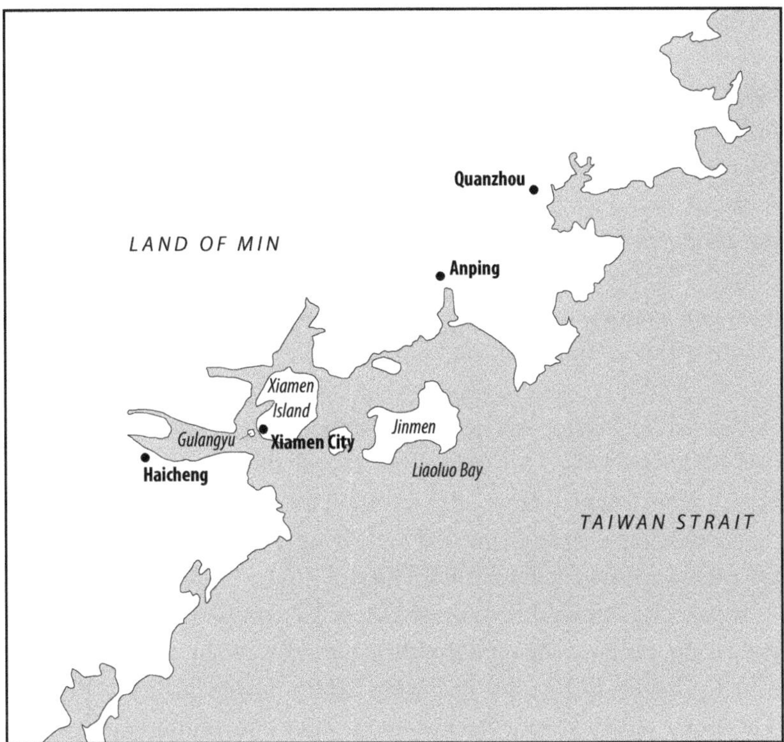

Figure 9. Zheng family base: Xiamen and Jinmen. The Zheng family based itself on the two islands of Xiamen and Jinmen. Xiamen boasted a harbor so deep and well-protected from ocean swells that Italian missionary Victorio Riccio referred to it as "unrivaled in all the world."

A SNEAK ATTACK

This fleet was being built at Zhilong's headquarters in Xiamen, a steep island that lay almost within yelling distance of mainland China (figure 9).[16] Its deep harbor was one of the best in southern China. An Italian missionary described it as one of the best in the world.[17] It was protected from sea waves by a small green island called Island of the Drumming Waves, or Gulangyu. Today, a huge concrete statue of Koxinga stands on Gulangyu staring out toward Xiamen's glassy skyline, but in those days there was no statue and no one paying much attention to the nine Dutch vessels that anchored late at night on the other side of Gulangyu, just out of sight.

At dawn the next morning, Putmans divided his fleet into two squadrons.[18] One sailed around the eastern side of Gulangyu and the other around the western side so that Zhilong's ships wouldn't be able to escape. As it turned out, he didn't need to bother. He met no resistance. His ships were allowed to sail, flags waving, right into the midst of Zhilong's fleet. Hundreds of black-haired people were milling about on the new ships. They didn't raise an alarm because they thought the Dutch were friendly. Zhilong's last letter to Putmans had been conciliatory, promising eight licenses per year for Chinese ships to sail to Taiwan full of silk and porcelain. Putmans hadn't replied, but Zhilong had no reason to expect what happened next.

Putmans's flagship opened fire. As the barrage thundered over the bay, he lowered the Dutch flag and raised the Blood Flag. It was a classic pirate maneuver: change your colors after you attack. Soon all the Dutch ships were flying red and firing away. The junks' workers jumped overboard and swam for shore.

It was clear there'd be no resistance. To save powder, Putmans silenced his cannons and ordered his men to row out and destroy the fleet by hand. The junks that were safely downwind were burned. The ones upwind were hacked to pieces. The Dutch were disappointed to find no booty—the vessels were empty except for powder and ammunition—but they salvaged what they could, taking fifty iron cannons and converting the vessels to firewood. Only three large junks survived the attack. The Dutch suffered only one casualty, when a sailor died setting a fire.

Zhilong was shocked.[19] "You've behaved like a pirate!" he wrote to Putmans. "Are you proud of yourself? Attacking without warning . . . ? If you had told me in advance, I would have come out like a soldier and fought openly, and whoever won would have deserved the victory, but I thought you had come as a friend, to trade and do business."[20] Zhilong promised to get even: "I'll bide my time. Don't believe that you and your forces will be allowed to remain here in the imperial waterways for long."[21]

But Putmans roved the waterways with impunity, pillaging villages and capturing vessels. The Chinese commanders couldn't drive him away, because, as one of them wrote, the red-hairs' cannonfire is too intense and their ships "are tall and large, while ours are low and small, so we can't attack them from below like that."[22]

Putmans wasn't just seeking booty. He was blockading the coast to force Zhilong to agree to his demands: free trade in China, a trading base on Gulangyu, and a permanent ambassador in Fuzhou, the capital of Min.[23] (These were demands strikingly similar to those the British would make two hundred years later in the Opium War.)

He felt sure his blockade was working. "Zhilong," he wrote, "wishes that peace had already been reached, because you can't spin silk during a war."[24] He figured that Zhilong was "very frightened,"[25] not just of Dutch ships but also of the pirates he was luring to his side.[26] By the end of September, four hundred and fifty pirates had joined the Dutch fleet, and more were arriving each day.[27]

"We believe," Putmans wrote, "that this enterprise will be carried out and brought to its desired conclusion primarily by the pirates, although our ships will have to remain here to help."[28] Sometimes Zhilong tried to lure the new recruits away, but Putmans wasn't worried. "The pirates are so jealous of each other," he wrote, "that nothing happens here among their leaders that we don't hear about."[29]

Yet Putmans's surprise attack had an unintended consequence: it brought together Zhilong and Zou Weilian. The two men, so different in background and demeanor, didn't like each other. Their mutual recriminations had been redounding up to the faction-riven imperial court in Beijing, Zou accusing Zhilong of not taking coastal defense seriously, Zhilong using his contacts to slander Zou.[30] But now they worked together to defeat the Dutch.

Usually a governor would stay in Fuzhou, several days to the north. But Zou moved his court to the harbor town of Haicheng, just upriver from Xiamen.[31] While Zhilong rebuilt his junks, Zou summoned help. Commanders from up and down the coast began arriving with armadas large and small. All of them—and Zhilong too—swore an oath before Zou to fight to the death. There would be no retreat from the red-hairs.

Putmans knew nothing of these preparations and kept plundering, keeping careful records. Small vessels carried only watermelons or rice or salted fish. One junk had furniture: twenty-four lacquer tables, sixty-eight chairs, twelve round tables, six writing boxes, a box of ink-stones. More lucrative were large ocean junks laden with cloves and pepper, ivory and deerskins, silk and sandalwood. But the richest prize of all was a vessel that had come from Manila and held 27,994 pieces of eight, worth around six million U.S. dollars in today's money. In the six weeks after their sneak attack, Putmans and his accountants estimated that they'd pillaged goods worth 64,017.25 pieces of eight, on the order of thirteen million U.S. dollars.[32]

Zhilong knew the autumn winds brought storms, so he bided his time.[33] Indeed, in October, while Putmans and some pirate allies considered how to raid a coastal island, they encountered a tree-tearing gale.[34] His flagship collided with another vessel and lost its anchor. There was a crash and a crunch. The hull was smashed to pieces on sharp reefs.[35]

He thought he'd sink and die, but some of his crew got ashore and then helped him pull himself to land, hand over hand. "Thanks to God's grace," he wrote, "nearly everyone made it ashore."[36] One of his other ships came to a similar end, along with some smaller vessels. The pirates lost twenty or so junks.[37] He was disheartened: "What a damaging misfortune this was for the company," he wrote, although he was consoled when the pirates said the storm had been worse for Zhilong.[38] It seems, though, that that news wasn't true, that it had been propogated by Zhilong to provide a false sense of security.[39]

Putmans led his fleet north to safer waters. As he passed near Xiamen, scouts told him there was a Chinese fleet anchored there. He didn't think it was anything worrisome: five or six large warjunks and twenty smaller ones. But the pirates said there was another fleet hidden behind the city. They urged him to launch a preemptive strike, to smash this fleet before Zhilong and Zou Weilian could finish preparations.

Putmans said no. He probably should have said yes.

"War Is the Art of Deception"
—Sun Zi[1]

Shortly after Putmans declined to launch another sneak attack, a messenger arrived with a challenge: "How," Zhilong wrote, "can a dog be permitted to lay its bitch head on the emperor's pillow? . . . If you want to fight, bring it to us here in Xiamen, where the high officials of China can watch our victory over you."[2] The letter was signed by twenty-one Chinese generals.

This was an abrupt change of tone. While Putmans had been pillaging, he'd received some letters from Zhilong, most of which had been unthreatening. He'd also received letters signed by Chinese officials. They were polite, albeit vague and unyielding. In fact, Zhilong had been forging these letters, keeping Putmans thinking he might be on the verge of winning concessions.[3] Putmans had even made embarrassing replies to the fake letters: that once peace was reached, the two sides could live for all time in friendship, and that he'd rid the entire coast of pirates and supply his Majesty the Emperor with Dutch musketeers and "new inventions of cannons, with which great force can be exercised."[4]

So Zhilong's challenge surprised Putmans. He found it rude and insulting, filled with bragging and boasting. "If they come attack us," he wrote, "let God help us achieve a victory in His Holy Name over this devious nation of sodomites."[5]

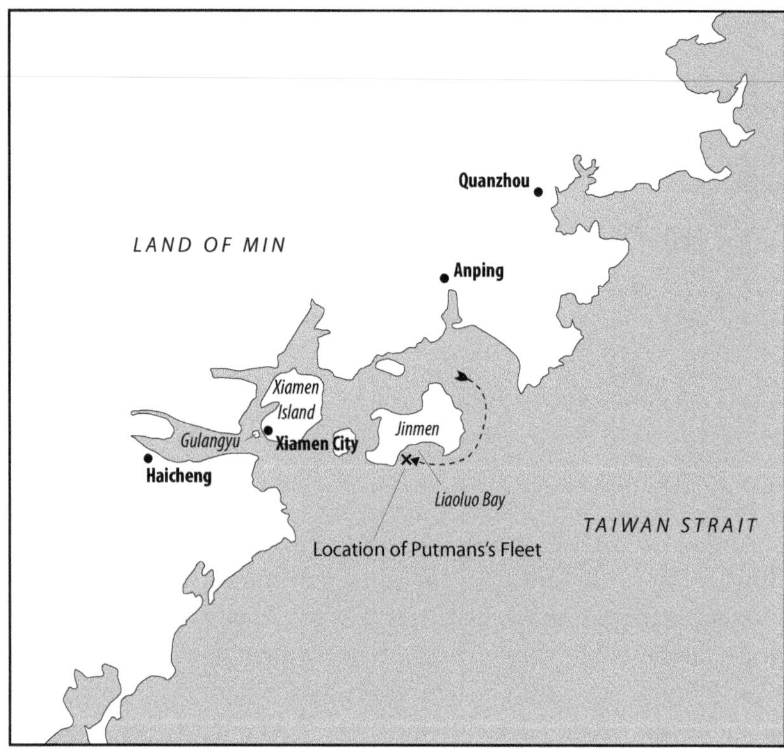

Figure 10. The Battle of Liaoluo Bay, October 1633.

Putmans anchored a few miles seaward of Xiamen, off the Isle of Jinmen, where there was a beach-lined crescent called Liaoluo Bay (figure 10). It seemed perfect. It provided shelter from the winds but was open enough to allow access to deeper waters, where Dutch ships had the advantage, their complex rigging allowing them to sail close to the wind. He and his allies anchored and waited, the pirates flying blue pennants that sported the company's acronym, VOC, for Verenigde Oost-Indische Compagnie. That way they could be distinguished from Zhilong's junks.[6]

Early in the morning, he heard warning shots from a sentry vessel. Zhilong's fleet hove into view around the corner of Jinmen. Putmans estimated that there were around a hundred and fifty junks. Fifty or so were large, but he was confident he could blast them into driftwood. He gave the order to stand and wait.

When Zhilong first spotted Putman's ships, he found their posture arrogant. "It was just daybreak," he wrote, "when we saw the barbarians' decked ships there, nine of them, cocky and self satisfied with the cliffs at their back, accompanied by fifty pirate ships sailing back and forth around them."[7] He knew the Dutch would have the advantage in a straight-up firefight. Maybe if he'd still had the huge junks he'd built earlier, with their reinforced cannon decks and European-style cannon mounts, he would have met Putmans head to head, but instead he had a motley fleet: a few imperial ships, some merchant ships, and some of his own vessels.

So he and Zou had prepared a fleet of firebombs. One Chinese account, the *Taiwan wai ji,* which is based on real events but takes liberties, provides delightful details.[8] Zhilong said to his captains, "The decked ships are sturdy and hard to destroy, so the only way we can achieve victory is to attack with fire. Let's select some people who are good at swimming. . . . We'll get a large piece of bamboo and saw it into tubes, and each person will carry two of these tubes around their waists."[9] With the bamboo serving as life preservers, the men were to crash their boats into the Dutch ships, set them alight, and then jump overboard to be fished out by comrades. The fireships themselves were filled with inflammable material: grass and bamboo, sesame oil, palm oil, saltpeter, and sulfur.[10] A list in another Chinese source is bafflingly esoteric: gourd tubes, magic smoke, cannon stones, magic sand, poison fire.[11] The fireships were also equipped with "wolf-teeth": chains with hooks and spikes that could be used to grapple the fireship to the enemy vessel.

Usually fireboats were small, expendable vessels. But Zhilong wanted to trick Putmans into thinking this would be a standard battle. So he'd made fireships out of his largest warjunks. Like a good illusionist, he'd started his misdirection with words. In his challenge, he'd bragged about his fleet and said he wanted everyone to see him defeat Putmans so all could judge who was the better commander. His floating bombs were equipped to complete the deception. Not only did they look like powerful warjunks. They were also filled with cannons and soldiers.

The trick worked. "We could see," wrote Putmans, "that they were extremely well supplied with guns and men, and they comported themselves bravely and without fear, so we concluded that these were all warjunks and therefore expected that—with God's help—we would be victorious."[12] He was confident that his nine vessels, along with his pirate allies, could destroy a Chinese battle fleet of a hundred and fifty junks. He even thought that he could do it by firing from his anchorage.

Before the battle Zhilong had quoted to his officers an ancient adage: "A warrior prizes speed above all else." The line appears in Sun Zi's *Art of War,* written more than two thousand years before. Zhilong explained how important it was to get the firejunks near the Dutch warships before the Hollanders' cannon and musket fire caused casualties and frightened the soldiers. To keep up morale they needed to inflict damage quickly.

Indeed, the junks came fast. Putmans considered trying to break for deeper water but realized there was no time to raise anchors. "We stayed lying there," he wrote, "to see what kind of advantage we could get over them."[13]

He didn't expect the Chinese to head right for his fleet, but they did.[14] Dutch muskets and cannons roared forth, "the cannonballs flying as thick as rain," in the words of one Chinese participant.[15] Another wrote, "the great cannons and fire machines were all going off at once, but our people advanced bravely on the decked ships."[16] What the Chinese described as bravery, Putmans saw as madness: "The Chinese came forth like insane, forsaken, crazy, desperate men, who had already given up their lives, showing no fear of any violence of cannons, muskets, fire, or flame."[17]

Junks collided with a Dutch ship and were immediately set alight, becoming a wall of fire.[18] "The junks," wrote Putmans in his diary, "went up in an instant in such terrifying tall flames, burning so vehemently, that it seemed nearly impossible."[19] To Putmans this self-immolation was insane. "It was as if they were crazy drunk or out of their minds, showing no concern for the welfare of their own people."[20] The fire reached the powder room located in the stern. The ship exploded and sank with its crew and dozens of Chinese attackers.

Zou Weilian had made clear that the highest honors in battle would go to those who could capture a Dutch ship, so while the first was sinking, soldiers boarded another, hacking at the crew. They were driven back once, twice, but the third time they surged over the decks, "slashing and burning and drowning countless barbarians."[21] Scores of Dutchmen were captured. Dozens were killed. "When the decked ships were burning," Zhilong wrote, "the fire and smoke soared up to the heavens, and our eyes were filled with the sight of floating corpses, while the bodies of those who were captured and beheaded piled up in heaps."[22]

"At this point," Putmans wrote, "we understood the truth: that this entire fleet had been prepared as fireships and they'd had no intention of doing battle, planning instead to come up against us and set fire to our ships. This was despite the fact that these were well-armed and large vessels, the very best warjunks."[23] His captains were panicking, sawing through their anchor cables. "We had no chance of victory," Putmans wrote, "since they enjoyed odds of twenty against one and didn't care about their own lives."[24]

Putmans set out for deep water, under close pursuit. Zhilong later reported that he nearly captured Putmans: "The impostor barbarian king's ship was nearly in our grasp, and we were nearly at the point where we could truss him up. But who would have expected that the sea wind would suddenly become wild and the waves would become rough and treacherous? The barbarian ships tacked against the wind toward the outer seas."[25] Zhilong and his men kept pursuing, but, Zhilong wrote, "the more we chased them the farther they got away."[26] Sailing into the wind, it seems, Dutch ships had the advantage.

Only five of the nine vessels Putmans commanded that morning made it out. Three were lost—two ships and a junk—and the other had been left behind when it had been surrounded and unable to return fire. Once Putmans had reached a safe distance and turned around to look, he saw it still flew Dutch colors. He sent his fastest ship to try to help it if it managed to escape. Then he promptly set sail for Taiwan.

TO THE VICTOR GO THE SPOILS

Zhilong had won a glorious victory. In his official report, he wrote that the attack went so well that "it was like destroying something that was already decaying."[27] He praised the commanders for working together and the troops for their bravery. "The men," he wrote, "were courage from head to toe, everyone lending a hand."[28] He listed the prizes: six large cannons, two little cannons, sixteen muskets, eleven barbarian swords, one iron helmet, six tubes of gunpowder, seven barbarian books, one sea chart, three suits of armor.[29] He listed the prisoners, their names transcribed into Chinese characters. That list doesn't survive, but Dutch records indicate that ninety-three company employees were lost that day.[30] How many were killed and how many were captured isn't clear, but Zhilong and Weilian boasted that they caught the "impostor barbarian king's sea-expedition commander, Capitan Paets."[31] They also captured pirates, including two pirate wives and some Japanese pirates, whose hair was rolled on the head Japanese style.[32]

Ming officials hailed the victory as a "miracle at sea."[33] Zou Weilian wrote: "People say that ever since the red barbarians arrived in the Land of Min and the Land of Yue several dozen years ago, this kind of victory has been extremely rare."[34] Zhilong was less modest but more accurate: "It seems that this victory is enough to reestablish the prestige and authority of China and, in contrast, to lower the spirits of those crafty barbarians."[35]

The barbarians were disheartened. Putmans's bosses called it a disaster.[36] Putmans recognized that his plan had come to naught. "This defeat," he wrote, "has weakened us so much that we realized there wasn't anything else we could do this season here on the coast."[37] He felt equally weak the next season, and his superiors ordered him to be careful: "Carry out nothing other than flying sorties and keep our main ships away from China and out of harm's way so they won't be exposed to the kind of fury and resolution the Chinese displayed at Liaoluo Bay."[38]

Fortunately for him, further fighting wasn't necessary, because Zhilong still found the Dutch useful. After all, they'd made him famous. He was hailed as the only one who could control them. Now he just needed to keep them happy enough that they wouldn't start fighting again. The task was facilitated by his new fame. Previously, he'd been obstructed by Chinese officials like Zou Weilian, who insisted that the Dutch be gotten rid of altogether. But one of the first things he did with his new influence was to get Zou Weilian fired.[39]

Poor Zou had been partially responsible for Zhilong's new respect. Despite their earlier disagreements, he wrote to Beijing and extolled Zhilong. To be sure, Zou wrote, the former pirate had seemed at first to be insincere about getting rid of the barbarians, seemed even to be consorting with them. But then Zou had admonished him to stand up to them, and Zhilong had eventually recognized Zou's wisdom and rectitude. Zou wrote

> Zhilong is a fervent man. He recognized his errors and repented, swearing before Heaven to extirpate the barbarians, bankrupting his family to reward his soldiers, and if he waited for so long to take action, that's because he only wanted a perfect plan. . . . He braved death to be in the first wave of attack. His suffering and labor and achievements are high, and the stains on his heart are already gone. It behooves a virtuous official to ask for glorious promotions on the part of rebels-made-good in order to recompense these miraculous achievements.[40]

In fact, Zou had been nearly as responsible for the victory as Zhilong. He'd provided the coordination, summoning forces from elsewhere and putting them under Zhilong's command. And he'd provided much of the financing. So it's not fair that Zou was ousted. The emperor realized his mistake only later and, as recompense, sent Zou a special tablet written in his own hand proclaiming that "Zou Weilian is the purest and most loyal minister on earth," as well as a decree raising him three ranks and an important new bureaucratic post. Zou died before he could start work. The emperor's pronouncement was etched into his tomb, and some say it's still legible, although the stone images of men and horses have worn away.[41]

By getting rid of Zou, Zhilong made a point: It wasn't wise to cross him. In fact, one Chinese historian thinks that if the emperor had left Zou in office, Zhilong might have been kept in check, his power wouldn't have grown so quickly, and world history would have turned out differently.[42]

But Zhilong was now on top. With no opposition from Chinese officials, he offered the Dutch the trading privileges he'd probably always wanted to provide, keeping them from armed opposition but available as a manageable threat to bolster his power. Sometimes he let them trade on the coast. More frequently, he sent ships to Taiwan, each vessel flying a flag with Zhilong's surname, Zheng, embroidered on it. He and his agents could control how much silk the Dutch got and how much they paid. Generally he felt it was in his interest to keep the Dutch satisfied.

Under the new trading regime, Taiwan flourished, and Putmans turned his martial energies to the colony. He quelled headhunters, overcame smugglers, and laid groundwork for growth. Working closely with Min investors, he oversaw the establishment of rice paddies and sugar plantations, inviting thousands of Min settlers to Taiwan. They worked the fields, processed sugar, hunted deer, made bricks, constructed houses, built roads, ran ferry services, and generally made the colony prosper. He and his successors expanded Fort Zeelandia and built a new fort on the other side of the bay, with a botanical garden and a guest house and a gazebo to hold court over the aborigines. The Min villages near each fort bloomed and became towns with roads paved in stone and tile-roofed houses, their markets bustling with goods from all over the world.[43]

Zhilong's agents were in those markets. In fact, his agents were everywhere. His hegemony over Chinese overseas trade was soon undisputed. He had to fend off one more major challenge to his dominance, a pirate named Liu Xiang who came close to defeating him, but he prevailed with his usual verve, and by the 1640s his flag flew on nearly every ship that sailed into or out of the ports of Min. Not all these ships were his (although he claimed that his own merchant marine numbered a thousand), but nearly everyone had to fly his colors and pay for the privilege.

He collected tolls on all the shipping that called in his ports. Chinese sources suggest he got three thousand taels for each oceangoing ship, or around ten million taels per year.[44] If those figures are correct, his annual income from tolls alone was around the same as the Dutch East India Company's total yearly earnings, not just for the Taiwan colony, or Batavia, but for all its dominions, from Japan to the Spice Islands to India to Africa to Amsterdam.[45] Of course, Dutch sources are extremely detailed and reliable, whereas Chinese sources for Zhilong's earnings are qualitative and scanty and we have to be careful making comparisons. Still, those ten million taels would have represented only one aspect of Zhilong's revenue machine. He also earned money from direct trade in Japan and Southeast Asia, probably on the order of twenty or thirty million taels per year.[46] In addition he had other sources of revenue—rents and land income and bribes—about which we know little but which surely amounted to large sums. It seems likely that he earned three or four times as much per year as the world-famous Dutch East India Company.[47]

By all accounts, he was one of the richest men in China, his coffers "contending with the imperial treasury."[48] He built a walled compound south of Quanzhou in a place called Anping (see figure 9). "The troops defending these walls," a Chinese source notes, "were paid for by him himself and not by the government. His flags were bright and manifold, his swords and armor sharp and strong."[49] A canal led directly to his personal residence, and it was said that it even stretched to his own bedroom so he could board a ship at a moment's notice.[50]

His wealth bought influence.[51] "All of the grandees and worthies," one source notes, "had traffic with him, so that he gradually became a person of great illustriousness and power."[52] He made sure his brothers and clansmen and protégés were promoted. In 1640, he himself was raised to the position of Governor-General of Fujian Province, one of the highest posts in the imperium.[53] His family's wealth and power "shook the Land of Min,"[54] says one account, and another states that "the people of the Land of Min saw the Zheng clan as their Great Wall."[55]

This was quite a rise for a stone-throwing, lychee-loving pirate. But just as everything was looking bright, the world changed. There were famines and floods, plagues and pestilences, droughts, locusts, and raging bandits. The dynasty that had given him his position crumbled, and into the breach swept bald men on horses.

The Wrath of Heaven

The collapse of the Ming was part of a global crisis. Historian Geoffrey Parker writes, "The mid-seventeenth century saw more cases of simultaneous state breakdown around the globe than any previous or subsequent age."[1] These words are bold for a scholar, and Parker is a careful researcher, a historian's historian. Yet he and others are convinced that the seventeenth century saw revolutions, revolts, and wars on an unprecedented scale. In fact, they believe that there were more wars in the mid-seventeenth century than in any other period until World War II.[2] They label this period the "general crisis of the seventeenth century."

Why was the mid-seventeenth century so chaotic? The answer is simple and frightening: climate change. The weather didn't change much, certainly nothing compared to the massive dislocations that seem likely in the twenty-first century. It became merely a degree or two cooler. But it was enough to shake societies and economies from one side of the world to the other. The ensuing turmoil killed millions upon millions of people. China's population alone dropped by as much as fifty million in the mid-seventeenth century, more than the combined populations of today's California, Oregon, and Washington states.[3]

It started with volcanoes. In January 1641, some Spanish soldiers in the Philippines heard explosions. They thought Islamic militants might be attacking. Then the sky darkened. By noon the sky was blacker than night. They couldn't even see their hands before their eyes. Ash rained down. The men were far away from the blast, which was so huge it was felt as far away as Vietnam and Cambodia, nearly a thousand miles distant.[4]

Scholars today classify this Philippine eruption as a force six volcanic eruption, and it wasn't the only one in the mid-1600s. Twelve major eruptions shook the Pacific Rim between 1638 and 1644, an all-time record. The millions of tons of sulfurous ash they spewed stayed in the atmosphere and blocked the sun.[5]

Even as the sun's rays were being blocked, the sun itself was getting dimmer. Solar activity dipped to the lowest level ever recorded starting in 1645 and stayed at this low level for seven decades. This was measured by a fall in the number of sunspots, a phenomenon that astronomers in Korea, China, and Europe recorded with fidelity.

The dual phenomena resulted in cooling that affected most of the globe. Settlers in the Massachusetts Bay Colony were shocked when the Massachusetts Bay froze into ice so thick and sustained that the Indians said nothing like it had been seen for generations. In America's west, cold temperatures made for short growing seasons, reflected in remarkably dense tree ring patterns, patterns similar to those in northern Italy, which may be why the violins created by Stradivarius in the early 1700s from trees grown in the mid-1600s have a resonance that has never been replicated. In Scandinavia, 1641 was the coldest year ever recorded. In the Alps, glaciers invaded farms and villages. In France, the cold weather retarded agriculture. French grape harvests between 1640 and 1643 began a full month later than usual. Central Germany froze in August of 1640—*August.* In Japan, ice a foot thick covered the fields, and unusual snowfalls occurred in 1641 and 1642.[6]

But it wasn't just the cold. Rainfall patterns changed. No rain fell in the Valley of Mexico in the summer of 1641 and very little the following summer. Crops withered and the price of corn rose to famine levels. Droughts hit the Philippines, the Indonesian Archipelago, Vietnam, Korea, Taiwan, and parts of Japan. Citizens prayed for rain in Barcelona and Madrid. Many parts of sub-Saharan Africa were parched, with Lake Chad at the lowest level ever recorded. In 1641 in Egypt, the Nile dwindled to the lowest level ever recorded.[7]

Elsewhere, the problem was too much rain. In 1640 and 1641, the Rhine reached two of the highest levels ever registered. The Netherlands were struck by huge floods in 1643, with water so high that afterward one saw the bodies of cows, sheep, and chickens tangled in tree branches.[8] England, Scotland, and Ireland had some of their wettest weather ever, while on the other side of the planet Japan's 1641 rice harvest was destroyed by constant rain.[9]

But China was hit worst of all. It was colder in the mid-seventeenth century than at any other time from 1370 to the present. It was also drier. 1640 was the driest year for north China recorded during the last five centuries. The following year, 1641, was nearly as bad, one of the worst droughts on record. In July the Grand Canal dried up in Shandong Province, something that had never been recorded before. That same summer, locusts devoured harvests throughout eastern China. In 1642, in parts of China's subtropical south, places where it rarely froze, the ice on fishponds went five inches deep. Usually regions like this could harvest rice twice per year, but not now.

Famine followed. There were reports of people digging up corpses for food.[10] A magistrate in Henan Province wrote about how his area suffered eleven months of drought, locusts, and floods. "The people," he wrote, "all have yellow jaws and swollen cheeks; their eyes are the color of pig's gall." He wished he could adequately communicate their screams of hunger and freezing howls.[11] The cities were filled with starving people, opulent mansions abandoned. Wealthy Suzhou, with its elegant canals and famous gardens, suffered cannibalism, despite penalties imposed to prevent it. "I never dreamed," wrote one observer, "that I should have to witness these misfortunes in my lifetime."[12]

THE FALL OF THE MING

The best government would be tried by such conditions, and the Ming had once been great. It had ruled the seas, built the largest palace complex in the world, rebuilt the Great Wall and the Grand Canal, overseen long periods of peace and economic growth and demographic expansion. But by the mid-seventeenth century, its officials were divided into factions, and the man who sat on the dragon throne, the

Chongzhen Emperor, was unable to bring them to order. He was better than his predecessor, a man who refused to meet with his ministers at all, preferring his carpentry studio. But he didn't know whom to trust, since his ministers kept vilifying each other. He dismissed one after another. He was the one who fired Zou Weilian because of Zhilong's slander. In the nearly three hundred years of Ming rule, there were a hundred and sixty Grand Ministers. Fifty were appointed during Chongzhen's seventeen-year reign, an average of three per year.

Chongzhen tried responding to the crisis. He sent inspectors, organized relief, and conducted special prayers for rain.[13] Such prayers were part of his job as Son of Heaven, the intermediary between earth and the divine realm. According to tradition, Heaven had bestowed its blessing upon him and his dynasty, a divine right to rule the earth that was called the Mandate of Heaven. As Heaven's chosen ruler, he was supposed to intercede for harmonious conditions.

His prayers didn't work. The droughts and freezes continued. Starving people became bandits. China's history is full of brigands, but never had there been so many at once.[14] Ragtag bands coalesced into huge armies. In 1644, one army entered Beijing.

Emperor Chongzhen rang his bell, but his officials didn't come. He walked to the bottom of a hill he used to like to sit on, cast a cord around a tree branch, and hanged himself.[15]

Shortly afterward, thousands of shaven-headed warriors galloped through the pass where the Great Wall met the sea, descendants of nomadic horsemen who called themselves Manchus. "When I heard," their leader wrote to a powerful Chinese general, "that roving bandits had attacked and captured the capital and that the Ming Emperor met a miserable end, I was unbearably angry! So I am leading a righteous and compassionate army. I've sunk my boats and broken my woks [so there is no retreat]. . . . I vow not to lower my flags until I have . . . rescued the people from this disaster!"[16] The Manchus claimed the Mandate of Heaven, and many Chinese supported the claim, including the general to whom this Manchu leader directed these words.

The Manchus defeated the brigands and moved into Beijing, installing their Khan, a six-year-old boy, on the throne. He was given the reign title Shunzhi and a new dynasty began for China: the Qing.

Although millions of Chinese shaved their heads in the Manchu style, bald in front with a long pigtail in back, Zheng Zhilong kept his hair long and declared that he would try to restore the Ming. At first, he recognized a Ming claimant based in Nanjing, China's second imperial city, but that regime collapsed in infighting in less than a year, falling to a Manchu army. He transferred his allegiance to another Ming claimant. This one was based in Fuzhou, capital of the Land of Min.

This new Ming emperor seemed promising. He wore plain clothes, ate common food, and declined the usual trappings of opulence, refusing to have a palace built for him or to keep concubines. Determined to avoid his predecessors' mistakes, he took an active interest in policy, listening closely to his childless empress for advice. His only luxury was books, which he received gladly as gifts. He would take thousands of volumes with him when out on campaign.

And campaign was what he most wanted to do. His reign title was Longwu, which means Abundant Arms, and he vowed to drive the Manchus from China. Unlike other Ming princes, he'd already had experience with war. Years ago, he'd tried to raise an army to fight bandits, but Beijing had gotten nervous. He'd been imprisoned, spending much of his adult life in captivity. Now he was free and wanted to fight. Immediately after acceding to the throne in August 1645, he declared that he would lead a campaign from Fuzhou, passing out through the Min mountain passes to check the Qing advance.[17]

Zhilong thought it would be foolish to move so quickly. He proposed an alternative plan: build an army, drill it carefully, and only then attack northward. Two hundred thousand troops would be needed. Zhilong said he could certainly pay for some of them from his trading income, but additional funds were necessary, so he proposed new revenue policies: new land taxes, the sale of offices, and strong encouragement of voluntary contributions from officials and wealthy families (those who demurred would have signs posted on their doors: "Not Righteous").[18] Many of his suggestions were acted on, but the policies didn't provide enough revenue. He complained constantly that he lacked funds.

Even worse, the factions that had destroyed the Ming in Beijing and Nanjing also divided Longwu's court in Fuzhou. On one side were Zhilong and his clan. On the other were civil officials, men who'd passed the exams. There were fights about who should bow to whom and about seating arrangements. Accusations were submitted. People were fired. Others resigned in protest. One official who denounced Zhilong had his ear hacked off by bandits under mysterious circumstances. Zhilong was accused of beating an imperial minister with a wooden tablet.[19]

The factionalism affected the war. When the emperor ordered Zhilong to send forces out through the passes, the former pirate and his brothers resisted or procrastinated or complied halfheartedly, saying they lacked provisions.[20] The emperor suspected that Zhilong was having treacherous thoughts.

He was right. Zhilong was secretly talking to the Manchus. When he told his relatives he was planning to join the Qing, they urged him to reconsider. But it was his son who was most opposed.

The child Zhilong had deserted in Japan had been brought to China and had grown into a strapping and talented young man. Whereas Zhilong still had much of the pirate about him, pragmatic and interested above all in his own and his family's fortune, the son embodied different ideals: he proclaimed that honor and loyalty should come before family and filiality. It was a major difference, which helped lead to Zhilong's death. But what else can you expect when you abandon your son to be raised by samurai?

The Samurai

The boy who would become Koxinga was born in Japan in 1624, precisely when the Dutch were constructing Zeelandia Castle. Three days before his birth, a sea creature with glowing eyes surfaced near his mother's house. It heaved and tossed, thrashed and danced, sprayed water like rain. When his mother was in the final stages of labor, it disappeared. The silence was broken by a cymbal's chime. A fragrance suffused the streets. His mother fainted and dreamt a huge fish was swimming toward her belly. A beam of light illuminated her house, rising up to the sky. Afraid it was a fire, neighbors ran to help, but when they got there they were confused to find no smoke, no flames, just a delighted Zhilong, who told them a son had been born. They smiled. "This boy," they said, "will be important someday."[1]

Probably it didn't really happen that way. Zhilong wasn't even around for his son's birth. And we can probably treat as myths other stories about Koxinga: how he turned a monstrous sea turtle into an island, how he made wells by striking his sword into the ground, how he vanquished demons and monsters.[2] We're also free not to worship him as a god, even though they do in many places in Taiwan.

But how do we deal with the more subtle aspects of his legend? It's almost impossible to resist the dramatic stories about him because his life *was* dramatic. He and his father chose opposite sides in a civil war. This would be stirring in any setting, but it was particularly so in Confucian China, where filiality was a core virtue. A son was supposed to be obedient, to put family—particularly his father—first. But a hero is supposed to be upright and righteous. In Koxinga's life, loyalty to father conflicted with loyalty to the Ming. As the great scholar Donald Keene wrote, "The lives of few men in history are richer in dramatic possibilities than was Koxinga's."[3]

So it's no surprise that historians have been seduced by what Keene calls "colorful tales which have every merit save that of truth."[4] The most vexing problem is the nature of the sources. Nearly all the records Koxinga and his clan generated—tax registers, troop tallies, correspondence—were destroyed by the Manchus more than three hundred years ago. Qing, Dutch, Iberian, and Japanese sources help, but they provide an outside perspective. For a glimpse at the inside of his organization, we must rely on a few early accounts written either by people who were part of Koxinga's organization and had a stake in the legend, or by people who based their accounts on hearsay and interviews. Authors of both types of account liked dramatic stories, which were passed around like coins, getting shinier each time they were handled.

Koxinga himself seems to have encouraged such tales. He built a public persona as an upright soul who sacrificed family interest for the greater good. It's possible of course that he *was* an upright soul who sacrificed family interest for the greater good, and many historians think so. But others say he wasn't really as deeply committed to the cause as he pretended.[5] There's no way to be sure. Koxinga himself liked to cultivate inscrutability. As he once wrote to Coyet, he didn't like people to know what he really thought or intended. "How," he wrote, "can one know my hidden thoughts and tell what are my actual intentions, when I reveal them to nobody?"[6]

I tend to side with those who feel Koxinga was sincere. Most evidence favors that view. And though I may be yielding to the seduction of the story, led down the path that Keene decries, I can't help but feel that Koxinga's boyhood in Japan may have laid the groundwork by inculcating the virtues that defined his life: righteousness and a warrior's loyalty to his lord. These are key virtues of the samurai code, and there's reason to believe that he underwent samurai training as a young boy.

We know next to nothing about his early life, but it does seem that after his father abandoned him, he was raised by his mother and her family.[7] Some writers have tried to prove that his mother was a daughter of the shogun or a high noble, but she seems to have been from a low-level samurai family, of the class of warriors known as *ashigaru*, foot soldiers who didn't have the right to ride horses. There's no doubt that Koxinga's younger half brother, whose name was Tagawa Shichizaemon, was an *ashigaru*.[8]

In those days, Japanese boys as young as two or three wore swords.[9] Their training began early with lessons in martial arts and letters—the two pillars of samurai education. On Japan's Hirado Island, where Koxinga spent his boyhood, it's said that he studied swordsmanship with a teacher named Master Hanabusa.[10] An old tree there has a plaque that reads, "This tree was planted by Koxinga in the olden days, when he trained in martial arts and studied language to forge his indomitable will [literally his 'stomach of steel']. This tree he planted himself in those days and today it is firmly rooted and verdant and old and hoary."[11] Tradition has it that he planted the tree in honor of his teacher when he left Japan.

There's also a painting of Koxinga at six or seven years old. The boy has long hanging hair and holds a samurai sword, his back straight and legs slightly bowed as though pretending to ride a horse.[12] Scholars interpret this painting as evidence that Koxinga was schooled in military arts in Japan even before arriving in China.[13]

His training was interrupted at the age of seven when his father sent for him. Leaving his mother behind, he arrived in a China on the verge of dynastic collapse. What did the young swordsman make of this Ming realm? In Japan he'd lived in a modest house. Now he was brought to a huge mansion in the richest country in the world. His family's own flag flew on its walls, on the masts of the ships that sailed its private canal, and from the standards carried by the troops that guarded its gates.

Wealth bought great teachers, and Koxinga, despite the fact that Chinese may have been a second language for him, was a better student than his father. By the age of eleven he mastered one of the most difficult books in the Chinese canon, the *Annals of the Spring and Autumn*

Period. It's the most martial of the classics, portraying an ancient world of loyalty, honor, and valor, not unlike the samurai world he'd left behind. In samurai tales, a warrior would sooner kill himself than betray his lord or commit an act of dishonor. Loyalty and righteousness, which were part of the samurai code, were qualities he seems to have felt were lacking in the China of his day. Indeed, they were qualities he would come to feel were lacking in his own father. "In ancient times," he later wrote to Zhilong, "righteousness was always more valued than family loyalty . . . and ever since I learned to read I always admired the righteousness of the *Spring and Autumn Period*."[14]

The boy studied hard and was even able to read ancient texts in their original form, without punctuation or diacritics—likereadinghomerintheoriginalgreekwithalltheletterstogether. He passed the first stage of China's rigorous examination system at the age of fourteen. He passed the much more difficult provincial stage, too, although there's some evidence that his father tried to bribe the exam officials.[15] He was sent to Nanjing, one of the centers of scholarship, and an older scholar is said to have exclaimed, "This is no normal boy. He's a person of destiny, an outstanding talent."[16]

In Nanjing he studied with one of China's most famous scholars, Qian Qianyi, who nicknamed him Damu, which means Great Wood, a reference not to his physical endowments but to his potential as a scholar. It was an allusion to a famous story about Confucius, who compared teaching to carving wood: in both cases you need to start with good material. Once, when one of Confucius's students fell asleep in class, the sage cried out that trying to teach him was impossible. "Rotten wood," he exclaimed, "can't be carved."

Teacher Qian turned out to be a poor model for the ancient virtues of uprightness and loyalty. When the Manchus stormed Nanjing in 1645, he was one of the first eminent scholars to join their side.[17] According to various Chinese sources, his concubine urged him to stay true to the Ming, saying he should commit suicide as a sign of loyalty. Qian's decision to join the Qing haunted him for the rest of his life. Even today, he's remembered as a figure of disloyalty.[18]

Koxinga, however, stayed true to the Ming, as did his father for a time. After the fall of Nanjing, Koxinga went to Fuzhou to serve the new Ming emperor, Longwu (the one of simple ways who loved books). According to one source, in their first meeting, Longwu rubbed his back and said, "I wish had a daughter to marry you to so that you could be completely loyal to my family and we would be linked forever."[19] And in a rare gesture, Longwu symbolically adopted him, bestowing upon him the imperial surname and a new appellation: Chenggong, which means success. Today the Chinese and Taiwanese refer to him as Zheng Chenggong, but in his day most people, including Longwu himself, called him "Imperial Surname."[20] It's by that name that the Dutch and English and Spanish and Portuguese came to know him, and since it was pronounced Kok-seng, he became known in the West as Koxinga. I use the term in this book because it's a fitting title for someone who devoted himself and his fortunes to the restoration of his dynasty. It's also the name he himself preferred.

Longwu treated him as a relative, receiving him with protocols usually reserved for an imperial son-in-law.[21] He gave him an imperial sword, an ancient symbol of regal authority, and a seal inscribed with the words Great-Rebel-Quelling-General,[22] a title Koxinga preferred over all the other honors he received in his life. Maybe he liked the way it sounded similar to the title of the Japanese shogun, which means "Great Barbarian-Quelling General."[23]

CHOOSING SIDES

But Koxinga soon faced a difficult choice. According to one of those dramatic stories that historians are warned against, one day he found the emperor sitting dejectedly on the throne. "Your Majesty," he said. "You seem so unhappy. It must be because my father has subversive schemes. I have received great kindnesses from you, and honor demands that there be no shrinking back. I solemnly swear that I will repay this debt to your Highness unto death."[24] The emperor smiled. Comforted by these words, he named Koxinga commander of the imperial elite troops and ordered him to guard the Xianxia Pass, one of the main mountain passages into the Land of Min.

Zhilong ordered his son to withdraw and let the Manchus in. It was the autumn of 1646, and Zhilong wanted to show the Qing that he was on their side. Koxinga refused. One of his father's men visited the camp, and Koxinga told him there was no way he would leave his post and that his father must send supplies. "My wives and concubines," Koxinga said, "will be giving up their jewelry to buy food for my troops."[25] To make the point, the women took off their jewelry. The frightened man proceeded to Zhilong's headquarters. When he delivered the message, Zhilong was livid. "My boy is crazy to insist like this!" he yelled. "Let's see how well he conducts war on an empty stomach!"[26] He refused to send provisions. Without food, Koxinga's troops deserted. Koxinga returned from the mountains in failure.

Feeling deserted, Longwu decided he'd have to do without Zhilong's help and resolved to go out on expedition on his own. Koxinga begged the emperor not to go, lying flat on the ground, sobbing and pleading: "The best strategy now is self preservation!" Longwu wiped a tear from his eyes and ordered Koxinga to stand up.[27] He said he was determined to proceed. He set out on his own and was surrounded by Manchu forces. He killed himself by throwing himself into a well.[28]

This story—Koxinga reassuring the emperor, Zhilong withdrawing support from his son, Koxinga begging Longwu not to go fight—may be fanciful, but it accords with known events: Zhilong did insist on vacating the mountain passes. Longwu did go out on his own and get killed. And there's good reason to believe that Koxinga was entrusted with military commands by Longwu.[29] Yet the story may be too simplistic. Other sources cast doubt on Koxinga's loyalty. "Longwu," one author wrote, "told many things to Koxinga, who immediately passed them along to his father," causing disorder in the court.[30]

To what extent Koxinga, in these early days, chose his sovereign over his father is impossible to know. But what is clear is that he did break with his father soon enough.

After the Manchus stormed into Min, they sent Zhilong a letter: "We've had engravers prepare seals of authority for the position of Governor-General of The Lands of Min and Yue, and are prepared to give it to you."[31] It was a compelling offer. Zhilong would be even richer and more powerful than he'd been in the Ming.

He told his son he intended to accept. Koxinga protested. "Father," one source has him saying, "you've taught me to be loyal and not to tolerate duplicity! And in any case, how can you be sure you can trust the Qing?"[32] He cried and pleaded, but Zhilong was adamant, and other accounts have him admonishing his son: "In times of such chaos and disorder everyone always looks out for himself and nothing can be constant. You are just suffering from the idealism of youth."[33]

Zhilong set out to meet the Qing with an honor guard of African soldiers, men Zhilong had recruited through his ties with the Portuguese, and who served not just to protect him but as a status symbol.[34] A Qing prince welcomed him with a handshake. They drank and laughed. But the prince was worried because Zhilong's son and many Zheng clansmen were still at large.[35] So late at night, Manchu soldiers attacked Zhilong's armed camp.[36] According to European accounts, his African soldiers defended bravely but failed to keep their master safe.[37] Zhilong was taken to Beijing, where he lived under house arrest.

The Manchus marched southward and stormed the City of Quanzhou. This was where Zhilong had grown up throwing rocks at lychees, and now it was home to Koxinga's mother, who'd finally been brought to China. Some accounts say the Manchus captured and raped her and that she then hanged herself and Koxinga obtained her corpse and personally cleansed it of Manchu filth to prepare for burial.[38] This story, whether or not you believe it, added to Koxinga's legend because it portrayed him as fiercely devoted to his mother and served to explain a lifelong animus toward the Manchus.

Afterward, Koxinga apparently performed another dramatic act. He removed his scholar's cap and robes and burned them in front of a Confucian temple. Kowtowing four times to the Confucius altar, he proclaimed, "Up to this point in my life I was a Confucian student, but today I am an orphan official. Today I respectfully renounce my scholar's robes. I beg for the sage's blessing in this."[39] He held his arms above his head, placed his fist in his hand, and bowed, a traditional gesture of respect upon parting.[40] This episode, if it occurred, was like a dramatic scene in a Chinese novel: the hero devoting himself to a desperate cause.[41]

The cause certainly looked hopeless. The emperor was dead. The Manchus were striding southward. The Zheng clan was in disarray, and Koxinga's uncles were in charge of the armies, the ships, and the money. All Koxinga had were a few men and some grandiose titles: Great Rebel-Quelling General, Loyal and Filial Earl, Bearer of the Imperial Surname.

Yet he managed to become one of the most feared generals in China, commander of more than a hundred thousand troops, and the Manchus' most fearsome adversary. He came close—but not close enough—to toppling the formidable Qing.

The General

Koxinga had two ships, or maybe just one little boat, depending on whom you believe.[1] He had little money—perhaps a thousand gold taels[2]—and no sure way to get more because his uncles controlled the bases of Xiamen and Jinmen and their revenues. His uncles also controlled the Zheng army and navy, leaving him just a few dozen men.

Most important, he had little experience. It's not true, as some sources suggest, that until this point he'd been nothing more than a Confucian scholar and had "never practiced arms for a single day."[3] But it does seem that his one major command—guarding the Xianxia Pass against the Manchus—had ended in failure after his father refused to send supplies and his troops ran away. Despite his grand titles, he was what the Chinese called a "paper general."[4] He'd read about war and knew the histories and adages of China's rich military tradition, but it was another thing to put them into practice.

He led his followers to a little island near Xiamen.[5] They held a ceremony and vowed to restore the Ming.[6] He wasn't the only resistance leader. All through China's coastal provinces similar bands were springing up, similar oaths were being sworn.[7] Having learned that a new Ming emperor had assumed the throne far away in China's interior and called himself the Yongli Emperor, these people were declaring their loyalty and raising recruits. Koxinga proved the most successful.

At a place called Nan'ao, he recruited followers, increasing his band to three hundred.[8] Some of his father's old commanders decided he was promising and pledged allegiance, but at this point his troops were few, his ships were poor, and his first battles went badly.[9] He was defeated at the harbor city of Haicheng and again in Quanzhou and again in the nearby town of Tong'an, where Qing forces retaliated against him by massacring the locals so that "blood flowed in the gutters."[10]

It was around this time that he was joined by an obscure figure named Yang Ying. Chinese scholars don't even know where he was from, information considered so important in Chinese biography that it's usually noted right after the name, even before birth and death dates. Yet he's one of the most important people in Koxinga's history because he kept a journal.

In 1922 a battered and mildewed copy of this journal turned up near Quanzhou, having been preserved through the centuries by Koxinga's descendants. It's worm-eaten, it's missing pages, and its vocabulary is sometimes odd, but it provides an accurate account of Koxinga's enterprise.[11] "I've recorded," Yang Ying wrote, "all the facts as they occurred, month by month, year by year, as I followed my lord along on the campaigns of war."[12] He had a privileged understanding of Koxinga's organization because he was a revenue officer who rose gradually through the ranks. His *True Record of the Past King's Expeditions* is our best source on Koxinga, the only extensive primary source we have that survived the Manchu flames.

Yang Ying followed Koxinga as famine and failure chased his band southward from Min to an area called Chao, whose marshy bays and craggy islands were claimed by bandits, pirates, and warlords. These strongmen ruled over fortified villages that recognized neither Ming nor Qing, keeping local taxes for themselves. Koxinga wanted those revenues for his cause.

We can see through Yang Ying's eyes how Koxinga learned to apply the principles of Chinese warfare. Ancient adages are strewn throughout the account—*Geography is the root of strategy. War is the art of deception. Always use local guides.*—and we see Koxinga utter and employ them in a series of striking successes. When fighting against the three villages of Dahao, Xiamei, and Qinglin, with their powerful cannons and thousands of armed men, Koxinga used local guides to understand the terrain, set up an ambush, and commanded his troops to *feign weakness and lure*, drawing the enemy out so his troops could erupt from their hiding places and attack the enemy's flanks, *cutting the tail off from the head.* The one village was defeated so roundly that the other two soon submitted.[13]

Koxinga was an active commander, involved in the fighting, which could be dangerous. Once, some bandits pretended to surrender but suddenly drew swords and rushed at him. His horse started and he fell to the ground. His men saved him, but it was a close call.[14] Another time, he stood surveying the forbidding terrain of a village called Heping with an advisor when a bullet hit his advisor's right hand. It would have struck Koxinga if he hadn't turned away just in time. He was shaken and wanted to give up the attack, but one of his commanders insisted on pursuing it, and his forces scaled the village walls and slaughtered the inhabitants.[15]

Successful against villages, he went after harder targets. The most difficult was a general named Hao Shangjiu, a powerful commander who claimed to be a Ming adherent but whose loyalty Koxinga found reason to suspect. Koxinga used what was becoming his favorite tactic: *feign weakness and lure.* He surveyed the terrain, found good hiding places for his troops, and then attacked with a credibly large contingent to lure the general from his walls. It worked. When the trap was sprung the general was routed, his top commander was captured, and his men fled in disarray, their dead splayed out over the countryside.[16]

General Hao retreated into his stronghold, the port city of Chaozhou. It was a prefectural capital, with revenues from agriculture and trade. Koxinga besieged the walls. At one point he was drinking wine with some of his commanders beneath a hill called Turqouise Stone Mountain when one of General Hao's spies spotted them and reported their position. Koxinga's butler Ah San was raising a pitcher to pour a cup when a cannonball slammed into him and blew him to pieces, but Koxinga was unharmed. The spy was supposedly awed by this miracle, exclaiming that "This is a case of Heaven preserving the kingly."[17] Yang Ying liked this story because it indicated that Heaven looked favorably on Koxinga's cause. But Koxinga didn't manage to capture Chaozhou. General Hao decided to shave his head and join the Manchus, who sent reinforcements. Koxinga had to lift the siege.

Still, in the two years he'd spent fighting bandits, Koxinga gained experience, manpower, and a source of revenue. Now it was time to regain his birthright.

A STABLE BASE

The twin islands of Xiamen and Jinmen had served not just as his father's military base, but also as his family's main source of revenue, because they were the termina of China's richest sea routes (see figure 9). Koxinga wanted them back, but they were occupied by his uncles.[18] "These islands," Koxinga is reported to have said, "are like the two sides of my family's bed. How can I permit others to snore there?"[19] Sources indicate that relations between the various leaders of the Zheng clan were growing increasingly fractious.[20] Koxinga complained that his uncles were "crouching [in the islands] like ravening tigers."[21]

In the autumn of 1650 he sailed for Xiamen. According to one account, he arrived during the midautumn festival, when people look at the moon and celebrate with family, and his uncle Zheng Lian was passed out drunk at a cliffside cave not far from Xiamen city. Uncle Lian's men couldn't rouse him. When he finally awoke, still drunk, he found that Koxinga had already seized power. He went to see his nephew. The two men exchanged bows. Koxinga smiled and said, "Would uncle be able to lend me his troops?"[22] Lian didn't know what to say. Koxinga's guards came forward with swords drawn. His uncle stuttered his assent.[23] His other uncle, who controlled Jinmen, fled out to sea, leaving behind many of his commanders, who came over to Koxinga's side. Only one other uncle continued to command significant independent forces, the Jianguo Duke, Zheng Hongkui, but Koxinga was on good terms with him. In any case, Hongkui was based far to the south, holding the bandits and pirates in sway.[24]

Thus, in little more than a day, Koxinga gained the most important trading port in China, an army of forty thousand troops, and a powerful navy.

Then he received a plea for help from the new Ming emperor, whose court was far away, deep in China's inaccessible, forested southern interior regions. The Qing were advancing.

Koxinga declared he'd leave at once. His commanders didn't like the idea. "Your Lordship," said one, "it is certainly praiseworthy to lead troops to save the emperor . . . , but I fear that this may not be a favorable occasion. The base of Xiamen should not be abandoned."[25]

Koxinga was adamant. "Even if I sacrificed my own life I wouldn't be able to repay the kindnesses of the emperor to me and my family. Today I have been commanded to go there with my troops. How can I tarry and scheme for my own safety and that of my family? It is only right that I must go forth as quickly as possible."[26] I use the English word "right" to translate Koxinga's intent, but Koxinga used the Chinese word *Yi,* a term meaning righteousness, which in Chinese was often opposed to self-interest. This was the word used in the samurai code, and it was the same righteousness Koxinga admired in the ancient classics, a quality of heroes. Koxinga was making an explicit contrast between self-interest—or the interest of his own family—and virtue.

Another commander also begged him not to go. Shi Lang, one of his most talented officers, whose advice had helped Koxinga understand the use of signal flags, watchtowers, and drilling methods,[27] said he'd had a dream that the trip to the south would end badly. He begged Koxinga to think again.[28] Koxinga didn't answer.[29] He stripped Shi Lang of his command and set forth.

As Koxinga's navy sailed, a storm exploded over the sea. Koxinga's ship, filled with silver and rice and tax registers, was blown before the wind, its mast cracking, straight toward dangerous reefs. Koxinga climbed into a launch and was rowed through towering waves to another other ship, which set out to sea away from the reefs. Waves swamped the decks, sweeping tools and charts away. By dawn, the storm had abated, and when Koxinga came up on deck to look around, anxious about the rest of his fleet and about the money and men and tax receipts that had been lost in the storm, the ship's commander consoled him: "It was thanks to Your Lordship's loyalty and honor and the protection of Heaven that we came out of this alive."[30] Nearly everyone survived the storm, but bad news soon arrived from Xiamen.

Koxinga had left his base in charge of one of his many relatives, a cousin named Zheng Zhiwan.[31] But a Manchu army had launched a sneak attack on Xiamen, and Zhiwan was afraid he couldn't hold them off, so he loaded his things onto ships and sailed away, leaving the island undefended. Koxinga's wife and children fled with a few belongings. Manchus got the rest and burned the city, the flames lighting up the night sky.[32]

Koxinga's men wanted to go back to Xiamen immediately. Koxinga said no. "I've received the emperor's decree to save the imperial house . . . and am already so near the imperial presence. How can I turn back halfway there? The sorrows of my country haven't been redressed. How can I worry about the care of my own family?"[33] According to Yang Ying, Koxinga was under great pressure from his men. "The sound of crying could be heard everywhere,"[34] and officers pleaded with him: "Everyone in the armies cherishes their families, not just you. There's also a danger of desertion."[35] Feeling that he had no choice, Koxinga faced south, toward his emperor's court, and kowtowed, tears in his eyes, saying, "I, your humble minister, have braved great waves to approach the Imperial Visage and help restore the empire, not caring that Xiamen has been lost to the enemy. But my generals all want to turn back. It's hard to prevent them from deserting. It's not that I'm not loyal. It's that I have no other choice."[36]

When he got home, he found that his entire treasury had been sacked—a million ounces of gold and hundreds of pounds of pearls and jewelry, his family's life savings.[37] When he learned that his relatives had not only failed to defend Xiamen but had actually helped the Manchus ferry their troops there and back, he was furious.[38] According to one account, he grabbed the sword the dead emperor Longwu had given him and hacked at his hair, a gesture of frustration aimed at his elders, because hair is a gift given us by our parents and cutting it was an unfilial act. One of his uncles tried to excuse himself, saying that he'd had no choice but to help the Manchus because elder brother Zhilong was being held by the Qing, who'd threatened to harm him. Filiality, the uncle said, demanded that one protect one's elders. But Koxinga made clear that righteousness was more important than filiality. He summoned cousin Zhiwan and called for his sword. His generals begged him to reconsider, but Koxinga had Zhiwan and a general beheaded and their heads displayed on a stake.

Among the booty the Manchus seized in Xiamen were hundreds of thousands of bushels of rice.[39] There was nothing to feed the soldiers. Desperation drove Koxinga to launch a new series of attacks, achieving his first compelling victories against the Qing.

He and his men knew each hidden cove and narrow canyon of the Land of Min. They used their connection with the locals to implement bold stratagems: *Use leisure to await the enemy's exhaustion. Use full stomachs to await the enemy's starvation.*[40]

It was in this period that Koxinga came into his own as a commander, personally leading assaults, riding to the front of the ranks to rouse his men with speeches, adapting quickly to Qing tactics, reorganizing his forces and developing new units: teams of strong men with quilted shields two inches thick that offered protection against Manchu arrows and afterward could be rolled up so the troops could use long saber-staves to slash at Manchu horses. He set up a special bureau to oversee the production of these shields and other weapons: fire-arrows, firetubes, bombs.[41] He learned to outthink and outfight Qing leaders, delivering blow after blow.[42]

His success convinced independent commanders to declare their loyalty to him. Some bore impressive imperial titles: the Marquis of Western Pacification, the Marquis Who Pacifies the Barbarians, the Earl of Heroic Righteousness. Others were local leaders who opened their gates. At first these gates led mostly to smaller villages and towns, but early in 1652 the Qing general in charge of defending the city of Haicheng, one of the most important ports in China (it was the place where Zou Weilian had planned his assault against Hans Putmans twenty years before), sent Koxinga a jade archery thumb-ring and declared he was ready to surrender the city. Koxinga arrived with impeccable timing. "Usually," Yang Ying writes, "the harbor's waters were shallow and large ships had trouble entering, but on that day the tide surged, rising several feet, and Koxinga's ship was able to enter directly and moor just below the gate of the central administration. The people of Haicheng were astonished and said that never in history had such a thing happened."[43]

The people, Yang Ying says, compared the incident to an ancient miracle. Once upon a time, a hero named Liu Xiu was fighting to restore the great Han Dynasty, which had fallen to rebels and palace intrigue. His forces were fleeing from a larger army. Cutting off their escape was the Yellow River. But just when it seemed that all was lost, the river froze, allowing them to cross. Afterward it melted so the enemy couldn't pursue.[44] Liu Xiu went on to help restore the Han Dynasty, which ruled for another two hundred years. It's an episode much like the story of the parting of the Red Sea, when God intervened to let the Isrealites cross to safety. The fact that the tides of Haicheng had risen just for Koxinga was taken as a sign that Heaven supported Koxinga and that he was fated to restore the Ming just as Liu had restored the Han. Of course, Koxinga's mariners knew their tides. It wasn't the last time they'd use a high tide to help land troops, as Coyet would learn to his astonishment years later.

Yet it did seem that the tide was turning for Koxinga. His battles got larger and his victories more decisive. He developed new command structures and signal systems to coordinate his growing armies. When his camps lay far from each other or were separated by mountains, flag signals didn't work, so he developed smoke signals, building watchtowers thirty or forty feet high for skywatchers. One signal meant that the enemy was preparing to advance, another that the enemy's approach was imminent, a third that it was time to attack. There were systems of bugle calls to carry detailed orders: when to shoot arrows, set off rockets, and fire cannons; when to use shields and guns and swords.[45] The first major test of these new signaling systems went well; the enemy "scattered like chaff before the wind . . . their corpses spread about the fields."[46]

Having gained control of much of the countryside of the Land of Min, it was time to target the largest cities.

A SIEGE AND A REVERSAL

The most important city near Koxinga's base was Zhangzhou, which had nearly a million people (see figure 5). Like most Chinese cities, it was defended by massive walls. In fact, the walls were so thick and high that Koxinga decided not to try to storm them but rather adopted a "strategy of long-term blockade," closing all access to the city.[47] He oversaw the construction of extensive siegeworks—moats, wooden stockades armed with cannons, short earthen walls. He began damming the river and digging a canal to flood the city out, although he abandoned the plan when it turned out to be too difficult. The Qing sent armies to drive him away, but he defeated them. The Qing launched a naval assault against Xiamen, but he routed them.

For six months the blockade went on, and the citizens ran out of rice. Survivors' accounts are, as one Chinese writer noted, "so painful and difficult to take that who can bear to read them?"[48] People were desperate for food, paying four pieces of gold for a bowl of thin gruel.[49] They ate mice, sparrows, tree roots, leaves, leather, paper.[50] They ate each other, fathers eating sons, brothers eating brothers, wives eating husbands, mothers eating children.[51] "At night," one survivor recalled, "you could hear the knocking of bones, which sounded like the clacking of tiles. The houses were abandoned, the streets and alleyways empty and hollow. It was like walking through a graveyard. Greedy rats and starving birds crouched brazenly on benches in broad daylight."[52]

One memory is particularly disturbing. A scholar—a beloved and magnanimous man—locked himself in his room so he wouldn't consume the family's food, telling his wife and sons not to open the door no matter how much he cried. After the wailing stopped, a neighbor boy got ahold of the man's corpse and was about to eat it when he noticed that he could dimly make out words through the stomach wall. The man had eaten his books. The boy threw aside his chopsticks and chose to die.[53] Perhaps as many as seven hundred thousand starved, or seventy to eighty percent of the inhabitants.[54]

After six months of this, the Qing sent a cavalry force to lift the siege. Koxinga fought with his usual wiles, allowing his main force to clash openly and then, when the enemy had exposed its flank, springing an ambush from the woods. The Manchus scattered but quickly regrouped. He occupied the upwind position and blasted their ranks with fire-arrows, rockets, guns, and cannons, but suddenly the wind shifted. Smoke was driven back toward his side. His men couldn't see each other or recognize flag signals. When the Manchus charged, they ran. He tried to rally them, leading an assault with his elite troops, but it was too late. Many of his top commanders were killed.

The Qing advanced on Haicheng, knowing that if they could take it, they could stop his momentum and crack his control of Fujian. His career could have ended here. But he recruited locals to reinforce walls and build stockades. Workers were busy on the Qing side too—twenty thousand of them carrying provisions and heavy cannons and setting them up across a small river[55] from Koxinga's camp.

The Manchus opened fire, bombarding his camps day and night for a week. He couldn't dislodge them. They flattened his stockades, keeping his men cowering in holes. His messengers were too scared to transmit orders. Troops and officers "began muttering to each other."[56]

According to Yang Ying, Koxinga read the fright on his officers' faces and said, "If we don't succeed here, how can we hope to restore China?"[57] He said that those who wanted to leave could go. "But I'm staying here. I'll live or die on this ground."[58]

"Your Lordship," said his main advisor. "You may wish to stay here, but I'm afraid your generals and commanders won't be able to persuade their troops of your intent."[59]

Koxinga got out the seal the emperor had given him, with its characters Great Rebel-Quelling General. It was the embodiment of his authority, the way he signed letters and orders. Seals were carefully guarded because their seizure marked total defeat. "Take this seal," he said, "and go show it to the officers in the other camps. Tell them the emperor gave it to me and I intend to die for this cause. I have no intention of leaving."[60]

It worked. When the officers saw the seal, they braved the cannonfire and came to Koxinga to confer. He served wine. Stirring speeches were made. The brave commander Gan Hui quoted a patriot who'd fought the Mongols hundreds of years before: "Since time immemorial, no one has escaped death. My faithful heart may stop beating here today, but let my loyalty be a beacon through history!"[61] The officers found their courage: "Let us die here together in loyalty!"

Maybe they drank too much, because Koxinga climbed up a watchtower, ignoring pleas to stay down below where it was safer. "Life and death," he said, "are determined by Heaven. What meaning do cannons have to me?"[62] Enemy soldiers saw him gesturing down at their positions, protected only by a servant with a quilt shield. They vied to shoot him. His officers got him down just before a cannonball splintered his chair.[63]

Below, he laid out a plan:

> The enemy has been firing for several days and nights with their big cannons, thousands upon thousands of shots. Yesterday our spies reported that their camp is running out of powder and grain and their supplies will soon be gone. I predict that tonight they will fire a massive barrage and tomorrow morning will storm our positions with all their forces, hoping for a decisive victory. If they do not win they will have to retreat. The enemy's tricks and tactics are all known to me, and I have considered them carefully, so tomorrow, when they cross the river to attack our positions, they will try to fool us with empty cannons, but they will have no way of actually using them to attack.[64]

He ordered munitions expert He Ming to bury a network of bombs and bamboo fuse pipes along the riverbank and told his other commanders to fortify themselves in trenches to wait out the bombardment so they'd be ready when the Manchus forded the stream the next morning. Sun Zi says that when defending a riverbank, one should always let the enemy get at least partway across before attacking. Koxinga followed this principle, ordering his generals not to attack until the Manchus had crossed. "If everyone follows orders," he said, "this plan will work."[65]

When evening fell, enemy cannons thundered forth as he'd predicted. His camps were "smashed flat as the flat earth,"[66] but his troops were safe in trenches.

Just before dawn, the Manchus began crossing. First came porters with carts on their shoulders. Then came armored troops. Koxinga's men opened fire. The Manchus shot back. "The arrows fell like rain," Yang Ying wrote, "but sitting or standing, our people resisted as best they could."[67]

As the skies lightened, the Manchus began mustering on the bank. Koxinga gave the order to light the fuses. One after another, the mines exploded. Bodies flew into the air. When the smoke cleared, he saw corpses filling the stream. His troops charged out from their holes and routed the survivors.

It was the sort of triumph from which legends are born. "This battle," Yang Ying wrote, "was a case of snatching life from death and achieving victory in a desperate battle. Without our lord Koxinga's skill and personal leadership, it would not have turned out this way."[68]

RECOGNITIONS

The Battle of Haicheng made Koxinga's name. Shortly afterward, he received letters from two rival emperors. The Ming emperor Yongli promoted him to the highest noble rank: prince. Koxinga declined to use the term, saying he wasn't yet worthy, and instead he asked for titles for his generals. The other letter came from the Qing emperor. It offered Koxinga a title and asked him to join him and rule over Fujian Province, saying he could keep several prefectures for himself and retain control over seaborne trade.

The Qing emperor, Shunzhi, was still a teenager. His letter tried to use Confucian morality to persuade Koxinga to switch sides. "I cherish the importance," Shunzhi wrote, "of father-son relations. Compassionate filiality is a natural and Heaven-born thing. Your father has already chosen to serve us. Why do you choose to continue in enmity?"[69] Shunzhi also dispatched letters from Koxinga's father, who commanded and urged and cajoled Koxinga to defect. Some of Koxinga's younger brothers also came from their father in Beijing. They laid it on thick. If Koxinga didn't accept the peace offer, they cried, father would be killed.

In the Confucian tradition, loyalty to family was considered naturally more important than loyalty to one's sovereign. A famous passage in Confucius's *Analects* tells about a man who bragged that people were so righteous in his homeland that if a father stole a sheep, his son would turn him in. Confucius replied, "True uprightness is to be found when a son conceals his father's crime or a father conceals his son's."[70] Family loyalty should naturally trump political loyalty.

But Koxinga had none of it. "You youngsters," he said to his brothers, "don't know the ways of the world. . . . Father is only safe so long as I am at large. If I shave my head and accept the Qing's deal then father and you will be headed for ill fates. Stop speaking to me of these things! Do you think it's easy to deny my humanity and abandon my father? Doing the right thing is not easy! It's not easy!"[71]

Even so, he kept negotiating with the Qing, and some historians have argued that he was considering accepting the peace offer, that his loyalty to the Ming wasn't entirely sincere. "One shouldn't," writes one historian, "overestimate Koxinga's patriotism."[72] Other historians vehemently disagree, saying that Koxinga's commitment to the Ming was deep, even "fanatical."[73]

Which side is right? I incline toward the latter view. For one thing, it's clear that he used the ceasefire to shore up his position and gather provisions.[74] Knowing that the Qing would find this suspicious, he sent letters to them: "When you have several hundred thousand troops, getting them to take off their armor and wait for peace is easy, but getting them to accept the pressing needs of an empty stomach is not."[75] He was allowed to proceed.

For another thing, his public persona stressed loyalty and righteousness. He seems to have seen something wrong in a China where self-interest and familial interest trumped morality. Perhaps this reflects his Japanese upbringing—that's certainly what Japanese authors suggest.[76] In any case, his statements placed righteousness above family interest. When the Ming emperor had asked him to sail south and save the court, Koxinga immediately complied. His generals urged him not to leave Xiamen so thinly defended, but he replied that the wealth and safety of his family were less important than doing the right thing.[77] When Xiamen was sacked and his family fortune stolen, he still refused to turn back. "How can I worry about the care of my own family?"[78] His generals persisted and eventually he did return to Xiamen, but he made a show of reluctance, saying he feared desertion.

He also expressed admiration for the righteousness of the ancient classics, as though the China of his own time had lost its way: "I always admired the righteousness of the Spring and Autumn period."[79]

He used public occasions to make clear his feelings. In 1652, a man named Ku Chengdong brought him the severed head of a Qing general.[80] Ku had been the general's servant, but he'd assassinated his master and expected Koxinga to reward him. Instead Koxinga said, "A servant killing his master is a grave transgression. What does it teach those who follow after?" He ordered Ku to be decapitated. When Ku heard about the order he was shocked. "Shouldn't I serve as an example?" he said. "Don't you want others to copy me? If they do, the Land of Min will all soon be yours!" Koxinga's generals asked Koxinga not to carry out the execution.

But he was adamant. "Winning the Land of Min," he said, "is just a temporary private interest, but punishing great betrayals serves the cause of righteousness for all time. I'm not willing to pursue my current interest at the expense of eternal righteousness!" Ku was beheaded.[81] This wasn't the only time that Koxinga made a public point of prizing loyalty and punishing selfishness.[82] He did so to prove he stood for something more than winning a war: he wanted to restore values and virtues to China.

We'll never know for sure to what extent Koxinga considered accepting the Qing offer. In letters to his father that he knew the Qing would read, he said he was willing to defect but didn't trust the Qing or didn't like their offers. Probably he did this intentionally to keep envoys running back and forth with new offers, because it seems that privately he expressed more certitude. According to Yang Ying, his brothers cried and pleaded: "If we return and report that the negotiations have failed, then we'll have no hope of survival! And father, too, will have it hard!"[83] Koxinga replied, "My mind is made up! No more words!"[84]

Even as he expressed such clarity, he kept the negotiations alive for another year. There were more letters, more envoys, more scenes of weeping, "tears cast for a day and a night."[85]

Some accounts suggest that this negotiation depressed him—that although his mind was made up, he still felt anguish: "Koxinga was righteous and didn't accept recruitment, but he couldn't extinguish his own feelings about his father. Deep into the night he stood awake, looking toward the north [where his father was], privately feeling profound sadness."[86]

This is one of those dramatic stories that's supposed to make historians nervous, but there is a strong argument against those who believe Koxinga was considering switching sides: while the negotiations were going on, he was creating a government, strengthening his armies, and preparing for a massive assault into the heart of China.

The Sea King

In the spring of 1655, while peace envoys ran back and forth, Koxinga and his advisors "sat down to discuss being the Sea King."[1] They created a government. They changed Xiamen's name to Ming Memorial State and established there the six ministries of the traditional Chinese administration: the Ministry of War, Ministry of Personnel, Ministry of Rites, Ministry of Works, Ministry of the Exchequer, and Ministry of Punishments. It was a Ming mirror site, a copy of the government that the Ming Yongli Emperor ruled a thousand miles to the west in Yunnan Province.[2] They founded schools and academies.[3] Important people arrived: high Ming officials, famous scholars, noblemen. "On the islands," a source records, "the number of men in silk and hats multiplied and there was an ambience of peace and prosperity."[4] Even the Ming Prince of Lu, who had once been considered a candidate for emperor, came to Xiamen and was given a palace on the neighboring island of Jinmen.[5]

Koxinga focused most on forging his military. He built a training complex with a a multistory building to house instructors and an observation deck that looked down on a drilling field. He named it "The Pavilion of Military Drill."[6] As soon as it was finished, he climbed to the top and watched each division perform.

He wasn't impressed. So he personally revamped the drills, developing a regimen he called the Five Plum-Flower Drill Method. He taught it himself, following squads around and pointing out their shortcomings. He wrote it out and had it printed in manuals.[7]

He held grand inspections. The first time he found that one division was lax and ordered its commander, one of his highest ranking officers, to be punished with forty lashes in the middle of the field. Other commanders kneeled and begged him not to go through with the penalty, so instead he demoted him by one rank. But the man was so depressed and worried he got ill. Others who failed were beaten or had arrows driven through their ears.[8]

They were lucky compared to commander Cai Fei, who came and reported that the Manchus had routed him on the battlefield. Koxinga ordered him beheaded. His head was put on a stake and displayed to the troops.[9]

Heads on stakes were an accepted part of military discipline, but Koxinga was gaining a reputation for severity. He named inspectors to follow on campaign and report those who failed to uphold discipline. They carried red flags with grim words: "In the front ranks, those who disobey will be beheaded. Those who retreat will also be beheaded."[10] Commanders and generals wouldn't be spared. Punishments would follow a simple dictum: execute first, then report.[11]

The boundary between severity and cruelty is easy to cross, and Koxinga seems to have crossed it. "In the fifteen years that he ruled," wrote a Spanish missionary who lived in Xiamen, "it is estimated that he executed more than five hundred thousand people, many of them for light offenses, and this doesn't even count the innumerable souls killed in battle."[12] (The missionary attributed this penchant for violence to his Japanese heritage.[13]) The missionary's tally is an extreme exaggeration. Yet even pro-Koxinga accounts note that Koxinga had a bad temper. Usually he would yell, but sometimes, and even worse, "he showed his anger not through threats or reproaches but through a terrifying false laugh."[14]

His severity sometimes cost him the support of his own men. In 1656, Su Mao, one of his top commanders, lost a battle. He'd made a poor decision, and more than five hundred men died. Koxinga got furious and had him beheaded. He also punished others he deemed to have failed in the battle. One, a man named Huang Wu, was demoted and reposted to Haicheng City, which also happened to be the post of a cousin of the recently beheaded Su Mao. Huang Wu and the cousin conspired and surrendered Haicheng to the Qing.[15] It was a serious blow to Koxinga. Not only was it an important port and significant source of tax revenues, but its warehouses also held a quarter of a million hectoliters of grain and innumerable amounts of cannons, guns, and equipment.[16]

The loss of Huang Wu, however, proved even more devastating in the long term. He bore a grudge and became an eager collaborator.[17] He told the Qing about Koxinga's secret networks and how they stretched into Qing territories. The information allowed the Qing to cut off sources of income and intelligence.[18] Huang Wu also authored more aggressive plans. He advised the Qing to dig up the Zheng family graves and desecrate the bodies. He advised them to interdict Min trade. It was thanks partly to Huang Wu's advice that the Qing adopted a draconian coastal evacuation policy, which forced all coastal residents of Fujian to move ten kilometers from the shore.[19] These policies came later—the coastal exclusion policy didn't get under way until late 1661—but the loss of Huang Wu was a major setback. It wouldn't have happened if Koxinga hadn't been so severe.

Koxinga also seems to have become prouder and more brittle. While Su Mao's troops were dying on the bridge, a young Manchu prince was marching into the Land of Min with an army of thirty thousand. Most of Koxinga's troops were out on campaign and Xiamen was undefended. Instead of calling them back, Koxinga ordered a mass evacuation, making officials and grandees pack up their inkstones and move. Two officials complained, saying that he should bring his armies back from the fields.

He was furious and ordered the men beheaded. His uncle Hongkui persuaded him to commute the punishment to eighty lashes, still extremely severe. Koxinga didn't like the challenge to his authority and wrote a strident letter, saying that the two men were interfering with his rule, needlessly frightening and stirring up the people. "Don't you think," he wrote, "that the Qing has more experienced generals than this cute little child-prince who still smells of his mother's milk? . . . It's just a gambit. They're trying to pressure me into peace. That's all. . . . I've only ordered the evacuation to cause them to hesitate."[20] He compared himself to China's most revered strategist, Zhuge Liang, who, in a famous story, once found himself in a similar position. His armies were on campaign and his headquarters was about to be attacked by an enemy. According to the story, Zhuge Liang opened the gates and sat on the wall sipping wine and playing the zither, a couple of children playing next to him for effect. The enemy commander saw the scene and was afraid there would be an ambush, so he retreated.

Koxinga said he was doing the same thing. Yang Ying states that when people heard Koxinga's explanation, they exclaimed, "The lord's brilliant stratagems are flawless, way beyond what us little people can understand."[21] Present-day authors have taken their cue from the chronicle and written admiringly of Koxinga's brilliant stratagem, but I'm not sure Koxinga's behavior is praiseworthy.[22] In the story, Zhuge Liang is confident and serene, whereas Koxinga appeared anything but calm. Evacuating his capital certainly didn't make him look confident. As it turned out, this Manchu army was easily defeated, thanks to Koxinga's navy, but the angry incident suggests that Koxinga was becoming increasingly arrogant. Indeed, one historian suggests that when he won that naval battle, he became overconfident, convinced "that the Qing grip was infirm and slipping."[23]

Overconfidence would mar his next endeavor: to "attack right at the enemy's heart and guts."[24]

THE NORTHERN EXPEDITION

Koxinga's plan was simple: to push deep into Qing-held territory and capture Nanjing, China's Southern Capital, the original seat of the Ming Dynasty. He believed this would persuade his countrymen to turn against the Manchus and flock to the Ming cause.[25]

He ordered more ships, larger ones, and reorganized them so that each one had a special license plate. He drilled his troops, held special inspections. Were the guns, cannons, cannonballs, suits of armor, fire arrows, shields, swords, and lances all in good repair? Were the ships strong enough to endure the winds and waves of the open sea? Were the flags clean and bright?

There were parties and banquets. His first wife feted the wives and mothers and sons and daughters of the officials and officers and men, but there were so many she had to hold seven different banquets.[26]

The expedition got under way, but a Qing army marched on Xiamen, and Kozinga's forces had to turn back.

The next year he tried again. This time he created a new force of soldiers garbed in heavy steel mail from head to knee. People called them the Iron Men, but their official designation was the Tiger Guard, and they had terrifying tiger faces painted on their shields and helmets. Only men who could carry a five-hundred-pound stone lion around a circuit could apply and, of these, not all were selected. They had to prove skill with lances, shields, and bow and arrow. They had to demonstrate swordplay with a fifty-pound sword.

He loaded everyone onto the ships, even wives and children, even high officials. After all, when the new capital was founded, they had to be ready to start ruling it.

Italian missionary Victorio Riccio saw this invasion force when it was about to depart in June 1658. "It was," he wrote, "the most powerful fleet that had ever been seen in the Chinese seas." He estimated that there were fifteen thousand vessels, "although others insisted that there were even more than that." There were a hundred thousand armed soldiers, eight thousand cavalry horses, and all manner of supplies, as well as thousands and thousands of sailors. Some Chinese sources have even higher estimates. One indicates that the fleet consisted of fifty thousand vessels, a hundred and seventy thousand armed troops, five thousand cavalry, and eight thousand Iron Men.[27] The consensus opinion is that the expedition had about a hundred and fifty thousand troops.[28] One can imagine the impression such a powerful army—one of the largest in the world—would create on observers. "It was a shocking and awesome sight," the missionary wrote. "The fleet occupied the waters in such a way that the ocean looked like an immense forest of bare trees."[29]

The forest sailed northwards, but once again Koxinga didn't make it to Nanjing. This time the problem was dragons, or at least that's how Yang Ying explained it.[30]

There were two small islands where the Yangtze debouched into the ocean. They were the best place to rest before sailing upriver. One was called Monkey Mountain, and the other was called Sheep Island. They were uninhabited, but Sheep Island had the ruins of an old temple called the Temple of the Sheep Island King.

Koxinga's chief navigator[31] said it was a place of deep magical power, where two dragons dwelled, deep underwater. One was called Dimsighted and the other was called Blind One. They were sensitive to loud noises, so he warned Koxinga to keep his troops quiet. There should be no banging of gongs or burning of spirit money, things that superstitious sailors liked to do to pray for good weather.

There's no sense in tales like this, said Koxinga, because the march of righteous armies is supported by the Will of Heaven. In all his years on the seas he'd never seen demonic influences like these dragons. He let his troops bang gongs and fire cannons.

A black cloud covered the sky. Thunder roared. Lightning flashed. Huge waves thrashed the ships. Rain poured from the sky. You couldn't see, not even a few feet in front of you, and you heard cries for help, horrible sounds of rending and tearing, beating and crashing.

One of Koxinga's generals knelt down and said to Koxinga, "Your lordship is close to the Emperor, the Son of Heaven. Please pray to stop the winds and waves!"

Koxinga refused. "If the Will of Heaven is with us, what use is it for a man to beg and pray?"

The storm worsened. Soon many officials knelt before him on the heaving ship.

He relented. He made four deep bows in prayer. The storm lifted. The sea calmed.

This devastating typhoon, whether or not it was caused by myopic dragons, was a major setback. His fleet was scattered, scores of vessels lost.[32] Thousands of people were missing, including more than two hundred from his own household, among whom were six of his concubines and three of his sons.[33] Scholars estimate deaths in the thousands.[34] Hundreds of others made it ashore but were captured.[35]

Koxinga gave a bitter laugh and ordered that the corpses be found and buried.[36] He turned back, held some executions, and began repairing his ships.

The next year, 1659, he tried again. This time he made it past the dragons and entered the Yangtze (figure 11).

Koxinga had once warned his father, when the latter was about to defect to the Qing, that "a fish cannot survive for long out of deep

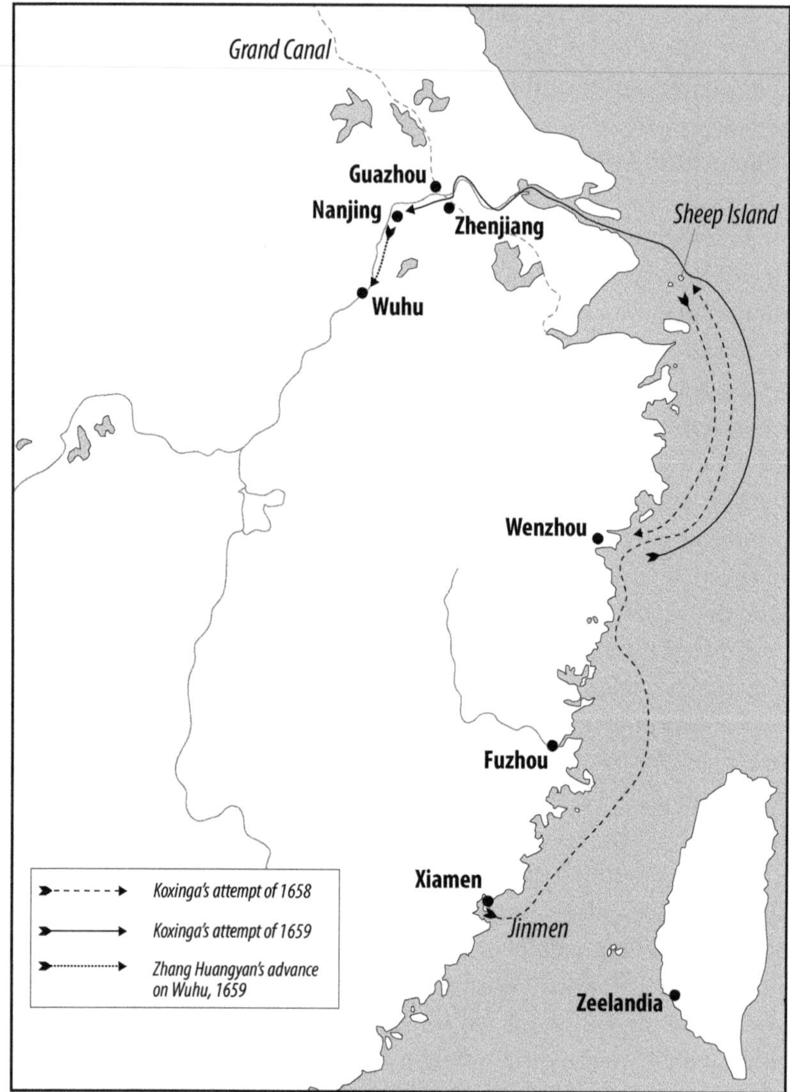

Figure 11. Koxinga's attempts to attack Nanjing, 1658–1659.

water." Now he himself was leaving the ocean behind. On the coast, he'd held an enormous advantage because the Qing didn't understand naval warfare. His ships could navigate the Yangtze River, but it was quite a different sort of sailing, and for the first time he was penetrating deep into Qing territory.

Equally important, this was a foreign land. The inhabitants were Chinese, but they spoke a different language, as different from Min as Spanish is from Romanian, and they had different customs. Up to this point, Koxinga had been able to rely on his Min contacts, who knew each hillside, each hidden cove, each mountain stream. He no longer had the geographical knowledge.

But there were locals who could help him. Not just fishermen and merchants, but loyalist leaders who were as committed to the cause as he was.

One of them was Zhang Huangyan, a man who'd been fighting against the Qing even longer than Koxinga. Zhang had even been part of assaults up the Yangtze River led by other Ming loyalists. Koxinga was wise to choose him as his main advisor.

Too bad he didn't listen to him.

THE STONE CITY

When Koxinga's main fleet arrived in the mouth of the Yangtze, Zhang said, "This area is the sea gateway to the river. It would be wisest to consolidate control here and use it as our main base, because from here we can control various prefectures."[37] Koxinga said no and pushed forward.[38]

To reach Nanjing he would have to gain control over the Guazhou region, where the river narrowed and flowed faster. Across it, the Qing had stretched an iron cable called a Roiling River Dragon. Someone would have to cut it before the fleet could pass, and they'd have to do it under fire, because the Qing had placed floating cannon fortresses on the banks. Koxinga dispatched Zhang to help with this difficult job. "Thinking of my country," Zhang wrote, "I dared, out of love, to bow and receive this order. Then I raised my sails and sailed against the current."[39] He took the vanguard, moving upriver in swift vessels called sandboats, leaving behind flags to mark sandbars for Koxinga's main fleet (figure 12).

It was a bright day when the loyalists got to Guazhou, but the wind was hard, the current swift, and the Manchu cannons roared out. "The troops were badly wounded," Zhang later wrote. "Bones flew and flesh jumped."[40] He shouted out his orders. Beat the drums! Row

Figure 12. Picture of sandboat, 1646. This woodblock print depicts a sandboat, a sturdy vessel that Zhang Huangyan used when launching his assault of the "Roiling River Dragon" in 1659. The text on the left notes that "the bottom is flat, and the body is light, so that it fears no shallows. It can be employed to go upwind, for it defies the wind." On these sandboats, Zhang Huangyan sailed swiftly up the Yangtze, well in advance of Koxinga's main fleet. From Zheng Dayu, *Jing guo xiong lüe*, "Wu bei kao," juan 18, quote from folio 7v. Used by permission of Harvard Yenching Library.

in rhythm! Divers held their breath underwater and tried to cut the cable, while soldiers in boats attacked the floating forts. They were massive structures, made of thick fir planks and carrying five hundred troops and forty huge cannons each. "They were extremely deadly things," Yang Ying wrote, "able to blast to pieces any ships that encountered them."[41] Only seventeen of the several hundred vessels attacking the cable survived the encounter, but eventually the cable was cut. Three floating fortresses were captured.

With the Roiling River Dragons vanquished, Koxinga could press his attack against the town of Guazhou. His land troops pummeled the Manchu armies while his cannon ships blasted away from the river. A brave detachment scaled the walls and planted their flag on top, at which everyone surged forward at once. The enemy broke and ran, but Koxinga had sent a force around behind the city. The fugitives were captured and killed. Koxinga ordered the city searched. All the Manchus found were immediately killed. Corpses filled the moats and wells.[42]

It was a vital victory because Guazhou squatted on the Grand Canal, the main artery of transport between Beijing and the wealthy regions to the south. But right across the river was another important target: the garrison town of Zhenjiang, which they'd have to seize to control the river. As Koxinga prepared to besiege it, Zhang came forward with more advice: Why not send a small naval force upriver to "pound on Nanjing's door"[43] just enough to distract the enemy?

Koxinga thought this a grand idea. And why shouldn't Zhang himself lead the force? And, why shouldn't Zhang, after pounding on the door, continue upstream, well past Nanjing, and try his luck at the river port of Wuhu? This would confuse the enemy, and on the off chance that Zhang might be successful in capturing Wuhu, Ming forces would then control both the upstream and the downstream approaches to Nanjing, making it even harder for the Qing to send reinforcements.

Zhang wasn't eager for this job. Wuhu was a major metropolis, "the throat of seven provinces, a place for merchants and traders from all areas to assemble."[44] He would have to penetrate deep into enemy territory. "I'm just a scholar," he wrote, "and my troops were weak and few. How was I qualified for such a responsibility?"[45] But he accepted.

He embarked on a small fleet of flat-bottomed sandboats and poled his way upstream.

He was surprised at how enthusiastically the people along the river greeted him. Small boats weaved in and out of his fleet, bringing fruit and melons, not at all afraid, as though they didn't even know this was an army. "I saw this and felt joy," Zhang wrote, "thinking it was a dignified scene of a princely army."[46] But he also noted that the people were frightened. They said they wanted to be loyal to the Ming but needed troops for defense and officials to govern. In one place they burned incense and knelt in the rain, kowtowing, begging him to come ashore and set up command in their city. He had no men to spare and was afraid he was behind schedule, so he pressed on.

The Yangtze was full and swift this year. His nimble boats made slow progress. He worried that Koxinga's main force would be even slower and the enterprise would be jeopardized.

He was happy to hear Koxinga had taken Zhenjiang in a decisive victory, the enemy completely routed, corpses spread out through the countryside, blood filling the ditches, survivors scattering like rodents to the four directions, and so on.[47] But then he learned what Koxinga decided to do next: to tarry in Zhenjiang so that the locals could get a good look at his forces. Koxinga dressed his ministers and officers in special red robes with caps and belts, and marched them and his troops into the city, drums beating, horns playing.[48] The people came out to watch, filling the streets and marketplaces, as the procession marched around the city, from the great sluice gate to the Ganlu Temple.[49] "Those who saw them," wrote Yang Ying, "said that this was truly an army from Heaven."[50] Afterward, Koxinga stayed even longer, preparing a feast. Day and night they ate and drank, playing music and dancing.[51] This display of wealth and power was his strategy, so that the decisive victory in Zhenjiang would resonate, would shatter the enemy's resolve, would "destroy their courage, and then Nanjing will fall of its own accord, with nary a strike against it."[52]

Zhang didn't share Koxinga's confidence that the Qing were ready to crumble. He worried that the longer Koxinga took to reach Nanjing, the more time the Manchus would have to send reinforcements. He wrote and urged Koxinga to move quickly. "In war," he wrote, quoting Sun Zi, "speed is the most important thing."[53] He estimated that Koxinga's Iron Men could march about ten miles (thirty li) per day. This was slow, but if they pushed themselves they could still reach Nanjing within five days, soon enough to keep the initiative. But he warned Koxinga not to advance upriver by water. "The big ships," he wrote, "would be ponderous moving upstream. That's no strategy."[54]

Gan Hui, one of Koxinga's most loyal and experienced generals, advised the same thing. He, too, quoted an ancient adage: *In war one must capitalize on one's thundering reputation.*[55] "We should," he said, "take advantage of this great victory [in Zhenjiang]. While the enemy is confused and panicked and unprepared, we should make a long drive, marching day and night overland, taking multiple routes and pressing directly on Nanjing. If they dare to meet us in battle, we'll break them like we would snap a little piece of bamboo, capturing the city in one beat of the drum."[56] Like Zhang, he warned that going by water would be slow and give the enemy time to reinforce.

Koxinga tried going by land for a time, but many commanders complained.[57] The troops were in unfamiliar territory. It was hot. They were tired and many were ill. The commanders felt it wasn't wise to march overland at double speed, especially since there had been so much rain that the streams and rivers were hard to cross. Koxinga decided to override Zhang's and Gan Hui's advice. He embarked the troops on the ships.

Zhang was astonished when he heard about this decision. He'd already arrived at Nanjing, pulled his sandboats up on the flats beneath the great Guanyin Gate, and begun skirmishing with the Qing. For two nights he'd camped there, but not a single one of Koxinga's ships had arrived. Meanwhile, the enemy was moving fast. Some powerful Manchu units happened to be returning from campaigns far to the south. Learning that Koxinga's main forces had still not arrived in Nanjing, they'd embarked these units on swift boats and sent them downriver toward Nanjing. "There were more than a hundred of these boats," Zhang wrote, "loaded with crack troops. . . . They floated downstream with the current, rowing as rapidly as though they were flying."[58] Zhang tried to stop them, but they got by.

Since Koxinga was taking so long, Zhang sent people upstream to Wuhu as ordered and then dashed here and there with the Ming banner. It seemed like Koxinga's strategy might be working. Envoys were arriving from all over to declare their loyalty outright, or to say they were interested in discussing coming over to the Ming side. They were thrilled by Koxinga's huge forces, and by the victories they achieved, some of them miraculous, like when four of Zhang's troops and four Iron Men scared away a hundred Qing troops and captured the riverside port of Jiangpu.[59] The episode was made into a nursery rhyme: "Is that a tiger? No! It's just eight iron generals, scaring away a whole town of Manchu guards."[60] (It sounds better in Chinese.) Wuhu fell, and Zhang went there to coordinate, receiving more envoys. Seven prefectural capitals, three subprefectural capitals, and thirty-two county seats sent representatives to Zhang or Koxinga.[61] Zhang had his hands full trying to coordinate them. "Truly," he wrote, "I was constantly on the go."[62]

But Koxinga evinced no urgency. His troops reached Nanjing two weeks after they'd paraded around Zhenjiang. Then they did nothing.

Koxinga was persuaded that the city was about to surrender. His men had captured letters describing how things were within the stone walls. One letter fearfully described Koxinga's troops—"more than two hundred thousand strong, with war ships of more than a thousand vessels, their bodies completely armored in steel so that arrows and swords can't penetrate."[63] It mentioned how Manchu refugees from the battles of Guazhou and Zhenjiang were "shaken to their souls."[64] It begged for help from Beijing: "The situation is as precarious as a pile of eggs, and so we ask that a great army be sent southward to reinforce us and stamp out [the enemy], to prevent the plains from being set afire and creating a pyre reaching to Heaven!"[65]

Koxinga took this letter as evidence that his strategy was working. "If it's like this," he exclaimed, "then Nanjing must certainly surrender!"[66] He ordered the city's leaders to submit. He had little notes copied out and tied to arrows to shoot into the city for the populace to read.[67]

His generals were less optimistic. Gan Hui was brave enough to voice his worries. "Our great army," he told Koxinga, "has been camped here for a long time beneath the walls and things have grown stagnant. . . . Please let's quickly storm and capture the city!"[68]

Koxinga said no. Attacking would cost many lives. It would be better to let the enemy go ahead and gather reinforcements. There would be a great battle and a great victory and Nanjing would surrender. In the meantime, Koxinga said, the areas around Nanjing were coming over to the Ming side. The city would become isolated. It would have no choice but to give up.[69]

Gan Hui returned to his camp and waited while Koxinga entertained envoys. Four eager young men came from the town of Mingguang, fifty miles away, asking for seals and letters of marque so they could raise forces on their own. Koxinga was proud when they said, upon seeing his troops, "What people are saying isn't an exaggeration! Truly this is an army of Heaven. The enemy won't be able to withstand this!"[70] Everything seemed to indicate that he was on the brink of victory.

"For half a month," Zhang Huangyan wrote in frustration, "Koxinga wouldn't even hear of firing a single arrowhead into the city!"[71] Zhang was shocked to learn that Koxinga wasn't even sending troops out from Nanjing to secure other strongholds, so important places still remained under Manchu control. "Jurong and Danyang," he noted, "which truly are the strategic keys to Nanjing, were not captured."[72] This meant that the Qing could still send reinforcements into Nanjing, several hundred here, several hundred there. They were starting to add up. They also sent supplies—food, transport boats, even steeds for the Manchu reinforcements who'd had to leave their horses behind when they'd boarded the swift boats that had sped them to Nanjing in advance of Koxinga.[73]

Huangyan wrote again to Koxinga. "It's absolutely vital," he wrote, "to send out some of your commanders to capture the cities around Nanjing so they can intercept enemy reinforcements. Once we've reduced all the places around Nanjing we can concentrate all our forces on the city and the enemy will be like sheep awaiting slaughter."[74] In any case, he urged Koxinga to do *something* soon: "Encamping troops at a strong city you have to be careful. The longer one remains camped out, the more likely it is that accidents will happen."[75]

He was right. After Koxinga had camped at Nanjing for two weeks, one of his officers defected to the Qing. Some sources say he was a gambling man who owed tens of thousands of copper pieces,[76] others that he'd disobeyed an order and was afraid he'd be beheaded.[77] He called up to sentries on Nanjing's massive walls, climbed up the rope they let down, and began telling the Qing where the landmines and cannon placements and hidden crossbows were. He said it was a good time to attack: "Within the camps they've commanded that for two days everyone will relax and take off their armor to celebrate Koxinga's birthday with toasts to his longevity."[78]

Just outside the city, where the walls turned away from the Yangtze River, Koxinga had placed strong encampments, some on a hill called Monkey Mountain and others below. The defector said the troops there were lax, that each day they took off their helmets to bathe and watch plays.[79]

Koxinga seems to have known that that camp was weak. He'd heard that its commander, Yu Xin, had been letting his men go fishing. He sent someone to investigate, but Yu Xin explained that his apparent carelessness was a cunning plan. He was luring the enemy out. He'd placed cannons to seal off the road that led out from the walls, so his camp was actually as tight as a steel bucket. He said if he didn't feign weakness, the enemy would never dare come out because he'd defeated them before and they were scared. He said his plan was just like an ancient story, when the famous general Zhang Fei pretended to be weak and tricked his enemy into attacking him, leading to the enemy's defeat. Koxinga replied that he wasn't convinced that Yu Xin was of the same caliber as Zhang Fei, He warned him not to be too ambitious, that sometimes if you try to draw a tiger you end up with a dog.[80] He even started sending reinforcements but changed his mind, thinking that there was no way a failure in one camp could spoil his entire enterprise.

But the Qing were preparing a surprise attack. Long ago there'd been a gate through the wall right near Yu Xin's camp, but it had been filled in nearly two hundred years before to shore up the city's defences. Now workers chipped away quietly through the night. They finished their tunnels just before dawn.[81]

With the defector as their guide, they attacked. One detatchment climbed the walls and descended on Yu Xin from above, coming over the rooftops of houses built up against the walls outside the city, yelling at the top of their lungs. Others charged out through holes in the now-open gate. Some of these holes, it seems, emerged within houses, and so shouting Qing soldiers seemed to be pouring out of habitations.

It was chaos: smoke, roaring cannons, war cries, screams as Yu Xin's men were caught and killed, sounds of splashing as they tried to swim away. Some made it, but most were killed or captured. Most of the officers were killed. Yu Xin himself was caught alive.[82]

Koxinga sent reinforcements, but it was too late. The Qing had established a position outside the walls.

The next day he made a stand at Jiangjun Mountain, just south of the city, but he and his commanders didn't know the territory.[83] They placed their positions too far from each other and had trouble coordinating. The Qing came around from behind and struck.

It was a hard-fought battle. The Qing cavalry dismounted, captured the mountain, and then swept down and chased Koxinga's forces to the river, where they were saved by boats.

A few of Koxinga's commanders held the rear, perhaps to allow an orderly retreat, or perhaps because they were trapped and couldn't break through to the river.[84]

One was Gan Hui, whose advice Koxinga had ignored. He was captured. According to one story, when he was taken to Nanjing for interrogation, he refused to kneel before the Qing high commander.[85] When he saw Yu Xin and other comrades kneeling, he kicked them and yelled that they should stand up: "You stupid Chinamen! You still think you can beg for your life?"[86] Right again. The Qing executed all of them.

Koxinga sailed downriver, reaching Zhenjiang the next day, and that's when he realized that Gan Hui was gone, along with so many others. According to Yang Ying, as he realized the extent of the damage, he sighed and said, "I've been so successful tricking the enemy in the past that I believed Yu Xin's words."[87]

But he was nothing if not resilient. He quoted another adage: *A general knows that victory and defeat are facts of life*. There was nothing to do but get on with things. What should he do?

Zhang Huangyan had strong opinions. "I felt," he wrote, "that just because the Nanjing forces had suffered a setback they didn't have to immediately climb aboard their ships. And then I felt that just because they climbed aboard their ships they didn't have to immediately raise their sails. And then I felt that just because they raised their sails they didn't have to leave entirely—they could still defend Zhenjiang."[88] He got out his brush, composed a letter on silk, and gave it to a monk to rush to Koxinga. "I still hold the upper reaches of the river," he wrote. "All of the prefectures are still on our side! If you can spare a hundred vessels to help, we can still try to achieve our great intentions. But if you just give up and leave, what will become of the hundred million souls of this land?"[89]

If Koxinga got the letter he didn't follow the advice. He kept floating downstream. According to some accounts, one of Zhang's protégés, a poor scholar from near Zhenjiang, saw the fleet sailing by and rowed out to see Koxinga. "Your Excellency," he said, "how can you give up on ten years of struggle and disappoint the hopes of the world?" Koxinga didn't answer. He spoke again, tears in his eyes: "But your military strength is still strong! Why not use this little defeat, when the enemy has won a victory and is complacent, to turn the ships around and advance again? Nanjing would surely fall. If you let this opportunity pass, you may never get another chance." He held Koxinga's hand, wailing. Koxinga had him removed.[90]

The fleet reached the sea. Fighting here and there to confuse the Qing, it made its way back to Xiamen.

Zhang Huangyan was up a creek without a paddle. All the places he'd gained were going back to the Qing or being captured. Unable to pass downstream, he fled upriver. Eventually he abandoned his sandboats and marched through the mountains. It was a difficult trek. He had to go into disguise. A thousand miles later, he reached the coast. He didn't give up. He kept urging Koxinga to launch new attacks. But Koxinga had settled on a new plan: to invade Taiwan. Zhang thought it was a terrible idea. So did Koxinga's generals. So did the Dutch.

Heaven Has Not Tired of Chaos on Earth

When Koxinga's tattered army regrouped in Xiamen, the Qing began advancing through the Land of Min. To make matters worse, the Yongli Emperor, the man they'd been fighting to restore to the throne, was missing. Qing forces had chased him over the border to Burma. There was no telling if he was even alive.

In early 1661, Koxinga summoned his commanders to a secret meeting. "Heaven," he said, "has not yet tired of chaos on earth. . . . Although we have achieved important victories, the impostor dynasty—the Qing—is by no means ready to give up."[1] He told them it was time for a bold move. "I want to pacify Taiwan. We'll settle our families and dependents there and use it as our new base."[2]

The commanders were silent, but their faces wore "embarrassed expressions."[3] China traditionally ended at the ocean. Overseas lands were considered off the map.[4] Most Chinese who bothered to think about Taiwan at all thought with some justification that it was filled with violent headhunters and miasmal swamps.

A man named Wu Hao spoke up.[5] He said he'd been to Taiwan and could attest that it was a cesspool of illness. Its bays were shallow, and the great warships would have trouble entering.[6]

But Koxinga had other sources of intelligence. In fact, he had at his disposal a man who'd lived in Taiwan his whole life and had worked closely with the Dutch. In fact, the man even knew the Dutch leaders, including Frederick Coyet himself.

His name was He Bin. He was clever and resourceful. And although he's often portrayed in China as a hero, he seems actually to have been a scoundrel, a liar, and a cheat.[7]

HE BIN

He Bin had started out much like Koxinga's father, as a translator for the Dutch. And just like Koxinga's father, He Bin used his bond with the Dutch to get filthy rich. But whereas Zhilong had made his fortune outside of Taiwan, He Bin found opportunities on the island itself.

In the 1620s, when Koxinga's father was pursuing piracy, Taiwan was still a wild land, inhabited by headhunters and a few bands of Chinese pirates. But by the 1640s and 1650s, when He Bin was building his fortune, Taiwan had become one of the wealthiest colonies in the Dutch Indies. There was a large and growing Chinese population. There were stores, workshops, smithies, churches, schools, orphanages, hospitals, city halls, and stately homes. There was a new harbor complex with wharves and a shipyard and stone piers. The streets were paved in brick and the roads in stone. There were ferry ports and canals and covered marketplaces.

Most important, rich fields of rice and sugar spread out across the plains. He Bin himself owned some of that land. It had come to his family out of a scandal, the first of many that swirled about him. His father had been a translator too, and at one point the Dutch caught him collecting secret fees from Min merchants, commissions for each transaction he helped them conclude with the Dutch. It was illegal, but he'd been doing it under the Netherlanders' hawk noses for years before they'd found out. Yet although they were upset, they also realized they needed him, so they decided not to punish him. They determined that he'd acted this way only because his official salary wasn't enough to pay his debts, so they supplemented it with a large tract of land where he could grow rice without paying taxes. It was a generous gift. He Bin inherited it after his father's death.[8]

But these rice fields were only a small part of his growing fortune. He became involved in many parts of Taiwan's booming economy:

trading, revenue farming, money lending, investments with other Chinese or with Dutchmen. He seems to have gotten involved in real estate. The streets of the colony's busiest city—Zeelandia City—were dotted with his projects. He had a big house on the waterfront, and one of his most important achievements—and sources of revenue—was a municipal scale.

In those days many Dutch cities had municipal scales—some are tourist attractions today because they tend to be grand buildings—but the one in Zeelandia was He Bin's creation, and it was also the source of another scandal. He proposed the idea of a scale to the Dutch Council of Formosa, the island's ruling body, in the early 1650s, saying it would help poor Chinese traders who were being cheated by false weights. The councilors thought it was a wonderful idea. They gave the okay to construct the building and made him the official weighmaster. It was such a lucrative position that the High Council of the Indies in Batavia decided the company should get a bigger share of the proceeds. So the High Councilors ordered Taiwan to hold an open auction for the post of weighmaster. Somehow, He Bin arranged to prevent the auction, probably by bribing the governor of Taiwan, Coyet's predecessor, who awarded him a three-year term as weighmaster for a sum much lower than the position's value. A Dutch tax official got mad and lodged a complaint. He Bin was stripped of his position, and an auction was held. Three Chinese merchants entered the highest bid, but He Bin persuaded the Dutch to let him remain weighmaster anyway, saying he'd be happy to match the winning bid. The three Chinese men were upset and protested, but He Bin nonetheless kept his position. The three Chinese men nursed their grievances.[9]

They weren't the only Min merchants who were upset with He Bin. Seven others joined them to write an unprecedented complaint letter to the Dutch. He Bin, they wrote, "faked goodness and honesty when he was around Dutch officials" even as he engaged in illegal practices to "satisfy his greedy appetite and fill his bottomless stomach."[10] They said he bribed tax collection officials and stole money from poor laborers. They said he lured newly arrived Chinese merchants to his home and tricked them and stole their goods.[11] They accused him of lying, blackmail, theft, and extortion.

Dutch officials never investigated the charges. He Bin got richer.

There were other scandals—suspicious trading ventures, cheating in auctions—but He Bin always came out on top. That's partly because the Dutch needed him. He had ties to Koxinga, and Koxinga's rising power in China was causing tremors in Taiwan.

In the 1650s, Koxinga needed more income to pay for his armies, so he began expanding his trade routes, sending junks directly to places like Tonkin, Cambodia, Palembang, and Melaka. These were ports in which the Dutch had trading interests. Officials in Batavia worried that he'd undermine their profits.[12] They wrote to him and requested—politely, they thought, and with gifts—that he keep out of their markets, and threatened—also politely, they thought—to take measures if he didn't.[13] He didn't listen, so they captured two of his ships. One escaped. The other's rich cargo was impounded.[14]

Koxinga responded by levying an embargo on Taiwan, forbidding Min ships to sail to Taiwan, "not even the smallest vessel or piece of wood," saying that any vessel that did would have its crew executed and its cargo confiscated.[15] He made an example of one junk captain who disobeyed the order. The man was executed in Xiamen and his crew had their right hands cut off.[16]

Taiwan was so dependent on junks from China that the colony's economy collapsed. The shelves of Chinese shops were bare. Farmers couldn't sell their crops. Laborers were laid off and begged for food. Schools ran out of paper. Merchants went bankrupt. Company revenues plummeted. "If it should continue like this for much longer," Dutch officials wrote, "it would spell total ruin for the company in Taiwan."[17] They prayed that God would destroy that "proud tyrannical bastard of Zhilong."[18] But this was 1656, and Koxinga was at the top of his game.

It was at this point that Frederick Coyet became governor of Formosa, and his first order of business was to try to restore Taiwan's economy. He and his advisors decided to send He Bin to Koxinga's court as a special envoy.

He Bin's performance was wonderful. After he returned, he told Coyet he'd managed to clear up all the misunderstandings. He said that every time he mentioned Taiwan's previous governor, Koxinga became upset and violent. So, He Bin said, he'd simply told Koxinga that Taiwan had a new governor, a man named Frederick Coyet, who was "just, good, and intelligent, . . . loved and praised by all."[19] Koxinga was delighted and would reopen trade at once. He would insist, of course, that the Dutch stop capturing his junks and on a few other minor issues, but the embargo would end.

He Bin didn't tell Coyet what really happened. According to Yang Ying, He Bin actually told Koxinga that the "chief of the red-haired barbarians, Coyet," wished "to present tribute and open trade relations, and to display foreign treasures."[20] Presenting tribute and displaying foreign treasures was an old Ming practice, in which inferior countries (all countries were inferior to China) sent ambassadors to kowtow to the emperor, recognizing him as a sort of geopolitical elder brother, their superior in a global hierarchy of governments. Coyet wouldn't have been pleased to know that He Bin had represented the Dutch as inferior, as willing to pay tribute to Koxinga.

But that's not all He Bin had promised on Coyet's behalf. Yang Ying indicates that He Bin said the red-haired barbarians were willing to pay Koxinga a yearly tax of five thousand taels of silver, a hundred thousand arrow shafts, and fifty tons of sulfur.[21] The idea of paying a tax to Koxinga would have incensed Dutch officials.

Having made these promises, He Bin had to deliver the goods, and without alerting the Dutch. So he began to pay the "tribute" himself, financing it with a secret toll on all junks departing for China.[22]

Coyet heard rumors about the toll and confronted He Bin, who denied the charge. Coyet believed him because, as he wrote, "there's no way such a thing could occur here without causing great tumult among the residents."[23]

Coyet had little incentive to investigate further because he was getting kudos from his superiors in Batavia for reopening trade to China.[24] Coyet needed He Bin, who sailed frequently to Xiamen on his behalf, bringing official letters to Koxinga. He Bin's ships also carried war materials: arrow shafts, fish intestines, feathers, and hemp. And they carried the "tribute" of silver supposedly sent from Coyet.

The scheme collapsed in 1659 when a nervous Min merchant asked to speak with Coyet. The man had been a signatory of the letter of complaint against He Bin years earlier. He told Coyet that the rumors were true, that He Bin had indeed been collecting tolls from junks departing Taiwan. The merchant provided such details that Coyet could no longer ignore the evidence. He arrested other Chinese entrepreneurs, who revealed under torture that it was all true. Coyet was shown toll receipts signed by He Bin himself. The tolls were high. Many traders had been driven out of business. Others had borrowed money from He Bin at interest.[25]

Coyet arrested He Bin.[26] He was tried and found guilty. He was fired from his job as translator, dismissed from his other positions, and assessed a fine of three hundred reals. It was a remarkably light punishment. Coyet clearly hoped that He Bin could be persuaded to keep working with him.

But He Bin ran away to Xiamen. He left behind huge debts and brought with him a map.[27]

INVADING TAIWAN

When Koxinga called his generals together to discuss invading Taiwan, he referred to this map. "He Bin," he said, "presented a map of Taiwan showing that the island is vast and fertile, its fields and gardens stretching out for a thousand li, its potential tax revenues worth hundreds of thousands of ounces of silver."[28] Clearly, he said, Taiwan could serve as a new base. He Bin had also pointed out that less than a thousand red-haired barbarian troops guarded the island. It could be captured "without lifting a finger."[29]

His generals knew it was foolish to arouse Koxinga's temper. Only the commander Wu Hao spoke against the idea. (He was later executed, ostensibly for an unrelated offense.) Another man, Yang Chaodong, spoke in favor, saying it was a grand idea that could certainly be carried out successfully. He was later promoted to governor of Taiwan.

Koxinga's commanders weren't the only ones uneasy with the idea. His soldiers weren't told the destination of the new expedition, but they observed the preparations with growing unease. The staging ground was Liaoluo Bay in the Isle of Jinmen, the beach-lined cove where Koxinga's father had defeated Putmans twenty-five years before. As the ships were readied and supplies loaded—supplies that included plows and farm tools—they began to realize that it wouldn't be the sort of coastal voyage they'd undertaken before.[30] They began running away. Koxinga appointed someone to hunt them down.[31]

He made sacrifices to the river for Heaven's blessing and ordered the officers and troops to quickly embark, perhaps worried about more desertions. He Bin embarked, too, to serve as a guide. The ships set out, filling the sea with masts.

Crossing to Taiwan was dangerous. Even the Dutch, with their sturdy ships, considered the Taiwan Straits "hard and heavy waters"[32] (figure 13). Chinese sailors concurred. According to Chinese sailing accounts, you first crossed the so-called Redwater Trench, an area of reddish seas that posed no danger, but then, if the wind was good, you soon reached the fearsome Blackwater Trench,[33] a twenty-mile

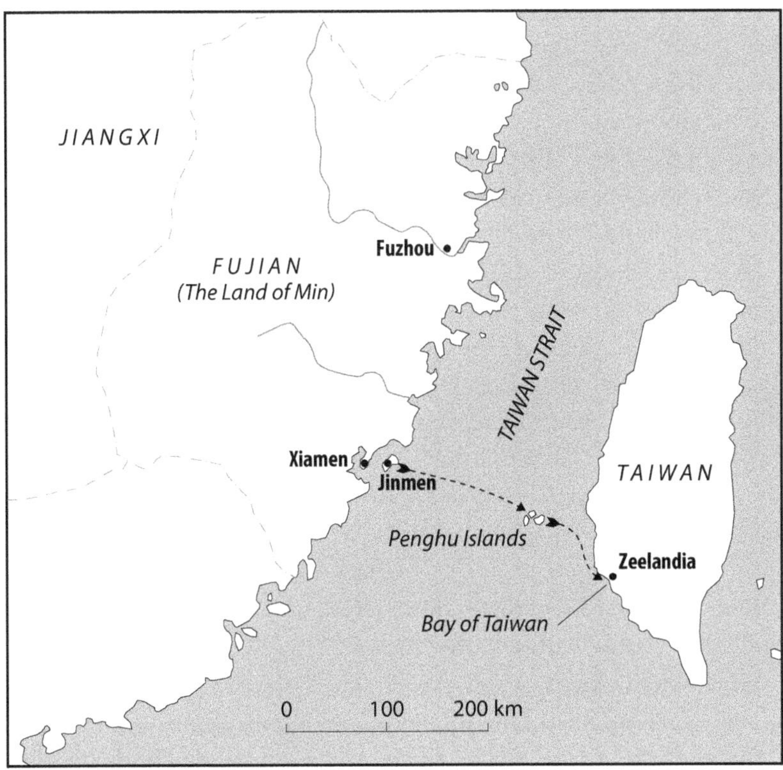

Figure 13. Koxinga's crossing, April 1661.

(eighty-li) band of water that was unfathomably deep and with swift and confusing currents. It was said that the Blackwater Trench had foul vapors and two-headed snakes. To buy safe passage, it was customary to drop paper spirit money into the trench while holding one's breath.[34]

Of course, the sea wasn't all treacherous. One Chinese source about the Taiwan Straits notes the wonder of bioluminescence. "The night sea's moving waves sparkle like liquid fire, and when the heavens are dark it's even more brilliant. On a vessel in the middle of the ocean, one can strike the water to see it. Hit the water once, and liquid sparks fly in splashes, like gallons of shining pearls. Pour them out onto the water's surface, and the glittering light shimmers and twinkles, lasting a long time before fading away."[35]

Koxinga's crossing went well at first. The wind was good, and by the end of the second day they'd reached the Penghu Islands, where the ruins of the old Dutch fortress were, the one that Koxinga's father had helped persuade the Dutch to vacate before they moved to Taiwan. That was the year Koxinga was born, thirty-six years ago.

But the weather got blustery and they couldn't go on. For three days, it rained and blew. Finally it cleared and they set out, but when they reached the last two islands in the archipelago, the Eastern and Western Good Fortune Islands, they met headwinds and turned back.

Koxinga was worried. He Bin had said the crossing took only a few days and that Taiwan's granaries were bountiful, so the expedition had only a few days' worth of provisions.[36] Supplies were dangerously low. Koxinga ordered Yang Ying to tour the islands and look for supplies, but Yang returned with bad news. The inhabitants didn't grow grain or rice, just sweet potatoes, barley, and millet. Bushel by bushel, cup by cup, he'd gathered all he could, but it amounted to just a hundred hectoliters, "not enough for even one dinner for the great army."[37]

This was frightening news. Koxinga decided to take a chance. He ordered the fleet to set forth. Some of his officials kneeled before him and asked him to wait for clear weather.

He responded with a rousing speech. He evoked the ancient story of the freezing river, how the hero Liu Xiu, fighting to restore his dynasty, knew his way was blocked by the river but had faith and continued and the river froze and let his army cross, a sign that Heaven was on his side.[38] Koxinga didn't need to say what happened next, because his officers knew that the hero went on to restore his dynasty. In fact, Koxinga needed only four words to evoke this whole story. This sort of classical knowledge is one of the delights of Chinese, a weaving into today's world of the ancient past in a way that we westerners no longer understand. Victorian schoolboys might have been able to employ Caesar's phrase "*veni, vidi, vici*," on the rugby field with some resonance, but modern westerners—or Americans at least—have lost touch with this tradition, whereas modern Chinese is still filled with resounding classical references. Koxinga said this to the men: "The freezing river allowed passage—this showed that Heaven supported the cause. If Heaven supports our pacification of Taiwan, then today, after we set sail, the winds will become still and the waves will lessen. Or would you rather stay here trapped on these islands and await starvation?"[39] They understood and submitted to the order.

Another version of Koxinga's address to his men before leaving Penghu has him setting up incense and praying to Heaven, saying, "If Heaven's Mandate is already settled [and the Qing have thus been chosen by Heaven], and I am merely deluded [in my desire to restore China to the Ming], then may wild winds blow and angry waves storm, and may all our troops be overcome and perish. But if the future holds a ray of hope, then I pray that Heaven will show some modicum of mercy, and the ancestors will silently offer their help and aid us with a tide, so that we may advance our boats, and directly arrive without trouble, and our army may calmly go ashore."[40]

Whatever he said, the rain was still falling when he set sail. Rain fell and waves tossed the ships. But during the night the rain stopped. The ships sped forward. Heaven, it seems, had blessed the venture. Soon his huge fleet would surprise and frighten the Dutch.

He didn't know it, but Heaven had prepared the way five years previously, when a terrifying storm had flattened a Dutch fortress that had once stood guard over one of two entrances to the Bay of Taiwan, seat of the Dutch colony.

TWO

An Extreme and Terrifying Storm

The most terrifying storm Coyet had ever seen occurred five years before Koxinga's invasion. It began after an unusual stillness. The light changed and a few raindrops spattered on the tile rooftops. Then the wind picked up. After dark you could hear the waves thrash the shore outside the castle, just beyond the dunes. The wind bellowed from the south, which was odd, because at this time of year it should have been coming from the north.

The wind roared through the night and into the dark, wet morning. From the castle you could see the sea heaving to the east, while just to the north the Channel that led past the walls into the Bay of Taiwan churned itself white. Some Chinese boats had capsized, so Coyet sent a few men down to the pier to lash the company's craft—a yacht and a galiot that were waiting to be loaded—to the stone walls fore and aft. Out at sea another galiot, the *Red Fox*, bucked at anchor and its ship's launch was captured by a wave.

Typhoons rotate counterclockwise, so with the wind coming from the south, the typhoon must have been off to the west, in the Taiwan Straits. Most typhoons strike Taiwan on its sparsely populated east coast, so those who live in the densely populated western plains are usually spared direct hits, receiving storms blunted by the island's high mountains. In this case, though, the typhoon took aim right at the western coast, the core area of the Dutch and Chinese settlements.

As the second night fell, the howling intensified. Within the governor's mansion, Coyet heard it turn into "a tempest so extreme and terrifying that no one could remember living through anything like it before."[1] The buildings shuddered and shook. Winds like this could rip palm trees out by the roots and sling them through walls, but the greater concern was water. Zeelandia Castle was built on a tendril of sand that snaked out into the ocean (figure 14). As it stretched northward, the island got bumpy with dunes and then suddenly, as if changing its mind, turned back and pointed toward the mainland like a skeletal finger. Zeelandia Castle was built on this crook, its back up against some dunes and its front gates opening onto the water that usually brought its treasures—cotton, pepper, porcelain, silk, and silver—but which was now hurling itself against the stone pier. The main part of the castle would probably be safe because it was built on a high berm, its thick walls enclosing a large plaza in which there were houses, barracks, and prisons.

But the governor's mansion and the church and the main warehouses and residences were in what they called the lower castle. Originally, the long row of structures built shoulder to shoulder had faced the piers directly. Later a long, thick wall had been built between the piers and the buildings. It had been designed to defend against pirates, samurai, and Spaniards. Now it protected against the waves (figure 15).

All night the storm raged, ripping through gaps in doors and windows. It reached a crescendo around midnight. Several hours later it began to wane.

In the morning, when the Dutch emerged blinking into the light, they were relieved to find the upper and lower castles intact. There were broken windows and torn roofs, but no major damage.

But when they opened the gates they saw devastation. The pier beneath the lower castle had been completely torn away. The shore wall that led along the bank leftward toward the beach and rightward toward the town of Zeelandia had been ripped apart, some of its stones cast high up onto the land, and the stone path that led along it had been scoured away by the water. Some of the huge stones that were meant to guard the bank against erosion had been swept away entirely, and the ships that had been bound to the stone wall were battered, masts

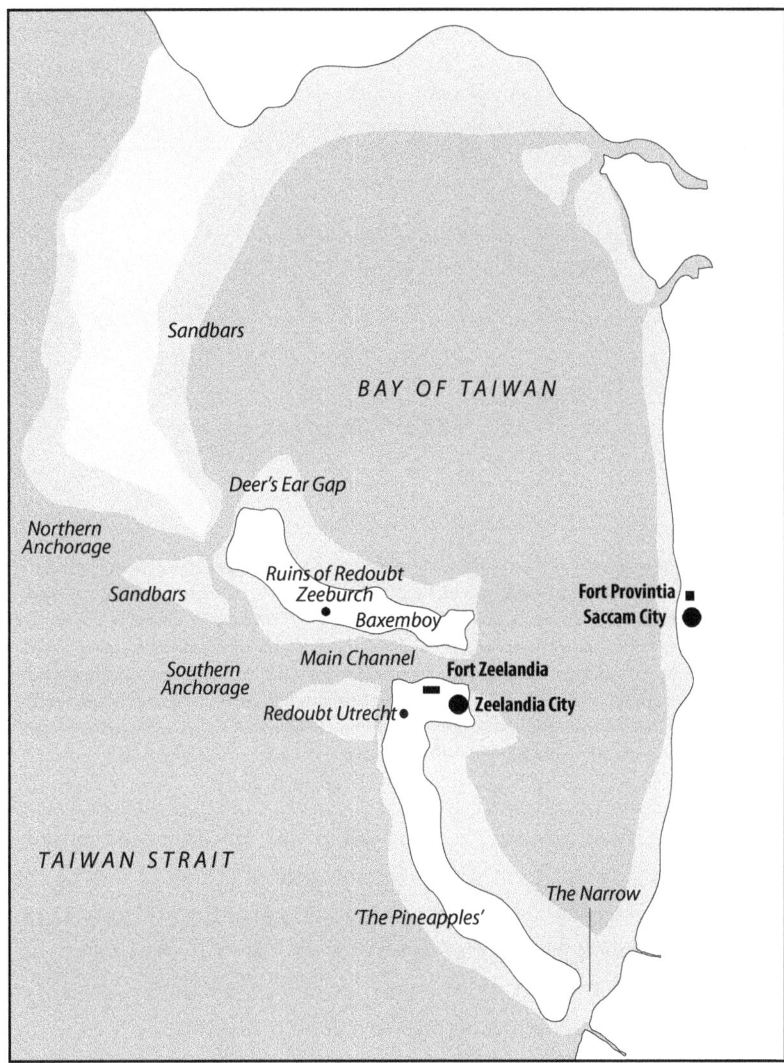

Figure 14. The Bay of Taiwan. The Bay of Taiwan no longer exists, having been filled in by alluvial deposits over the past three centuries. There are a dozen-odd seventeenth-century charts of the bay, but they differ from each other, sometimes drastically. Partly that's because the landscape was changeable even then. Each new storm could throw up an island or destroy one. This reconstruction, based on a chart from 1635 (see figure 18, later), shows Zeelandia Castle on its long, thin island. Across the Channel lies Baxemboy Island, where the Redoubt Zeeburg stood. This redoubt was destroyed in the Extreme and Terrifying Storm of 1656, leaving the way open to Koxinga, who would later sail in through the shallow and tortuous Deer's Ear Gap.

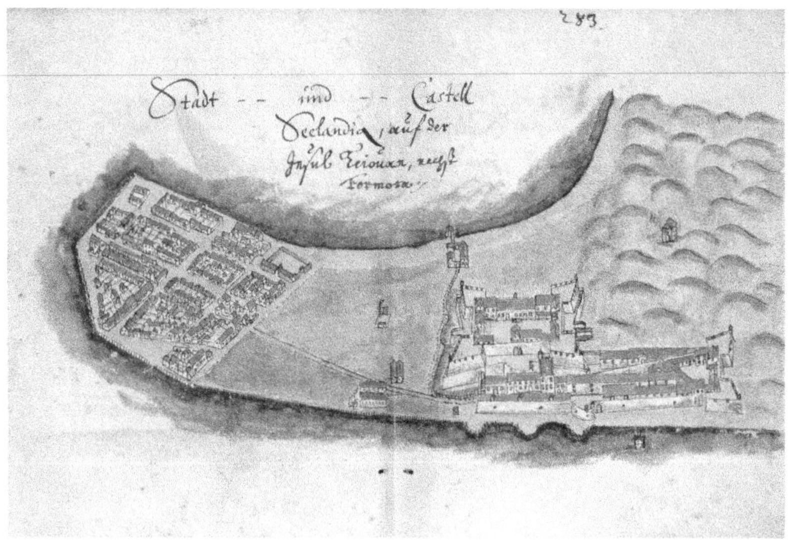

Figure 15. Bird's-eye view of Zeelandia, c. 1652. This wonderful map was drawn by German traveler Caspar Schmalkalden, who was in Taiwan in the late 1640s and early 1650s. In Taiwan, he wrote, "I handed in my gun and became a surveyor," so the drawing is quite accurate. By this point, Zeelandia Castle had grown from the square Upper Castle to encompass a Lower Castle as well, with the Governor's Mansion the most prominent of the many structures within. Also notable is the outhouse structure that perched over the Channel, below the Lower Castle, and the stone path that led from the castle across the plain to Zeelandia City. Used by permission of the Universitäts- und Forschungsbibliothek Erfurt/Gotha, Chart B, fols. 282v–283.

splintered. Out in the bay, a yacht called the *Maerssen* was standing nearly right side up. That would be unremarkable except for the fact that the *Maerssen* had gone down in another storm the previous month and been deeply buried under sand and silt. Now it stood more than a hundred meters from its previous location, something that, Coyet mused, "could not have occurred without terrific power."[2]

Zeelandia City, a hundred meters east of the castle, on the tip of the island finger, was "a wasteland."[3] Its brick-paved streets were filled with boards and sand and overturned boats. The houses along the harbors on all three sides were smashed to pieces, including beautiful ones that had just been built, such as He Bin's new mansion. But no part of the city had been spared. Every street had rubble and bodies. Many were Chinese women and children who'd been drowned or crushed under fallen walls.

Bells were rung and gongs beaten. Coyet had the town criers announce that anyone caught stealing or rooting through the wreckage would be thrown into chains for a year's hard labor. People began to clean up and rebuild.

But some things couldn't be fixed. Across a wide channel of water from Zeelandia Castle was another long sandspit of an island called Baxemboy. The fishing village that had once stood on Baxemboy's grassy bank was gone—not a trace of it left, not even a beam or foundation. Most worrisome of all, about halfway down the island, over some dunes and past a copse of spindly pineapple trees, an important fortress had stood guard over another channel into the bay, the Deer's Ear Gap.[4] The storm had flattened it. Nothing was left but a mound of sand and bricks. Five soldiers had been killed immediately. The rest managed to escape, the healthy ones pulling their broken-legged comrades to safety. They said the fort had collapsed at midnight, when the storm had been at its strongest.

Coyet sent workers to dig out the bodies and engineers to survey the wreckage. They reported that the fort would be impossible to rebuild because the storm had completely altered Baxemboy. For forty years navigators had used its tall dark dunes as a landmark, knowing that when they sighted them they were near Zeelandia Castle. But the dunes had been swept away, leaving only a flat beach.

Charts could be remade, but dunes couldn't. There was no place to build a new fort. How would the Dutch defend the Bay of Taiwan if an enemy should come? Zeelandia Castle still guarded the main channel, but the Deer's Ear Gap was now undefended. Coyet considered this to be the "most significant misfortune to befall the company in this tempest."[5]

Sometimes there's little to do but turn to a higher power, so Coyet and his colleagues decided to hold a general Fast and Prayer Day, "to beg the Almighty to lift His plague from the island, which we have felt here in Taiwan because of our many sins, for which He saw fit to bring to this island the terrifying storm winds and calamitous floods, in which at least eight hundred souls were drowned."[6]

That night, as if in answer, explosions resounded from Baxemboy Island. When people investigated the next morning, they learned that the explosions had come from the ground beneath the fallen fort, near where soldiers guarding the ruins had sat around a bonfire. Just as the flames were dying into embers the booms erupted from deep below the sand. The soldiers guessed that buried grenades must have gone off.[7]

Maybe these explosions can be counted as the first omens. Five years later, when Koxinga's arrival was imminent, there were many others.

A Foggy Morning

The last day of April 1661 dawned dark and foggy on the "earthly paradise" of Taiwan.[1] The brass cannons of Zeelandia Castle were clean and loaded, and sentries squinted into the mist. They knew—everyone knew—that Koxinga might be out there. Zeelandia City, a five-minute walk away, was nearly empty, its taverns boarded up, its houses locked and abandoned.[2] Most Chinese citizens had fled, hiding along the coast and waiting for boats to take them away.[3]

There'd been strange reports. Chinese wearing Dutch clothes were sneaking around at night.[4] A shaved Chinese was caught scouting in native villages. Chinese bandits broke into a farmer's house and branded him with fire. Some soldiers said a man had surfaced in the main channel in front of Zeelandia Castle, risen up three times and then disappeared. They'd gone down to investigate but found nothing, and there were no reports of anyone overboard or drowned. That same day some said a mermaid appeared, her long hair golden in the sun. She, too, came up three times before sinking away, as if in warning.[5]

Some people heard screaming in the plain that stretched between the castle and the town. Others said they'd seen a spectral battle there, armies of ghosts fighting with ghastly cries. When they looked out to sea they saw the three ships that lay at anchor beyond the harbor entrance burst into silent cannon fire. The odd thing was that sailors on the ships said they'd seen the castle fire a soundless barrage at exactly the same time, "but as soon as the day broke through, we all saw that it was nothing."[6]

Stories like this might be expected of common soldiers, drunk on their rice wine. But even Coyet's own official journal, usually a staid record, noted that a dog had given birth to two baby leopards that soon died, "this being something very strange, never before seen in this land."[7]

All of these occurences, a soldier would write later, were signs and omens of the disaster to come.[8]

Some people thought this worry was pointless, and they had good arguments on their side. After all, last year Coyet had also panicked that Koxinga would come, had insisted that an invasion was near. He'd sent an urgent request to his superiors for help, and they'd sent a reinforcement fleet. When it had arrived, its admiral, Jan van der Laan, had waited around, getting increasingly impatient.

He'd accused Coyet of paranoia, saying that there was no way Koxinga would attack, or that if he did, it wouldn't take much to stop him, because the Chinese "are not soldiers but effeminate men."[9] He felt Coyet was insulting him, refusing to listen. He began to hate him. Coyet hated van der Laan back, calling him Jan-against-all-reason (it sounds better in Dutch) and coming up with a long list of insults: "Van der Laan is as experienced in the affairs of state and politics . . . as the pig from Aesop's Fables, rude and brusque to the highest degree, self-important, egotistical, arrogant, stupid, stubborn, and of a very hostile and uncivil comportment."[10] There were angry scenes in the Council of Formosa. Van der Laan said he would sail away with the fleet and attack the Portuguese in Macau. Coyet refused to let him. One of Formosa's top military men, Captain Thomas Pedel, about whose questionable judgments we'll be hearing quite a bit, suggested that they just send someone to ask Koxinga what his intentions were and maybe see what kind of preparations he might be making.[11]

This was a silly idea. If, as Sun Zi wrote, "war is deception," then why should one expect honesty from a possible enemy? The envoy sailed to Xiamen and was received by Koxinga. When he asked about the warlord's war preparations, Koxinga replied, "I'm not in the habit of publishing my designs. In fact, I'll often circulate a rumor that I'm moving west when I'm really intending to move east."[12] This sounded cagey to the Dutch envoy, but in fact Koxinga was merely quoting a common adage: *feign east, attack west*. Koxinga gave the man a letter to take back to Coyet. "Your Honor," Koxinga wrote, "still remains in doubt about my good feelings toward the Dutch State. You seem to believe that I've been planning some hostile action against your land. But this is just a rumor propagated by evil-minded people."[13] Why, Koxinga asked, should he bother himself with "a small grass-producing land"[14] like Formosa when he was so busy attacking the mighty Manchus? He told Coyet that in any case he often spread rumors to deceive his enemies. "How," he asked, "can anyone know my hidden thoughts and true intentions, when I've revealed them to nobody?"[15] In fact, by this point, Koxinga had already considered attacking Taiwan and was just biding his time.[16]

His letter did little to calm the controversy in Taiwan. Jan van der Laan sailed away in anger, taking experienced officers and the best ships. He left just the three ships that had seemed to catch ghostly fire. It was shortly after he left that the omens started.

Now the morning sun burned through the fog and revealed hundreds of masts, so many that they looked like trees in a dense forest.

Cannons were sounded, bells rung, horsemen dispatched. Koxinga had arrived.

SIGNS OF HEAVEN'S WILL

By the time the fog was gone, it was too late to stop Koxinga from sailing into the Bay of Taiwan, the core of the Dutch colony. His ships were already starting to enter the Deer's Ear Gap, one of two channels into the bay.[17] The Deer's Ear Gap wasn't as deep as the Channel that led past Zeelandia Castle, but it was unguarded. The only Dutch cannons there were buried under tons of sand, near the ruins of the fort that had been destroyed in the terrifying typhoon of 1656 (figure 16).

The Deer's Ear Gap wasn't easy to navigate. It was shallow and tortuous, filled with sandbars that shifted with each storm. It was dangerous for deep-drawing ships like Koxinga's oceangoing junks. But Koxinga benefited from a miracle, or at least that's how Yang Ying describes it: "Previously this gap was very shallow, so great ships could

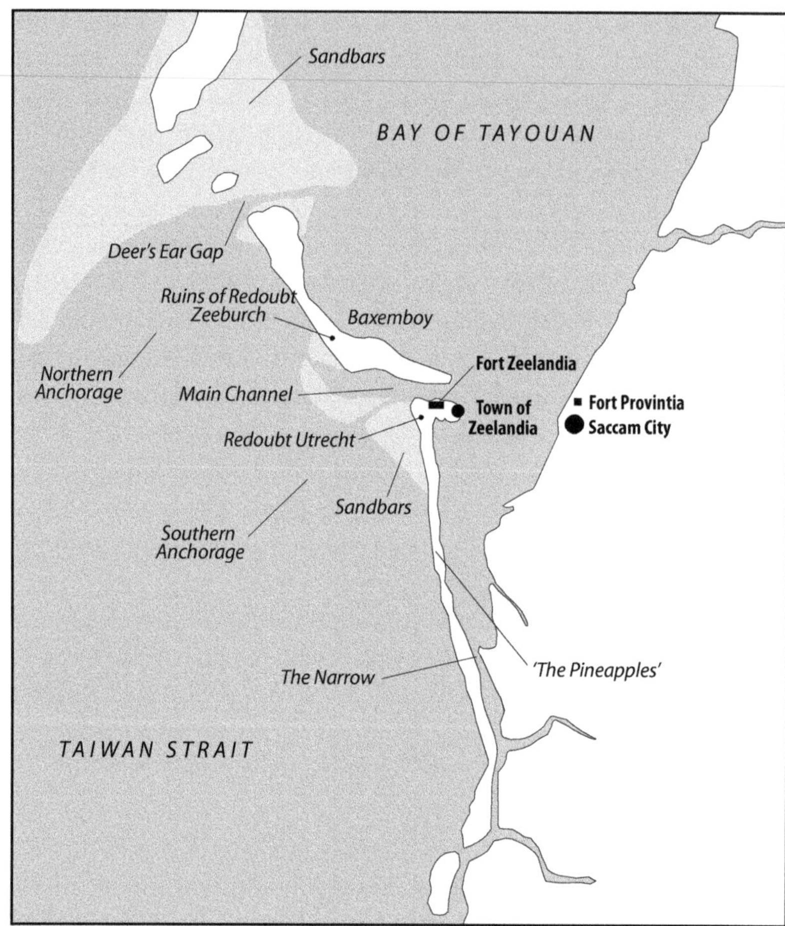

Figure 16. The Bay of Taiwan. This map shows the Bay of Taiwan c. 1656. There were two entrances into the bay. The Main Channel was protected by Fort Zeelandia. The Deer's Ear Gap was much shallower and more tortuous, but the Dutch had known they must keep it defended to prevent an invader from sailing into the bay, which is why they had built a fort called the Redoubt Zeeburg on Baxemboy Island. The Extreme and Terrifying Storm of 1656, however, destroyed the Redoubt Zeeburg and it was never rebuilt. So when Koxinga arrived, he sailed through the Deer's Ear Gap, bouyed by a high tide, bypassing Zeelandia Castle and landing his powerful troops on the mainland a few miles north of Fort Provintia. This map is based on a chart from 1656 (see figure 19, later).

not enter or exit, but on this day the tidewaters surged by several feet. Our ships—even the extremely large ones—could enter the bay without trouble. This could only have occurred because of the quiet aid of Heaven's Will."[18]

Yang Ying thanked Heaven, but in fact Koxinga had planned carefully. The day of his arrival—30 April—fell nearly on a new moon, when tides are high.[19] He'd done this sort of thing before. In 1652 his navy arrived in the City of Haicheng on a high tide and sailed right to the main governmental offices, surprising the inhabitants. Yang Ying portrayed the event as a miracle, a sign of Heaven's Will.

Koxinga nearly missed the tide this time. If he hadn't defied the rain and rushed to leave Penghu, he would have been stuck outside the bay, his ships exposed to the weather.[20] Maybe Heaven had helped a bit.

A FLURRY OF ACTIVITY

Coyet called the Council of Formosa to an emergency meeting. For now, it seemed, Zeelandia Castle was safe. That was good, because it housed most of the troops and cannon and many of the high officials. Others lived in Zeelandia City, just a hundred yards away.

But there were administrators, schoolteachers, missionaries, and soldiers who lived with their families in the countryside. Coyet's first order was to send horsemen out to warn them to flee to Zeelandia.[21]

Next, he ordered Dutch prisoners freed and chain-gangers released. Those who'd been soldiers were given guns and returned to their units. He dispatched slaves under guard to bring supplies from Zeelandia City to the castle. He ordered bakers to make hard bread.

He and his councilors considered what to do about the Chinese residents of Zeelandia City, the ones who hadn't boarded up their houses and fled, people among whom the Dutch had lived in mutual prosperity and, for the most part, peace. He sent soldiers to the city to arrest the wealthiest and bring them inside the castle. The rest of the Chinese were ordered to stay in their homes.

They disobeyed. A stream of Chinese refugees trekked out of the city, past the brick hospital and then southward along the long narrow island beneath the pineapple-tufted dunes.[22] Dutch patrols tried to turn them back, but many made it through, some by beating a Dutch corporal nearly to death. Coyet wondered, "If we meet such treatment from our Chinese colonists, who knows what evils the enemy has in store for our people in the countryside? God Almighty please protect them from the enemy's violence."[23]

What was Koxinga's next move? Watching from the castle, the Dutch noticed a few small junks scouting out landing places near a village called Smeerdorp, which lay on mainland Taiwan, across the bay from the Deer's Ear Gap. Shortly afterward, scores of Koxinga's larger ships sailed there, buoyed by the high tides, and began landing men.[24] Hundreds of Chinese who'd lived on Taiwan under Dutch rule greeted them with wagons full of weapons and supplies. It seemed as though they'd pledged allegiance long before.

Among the first to land were cavalry units. One Dutch rider reported to Zeelandia that he saw a hundred or more horses tossing their heads near Smeerdorp, each of them ridden by a powerful knight with weapons shining in the sun: a sword, a long frightening lance, and a bow. The leader of this cavalry—and one knew it was the leader because someone was carrying a red umbrella over his head—was dressed in European clothes.[25] This was probably Koxinga's general Ma Xin, a man who would play a major role in the war over the next months.[26]

It seemed clear that Koxinga was aiming at the other main Dutch fortress on Taiwan, Fort Provintia, which lay just across the bay from Zeelandia Castle, easily visible from the ramparts. Fort Provintia sat right on the bay, near the other major city on Taiwan—Saccam.

Sure enough, Koxinga's troops began marching toward Saccam and Fort Provintia, drums pounding and horns blaring, flags waving in the wind.

It was a brilliant move. Coyet and his colleagues had expected that Koxinga would have to contend with Zeelandia Castle first, but Koxinga had slipped past their defences. If he captured Provintia, mainland Taiwan would be open to him and Zeelandia would be surrounded.

Coyet was worried, but the people in Fort Provintia were terrified. Its commander, Jacob Valentine, tried sending the women and children to Zeelandia Castle by boat, but wives refused to leave their husbands, children cried, people screamed, and the plan collapsed. Meanwhile, Chinese forces had climbed the hill behind the fort and begun pitching their camp, hundreds of white tents sprouting beyond the horse stalls and the beautiful botanical garden.

Valentine decided to pray. The prayer had barely finished when the enemy's drums and trumpets started up again and more than a thousand Chinese soldiers charged the fortress, their steel helmets and lances flashing in the sun. The fort's gunners fired their cannons. More shots came from the bay, where a squadron of Dutch boats had sailed over from Zeelandia with reinforcements.

The Chinese soldiers scattered, dragging their dead with them, except for one man who'd fallen on the ground in front of the fort. He refused to surrender. The Dutch kept shooting at him, musketballs punching into his flesh. But he shot arrow after arrow at the brick walls, until finally an African boy in the fort shot one of his own arrows back at him and hit him in the belly. Then, rolling from one side to the other, the man crawled away on all fours. If this was the kind of courage they could expect of Koxinga's soldiers, it would be a difficult war.

A few dozen musketmen disembarked from the Dutch vessels in the bay and scrambled through the mudflats to Fort Provintia's front door, which opened to the waterfront. Coyet had sent two hundred musketmen, but the rest had turned back, either because it was too hard to land or because their leader had been frightened when a bullet whizzed past him.

When it got dark, Valentine sent soldiers out to set fire to the wooden granaries in Saccam so the rice wouldn't fall into Koxinga's hands. By the firelight, Dutch musketeers shot at enemy soldiers who showed their "mouse-heads" between the houses of Saccam. The fallen soldiers didn't whine or cry much.

Coyet saw the flames from Zeelandia Castle. He made a midnight inspection and then went back to the governor's mansion in the lower castle and tried to get some rest. The next day there would be fighting.

Koxinga's Victories

According to the Military Revolution Theory, Europeans owed their ascendancy over the world—or at least those parts of the world that they controlled before 1800—primarily to their superior guns, ships, and forts. So it's intriguing that during the first few days of Koxinga's invasion Dutch muskets lost to Chinese lances; Dutch ships lost to Chinese junks; and a Dutch fort surrendered to a Chinese siege. What do these defeats tell us about the military explanation for European expansion?

Let's start with muskets. The musket was introduced in Italy in the 1550s and gradually became "master of the battlefield," revolutionizing warfare in Europe.[1] Broadswords, halberds, crossbows, longbows—all of them hallmarks of traditional European warfare—disappeared, until by the middle of the seventeenth century most European infantry units were composed of musketeers protected by pikemen.

The key to the musket's success was its ease of use and its power: it could hurl heavy lead pellets more than a hundred yards and pierce heavy armor. But its main drawback was its low rate of fire. In the sixteenth century, even experienced musketeers could fire only once every minute or two. The rate increased in the course of the seventeenth century, but it was still an order of magnitude slower than a longbow.

There was a way to compensate: a technique called "volley fire." The principle was simple: draw your gunmen into long ranks, one in back of the other. The first rank fires and then steps back to reload while the second rank fires. The second rank steps back while the third rank fires, and so on. Volley fire seems to have been invented independently at least three times. The first recorded use of the method is China in 1387, when Chinese gunners employed volley fire against an enemy elephant brigade.[2] The next invention of volley fire occurred in Japan in the late sixteenth century.[3] The third time it was invented in Europe, and the inventors were the Dutch. The technique required intense coordination and discipline. Dutch commanders drilled their troops obsessively. The acts of firing and reloading were analyzed into a series of discrete steps, which were drawn out and published in military manuals. The first manual divided musket handling into thirty-two steps. Subsequent manuals added more steps. Military manuals like this proliferated widely, translated into all the major European languages, and Dutch drill inspectors were sought after throughout Europe. As a result, Dutch musket techniques spread rapidly.[4]

The Dutch brought their musketmen to the colonies. Most soldiers in Zeelandia were either artillery specialists, pikemen, or musketeers. They'd proven effective in the past. The rapid spread of Dutch power in Taiwan under Hans Putmans in the 1630s had been accomplished primarily by musketeers, whose deadly fire overwhelmed the aborigines.

Dutch musketeers had also worked against Chinese rebels. In 1652, a farmer named Guo Huaiyi had raised a Chinese peasant army of five or six thousand to oust the Dutch and take Taiwan for themselves. They massed in a field waving banners and spears and yelling, "Kill, kill the Dutch dogs!" They attacked the City of Saccam and captured some Dutchmen, cutting off their noses and ears, poking their eyes out, slicing off their genitals, and sticking their heads onto bamboo stakes.

Against these thousands, the Dutch dispatched a hundred and twenty musketmen. Ferried across the Bay of Taiwan to Saccam, where the enemy waited for them on shore, they disembarked in waist-deep water and waded in formation toward land. When they were sure they could keep their fuses lit and powder dry, they opened fire, volley after volley. The rebels could have overwhelmed them with one surge, but the corps kept its discipline. The rebels scattered. The Dutch pursued. Five hundred rebels were killed that day, and over the next days four thousand more. The musketeers returned to Fort Zeelandia in triumph, bearing the leader's head on a stake. Not a single Dutch soldier was hurt.[5]

Koxinga's troops were better armed than these Chinese peasant rebels, but they carried traditional weapons similar to those the musket had replaced in Europe: swords, saber-staves (long staves with swords at the end), bows and arrows (figure 17).

How, then, did these soldiers defeat the Dutch musketeers, who represented the most advanced firearm technology and techniques in the world? It's easier to ask how the Dutch musketeers lost, because the answer is simple: They were led by a foolhardy, overconfident captain named Thomas Pedel, whereas the Chinese were led by a wise and seasoned general named Chen Ze.

THE MUSKETEERS

We've already had occasion to question Thomas Pedel's judgment. He was the one who suggested sending an envyoy to ask Koxinga whether he planned to attack Taiwan. On this sunny morning, day two of the invasion, he was particularly reckless because he was angry. His son had nearly been killed by Chinese soldiers.

The boy arrived at Zeelandia Castle early in the morning, his arm hanging loose from the socket. Chinese troops had chopped his tutor to bits, and two other Dutch guardians as well, and he'd had to watch the whole thing. One had hacked his shoulder with his terrifying saber staff, but the boy had gotten away.

One of the few soldiers who survived Pedel's leadership that day described how furious the captain got after seeing his son. Immediately, the soldier wrote, Pedel ordered his drummers to beat their drums, lined up his best men, and then went to ask Coyet for permission to attack the Chinese with two hundred and forty musketmen, even though the Chinese numbered in the thousands.[6] Coyet agreed.[7]

So Pedel marched his soldiers through the courtyards of Zeelandia Castle, drums echoing off the walls, and through the arch to the pier outside, where they boarded an armed galiot and some abandoned sampans.

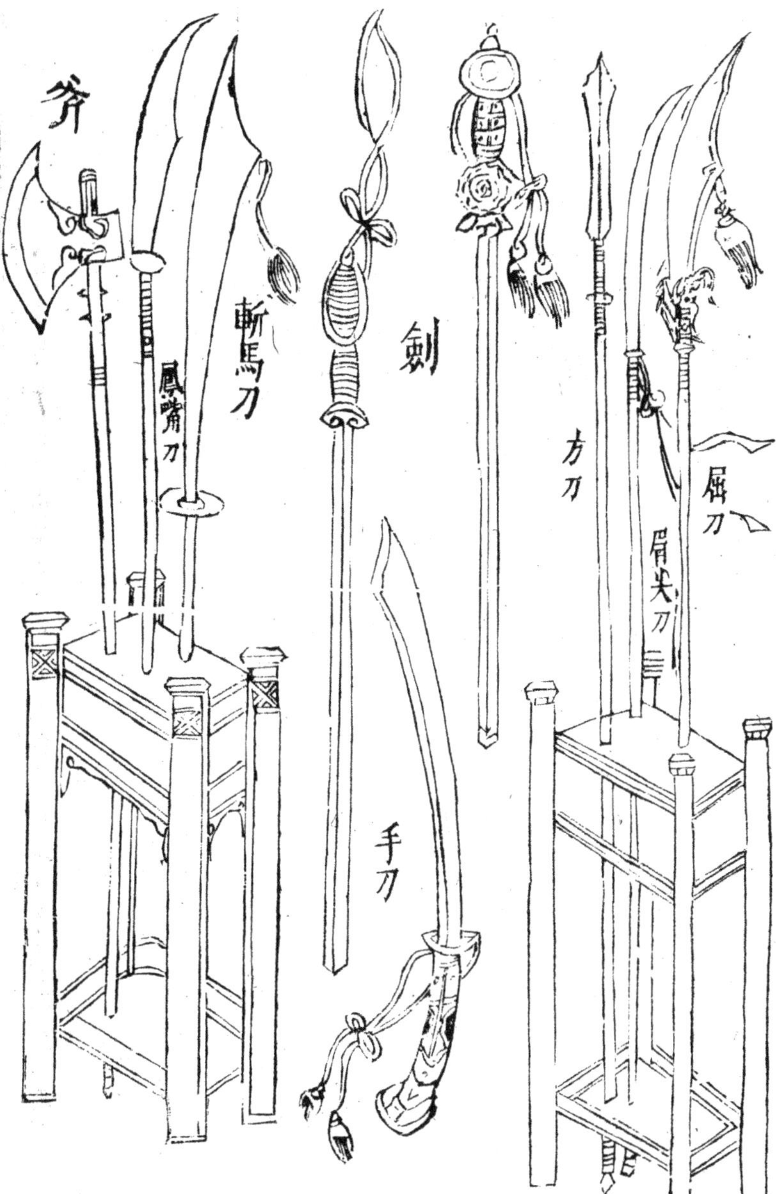

Figure 17. Picture of Chinese long-handled weapons, 1646. The third weapon from the left is one of the saber-staves that Koxinga's soldiers wielded. Known as "Horse Hacking Swords" (砍馬刀), they were deployed to great effect against Manchu cavalry. They also proved devastating to Thomas Pedel's musketeers. From Zheng Dayu, *Jing guo xiong lüe*, "Wu bei kao," juan 5. Used by permission of Harvard Yenching Library.

After a short passage across the Channel, he and his men disembarked on a grassy bank near some burned fishermen's huts. This was the southern end of Baxemboy, an island that stretched, long, thin, and bumpy with dunes, northward almost ten kilometers to touch the Deer's Ear Gap.

In times of peace, sandy Baxemboy appealed primarily to fishermen. But now, because it lay between the only two channels into the Bay of Taiwan, it was a strategic key to the war (figure 18).

The Dutch fort that had washed away in the Terrifying Storm of 1656 had stood toward the opposite side of Baxemboy. Koxinga's troops were raising tents near its ruins. An early governor of Taiwan, a crabby man named Pieter Nuyts, whom one historian calls the "bull in a China shop," had foreseen just such a catastrophe. "If," Nuyts had written, "the enemy," and by enemy here he was talking about Spain or Japan,

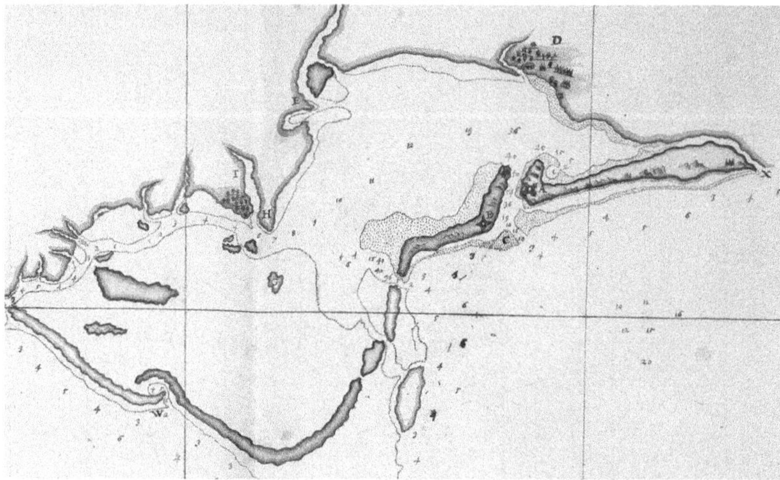

Figure 18. Early chart of the Bay of Taiwan and its two entrance channels, c. 1635. The island to the right is where Zeelandia Castle was located, marked with an A. The island to its left (i.e., to its north) is Baxemboy. The structure labeled B is the Redoubt Zeeburg, which was destroyed in the Extreme and Terrifying Storm of 1656. The Deer's Ear Gap is at the end of Baxemboy Island, between it and the sandbar island to the left. It was a narrow and tortuous channel, which Koxinga successfully navigated thanks to an unusually high tide. The battle between Captain Thomas Pedel and Chen Ze occurred near the ruins of the Redoubt Zeeburg. Used by permission of the Austrian National Library, Vienna, Austria, Atlas Blau van der Hem, vol. XLI, sheet 2.

"If the enemy were to sniff out the fact that this place [Baxemboy] is the strategic key of Taiwan, he would do his best to capture it, and then he would be able to strangle us, and we wouldn't be able to get ships in or out, and he would be able to attack us from inside and outside."[8]

That's what Koxinga had in mind. He knew if he controlled Baxemboy he would secure access to the Bay of Taiwan. So he put an entire regiment[9] there. Its commander was Chen Ze, a veteran of nearly fifteen years of war against the Manchus.[10] Among Chen Ze's units were the best troops in the army: the Iron Men. He also had cannon junks to defend by water.

He'd begun landing his forces the previous day. The troops must have been hungry, because the first twenty or so had walked a mile or two southward over the dunes and stopped at the fishing village just across the Channel from Zeelandia Castle. Tauntingly, they'd planted a flag near the huts and begun chasing down pigs and chickens. This was too much for Coyet to bear, so he'd sent soldiers to chase them away. Too few to offer resistance, the Chinese fled, dropping their prey but keeping their flag. Hunger brought them back. This time the Dutch let them cluster together before firing cannonballs and dispersing them. Coyet sent a team to burn down the straw huts.

Pedel's musketeers landed near the charred village. What was he thinking as he stood there, contemplating the odds? There were on the order of two thousand Chinese troops on the little island.

He addressed his men. We don't know exactly what he said, since he never made it back to give his report, but others say he said this: "The Chinese are cowardly and effeminate. They cannot bear the smell of powder and the roar of muskets and will flee at the first charge, as soon as a few of them have been shot down."[11] In the more than twenty years since Pedel was stationed on Taiwan, he'd risen from corporal to captain, the top military rank in the colony. He'd wrangled with rebels and put down pirates. Maybe he reminded his men about the Chinese Rebellion of 1652, when just a hundred and twenty Dutch musketeers—half as many men as now stood on Baxemboy—had defeated a Chinese force much larger than Chen Ze's. The victory had convinced most Dutchmen that, as Coyet would later write, twenty-five Chinese put together didn't match one trained Dutch soldier.[12]

Pedel led his men in prayer and then marched them toward Chen Ze's encampment. The route took them around dunes and through a little forest of spiky pandanus bushes, which the Dutch referred to as pineapples.[13] To their right was the Bay of Taiwan, where the three small vessels that had transported them to Baxemboy were following along by water, their cannons stuffed with musket shot to blast through the enemy. To the left the musketeers caught glimpses of the open sea, where three tall Dutch ships were sailing toward a fleet of junks.

Ahead of them, far down the beach, the enemy encampment was festooned with pennants and crawling with men in flashing helmets. The enemy began lining up marching toward them.

Pedel's musketmen passed more dunes to their left and then left the pandanus trees behind them. Here Baxemboy flattened out a bit and widened, becoming an open field, precisely the sort of terrain in which muskets excelled. Pedel ordered his men to spread out so more would be able to fire at once.

At this point, survivors recall, two cannon shots sounded from Zeelandia Castle. The musketeers turned and saw the flag on the huge mast in the upper castle being raised and lowered. It was a signal to turn back. Pedel's orders called for him to "do as much damage to the enemy in as careful a manner as possible, so long as he sees no unavoidable danger, it being preferable that he turn back without achieving anything than expose himself to too much danger."[14] Pedel ignored the warning.

Soon the musketeers got their first good look at the enemy. The Chinese marched in formation, hundreds upon hundreds of them, carrying silk pennants on steel pikes with sharp points. Some flags were long and thin, like ship's flags. Others were huge and rectangular, like army standards, and they were held up on taller staves. They were all colors—red, black, blue, silver, and gold—and many bore embroidered images, which looked to the Dutch like snakes and dragons, devils and demons. They wore polished steel helmets with sharp spikes long enough to stab a man clean through. They wore armor of steel down to the knees.[15] Behind and to the side, officers on horses yelled commands and gestured with swords.

They didn't have muskets. Indeed, Koxinga's men looked, as one Dutch observer wrote, positively ancient, like Romans with tufted helms. Although they had some guns, they were large and unwieldy.

Their main weapons were as ancient as their costumes: swords, saber-staves, bow and arrow.

At a distance, musketeers should have the advantage. Their highly disciplined volley fire was able to spew a constant hail of lead, a machine gun made of scores of men. The idea was to quickly cause major damage among the Chinese ranks so they would break formation and run. Then the musketeers could advance and pick off the runners, firing smoothly away. That's how it had worked with the rebels nine years ago.

When the two forces had closed to just beyond musket range, perhaps a hundred and fifty meters, the Chinese abruptly stopped, a wall of Iron Men. Pedel kept marching.

The Military Revolution Model proposes that Europeans' drilling and disciplinary tactics provided an edge in warfare and formed part of a "western way of war."[16] Chinese historians have recently found analogues to these techniques in Ming China.[17] And we've already seen how Koxinga developed his own drilling method and printed training manuals. We know how he liked to spend days at his Pavilion of Military Arts, watching his troops march, following them to make sure they moved in rhythm, punishing those who were sloppy.[18]

Pedel must have begun to suspect by now that these Chinese weren't like those he'd fought before. They stood stock still, peering out from steel helms. There's no mention in Chinese or European sources of the sounds he might have heard, but we know Koxinga's units used gongs and drums and reedy battle horns to coordinate their movements, just as the Dutch used drummers. There must have been a cross-cultural cacophony as his men approached.

A command was shouted in Chinese. From behind the ranks, new soldiers emerged and planted fifty large guns in a row in front of the Iron Men. Survivors called these guns *bassen* or *doppelhaggen*. They were large and looked primitive to the Dutch, heavy, slow to load, difficult to use.

At this point the Dutch galiot and sampans, which had been shadowing Pedel in the bay, opened fire, unloading cannonloads of shot and shrapnel into the Chinese ranks. Chen Ze's men reaimed their guns and fired at the vessels, but to little effect. The Dutch cannons, on the other hand, blasted large gaps into enemy ranks, scores of soldiers falling in piles on the sand.

But the gaps just filled up with new arrivals from the junks and camp, and the ranks stayed still. To the Dutch "their numbers seemed without end."[19]

By now Pedel's musketeers had arrived within effective range. Pedel gave the order to fire. They began firing in turns,[20] as trained musketmen did. When the first shots roared out, the Chinese surged forward with a terrible battle cry. The traditional war call is "Sha!" which means both "kill" and "attack."

We'll never know how Pedel's musketmen would have fared in a direct confrontation like this, two hundred and fifty muskets against a couple thousand troops, because Chen Ze was too smart for that.

Remember those warning shots fired from the castle? People in Zeelandia had seen junks sailing from Chen Ze's main flotilla southward along Baxemboy, hidden from Pedel's view by dunes. They couldn't tell what the junks were doing and suspected that they were planning to attack from the sea. So Coyet gave the signal to turn back, which Pedel ignored. What the junks actually did was even worse. They quietly unloaded a detachment of Chinese troops behind the dunes. As the musketeers marched blithely by, the Chinese quietly threaded their way through the hills and hid among the spiky pandanus trees, to Pedel's rear.

As soon as the Iron Men yelled "kill," the woods behind the musketeers also erupted in war cries. Pedel tried to keep order, commanding some of his units to turn around and fire, but the musketmen's famed discipline broke down. They dropped their guns and ran. Chen Ze's men strode into the Dutch ranks, swinging their saber-staves left and right.

The Dutch fled into the muddy bay water, to try to board the galiot and sampans, but there was such a rush that one vessel capsized. Those who couldn't swim drowned. Those who could began swimming back toward the fortress, miles away.

Pedel himself fought on with a small band, wading backward toward the vessels while firing away. He was struck once and fell. He climbed to his feet, yelled to his men to keep fighting, and was cut down by a Chinese saber-staff, at which the few musketmen who were still left splashed through the water and pulled themselves into a boat. Of Pedel's two hundred forty crack troops, fewer than eighty returned.

Why did Pedel ignore the signal to turn around? How did he so underestimate the enemy? How did he let the enemy get behind him? He was aggrieved, overconfident, and angry, but he was also outmatched. Chen Ze, who had never been to Taiwan before, understood the strategic possibilities of Baxemboy's geography better than Pedel, who'd lived on Taiwan for twenty years. Chen Ze and his comrades were masters at geographic war. They'd been inculcated with the idea—found in Sun Zi and other ancient texts—that terrain is the key to strategy and that a general should know the land he fought on. Yang Ying's chronicle is full of phrases like "be aware of the area's geographical advantages,"[21] "size up the area's geographical advantages,"[22] "divine an area's geographical advantages,"[23] "lose the geographical advantage,"[24] and so on.

Oddly, Pedel didn't even have scouts who might have warned him. In fact, it's striking that the survivors among his musketmen never quite understood how the Chinese got behind them. One later wrote that the Chinese had already been hiding while the Dutch marched by. "On Baxemboy," he wrote, "grow many pineapple trees, which are about half as tall as a man. Behind them were hiding many of the enemy, and the companies marched past them, unawares."[25]

I can't help but note here the few lines Yang Ying devotes to Chen Ze's victory. Here are European musketeers, armed with the latest gun technologies and trained in the soundest methods, roundly defeated, having completely underestimated their enemy, but Yang Ying was supremely unimpressed: "The barbarian leader Coyet, seeing that Chen Ze's camp at Baxemboy was not yet firmly established, sent the warrior general Demonspawn Ba [that would be Thomas Pedel] in command of three hundred men with bird guns to attack the camp, and the Forward General of the Resolution Brigade [Chen Ze] led his men against the enemy and annihilated them in one drumbeat. Demonspawn Ba died in battle, and the other barbarians were nearly all wiped out."[26]

This may have been a small battle for Chen Ze, but it was a significant defeat for the Dutch. Their best musketeers and most senior commander had proven useless against just a small part of Koxinga's army. Never again did the Dutch march out against Koxinga in direct battle.

DISASTER AT SEA

That same morning. the Dutch were also defeated at sea, where they ought to have been strongest. As Pedel and his men were marching toward death, three Dutch ships sailed toward Chen Ze's fleet. In front was a mighty war-yacht called the *Hector of Troy.* Next came a medium-sized yacht called the *'s-Gravenlande*. And last came a smaller yacht called the *Maria*, a ship we'll hear a lot more about. Their orders were to advance on Koxinga's junks and blast them with cannons. And cannons they had in superfluity. A well-equipped war-yacht of the *Hector*'s class often carried more than thirty large cannons and four or five huge bronze ones.[27] The medium-sized yacht carried twenty, and the *Maria* a dozen or so.[28] Koxinga's junks, in contrast, appear to have had only two cannons each, but what they lacked in size they made up in numbers. Chen Ze had about sixty junks available. And whereas the Dutch ships probably carried several dozen soldiers at most, he had thousands.

We're fortunate that one ship log survived—the *'s-Gravenlande*'s—so we have a firsthand account of the battle. The three ships sailed from their anchorage near Zeelandia toward where Chen Ze's vessels were anchored. Chen Ze tried to lure them into shallow waters but they didn't take the bait.

At first conditions were perfect, sunny, with a "sweet little breeze from the Northwest."[29] But the wind suddenly died, and the junks swarmed forward, shooting cannons and fire-arrows. The Dutch shot back with muskets and cannons, although much of their attention was devoted to putting out the fires that kept taking root on the decks and on the sides. If a fire were to reach the powder cabin, the game would be over.

The junks came right up alongside to try to board, grasping the ships' cables and lashing the junks fast to them.[30] When a junk managed to attach itself, other junks tied themselves behind it, forming chains six, eight, ten junks long. Chinese soldiers surged forward along these chains.

The Dutch cannons pointed from the sides of the ships, yet the chains of junks were attached to the ships' rears. So the Dutch re-aimed their cannons. The ship's log notes that they even brought one into the officer's cabin and pointed it out the porthole. They blasted at the enemy, "greeting them in such a way that the blood flooded out from the gutters."[31] For more than an hour they shot, but finally the Chinese gave up.

The Chinese junks were starting to retreat. The largest Dutch ship, the *Hector*, shot a couple more times at the retreating junks. Then there was an explosion so loud that in the castle, more than a mile away, the windows jumped in their frames.

Pedel's musketeers, who were at this point still marching toward disaster, heard it too, and when they turned to look they saw a massive ball of fire. When the smoke cleared, the *Hector* was gone. Only one man survived, clinging legless to a beam, where he was fished out by Chinese sailors. Much later he was returned to the Dutch as an act of good will, his wounds writhing with maggots. He told them what happened.

The *Hector* had been destroyed not by the enemy but by carelessness. A cannon had been fired in the cabin where the ship's chief gunner lived. In most Dutch warships there was a gangway from this cabin down to the powder room, where muskets, gunpowder, grenades, and other things with a tendency to explode were kept. In some ships, such as the famous *Batavia,* which has been the subject of considerable study, there was a room between the chief gunner's cabin and the powder room, which acted as a buffer (in the *Batavia* it was the bread pantry).[32] Perhaps in the *Hector*, however, the powder room was closer to the gunner's cabin, or perhaps the ports between the two were open. In any case, soldiers on the *Hector* must have brought a cannon into proximity with this powder keg to fire at the Chinese. Cannons tended to spew sparks to the side as well as out the front. It supplied just the sort of activation energy that piles of grenades and barrels of gunpowder need.

Chinese sources, which have few details about the battle, say Chinese forces sank the *Hector* themselves, a judgment that Sinophone historians have accepted.[33] Indeed, one of them, the usually careful Chen Bisheng, has suggested that the Chinese junks Chen Ze commanded were filled with the same sort of incendiary materials that

Koxinga's father used to defeat Hans Putmans in 1633.[34] Dutch sources, which are much more detailed, make clear that this wasn't the case. The Chinese were trying to board the *Hector*, not destroy it with fireboats. According to the legless survivor, the Chinese lost men in the explosion too. He saw boatloads of burned bodies being shipped from the junks to land.

Whatever the cause, the loss was devastating to the Dutch. They had just two oceangoing ships left. One, the *Maria*, was a dispatch yacht, swift and seaworthy but unsuited to war. The *'s-Gravenlande* was a decent warship, but it was nothing like the *Hector.* On its own, it couldn't keep Koxinga's navy from controlling the waters around Taiwan.[35]

So Koxinga's invasion was proceeding remarkably quickly. He had naval dominance and his army controlled Baxemboy.

He expected that Fort Provintia would soon fall as well.

Parleys and Capitulations

Yachts had failed against junks and muskets against sabers. Dutch soldiers irrigated their grief with rice wine and muttered mutinous words—"You can't catch a hare if your dogs don't care"—before collapsing in the streets snoring like pigs.[1] Victorious on land and sea, Koxinga turned to his next goal: to capture the Hollanders' chief stronghold on mainland Taiwan—Fort Provintia. Thousands of his troops were surrounding it.

Among the tents that metastasized on a hill behind the fort, Koxinga's own tent stood out, black with blue flames, larger than the rest.[2] Gunners in Fort Provintia shot a cannonball through it, blowing away the leg of one of his entourage.[3] The tent was moved out of range.

Despite this show of bravado, the Dutch in Fort Provintia were scared. They were a hundred and forty soldiers against an army of thousands, and they lacked supplies. The powder cellar held only a couple small barrels of gunpowder and a chest-and-a-half of fuse, much of which had spoiled in the damp. The granaries and storehouses outside the fort—those that hadn't been burned down—were full of rice, but there was little in the fort. Koxinga had gotten there so fast that they hadn't had time to bring more provisions into the fort and burn the rest, as any good defender should.

Worst of all was the water supply. The cook reported that the well was dry. Usually the fort's inhabitants got water from a well behind the fort or a nearby creek, and no one had checked to make sure the fort's own well worked. They tried digging it out, but it kept filling in with sand. They got only a couple urns of muddy water, enough to boil some rice.

As they were digging out the well, a message from Koxinga arrived, brought by an odd trio: a Dutch woman wearing Chinese clothes, her four-year-old boy, and a battered Dutchman.[4] They said they'd been captured by Chinese soldiers the night before. The man had been beaten and nearly hanged to death from a tree. She'd been stripped naked and "plundered."[5] They said they'd been saved by He Bin, who took them to Koxinga. According to Yang Ying, Koxinga "spoke consolingly to them and ordered that they be taken special care of."[6] (He mentions no "plundering."[7]) Koxinga gave the woman a Chinese dress and the man a large Chinese placard decorated with lions and dragons and stamped with Koxinga's huge red seal.

Translated, the placard was found to demand immediate surrender:

> I have come to reclaim my land, which my father loaned to the company. How can anyone deny my right? I come in person to improve it and build beautiful cities. So think now and quickly. If you accept my authority you will keep all of your wealth and lands and houses and goods, and I will take you wherever you wish on my own ships. But consider carefully, and do not think about attacking, because you, who are just a handful of people, cannot stand up to my multitudes. You would be defeated and killed, and it would be your own fault.[8]

The trio also brought a letter, addressed personally to the man in charge, Jacob Valentine. It had the same sort of demanding language as the placard, but also this delightful line: "You know well that it is not proper to insist on occupying someone else's land."[9] It promised rich rewards to him and other Dutch officials if they gave over the fortress and death if they didn't. To show his good will, Koxinga later sent ten more captives.

Valentine, commander of this fortress, chief-magistrate of Taiwan, had sworn an oath to defend the company's possessions with his life. If he surrendered without permission from Zeelandia, his countrymen might try him for treason, punishable by death. On the other hand, there were thousands of soldiers up the hill getting ready to kill him and his family and friends.

He decided to write a note to Coyet. He described the lack of powder, the dry well, and the tired soldiers, and folded into it a copy of Koxinga's demands. But how could he deliver it to Zeelandia Castle?

Fort Provintia's front gate opened onto a sandy shore where dozens of boats lay tipped this way and that. Zeelandia Castle stood on the other side of the bay, across a mile of calm water. A short walk southward was a ferry pier, which used to offer regular service from Saccam to Zeelandia City.[10] But now, Koxinga's junks were patrolling the bay. If you passed the ferry pier and kept walking southward along the shore, you would eventually reach the point where Zeelandia Island nearly touched the mainland and there was a shallow ford called the Narrow. If you waded across you could walk northward along a duney path past pandanus bushes and melon farms and fishing hamlets to Zeelandia Castle. But Koxinga's troops had camped near the Narrow and were starting to patrol the dunes on the other side (figure 19).

So Valentine's messengers decided to try the direct route. They ran out the front gate, pulled a boat into the water, and rowed as hard as they could to get within range of Zeelandia Castle's cannon before Koxinga's boats overtook them. They made it across, but Koxinga was determined not to let it happen again. Chinese soldiers ran out and set all the boats on fire. Junks began patrolling the bay.

Valentine also penned a note to Koxinga. You could fault Valentine for his management—he'd failed to keep his fort supplied, watered, and armed—but he certainly could write an ingratiating letter.[11] He "reverentially" thanked His Highness Koxinga for the letters and for having so "politely and mercifully" treated the prisoners. Alas, he said, he didn't have the authority to turn over this fort. Only his superior, the governor of Formosa, could make that decision. And how was he to learn of the governor's decision if His Highness was attacking any boats that tried to go through?

Valentine must have felt embarrassed about the sycophantic tone, because when he read it out loud to other high-ranking Dutch in the fort, as was the custom, he said he'd written with more courtesy than he really felt so the enemy would learn to treat the Dutch with

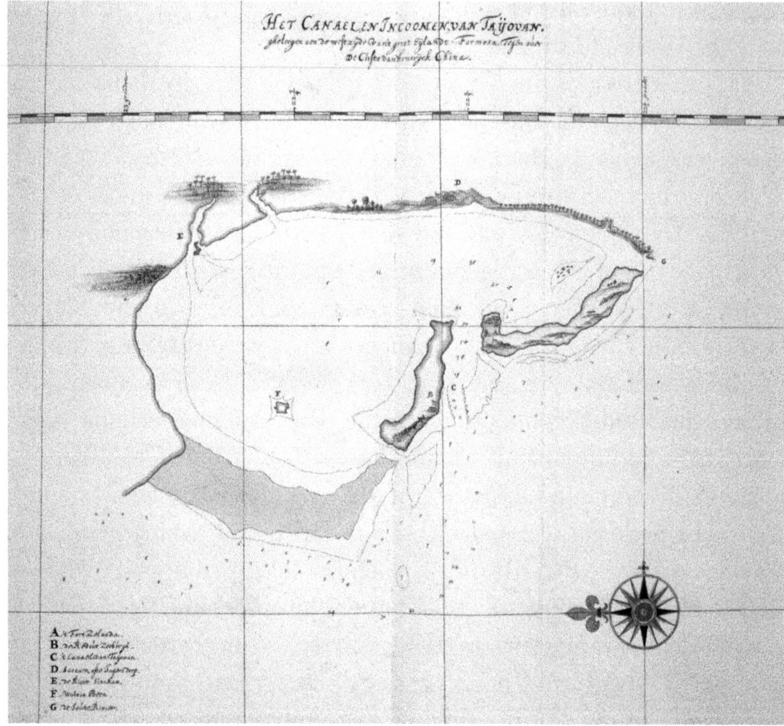

Figure 19. Later chart of the Bay of Taiwan and its two entrance channels, c. 1655. This chart depicts the Bay of Taiwan around 1656. Fort Provintia, where Valentine was surrounded, is marked by the letter D. It looked out onto the Bay of Taiwan, and one could easily see Fort Zeelandia on the other side, its huge flag waving in the wind. By walking southward from Provintia (to the right on this chart), one could reach the Narrow (marked by a letter G) and ford the water there to cross to the island the Dutch often called the "Pineapples," at the end of which stood Zeelandia. Koxinga put guards at the Narrow and patrol junks in the bay to intercept communication between the two forts. Used by permission of the Austrian National Library, Vienna, Austria, Atlas Blau van der Hem, vol. XLI, table 2.

respect, particularly those who were still in the countryside and might be accosted by enemy troops. Valentine gave the letter to two Chinese soldiers the Dutch had captured, who were given wine and steered outside.

Koxinga's response bristled with menace:

> In all the lands where I have led my people in war, I've always achieved victory. Think carefully now about your own strength compared to mine. The mighty Manchus, who have shields

> and swords and bows and arrows and armor as good as those of my own troops, quake when they hear my name. What can you hope to do against me, with just a handful of men? You trust in your ships, but now you've seen how I dealt with them, burning them up. And the people who tried fighting against me on Baxemboy, they've all been destroyed, not a single one surviving. So you people can't win on water or on land, and now all you have left is this little fort, which is like a dead dried out tree and cannot stand much longer.[12]

He chided Valentine for wanting permission from Coyet, saying that if the fort wasn't handed over right away he'd take it by force and would spare no one, not even women or children.[13]

The situation within Provintia was getting unbearable. The besieged were hungry and thirsty, and they heard the enemy all around, yelling orders, banging gongs, blowing horns, and, most frightening of all, hammering, sawing, and stacking. And it stank. The servants were too scared to empty the chamber pots outside the fort, so sewage piled up. Everywhere you walked, you stepped in it.[14] Most of the garrison had slept poorly and were getting careless. Soldiers forgot to clean their guns or load them properly, so their powder sometimes exploded, causing severe burns. Jangled minds mumbled dangerous schemes: set the gunpowder on fire and blow the whole fort to bits, people and all.

On the fourth day of the invasion, 3 May 1661, the besieged saw a boat rowing out from Zeelandia and figured it must be Coyet's response. But Koxinga had no intention of letting it through. Six little junks unmoored themselves and escorted the boat to the pier. A group of high-ranking Dutchmen climbed out, accompanied by four Dutch soldiers.[15] They walked toward the front gate of the fortress. Chinese soldiers stepped in front of them. The besieged couldn't hear what they were saying, but it looked like Thomas Pedel's eldest son, William, was translating—he was one of the few Dutch officials who could speak Chinese. They were motioning toward Fort Provintia. But the Chinese conducted them past the fort to Saccam City.

Valentine needed someone to go find out what was happening. He chose a man named Philip Meij, and we can be very happy with his choice. Meij later wrote a magnificent account of his experiences during the invasion.[16] It stood dusty and forgotten on various shelves for three hundred and fifty years before a Taiwan-based scholar recognized its brilliance and published it in Chinese translation.[17] It caused excitement among Sinophone scholars because it offers the finest firsthand descriptions of Koxinga ever discovered.

According to his account, Philip Meij stepped out of the fortress gate with a white flag and walked in the direction the Dutchmen had been led. They'd entered one of the houses that stood closest to the bayshore. When Meij got there, hundreds of Chinese soldiers were lining up. They seemed to be creating two long face-to-face rows stretching all the way up the hill to Koxinga's camp. He got himself shown inside the house.

The delegates told Meij that Koxinga had sent letters to Zeelandia Castle much like those he'd sent to Provintia, with threats and claims that Taiwan belonged to him. They'd been sent to tell Koxinga "in a gentle way" how displeased the governor was about his violent arrival in Taiwan and to see whether any kind of agreement could be worked out. But they were also supposed to tell Koxinga that Zeelandia Castle was well equipped with food and arms and the Dutch were ready to withstand him to the utmost if necessary, as good Christians, and that Batavia would soon be sending reinforcements. This was a lie, but it seemed like a good time for bluster.[18] They probably didn't mention that they'd sworn an oath to stand up to Koxinga's threats and reveal nothing about the Dutch situation, "except under unbearable pain."[19]

Meij told them that conditions in Provintia were getting worse. There was no water, little gunpowder, and few musket bullets. They said Coyet and the Council of Formosa had spent a long time considering what to do and wished "with all their heart" that they could offer some reinforcements and relief, but the bay was so tightly closed that not a single vessel could get through.[20] Coyet had therefore decided to give Valentine full authority to do as he wanted, either to brave a storm or surrender.[21] But there was no time for more talk. Two Chinese officers arrived, collected the Dutch envoys, and rushed them out the door. They grabbed Meij's flag as they left.

When he stepped outside, the long street was lined on each side with soldiers, four or six or ten men deep, all the way from the beach to the hilltop encampment.[22] They were fully armed, with bows, swords, and saber-staves. But what most intimidated Meij were the faces painted on their masks. They looked to him like rows of devils.[23] He later learned from a Chinese commander that the masks were designed not just to scare the enemy (they were particularly effective against Manchu horses) but also to prevent anyone—friend or foe—from seeing any sign of fear.

Meij made it back to the fortress, shaken, and found everyone busy stripping lead from windows and tin from the roof. They were collecting nails and screws and mugs—all the metal they could find—to melt into musket balls. Meij made his report to Valentine and then, barely able to keep his eyes open, collapsed into sleep.

While he slumbered, the envoys were having a meeting with Koxinga. It didn't go well.

THE AUDIENCE

After saying goodbye to Meij, the envoys were led up the street between the soldiers in their masks, which the envoys described as red-colored ape faces. When they crested the hill, they were met by He Bin, who offered his services as translator. They accepted.

He led them through the camp, choosing a roundabout route so they found it difficult to guess how many soldiers there were. He said there were twelve or thirteen regiments, each with nine hundred men. They found the troops imposing, but they weren't impressed by the cannons pointing at the fort. They were small, and the envoys judged them unusable because of the ridiculous mounts they lay on, unprotected by any kind of siegeworks.

Koxinga wasn't ready, so they were invited to tea in in an officer's tent. Their host ordered an underling to show off his sword by slicing through bamboo tent supports. Koxinga's blades were famous. One Chinese source describes, perhaps with exaggeration, how they were made: "A hundred blacksmiths take turns striking [the steel] in sequence, thus forming the sword, which is why they're so incredibly sharp."[24] The officer told another soldier to model his armor, and the envoys examined it closely. It had iron plates fixed with wire on either side of a heavy cotton cloth. The officer asked if the Dutch had mail like this. The envoys laughed out loud.[25] Armor of this type had gone out of fashion generations ago in Europe, ever since muskets had gained the ascendancy.

Word came that Koxinga was ready. They were led to his tent. He was sitting behind a small table. A thick red carpet lay on the ground in front of him. They removed their hats and bowed. They were told to sit on the carpet, "Malaysian style," as they later wrote.

Koxinga said something in Chinese. William Pedel and He Bin translated: Why had they come?

They replied as they'd been instructed to. Governor Coyet, they said, wondered why His Highness had suddenly appeared with so many junks and such a huge army, sweeping through Deer's Ear Gap and into the bay and through the land, and why he had sent threatening letters expressing such strange and mysterious demands. Coyet thought maybe there was some kind of mistake, that perhaps His Highness's letters had been misunderstood because of a lack of trustworthy translators. So he'd decided to send the envoys to hear the proposals from His Majesty's own mouth.[26]

Koxinga evidently expected a different answer because, as the envoys wrote, "the self-important pirate proudly raised his eyebrow and said with upturned nose that he had come to take the land of Formosa and the strongholds upon it from the Dutch, either with or without their permission, because the land was his."[27]

He gestured with his hand toward Fort Provintia, visible from the tent, and toward his troops, and then said, in words the emissaries found deeply blasphemous, "I can shake Heaven and earth with my might. Wherever I go I triumph. Didn't you see how my junks burned your great ships? Didn't you see how Thomas Pedel and all his soldiers were defeated on Baxemboy? Now I've got you cut off on land and sea. You have nothing left but two fortresses, which won't be able to withstand my troops. You Hollanders would be insane to fight against my thousands of soldiers with so few people."[28]

The emissaries stood up to make their reply, saying, calmly and with dignity (or so they later said), that they weren't authorized to hand over any fortresses. They advised His Majesty not to be hasty because there were plenty of weapons to go around, and both sides would suffer. In any case, they said, Formosa belonged to the Netherlands, and his Majesty's own father knew that. They brought out a peace treaty that his father had signed with the company in 1630, which to Dutch minds proved that the Zheng clan had agreed that the Dutch should hold Taiwan in perpetuity and that the Zhengs made no claim on it.[29]

Koxinga said he knew nothing of any treaty. He would take Formosa and its fortresses one way or another. If the Dutch came and begged him for mercy and paid obeisance, he would let them keep their property, and their debts would be paid, and he would make them into greater lords than the company could ever do. Or if they preferred he would give them junks to go to Batavia. But if he had to take the forts by force they shouldn't expect mercy.

He started yelling: If he had to use force everyone would be killed, the envoys first and in a most unpleasant manner.[30] In fact, he said, he would attack Provintia immediately and kill everyone right in front of their eyes. He called in some of officers and it seemed as though he were giving orders to start the attack.

The envoys begged him to wait, at least until they could report to Coyet. They promised to come back the next day.

Koxinga said they could have until morning but there was no need for more talk. If Coyet wanted to give up he should fly a white flag. If the Dutch flag stayed up, he would attack: Fort Provintia first and then Zeelandia Castle.

The envoys bowed goodbye. They were taken to the top of the hill, where they could see the entire camp. It seemed that Koxinga's troops actually were preparing for battle. They'd formed ranks, six or eight thousand of them, and the envoys saw various types of units: masked soldiers, archers, infantry with saber-staves and swords in beautiful long sheathes. Two hundred or so of the troops seemed to be a special elite, armed with guns. Swarming everywhere were thousands of workers and pages.

The envoys were fed a "very bad meal" and then, much to their surprise, they were left alone. They went to Fort Provintia to confer with Valentine.

SURRENDER

Valentine had to make an unpleasant decision: surrender, which might bring charges of treason, or resistance, which might bring death. He knew he'd choose surrender, so he did what any good bureaucrat does when he wants to cover his ass: he called a meeting. The envoys were asked to participate.

When he addressed the gentlemen gathered in the fort's Great Hall, he didn't say outright that he intended to surrender. He described the situation in six clear points. First, there was only enough food for five days. Second, the fort would withstand only one assault. Third, there were only two hundred pounds of gunpowder and little ammunition. Fourth, there was so little water in the well that you had to scrape it out with cupped hands, and it was impossible to dig it any deeper, and the enemy had discovered the well in the garden in back and filled it in. Fifth, the soldiers were exhausted, and everyone else, too. And, sixth and last, "the stench was getting more and more unbearable and causing severe illness."[31]

Everyone gave his opinion, but then Valentine realized Philip Meij was missing. Meij was woken up and led to the Great Hall. Valentine turned to him and said, "What do you think we should do?"

He blinked away his hour of sleep and said he was optimistic because Zeelandia Castle would be sending help soon, surely. Valentine turned to the envoys from Zeelandia, who reiterated that there would be no help. "When this news entered my mind," Meij wrote, "my thoughts went reeling from one thing to another. Finally I realized that things were so bad for us that that we would have to be responsible to God Almighty Himself if we insisted on putting so many innocent souls into danger and death. I also considered the fact that even if we held back one or two assaults and were to hold the fort for another day or two or three at the utmost, we would still have to give up and trust in the mercy of the enemy, who would be all the more angry and bitter."[32] Having sat pondering for a moment, he gave his answer: If the enemy was inclined to offer a reasonable accord, they shouldn't reject it. To Meij's relief, Valentine said that everyone else in the room felt the same way.

The decision made, the envoys said goodbye and got in their boat, while Valentine, ass suitably covered, wrote out terms of surrender: the Dutch would keep their money and goods and slaves; the soldiers would march out of the fort in honor, keeping their guns and powder; and everyone would be allowed free passage to Zeelandia. A translator began setting the terms into Chinese.

The sun went down. Outside, the enemy could be heard dragging and breaking and building things. The besieged passed the night worrying and in the morning awoke to find that the enemy had torn out the fence around the garden in back of the fort and ripped out trees and bamboo and anything that might hinder their approach. Beyond the garden and the burned-out horse stalls were thousands of Chinese troops, just beyond cannon range.

Valentine waited to send out his surrender letter. Last night, before the envoys had left, they'd promised to ask Coyet one last time to send aid. Valentine was supposed to look for a signal from Zeelandia Castle: a cannon shot and the raising and lowering of the flag.[33] That would mean there would be no aid and that surrender should proceed. But as the sun rose higher, there was no signal.

Around noon, music came from Koxinga's camp. Horsemen trotted downhill. The besieged guessed that the one with the red silk parasol was Koxinga. In front walked red-clad figures and behind marched drummers and horn players. The troops stood at attention as he passed. It looked like he was making an inspection. Shortly afterward, drums began pounding. Orders were yelled. The Chinese pressed forward.

Valentine handed the letter to Philip Meij, who once again found himself outside the fort. He and a companion, who carried a white flag, walked to Saccam City and were escorted into a house that Koxinga's officers had commandeered for a headquarters. He found a commander there, sitting alone at a table eating. "Are you surrendering the fort?" the man asked. Philip said he didn't know, that he was just supposed to give this letter to Koxinga. The general shook his head and said all the Dutch were going to die. He took the letter and turned it over in his hand, looking at the front and back. Meij and his companion were taken to Koxinga's tent.

As they approached, He Bin came out, smiling and shaking hands. He took the letter and led Meij forward, saying Koxinga would treat him well and that he wouldn't even have to kowtow and could just bow according to the European fashion.

Hundreds of soldiers stood before the tent, and Meij's description is too good to pass up:

> In front stood around six or eight hundred armored soldiers with scores of banners in three rows on either side, each outfitted in the richest way, their armor covered with black satin that was beautifully adorned with lions and dragon-heads of all colors of silk and gold. Their lances flashed like silver and their helms, too, each of which had a tuft of red hair around a foot high sticking out.

They walked forward between the rows. Halfway down, Meij's flag-bearing companion was held back and Meij proceeded the rest of the way on his own.

Koxinga was sitting behind a table covered in embroidered silk. He wore an unbleached linen robe and a tapered brown hat with a golden rim from which jutted a little white feather. Behind him, two "beautiful boys" in black satin robes waved fans with gilded handles eight feet long, and on both sides there stood black-robed officials. Meij estimated his age at around forty, which was quite a good guess, as Koxinga was thirty-six. Meij found him handsome, pale, with big black eyes that constantly flickered back and forth. When his mouth was open you could see four or five long filed teeth far from each other. A thin beard wisped to his chest.

Meij began to bow but was thrust onto his knees and into a kowtow on the red carpet. He Bin handed the letter to Koxinga, who opened it. At this point, behind and outside the tent, a shot was fired, some kind of signal. Koxinga huffed and mumbled to himself as he read the letter. Then he looked up at Meij and He Bin and the officials standing next to him and spoke in Chinese in a stern and booming voice, gesturing with exaggerated movements "as though he was about to fly away with his hands and feet."[34]

He Bin translated: "It seems that Heaven still favors you. I had already given the order to my officials to attack your fort and kill everyone inside if there was any resistance. Now I will not only let you live but also allow you to keep your land and houses and property, and you can keep living in them just like before."[35] Only one condition did Koxinga refuse to accept: he wouldn't allow anyone to go to Zeelandia Castle.

If Philip Meij really replied as he said he did, he must have been a courageous man, because he says he said, perhaps from his prone position on the red carpet, that if Koxinga didn't agree that everyone could go to Zeelandia then there was no deal. Koxinga asked him why everyone wanted so much to go to Zeelandia, when he would provide everyone with everything they needed here in Saccam. Meij replied that they were all Dutch, and that their parents, children, wives, husbands, brothers, and sisters lived in Zeelandia and they couldn't be so lightly separated from them. Koxinga said he'd never let people go to Zeelandia, so Meij and his countrymen should get the idea out of their heads. He said that when the Northern Monsoon began blowing the next year, he would arrange for everyone to be taken to Batavia.

Meij said he didn't have the authority to agree to that, so Koxinga wrote some red characters on the letter and made a gesture with his hand. A member of his entourage stepped forward and received the document with reverence.

A high-ranking official accompanied Meij back toward Provintia. He was Yang Chaodong, the man who'd spoken in favor of Koxinga's plan to invade Taiwan when all the other generals seemed against the idea. Within a month, Yang would be named prefectural governor of Taiwan.[36] At this point Koxinga wanted him to arrange the final surrender deal with Valentine.

Yang was too afraid to go all the way to Provintia. He stopped at the Saccam Town Hall, the last building before the plaza that lay between the town and the fort. Eventually, Meij arranged—by means of promises and hostages—for him to talk to Valentine through a cannon port in the fort. There was more negotiating, messengers sent to Koxinga and back, until finally Valentine himself went to see Koxinga, with Yang held hostage in the smelly fort.

Valentine didn't write an account of his audience, but it must have gone well, because soon joyful horns and drums and flutes and gongs sounded from Koxinga's camp, and then a merry procession wound its way down the hill. There was a retinue of musicians and a beautiful palanquin shaded with an orange parasol and heaped with silk and velvet and damask.

A figure on horseback occupied the place of honor. It turned out to be Jacob Valentine.

When he entered the fort, he spoke tersely to Meij and the others. They must vacate the fortress in two days, but no one could go to Zeelandia. They'd have to move into houses in Saccam, and Koxinga promised to provide food and everything else they might need. Valentine seemed embarrassed by the gifts. He said he tried refusing them but Koxinga had insisted.[37]

Outside, the celebration intensified. There was shouting and cheering. Guns were fired in joy. It was so loud that Coyet's soldiers heard it on the other side of the bay.[38]

Valentine had been given two yellow flags with dragons and lions on them. He had them raised above the fort.

Two days later, on 6 May 1661, Valentine held one more meeting inside the fort. He gathered all the soldiers together and asked whether they were sure they were ready to leave. They all called out "Yes." He asked the officers to sign a letter stating that the fort did indeed lack water and powder, that it did indeed stink too terribly to continue inhabiting, and they all signed, further covering his sychophantic ass. The exercise was nearly ruined when his top commander got drunk and started yelling about setting the powder on fire and blowing the whole fort to pieces with everyone inside. Valentine yelled back. The man abandoned his plot.

And so, as the sun sank below the sea, the officers handed Valentine their keys and mustered their men near the rear gate. The soldiers lit their fuses, put musket bullets between their teeth, and marched out into the dusk.[39] When they reached the botanical garden, which had once been a beautiful place filled with tropical plants and herbs but was now a trampled mess, they stopped, fired a salvo, and extinguished their fuses. The guns were taken by the Chinese for safekeeping.

Less than a week after arriving, Koxinga found himself master of the strategic core of Taiwan, the rich lands around the Bay of Taiwan.

Valentine and Meij and the others moved into nice houses in Saccam, while the soldiers were lodged near the waterfront. Koxinga sent rice and pigs, and special mutton for Valentine, and guards were set up to protect the Dutch from Chinese soldiers.[40]

Valentine said he had a good feeling about everything and was sure that Koxinga would honor his promises and it wouldn't be long before the Dutch were transported back to Batavia.

Koxinga was optimistic, too, sure the war would soon be over. As he wrote in a letter to Coyet, its words echoing those he'd written to Valentine: "All you have left is that little fort, which is like a dead tree that cannot stand up on its own much longer."[41]

Zeelandia Castle was indeed small compared to the great city walls Koxinga had overcome in China. It was even smaller than the little fortified villages he'd chastened over the years for refusing to pay taxes. So we can understand his confidence. After all, he'd nearly captured the Stone City of Nanjing. He felt sure that Coyet would turn the fort over. If not, his army would capture it in one battle.

He was wrong. Coyet's thousand-odd soldiers stopped Koxinga's army in its tracks for nearly a year, changing the dynamics of the war. How did they do it?

Renaissance architecture.

The Castle

We celebrate the Italian Renaissance for the *Mona Lisa*, the Sistine Chapel, and the poetry of Petrarch, but the Italians were also masters of the art of war. One of their most momentous inventions was a new kind of fortress. In the 1400s, as Europeans fired more and more cannons at more and more walls, it became clear that traditional castles were no longer effective. Medieval fortifications shattered.[1] The Italians began building different walls, lower and thicker, slanted to deflect and filled with earth to absorb cannonfire. Gradually a new architecture began to emerge, and in the early 1500s its form matured into a radical new design. Military historians have called it by various names, but I'll call it the "renaissance fort."[2]

The key innovation was an angled bastion that thrust out from each corner, a huge arrow of menace. With each bastion placed to complement its neighbors, the renaissance fortress could spew flanking fire like no other type of fort. Attackers used to be able to find a few islands of peace to place their ladders, which scholars call dead zones, places cannons couldn't hit.[3] But the renaissance fort covered all the angles. So long as it was fully manned and armed, it was nearly impossible to take by storm. Any troops foolish enough to try scaling the walls or battering a gate would be shredded by crossfire, from above, from below, from the left, from the right, even from behind, where bastions stuck out in back of them (see figure 2).

The new design spread rapidly, first within Italy and then beyond. Wherever it went, everything changed. Since the renaissance fort was so difficult to storm, you had to surround it and either slowly batter it into submission, a process that took weeks and required building counterfortifications, hundreds of yards of walls and trenches and batteries to protect your own troops and gunners, or starve it into submission, which required a tight cordon around it, and which could take months or even years. In either case, you needed a huge army. So wherever there were renaissance forts, armies tended to get larger. This was expensive. And the forts themselves were expensive, orders of magnitude more massive than medieval castles.

The renaissance fort may have changed not just the conduct of war and the size of armies, but also politics and society. To pay for the forts and armies, you needed more effective taxation policies and fiscal structures. The Military Revolution Model holds that the evolution of new social and political structures in Europe was catalyzed by—or at least the process was reinforced by—the military changes occurring in sixteenth- and seventeenth-century Europe, changes that were probably brought about by the renaissance fortress.

The renaissance fort also began appearing outside Europe. The Spanish and Portuguese were the pioneers, establishing forts from the Azores Islands in the Atlantic Ocean to the Philippine Islands in the China Seas. Then came the Dutch. During the seventeenth century, the Dutch Golden Age, Dutch engineers brought their advanced designs to the far-flung colonies of the empire.[4]

According to the Military Revolution Model, colonial forts like Zeelandia were, as Geoffrey Parker puts it, an "engine of European expansion," one of the prime technologies that allowed Europeans to establish a durable presence throughout the world. But the preternaturally prolific Jeremy Black argues that non-Europeans didn't have so much trouble capturing European fortresses when they wanted to. The Persians, for example, conquered a Portuguese renaissance fort with apparent ease in 1622, and Black quips that they "evidently had not read some of the literature on military revolution and did not know that European artillery forces were supposed to prevail with some sort of technological superiority over non-Europeans."[5] It's an important debate, and Parker and Black both make compelling cases. But it's been hard to resolve the question because we know so little about Europeans' wars with non-Europeans. Koxinga's attempt to capture Zeelandia Castle is a valuable test case.

By Chinese standards, Zeelandia Castle was tiny, but it was one of the larger forts the Dutch built in their Asian empire, as was only fitting for their largest Asian colony. Its high, slanted walls were made of tamped earth, much like Chinese walls. This earthen core was faced with a thick layer of red brick, which was itself covered by a layer of grey stone brought over from China and the Penghu Islands.

Zeelandia Castle was actually two forts stitched together. The upper castle was a square structure about a hundred yards on each side. From each corner jutted a huge bastion. As was customary with renaissance fortresses, each bastion had its own name—Vlissingen, Middelbug, Camperveer, Amsterdam—because it was a sort of minifort in its own right. Within the square upper castle stood buildings: barracks, a prison with torture implements, and houses, which before the war had primarily been inhabited by military officers but which now housed various officials too, including Coyet himself.

Nestled against the upper castle was the lower castle. It hadn't been planned as well as the upper castle because it had been built ad hoc around a row of buildings that lined the shore of the main channel into the Bay of Taiwan. Those buildings had been unprotected until in 1634 a Chinese pirate attacked the Dutch.[6] Afterward the inflammable straw roofs were redone in tile, and a new wall was conceived. It started just behind the northeast bastion of the upper castle, jogged down to the shore and then followed the shoreline westward for several hundred paces before doubling back on itself and rejoining the upper castle on its western wall.

The buildings within the lower castle proliferated through the years. The grandest was the governor's official residence, which stood in the middle, its back against the lower part of the upper castle. There was also a church, and other residences and offices, but the largest buildings were the huge warehouses filled with treasures from the Indies—pepper, porcelain, cotton, silks, cloves, nutmeg, tea, sandalwood, and

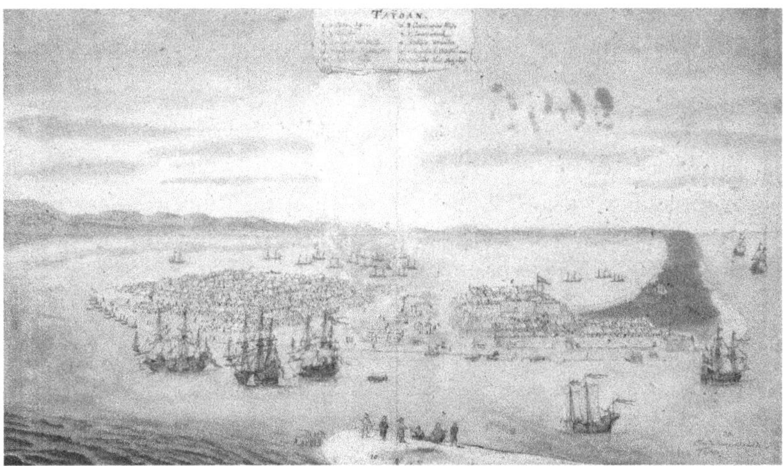

Figure 20. Zeelandia as viewed from Baxemboy Island, c. 1644. In the foreground is the southern tip of Baxemboy, where people seem to have just disembarked from a rowboat, some in Dutch and some in Chinese clothes. Still sitting in the rowboat is a woman in Dutch dress. It seems they've just rowed across the busy Channel, where Dutch ships are anchored. Behind them, on the other side of the Channel, lies Zeelandia City to the left and Zeelandia Castle to the right, a flag flying on the Upper Castle. By this point, 1644, the walls of the Lower Castle are complete, although they have only one bastion, which juts out toward the far right. In the dunes behind that bastion stands the redoubt that protected Zeelandia Castle, and beyond it the island stretches southward to nearly join the mainland at a ford called the Narrow. Used by permission of the Biblioteca Laurenziana, Florence, Italy, inventory number Castello 7.

silver. Near the main warehouses, a gate opened out onto the stone piers, where junks and sampans, yachts and fluytships docked to unload their cargos. Eventually, the walls of the lower castle got their own bastions, one for each corner. So together the two forts that made up Zeelandia Castle had seven bastions (figure 20).

Zeelandia Castle—particularly the upper castle, which rose imposingly on its berm—commanded a view in all directions. To the east clustered the tile rooftops of Zeelandia City, behind which, across an expanse of shimmering water, you could see Saccam and Fort Provintia, which now flew Koxinga's flags. Turning your gaze to the right, you could see the narrow island stretching southward, its dunes getting smaller as they approached the mainland at the Narrow. The Dutch called this part of the island the Pineapples, after a pineapple-like fruit known as pandanus that grew there. If you turned farther to the right, so you were facing west, you saw high dunes and beyond them the open sea. And turning to the north, you saw the main Taiwan Channel, on the other side of which was Baxemboy Island, where Thomas Pedel had been cut down by a Chinese saber-staff.

This was where Zeelandia Castle was most secure, because the walls came down to just a few meters from the water. Koxinga probably wouldn't try to attack there because his men would have to land on the waterfront. They'd be shredded by cannonfire before they even got close.

It was a bit more vulnerable on the other sides. If he came from the east, Koxinga could shelter his troops in Zeelandia City. But they'd still have to cross a large, open plain to get to the castle, and the plain was dominated by three of the castle's bastions, two in the upper and one in the lower castle. Over the decades a few structures had cropped up on this field—an enclosed market, a smithy, the gallows—but it was still open enough that anyone rushing through it would be exposed to lethal cannonfire.

The most vulnerable side was the west and southwest, where dunes rose behind the fort. One was particularly high. The Dutch had realized early on that an enemy might place cannons there and fire directly down into the castle, so they'd built a small fort on top, which they called the redoubt. So long as the redoubt stood, Zeelandia Castle was safe from attack from the dunes.[7]

Thus, Zeelandia Castle, although small, inspired Coyet's and his officials' confidence.

Koxinga was unimpressed. He expected Coyet to recognize that he faced impossible odds.

KOXINGA PRESSES FORWARD

When Coyet didn't offer an immediate surrender, Koxinga thought maybe he was just pretending to be confident. After all, Valentine had waited until the war gongs sounded before raising the white flag. Maybe Coyet needed more pressure. So on 4 May 1661, the day Koxinga's flags were first raised over Fort Provintia, his troops began pressing on Zeelandia Castle from two sides. Some crossed the

Narrow and marched toward Zeelandia Castle from the south. Others began preparing junks to sail across the bay, capture Zeelandia City, and assail the castle from the east.

There were still Dutchmen living in Zeelandia City, and to this point Coyet had resisted letting them into the fortress, which wasn't designed to hold so many people. The women and children had been allowed in, of course. They'd said goodbye to their husbands and fathers and walked through the narrow streets past the church and City Hall and out along the stone path that led to the castle, past the toll-house and municipal scales on their right, past the graveyard and fish market on their left, past the execution grounds with the gallows, and finally past the company's blacksmith building, entering a gate to the lower castle.[8]

Their men stayed to defend Zeelandia City, which had no walls, forming a night watch to help the soldiers patrol the streets, although the soldiers had a tendency to use the patrols as a pretext to harass the few Chinese who remained and to break down doors to find rice wine.

Toward the evening of 4 May, the men marched to the fortress. Their spokesman, a young but fast-rising company official named David Harthouwer, told Coyet it was too dangerous to spend another night in the empty city. Koxinga's junks were anchored just out of musket range and might attack at any time. They demanded to enter the castle. Coyet was displeased, but he ordered the drummers to pound out the signal for everyone to clear the streets and come to the castle.[9]

As they moved their belongings into cramped quarters, a Chinese emissary arrived with an ultimatum. He said Koxinga would prefer to avoid bloodshed and that the sooner Coyet surrendered, the sooner everyone could be friends again. At this, one of the Dutch officials asked, "What kind of friend invades his friend's country?"

The emissary replied that the Dutch must put this all in perspective. Suppose, he said, that the positions were reversed, that it had been the Dutch who'd invaded Koxinga's headquarters in China with overwhelming force. In that case, Koxinga would have had to accept the situation. In the same way, the Dutch simply had to come to terms with Koxinga's invasion. He was the strongest.

Coyet said he had no intention of surrendering and that the Dutch wouldn't let this aggression go unanswered. The emissary replied that if the company was strong enough to take this castle back again then they should go ahead and do it.

"Koxinga doesn't have the castle yet," said a Dutchman.

Well, said the emissary, he'll have it soon enough.[10]

Clearly, Koxinga and his people didn't think much of this little fort or the Dutch soldiers defending it. They thought they could capture it easily. The next morning, columns of troops—thousands upon thousands—forded the Narrow and marched northward through the Pineapples. Where the dunes got more ambitious, not far from the castle, they began planting flags and setting up tents.

This was too close. Dutch cannons made them scatter and "roll like handballs," but they didn't roll far. They pitched their tents again outside of cannon range. This was their new base camp, and it wasn't long before Koxinga himself came, ready to bear the discomfort of the heat and the sun to oversee the capture of the castle.[11]

While Koxinga's new headquarters assembled itself, his junks swarmed toward Zeelandia City. Musketmen tried driving them off but had to retreat. As they left, they set fires in the houses, the granaries, the shipyard, the firewood island just off the southern harbor. But Koxinga's men were pouring ashore near the ferry port behind the easternmost houses. They rushed to put out the fires. It's a sign of Koxinga's confidence that he also sent some forty soldiers to guard the houses of Dutch citizens in the town, so that after the Dutch gave him the castle they could get their possessions back.[12]

FEINTS AND SKIRMISHES

But Coyet didn't surrender. Both sides dug in. Chinese laborers made trenches in front of the city, using the sandy dirt to fill baskets and sugar crates, which they used to barricade the streets, Broadway, New Street, North Street. Dutch gunners shot at them, so the Chinese learned to cross streets at a full run.[13]

The Dutch leveled off dunes, dug trenches, strewed foot-spikes. They hammered together walkways to make the fort more defensible.

They used sugar crates and deerskins to construct arrow shields on the ramparts. They sent slaves and soldiers out to the smithy and the abandoned hospital outside the castle to scavenge planks and stones, doors and windows, bricks and roof tiles. Others gathered bamboo from the beaches.[14] Koxinga's forces sniped from windows, answered by cannonades from the fort, which brought showers of stone down upon their heads.[15]

Each day there were probes and skirmishes. The Dutch took pot-shots at houses and junks and Koxinga's new camp. Fifty-five cannon shots one day; one hundred sixty-six the next; forty-nine the next. A huge bronze cannon called Mad Meg (*Dolle Griet*) was the most effective, able to fire right into the enemy tents. "It was gratifying," Coyet's secretary wrote, "to see what a lively scene the shots made where they fell. We made thirty shots today with large cannons against the enemy and also celebrated the Sabbath."[16]

The Chinese pretended the shots didn't hurt, telling the Dutch, by means of a prisoner released to the castle, that "no one was much harmed by them. One man got a bit of a stiff leg from one, and another got a bit of a bump on his head in his iron helmet."[17] The freed man had been shown some of the large cannonballs that Mad Meg had hurled into the Chinese camp, but only so that they could tell him, with an air of insouciance, that they weren't much impressed because they had even larger cannons.

More frightening than Mad Meg were Dutch mortars, a relatively new weapon whose specialty was lobbing exploding grenades. They had short barrels, into which you placed what looks like a bowling ball with a fuse. Unlike a standard cannonball, mortar grenades were hollow. You filled them with gunpowder and bits of iron—bars, nails, specially designed shrapnel. To fire them you lit two fuses: the grenade fuse and the mortar fuse. Then you got out of the way. If all went well, the mortar came down where the enemy was gathering and then exploded, spattering the area with blood and bone (figure 21).

The Dutch aimed their mortars at the squares and intersections of Zeelandia City, wherever Chinese were in groups. Although mortars had been used in Chinese warfare, Chinese mortars may not have had exploding grenades, because Koxinga's men seemed unprepared for

Figure 21. Gunners using instruments to aim a mortar during a night battle, 1618. In this copperplate engraving, gunners use instruments to determine the proper angle of elevation for a mortar. Exploding mortar shells seem to have served the Dutch well in their war against Koxinga, causing havoc when they fell from above into Chinese encampments. As a Dutch prisoner noted, when describing his captivity among the Chinese, the Chinese were "very bitter [*vergramt*] toward our chief gunner, saying that it was as though he could lay the shots with his own hand, wherever he wanted." The image is from Leonhard Zubler, Nova geometrica pyrobolia, 1618. Used by permission of Anne S. K. Brown Military Collection, Brown University Library, Providence, Rhode Island.

them. One of the first grenades landed right in the middle of Broadway, and crowds of Chinese just walked toward it, trying to douse it with water. The fuse kept sputtering, and the grenade exploded right in the middle of them, killing and wounding many.[18] Another time, a Chinese official saw one land and went to have a look. As he leaned down to pick it up, it exploded, blasting away part of his silk-clad arm. He survived only because the largest fragments just missed his head, although his face and chest were heavily wounded.[19]

The grenades were safer to study when the fuses fell out or were asphyxiated in the dirt. On one occasion, Dutch soldiers watched as a Chinese man rolled an unexploded shell down Broadway toward the northern harbor, "perhaps to show it to his commander."[20] Another time, the Chinese took an unexploded grenade, unfilled it, and then refilled it with gunpowder. They lit its fuse and loaded it into a regular cannon, which exploded into pieces.[21] Later, a Chinese commander would try to send spies into the fortress to try to find out what kinds of cannons shot the exploding shells, but that was months in the future. For now, the Chinese learned to dive for cover when a mortar landed. The Dutch gunner seemed to them eerily accurate, gaining a reputation for uncanny precision: "it was as though he could lay the shots with his own hand, wherever he wanted."[22]

Mortars weren't just scary to those on the receiving end. They had a tendency to maim their owners, too. One sunny afternoon, a mortar delivered a grenade right where it was supposed to, near a house in Zeelandia City, but when it exploded, it shot a piece of iron high into the air. It plummeted into the castle and split someone's head in half.[23] Mortars' squat barrels also tended to spew showers of sparks, which had a way of finding other things that liked to explode, as occurred on another afternoon, when mortar sparks set off a cannon, killing one Dutch soldier instantly and four of his comrades over the next hours.[24]

DIPLOMACY

Through all of these skirmishes, Koxinga kept demanding surrender and Coyet kept refusing. Sometimes Koxinga tried to work through intermediaries, urging Dutchmen to persuade Coyet and the others to surrender. One promising mark he found in the grieving translator William Pedel, whose young brother had been wounded by Chinese troops and whose father had been hacked to death on the battlefield. He spoke Chinese, and so Koxinga told him to persuade his compatriots—particularly the women—to surrender the castle soon, so they could keep their wealth and slaves. He promised him riches and a high station if he did and threatened to kill his family in a painful manner if he didn't.[25] He didn't.

Koxinga tried using Jacob Valentine as an example. "The man who governed Fort Provintia was wise," he wrote,

> because as soon as he saw that my army was ready to storm his fort and attack him, he chose the best course and came immediately to my side, bowing and surrendering that fort, and so I bestowed upon him riches and presents and the rank of a high official. . . . Now then. Let this be an example for you. Put yourself under my authority as he did, and I'll promote you to high positions and give you everything you might desire.[26]

He made Valentine write to Coyet, although Valentine protested that "such letters will not now be given any respect and won't have any effect."[27] Valentine duly passed on Koxinga's message that surrender was better than death. Sometimes he wrote about potential deals Coyet might have found compelling: that if Coyet surrendered Zeelandia Castle Koxinga would give Fort Provintia back, that the Dutch would be given free trade, or, if they wished, they could have a place to trade in Penghu, where they could even build a fort. But Coyet was suspicious because the proposals didn't come directly from Koxinga. Most seemed to be thought up by He Bin. Valentine noted his own suspicions about He Bin, saying that the translator was making offers in the name of Koxinga, "so he says."[28] He Bin also asked Valentine to convey the discomfort Koxinga faced waiting for surrender "so many days outside Zeelandia in the sunshine and heat," as if Coyet cared much about Koxinga's well-being.[29]

Coyet knew his replies would be studied by the Chinese, so he used them to send messages to Koxinga.[30] "It is our duty," he wrote to Valentine, "to repel this powerful attacker, and we feel we have supplies and courage enough to do so, as well as God's help."[31] Sometimes he undermined Koxinga's claims about casualties in the skirmishes around Zeelandia Castle: "It is nice that yesterday only one of our men was wounded and none died in the skirmish . . . even though Koxinga tells you that we lost fifty."[32]

Koxinga's own letters adopted a tone of forthright menace:

> My soldiers always win, north, south, east, or west, and even the Manchus, as mighty as they are, with their multitudes of horses and armed troops, are terrified when they see my forces marching from far away. You overestimate your own power.

> You must realize that compared to the Manchus, you are only a handful of people who cannot stand up against my own soldiers. How can you fight against me, relying only on your ships, which I burned up in an instant, even as I defeated your people as soon as they set foot on Baxemboy, so that not even a single man survived? You people cannot last on water or land but will lose everywhere. Now all you have left is that little fort, which is like a dead and dried out tree that cannot stand on its own.[33]

He liked metaphors about dead trees. In another letter, he wrote, "For me, defeating the mighty Manchus is no harder than breaking off the branch of a tree. So you people, who are so fewer—how would you be able to stand up against me?"[34]

He seemed especially fond of belittling Zeelandia Castle:

> How can you people hope to resist me in that little fortress? I have long known the situation of your castle and the thickness of its walls, which are just like the walls of Fort Provintia. Yes, Zeelandia Castle is built on a higher hill, but what difference does that make? When I strike with my cannons the walls will collapse and crumble, without my having even to risk any of my soldiers.[35]

The Dutch had a reputation as powerful gunners, but Koxinga liked suggesting that it was overrated:

> It is true that you people are famous for playing artfully with cannons, but you have never had this many cannons leveled at you. I have brought hundreds of them, ready to use against you, but I find myself troubled by the idea of killing so many people, and so I'm first sending you this letter so that you can think carefully and come pay obeisance to me, and then I will raise all of you up to a higher position even than Valentine. But if you put off your decision until I have blown holes in your castle, then it will be too late and no one will escape with his life.[36]

Coyet responded that he wasn't afraid of Koxinga's cannons:

> Although Your Highness continues to demand that we surrender this castle, we don't feel that to be necessary. . . . Not even

> the hundred cannons that Your Highness says are pointed at us can persuade us, because we have even more cannons here in our fort to answer with. Your Highness will have to come up with some other proposition if you ever want to keep your friendship with the Company and your trade safe in so many diverse lands.[37]

All this communication didn't move the two sides any closer to peace. Coyet addressed Koxinga politely, using the term "Your Highness," but he didn't yield.

An Assault

Koxinga preferred intimidation to battle. Before attacking Zeelandia Castle, he tried to terrify the Dutch. The besieged had settled into a nightly routine, with Minister Kruyf leading evening prayers and Coyet making one last inspection of the bastions before going to bed in a big, crowded house in the upper castle. Late on a windswept night not quite three weeks into the war, when everyone but the watchmen were in bed or at their spot on the floor, a gong rang out from Zeelandia City and then, all at once, horns blared, pipes blew, drums pounded, soldiers yelled, and cannons and guns went off in mad profusion. Fire-arrows lit up the sky, although most barely reached the castle's outer walls. The bullets and cannonballs similarly flew harmlessly overhead. Then the gong sounded again and the attack ceased. No one was hurt, but nerves were rattled in the dark.[1]

A few nights later the Dutch were torn from their slumber by screaming, horns, and sounds of great wagons rolling about in the dark, "perhaps to scare us or maybe to hide the sounds of some heavy work."[2] The next night screaming started in Zeelandia City and then spread into the blackness of the sand dunes behind the castle. It seemed to come from everywhere at once and was accompanied by loud knocking sounds and rumbling and shrieking in the foremost houses of the city. The Dutch fired into the darkness, but it was impossible to see what was happening. As before, the noises stopped and no one was harmed.[3]

After a week of this yelling and banging, Koxinga sent Coyet a letter demanding immediate surrender. The man he chose to deliver it was a Dutch missionary named Antonio Hambroek. It was an inspired choice. Hambroek, a venerable figure, was one of the many Dutch people who'd been living in the countryside when Koxinga arrived. The fact that he was now in Koxinga's power meant that there was little hope that the hundreds of other Dutch men and women who'd been living in the country—wives, brothers, sons, and daughters of those in the castle—were still free. Some in the castle had hoped that these people might be conspiring against Koxinga with the natives and would lead an aboriginal army in guerilla warfare. Hambroek's appearance meant that that dream was over. Zeelandia was on its own.

The old man arrived on horseback at dusk and was led upstairs into the upper castle, where he gave Coyet the letter. It started out with promising insults:

> It is as though you Netherlanders are stupid and crazy, thinking that with just a few hundred people you can you fight against us, who are so incredibly many. It is the will of Heaven that everything live and remain safe from destruction, and so I am happiest when all men stay alive. That's why I have sent so many letters to you and given you so many chances.[4]

Koxinga wrote that his patience was at an end. He was ready to attack the castle, and if Coyet was wise, he would hand it over now. Of course, Coyet was welcome to wait until the cannons started firing, but then he'd have to be especially contrite:

> If you and others—people of high and low station alike—raise the white flag and say "Peace," then I'll say, "Stop shooting. It's enough." And as soon as you appear before me with high and low officials, with women and children, I'll immediately order my cannons to be taken away.

In that case, Koxinga said, he'd give the Dutch just one hour to vacate the castle, although he'd make sure his soldiers protected the fort and kept order, "so that not even the smallest piece of grass or hair from your belongings is taken." Koxinga concluded by invoking fate:

"In either case, it has come to pass that we can give you life or death, so it's up to you to make a worthy decision. If you let your thoughts range around too far then it's the same as seeking your death."

As Coyet began composing a defiant response, he heard disturbing sounds coming from outside the castle. Out in the dark Koxinga's workers were digging and stacking, hauling unseen heavy things, calling out to each other. Sentries told Coyet that another envoy had arrived. The man, a Dutchman whose name was Ossewayer, said Koxinga was getting impatient. He also said Koxinga had an important message that had to be communicated in person by a Chinese envoy.

Coyet asked Ossewayer what the Chinese were doing out there. Ossewayer said he hadn't been able to see much, but he had noticed that workers seemed to be piling up a mountain of dirt and clay in Zeelandia City, behind the row of abandoned houses that faced the castle. The dirt already reached up to the second floor windows and stretched as far as he could see up and down the street, from Jan Fonteijn's house in the south to the Chinese merchant Hocko's house in the north.[5]

Coyet sent Ossewayer back out to demand that all work be stopped, because it was contrary to the rules of war to conduct such threatening activity when engaging in peace talks. Ossewayer was also supposed to say that Coyet wouldn't receive the Chinese envoy until the next morning.

While Ossewayer walked with flag and lantern back across the plain, Coyet and the others asked Hambroek what had happened to the Dutch families in the countryside when Koxinga arrived.

Hambroek said he'd known something was wrong even before the invasion, because the natives had been unusually defiant. He'd worked among them for years, and many were going to church and school and could read and write. He and other missionaries had rooted out their "devilish" priestesses and gotten many of them to give up the custom of headhunting. But just before the invasion, men from Hambroek's village—a village called Mattau—had carried out a headhunting raid. When they returned in victory, they began celebrating as they liked to do, displaying the three heads they'd captured, dancing and drinking and leaping about all night long. Hambroek expressed his disapproval, but the villagers argued openly with him, which he thought was unusual and disturbing. Had these headhunters already been aware that things were changing? Were there already Chinese instigators in their midst? It was possible. Chinese had long had close links with the natives, and Koxinga had prepared the way to his invasion carefully, sending out advance agents to drum up support.

A few days later Hambroek learned that thousands of ships had arrived. The Dutch colonists gathered in a village called Soulang. It had been one of the company's first native allies. There was a church, a schoolhouse, Dutch houses. It should have been safe, but its people were no longer welcoming. The Dutch fled. Koxinga had cut off the roads leading southward to Fort Provintia and Zeelandia Castle, so they went north.

The refugees numbered well over a hundred. Most were civilians, and among them were women, children, and old people. They weren't used to marching a dozens of miles a day with heavy bags. They needed a safe place with food.

But Koxinga rapidly expanded his influence. He personally visited the native villages the Dutch had counted as their closest allies. According to Yang Ying's chronicle, "the men and women crowded the streets, welcoming him with food and drink. Koxinga thanked them and gave them gifts, and they were deeply happy."[6] The Dutch had made a practice of chosing village headmen, giving them staves and robes as symbols of authority.[7] Now Koxinga appointed these same people as "official border chiefs," giving them silk robes and hats.[8] It was astonishing how fast they switched sides.

So the refugees went north into wilder territory. The children were hungry, the officers were fighting with each other, the soldiers were refusing to obey orders. When a message arrived from Jacob Valentine urging them to give up, they were in a receptive mood. His letter said that Fort Provintia had surrendered—it was unavoidable he said—and that Koxinga would welcome other Dutch people. They would have places to live, food to eat, and a ride back to Batavia when the winds turned. They would even have their belongings restored to them. Valentine said Koxinga was treating him and the other Dutch very well.

Some refused to surrender, saying they'd take their chances on a march into the lands of the Great Prince of the Middag, a mysterious indigenous ruler to the north who'd been independent but friendly toward the Dutch. From there, they said, they'd be able to make it all the way to the northern tip of Taiwan, where two isolated Dutch fortresses guarded Taiwan's far reaches. But most of the refugees were too old or too young or too sick to undertake such a voyage. They trudged back, surrendered to Koxinga's soldiers, and moved into Saccam City with the other prisoners.

Hambroek said that at first Koxinga lived up to his promises. His men sealed Hambroek's belongings—and the belongings of other people—and brought them back to Saccam for safekeeping, promising to restore them soon to their owners. But the prisoners started going hungry. Even Koxinga's own soldiers lacked food.

Then Koxinga summoned him and other prisoners "of quality"—officials, merchants, surveyors, and surgeons—to his camp in the Pineapple dunes to witness his defeat of the Dutch, and to keep them out of trouble in Saccam.

Coyet wanted details about the camp, anything that might be useful in war. Hambroek said the Chinese in the camp showed him devastatingly large cannonballs—forty pounders. They said they had a hundred huge cannons ready to fire at the castle, but he hadn't seen any cannons capable of firing balls that large. In fact, he said, one of Koxinga's officials had confided in him that Koxinga wished he didn't have to assault Zeelandia Castle directly, that he'd prefer it if the Dutch would meet his forces out on the open field. Hambroek also overheard—vicariously through a comrade's Chinese servant—a group of Chinese soldiers saying that a direct attack on Zeelandia Castle wouldn't work, because the fortress was filled with cannons and had already showed its power, killing many Chinese, including the son of one of Koxinga's top officials.[9] But Hambroek said that most people in the camp believed Koxinga would attack the castle anyway, firing first from Zeelandia City and then from all sides, after which his troops would try to storm the walls, and any laggards would be executed on the spot.

While Hambroek answered questions, the yelling and digging got louder. It sounded like the workers were no longer behind the houses but had moved out into the open plain itself, approaching the castle. Ossewayer must not have managed to get them to stop. Coyet ordered his musketeers to fire a barrage into the dark. The bullets didn't stop the heaving and hauling, but they did whiz past Ossewayer, who happened to be walking back across the plain.

He arrived at the fortress, extremely rattled. Coyet asked him what in Heaven's name the Chinese were doing out there. Ossewayer said the whole area was swarming with workers. They seemed to be moving that huge mountain of earth from the street behind the houses to the plain in front, just across from the castle. They were shoveling it into sandbaskets. He presumed that they were going to use them to build barricades for an attack the next morning. Ossewayer said he'd transmitted Coyet's request that they stop this work, but they'd refused, and they kept pressing him for Coyet's decision about surrender. But, Ossewayer said, if Coyet planned to answer tonight, he'd have to find another messenger because there was no way he was going back out there.[10]

Coyet decided that Ossewayer and Hambroek would spend the night in the castle. He made a final inspection, told the soldiers to keep their cannons at the ready, and went to bed.

He didn't rest long.

THE BATTLE

Coyet no longer slept in the governor's mansion with its grand halls and paintings of sea scenes and royal portraits.[11] He'd moved to a house in the upper castle. It was meant to be safer, but it stood against the eastern wall, closest to the plain where the Chinese were placing their cannons. The house's top story and roof showed above the ramparts.[12] Around fifty people lived there: Coyet and his family, his secretary, the owner of the house and his family, one or two high-ranking military commanders, and some of the colony's most eminent women and their children.[13] Even on good nights they couldn't have been getting much sleep, with babies crying, children coughing, chamber pots tinkling, last-minute messages to and from the governor. But on this hot night you could hear the Chinese a few hundred feet away, yelling and moving things around. Now and then muskets and cannons roared from the bastions next door.

Whatever sleep they got was interrupted by cannonfire. It was still dark, hours before dawn. Cannonballs burst through windows, blasted through walls, crashed through the roof. Stones and bricks fell in showers of mortar. The enemy must have learned that Coyet slept here, because the attack was aimed squarely at the house. Maybe they'd seen him walking there at night, after prayers and inspections, making his way across the berm from the lower castle to the arched stairway that led up into the upper castle.

The shots were surprisingly accurate, given that they were aimed in the dark. Forty balls slammed into the house before anyone could get out. The top story collapsed, bricks and roof tiles shattering into the courtyard below.

A cry went up. The governor had been killed! But no. Coyet had escaped, "a sign of God's special protection," and was climbing the stairs to the bastions. The flashes of cannonfire revealed what the Chinese had been building: sandbasket barricades stretching from the southern harbor to the northern piers, all along the plain in front of the city, adorned with flags and banners. There were gaps for cannons—twenty or twenty-five of them of various sizes, some shooting twenty-four-pound balls, others eighteen-pound balls, and others smaller.

Having battered the house where Coyet had been sleeping, they were now shooting at the castle itself. "It was amazing how swiftly they fired, the one charge scarcely being off when the next was ready."[14]

It was dangerous up on the bastions. Cannonballs that struck the walls below weren't too worrisome. Although they could penetrate more than two feet into the walls, none caused structural damage because the walls were so thickly filled with earth. But the Chinese were aiming at the ramparts, trying to destroy the crenellations so the Dutch gunners couldn't shelter themselves or aim their cannons.

The chief gunners of the upper and lower castles "bravely leapt into action," aiming their cannons in the dark, with only the flashes of enemy cannonfire to guide them. Their job wasn't easy. Shrapnel and splinters of stone ripped past them. The chief gunner of the upper castle had his hat rim torn clean away. The chief gunner of the lower castle had his ear shot off. But they kept at it: swab, load powder, tamp, carefully insert cannonball, carefully insert fuse, aim, light, stand back. Again and again and again.

It was hard to tell whether their shots were doing any good because it was so dark. At one point they noticed that a huge group of Chinese had marched northward from Koxinga's camp and were preparing to rush the redoubt. They aimed at this host and managed to drive them away.

The firefight went on for two hours in the dark. When the sun rose, the gunners could aim better and fire faster. It wasn't long before the Chinese began fleeing from their batteries into the city, leaving their flags behind and their cannons in undignified poses: tipped to the sides, bereft of wheels, pointing impotently up to the sky with swabs sticking out of their barrels.[15]

Coyet sent a detachment of musketeers to investigate.[16] The men ran across the field, only a few bullets whizzing past their heads, and crouched behind the batteries. When they peeked around, afraid of being slashed by a saber-sword, they just saw cannonballs and corpses littering the ground.[17]

Some straddled the cannons and hammered spikes into their fuse-holes. Others gathered flags. Chinese bowmen tried to stop them, but each time they stepped out to shoot, the musketeers drove them back to shelter.[18] After the musketmen ran out of powder, they marched back across the plain with their prizes—thirty enemy flags. Maybe they were a bit too proud and careless, because the Chinese shot a couple on the way back.[19]

Coyet greeted them as heroes. He was happy to hear that no Chinese had dared venture out against them beyond the abandoned houses, concluding that "this was a clear sign of the enemy's great defeat."[20] His men admonished him for not sending reinforcements, because with help they'd have been able to spike all the cannons and capture even more flags. He apologized and sent out another force, to "further fan the burning courage of our men."[21] This time, Chinese troops came from hiding places behind the houses in Zeelandia City, brandishing their saber-staves. They were determined to prevent the Dutch from stealing more flags or spiking cannons. Gunners in the castle blasted through them—"one could see them swept away, legs up in the air"—and although their commanders kept driving them forward, they couldn't prevent the Dutch from spiking the rest of the cannons.[22]

The warriors returned to the castle with arms full of arrows, helmets, swords, and armor. Some had managed to sneak into the houses in the city and reported that they'd seen stacks of Chinese bodies covered with blankets. They hadn't ventured far, but it seemed that each of the houses they visited had more bodies than the last.

Coyet was delighted, and when he saw Chinese boats leaving Zeelandia City's piers riding heavy in the water, he suspected that they were filled with dead and wounded.

"It seems," his secretary wrote, "that the enemy has suffered a major defeat."[23]

HOW COYET WON

Koxinga had been supremely confident before the battle. How did the Dutch win such a resounding victory?

Coyet had an answer: great leadership. In his book, *Neglected Formosa,* he describes how he was awakened at daybreak by cannonfire and rushed up to the walls to survey the situation. His "practiced eye" saw right away that the enemy's cannons were unprotected and that the enemy troops had exposed themselves, "jubilant over the success of their firing, and very hopeful that a breach would be made in the walls." He calmed his men and ordered them to rearrange their cannons so their shots would cross one another. He told them to load their pieces with antipersonnel ammo: musket pellets, large iron nails, shrapnel. Then he told them to wait. When the time was ripe, he ordered them to "fire on the unprotected Chinese from above, below, and all sides, simultaneously." One barrage was all it took: "with the first charge, nearly the whole field was strewn with dead and wounded, the enemy being thus taught the lesson not to expose themselves so readily."[24]

Coyet's book was published more than ten years after the war, and he wrote it to defend himself from charges that he'd been responsible for the loss of Taiwan, so it's not surprising that he portrays himself as a hero. He changes a key detail: the time of day. Records of the battle—such as the diaries and resolution registers that Coyet himself oversaw—note clearly that the battle began while it was still dark, hours before dawn, and this is confirmed by an independent account by German artist Albrecht Herport. But Coyet's book says the battle occurred when it was already light. In this way, Coyet could portray himself as a daring commander surveying the field. Primary records do note that Coyet went up onto the walls and reassured the troops, who feared he'd died when the roof of his residence collapsed. But he wouldn't have been able to see any better than anyone else. Moreover, primary sources attribute the precision of the cannons not to Coyet but to the chief gunners of the upper and lower castle, who lost a hat and an ear respectively.

Still, one thing rings true about his account: the emphasis on crossfire. That was the key ability of the renaissance fortress, the trait that distinguished it from other fortifications. The ungainly bastions that thrust out from the walls were designed to cover all the angles. The key passages in Coyet's description note that "all of the cannons were arranged in such a position that their respective shots would cross one another" and that the Dutch "fired on the unprotected Chinese from above, below, and all sides, simultaneously."[25]

Koxinga's forces had faced many walls. They were among the most experienced, battle-hardened troops in the world. But they'd never encountered a fort like this.

Chinese walls were huge and tall and thick—thicker than the largest European walls, and much more impressive than Zeelandia Castle's. Nanjing's walls, for example, ranged between thirty and fifty feet thick, wide enough for three Humvees to drive abreast on.[26] Other Chinese cities, from the capital of Beijing to the capitals of minor counties, were also protected by walls much thicker than European fortifications. In fact, Chinese walls were capable of withstanding even industrial era cannons, as in 1841, when a seventy-four-gun British warship bombarded a fort near Canton: the modern guns had no effect on the fort's walls, because, as a British report put it, the walls were constructed in such a way "as to render them almost impervious to the efforts of horizontal fire, even from the thirty-two-pounders."[27] An expert in Chinese military history suggests that breaches in Chinese walls by artillery fire were exceptionally rare. One of the few examples occurred during a siege of the city of Suzhou during the pre-Ming wars. Suzhou's walls were unusually weak by Chinese standards, but it still took an artillery bombardment of ten months before the breach was made.[28]

Since bombardment didn't work, Chinese sieges were usually decided in other ways. Geoffrey Parker suggests that the most common methods were mass assaults, mining, and blockades.[29] In fact, however, Chinese commanders preferred to avoid even coming to that point. According to Sun Zi, the worst way to conduct a war is to storm walls and seize territory. "Thus," Sun Zi's *Art of War* notes, "the best policy for winning a war is to use tricky stratagems. The next best policy is to destroy the enemy's alliances by means of diplomacy. An inferior policy is to launch an attack on the enemy. But the worst way of all is to storm walls and seize territory. Sieges should only be used as a last resort."[30] Koxinga usually followed this advice.[31] Chinese historian Deng Kongzhao notes that Koxinga's favorite method was to surround an enemy and await surrender, a strategy that he believes Koxinga adopted straight from Sun Zi.[32]

Data I've compiled from a bit more than a decade of Koxinga's wars in China corroborates Deng's point. The most common way Koxinga got past walls was through open gates.[33] Nearly two-thirds (63%) of fortified places Koxinga gained were opened to him, either by conspirers within or by preemptive surrender.[34] The next most important category was mass assault, usually by scaling walls with ladders (16%). Four other methods were much less common: bombardment (6%), battle outside the walls provoking a surrender (6%), blockade (4%), and mining (4%).

When Koxinga did bombard walls, he usually focused his cannonfire on the gates. Indeed, according to a Dutch soldier who had been a prisoner of Koxinga's and had accompanied the warlord on campaign for eight months, Koxinga generally used his best troops not for storming, "but almost always for ramming doors open."[35] In fact, when the Dutch had an occasion to attack a Chinese walled city themselves—this was in 1662, and it was a small city with walls that were thin by Chinese standards—they found their cannons could make no dent, and so they had no choice but to aim their cannons at the gates, which, once they started to be shattered, the Dutch soldiers stormed into, through a hail of "stones, filth, nightsoil, . . . and also some dead dogs."[36] It was only occasionally that Koxinga tried to bombard Chinese walls, and usually those bombardments were levied against small fortified villages known as *zhais*, the smallest and most minor walled settlements in China. I know of only one case when Koxinga captured a proper Chinese town by bombarding its walls: the siege of Taizhou in 1658.

In most cases he used his cannons not to blow holes in walls but to destroy their crenellations and damage enemy cannons so his troops could storm. That seems to be what he intended to accomplish with Zeelandia Castle. His gunners aimed high, not so much at the castle walls themselves but at the crenellations on top of them that provided cover for Dutch soldiers. He succeeded in this. Most of the crenellations on the castle facing his cannons were destroyed.

Yet the tactic didn't work. Dutch gunners kept firing back. Koxinga's officers were shocked by the counterattack. In the heat of battle, when Dutch cannons were ripping through Koxinga's troops and cannon positions, Chinese officers pleaded with the "men of quality" Koxinga had summoned to his camp, begging them again and again to go to the fortress walls and wave their hands and cry out, "Stop shooting! Peace! Peace!"[37] The men had refused, saying that if they did they'd be shot to death.

The way Koxinga set up his cannon batteries seemed careless to Coyet: "I noted that the enemy's cannons were placed very poorly, entirely unprotected and easy to destroy."[38] This army had faced hundreds of walls. Why would they set up such vulnerable batteries? It's possible, as historian Deng Kongzhao suggests, that Koxinga was being hotheaded, that it wasn't a well-thought-out plan, adopted more out of momentary anger at Coyet's refusal to surrender than any larger strategy.[39] But Deng seems to have been unaware of the Dutch sources that show Koxinga's long, deliberate period of preparation—the building and scaring—that preceded the attack.

It seems more likely that Koxinga didn't realize what Zeelandia Castle was capable of. The renaissance fortress was designed to project a "defense in depth," to increase as much as possible the amount of area outside the walls that the defenders' cannons could control while maximizing the number of angles they could strike. The sandbasket barricades Koxinga's workers built were extensive, but they left gaps that the Dutch could target from multiple angles.

Koxinga's forces were used to walls without bastions, walls that couldn't spit flanking fire like this. Chinese walls did have outcroppings, but they weren't built according to the same principles as the renaissance angled bastions.[40] Instead they were square outcroppings with ninety-degree angles. Beijing's walls and Nanjing's walls were like this, as was Koxinga's own headquarters in China, the walled city of Xiamen. As a Dutch admiral wrote when he had a chance to tour Xiamen in 1663, the city had "uncommonly high stone walls strongly made out of masonry, with four gates that stick out beyond the walls but with no bastions or bulwarks."[41] Such outcroppings provided a bit of defense in depth, but not much.

It seems that Koxinga's troops, in their wars in China, frequently got quite close to walls, found dead zones, places where the defenders couldn't attack them. When attacking the fortified village of Outing, for example, his troops used shields to protect themselves while they went right up against the walls, bored holes in them, and set charges to blow them apart.[42] In Nanjing, his troops seem to have camped quite close to the walls, so when the besieged themselves bored through their own walls and poured out they were right next to Koxinga's camps.

In most cases, though, Koxinga's troops never needed to get that close. His favorite means of capturing a fort was intimidation. He'd array his army neatly below the walls, with their flags waving. He'd make a big show of setting up his cannons and building batteries. He sometimes deliberately instructed his support troops to make noises, to call and yell in the days before attacks, as he did in the week leading up to the Zeelandia Castle attack. Then he would fire a barrage. Usually these measures were enough to frighten defenders into surrender.

Did he expect his initial barrage to cow Coyet into capitulation?[43] It's possible, but evidence suggests that he intended to storm the castle. His siegeworks were extensive, his barrage intensive, and large groups of soldiers were massing in the dunes. Moreover, on the night before the attack, he sent someone to Saccam to warn the Dutch prisoners there that the next morning they would be forbidden to show themselves on the streets because he was going to attack Zeelandia Castle. In fact, they were forbidden even to look out the windows.[44] Testimony from a Chinese prisoner notes that Koxinga did order a storm against Zeelandia Castle.[45] Other evidence suggests that the man who led the attack was beheaded for his failure and another figure was the target of Koxinga's ire for not pressing the attack hard enough.[46]

In any case, Koxinga and his commanders were shocked at the fierceness of the Dutch counterattack. They'd never faced a fort like this before.

AFTERWARD

After the smoke had cleared, Coyet replied to Koxinga's letter, apologizing brightly for his tardy response: "I'd hoped to send our answer to your Excellency's letter of last night before now, but . . . was hindered from my good intentions until this afternoon because we had to devote considerable attention to defending ourselves. I won't bother to tell you how we answered the cannons you placed in the town. Your own soldiers are the best authority about that and we'll accord ourselves with their point of view."[47] He reiterated what he'd made clear before: the Dutch would defend Zeelandia Castle to the death. To add insult to injury, he didn't use the terms Your Majesty or Your Highness as he'd done before, but the simple honorific Your Excellency, putting Koxinga at the same rank as himself.

Hambroek said he'd take the letter to Koxinga. Two of his daughters begged him not to. They were afraid Koxinga would kill him. He said he had to go. He had three other children outside the castle, still in Koxinga's custody, and his wife was there, too. If he didn't go back they'd be killed. As the Swiss artist-soldier Albrecht Herport wrote, the daughters "had to watch, their hearts breaking, as their old father left them."[48]

Readers of Herport's account liked this scene and adopted it for their own books. Each time it became a bit more dramatic. A famous travel account by a Dutch surgeon tells it this way: "The missionary

Hambroek, driven by concern for his wife and three children whom Koxinga had in custody, had no choice but to return to the enemy and say his final farewell to the two daughters who lived in the castle. Oh what a sad parting! They watched, melting in tears, as their old father left them with overcast soul and headed out toward his inevitable death, because before long this worthy old man and others would all be beheaded."[49] The next book took the surgeon's scene and made it into a little drama. "Melting into tears" became "a flood of tears." And Hambroek became a patriotic hero, making a rousing speech urging Coyet and the rest to fight to the death and not to worry about him, that he was determined "with unflappable firmness to wait for God's further plans for him, and that he would be responsible for his conduct for all eternity before himself, the world, and God."[50]

From there the scene blossomed into an entire play, a tragedy called *Antonio Hambroek, or The Siege of Taiwan,* which ran in Amsterdam's equivalent to Broadway. In the play, Koxinga orders Hambroek to persuade Coyet to surrender, threatening him with execution if he fails. Instead of advising surrender, Hambroek urges Coyet to fight to the death. In the play, Coyet and Hambroek are good friends, and Coyet doesn't want to cause the missionary's death. Hambroek says everyone must die, and that if this is his time, then that's simply God's will. The Hambroek of the play has one daughter living in the castle. She begs him not to return to Koxinga. She embraces him. She falls to the floor. There are tears. He refuses. A Chinese emissary who has accompanied Hambroek into Zeelandia Castle is moved by the old man's faith and goodness. "In my country we imagine Christians to be fools, but now I see how Christendom gives birth to heroes."[51] He tells Hambroek that there's a way for him to avoid being killed by Koxinga: commit suicide. Hambroek says no, that God will take him when it is His will. Hambroek gives a final rousing speech about friendship and loyalty and God and goes outside. His daughter watches from the castle walls as Hambroek is executed, his head falling into the sand, lips still moving with words of reassurance. Then she throws herself over the walls. The play was a success. It inspired paintings and stories and bad patriotic poetry.[52]

In the play Hambroek is executed immediately, but in reality he wasn't killed that day. After sadly parting from his daughters, he walked down the stairs, found that the horse he'd tied up in the dunes the night before was gone, and began the long sandy walk to Koxinga's camp. If his daughters were allowed up on the ramparts to watch, they would have seen their father moving slowly toward Koxinga's camp, the sun bearing down on the white flag carried by his escorts. The last they would have seen of him was the deep, respectful bow he made to the Chinese watchmen before he was led into camp.

He was allowed to return with the other "men of quality" to Saccam, where he and other prisoners observed the fallout from the Dutch victory. One prisoner estimated the number of Chinese killed at around a thousand, and the number of wounded around eight hundred.[53] Hambroek and the other captives thanked God the Almighty for this victory, "even though it would more likely bring us trouble than benefit."[54]

They were right about that. This was the beginning of a time of troubles for Koxinga. In the next months, at least a third of his soldiers would die of disease and starvation, and he and his officers would take out their frustration on the Dutch prisoners, who hadn't been any use in persuading their comrades to surrender Zeelandia Castle.

The war had been pretty civilized so far, as wars go. But from this point, as both sides got desperate, there would be mutilation, crucifixion, vivisection, bodies crumpled in creekbeds, and corpses floating in the tides.

A Summer of Misery

A couple days after the battle, there was a perplexing exodus. Chinese soldiers vacated Zeelandia City and, to stay out of cannon range, waded through the bay toward Koxinga's camp in the dunes. They didn't try to look martial. They moved quickly, their flags rolled in their arms. Behind them trudged workers with chests, chairs, benches, and tables. The procession lasted three hours.

Coyet was puzzled. The battle had been deadly, but Koxinga still had the advantage—tens of thousands against a thousand. "On the one hand," Coyet's secretary wrote, "you might think the enemy is feeling terribly defeated, because their cannons have been made useless. But on the other hand, there might be some trickery or deceit here, an attempt to lure us into complacency."[1]

The Dutch peered out from the castle walls, carefully at first, because they were used to Chinese troops taking potshots at them and the crenellations had been blasted away, but once they were sure no one was shooting they gathered in groups, pointing and speculating. The city seemed empty. The flags were gone. Only a few Chinese scuttled across the streets.

Koxinga's base in the Pineapple dunes began shrinking too. The day after the exodus, it sprouted flags of white, the Chinese color of bereavement, and cries of sorrow issued across the dunes. The Dutch suspected that a high commander had been killed in battle and was being mourned. The next day the flags were gone and tents were being packed up.

Coyet dispatched parties of kidnappers to find out what was happening, promising fifty *reals* for each living Chinese they could capture. That was a small fortune, even split between several comrades, but it wasn't easy work. The most vulnerable enemy soldiers were night watchmen, who were usually stationed in small groups apart from the main camp. You had to know where the sentry post was and then you had to be patient and come at your target from behind, throwing a line around his neck so he couldn't scream.[2] This time no one captured a watchman, but one group caught a civilian.

The captive said his name was Ciko and that he was a thirty-six-year-old sackmaker. He'd lived in Zeelandia City before the war and fled after Koxinga arrived. Now that the city was empty he'd come back for his scissors. Coyet and the others asked him questions while a secretary recorded his answers. Where was Koxinga? He'd left the Pineapples and was now living in Fort Provintia. Why had Koxinga's camp sprouted white flags? A high official had been killed in the battle, and the flags had been to mourn his death. Were any other officials killed? Another official had had his arm shot off. How many soldiers were killed in the battle? Hundreds, he said, but he didn't know precisely. A lot had been buried in Saccam. What about the cannons the Dutch had spiked? They'd already been repaired and were waiting near the ferry pier to be shipped back to Saccam.

Ciko said he couldn't answer Coyet's most important questions: how many troops were in the city now, or what Koxinga was planning. So Coyet had him brought to the rack. It was a terrifying contraption: a wooden platform shaped like a huge reclining gingerbread man, arms and legs splayed.[3] At first they didn't strap him in, just used the rack as a backdrop "so he'd be less willing to play around with lies."[4] Ciko repeated what he'd said before and added new information, things that a sack-maker couldn't know much about—like Manchu positions and the number of troops Koxinga had available. Coyet and his councilors thought that was suspicious.

They strapped him in. Before they'd even raised him up he started talking, casting around for something to satisfy them. He tried giving them numbers—Koxinga had brought ten thousand troops, he'd brought five hundred pages, he'd brought forty or fifty cannons. He tried telling them what he thought they wanted to hear: that Koxinga wanted the castle and that whatever idea he got in his crazy head his people had to carry out. He said the Dutch prisoners were being treated well, that most of the Chinese who'd lived here before the war didn't like Koxinga, that they wished that Koxinga had never come to Taiwan, because he was persecuting the common people, demanding their treasure and tribute, and that things were so bad that even Koxinga's own troops were running away.

This was nice to know, but Coyet wanted more. Wasn't there anything else Ciko might know about Koxinga's current situation? Anything at all? He'd be very thankful and reward him well. But the only thing Ciko could say was that the common people felt that Koxinga would never dare to attack Zeelandia Castle now, and instead would just try to starve the Dutch out.[5] And, he said, in his opinion, Koxinga would have a hard time taking the castle anyway, because his troops were frightened of Dutch cannons. He was taken down from the rack and clanked into irons for labor, and just like that Ciko disappears from the historical record.

There were other prisoners in the following days, and the rack saw a lot of use, but no one could give Coyet what he wanted, which was news about Koxinga's intentions.

Thanks to Chinese sources, we know what Coyet and his counselors—and probably the Chinese prisoners—didn't know: Koxinga had given up on taking Zeelandia Castle for the time being. But his decision had little to do with the defeat.[6] He was worried about something generals fear more than forts: hunger.

HOW TO FEED AN ARMY

He Bin had had painted Taiwan as a land of plenty, filled with rice and sugar, so Koxinga had brought few provisions to Taiwan. Another wave of troops was arriving from China, and they also brought little rice. To find out exactly how much food there was in Tawan, Koxinga sent He Bin and Yang Ying out to do a systematic survey.[7] They came back with terrible news.[8] There were only six thousand hectoliters of rice and grain and three thousand hectoliters of sugar.[9]

Six thousand hectoliters of rice contains about a billion and a half calories.[10] It sounds like a lot, but it isn't. If we assume that Koxinga's forces on Taiwan numbered around twenty-five thousand people, and if we assume further that each person needed two thousand calories per day, then Koxinga needed fifty million calories each day just to feed his armies. That means that six thousand hectoliters of grain would feed his troops for about a month. The three thousand hectoliters of sugar would add another billion calories or so, which would provide another twenty days. But in total, Taiwan would feed his huge army for two months at the most. This wasn't what he'd expected.

The bad news arrived around the time that Dutch cannons foiled his assault on Zeelandia Castle.

So he decided he needed his men for tilling not killing, and there was no time to waste. As Coyet himself noted, "It's already gotten very late for planting. In our opinion, the Chinese won't be able to avoid starvation, because they can't have found enough grain to feed that huge army for long. We hope that God our Lord will continue to create obstacles for the enemy."[11]

Koxinga gave up the siege to devote his efforts to building up Taiwan as an agricultural colony. He left a small garrison to blockade Zeelandia Castle, which he felt was so "isolated and without hope of reinforcements that it would surrender on its own."[12] Then he took up residence in Fort Provintia (presumably it had been scrubbed of sewage) and declared it the seat of government of a new city: the Eastern Ming Capital.[13] He decreed that the island of Taiwan would now be a prefecture of the Chinese Empire, and he divided it into two counties, appointing to the prefecture a governor (the sychophantic Yang Chaodong) and to each of the counties a chief magistrate, just as in China.

Then he issued a heady decree:

> The Eastern Capital is where we are starting a country and establishing our families. It will become a stable and enduring base for us for ten thousand generations. These uncivilized reaches that I have opened up I now donate to you civil and military officials, to you generals and colonels, to you commanders high and low. All of you commanders and troops and

> your families will come together and choose sites to build your homes. You must establish there your fields and residences, things that you can pass on to your sons and grandsons and descendants. Thus, with one grand effort now we establish the foundation of eternal prosperity.[14]

He dispatched his troops out into the bush to "establish frontier garrisons and open up the land for cultivation."[15] Many of them were ordered into areas that had never been intensively cultivated, where there were no Chinese or Dutch towns. There were native villages, of course, but Koxinga ordered his troops not to harass them or take their fields. There were many other things his pioneers weren't allowed to do. He printed up a list. They couldn't harass Chinese settlers or take their fields. They had to report clearly all the land they planned to settle before starting to cultivate it. They had to list the land's natural resources and seek permission before exploiting them. There were specific clauses about fisheries and forests, about mountains and businesses. There were warnings about inspections and provisions for punishment.[16]

Koxinga gave each general a territory defined by a stretch of coastline eight hours long (about 45 kilometers).[17] They were supposed to build a large town in the center and a smaller garrison at the end. That way, there'd be a Chinese town at least every four hours. Ideally, they'd all be located close to the coast.[18]

For help measuring out these territories, Koxinga turned to his Dutch prisoners, among whom were several trained surveyors. The most experienced was Philip Meij, the man whom Valentine had sent to talk to Koxinga about surrendering Fort Provintia. Koxinga ordered Meij to accompany an expedition northward from the Eastern Capital. It was a large expedition, with translators, soldiers, servants, woodcutters, carpenters, and painters. Meij's job was to erect mile-poles along the route and, more importantly, to designate places for the frontier garrisons.

Meij's description of this miserable trip gives us a glimpse of the challenges Koxinga's troops faced. Before they even got out of town, his partner—another surveyor—fell ill and had to be replaced. Then they began their trek. It was "extremely difficult, because of the poor roads, the rain, the mud, and the bad treatment."[19]

He knew Taiwan well, and as the party tramped northward, he was surprised at how much it had already changed. The Dutch had had only a dozen or so troops in each of the main native villages, but Koxinga had stationed a regiment—around a thousand men—in each one. He'd ordered each man to plant enough potatoes to last him and his dependents three months, so even young boys were out in the fields putting potatoes into the ground. After that the men were supposed to prepare paddies for rice. First they had to clear the land. Then they had to make it flat and even. Then they had to build a dike all around to keep the water in. Only then, after they were sure the drainage was right, could they go barefoot into the water and plow it with an ox, after which, finally, they could plant the seedlings and tend them carefully. Koxinga was in the process of distributing oxen and plows to aid in tilling.

Meij was astonished by what he saw: "There was scarcely a corner of these lands that hadn't been enclosed and planted, and we were amazed by these heathen's industriousness and zeal."[20] Even the paths between the villages, which used to be sparsely traveled, were busy. "The whole way from Saccam we couldn't march five hundred feet, or even a hundred or two hundred feet without seeing three, four, five, or six, or even more people carrying and hauling, and this doesn't even count the Chinese soldiers."[21]

At the margins were Dutch prisoners, who were starting to die off. At first, Koxinga had housed them in Saccam, but he knew it was foolish to leave hundreds of Dutchmen in his capital while his troops were gone. So he sent the prisoners into the countryside, with each of his commanders responsible for a dozen or two. In one village Meij visited, dozens slept crowded in the church that Dutch missionaries had built. In another they had to sleep outside. In another they had little tents where they slept all mixed together "without regard to rank or status." They were dirty, ill, and hungry. Food was scarce, and they were pushed to the end of the food line.

One day he came across a Dutchman lying on a muddy path between two villages. The man was just skin on bones, as "naked as his mother had brought him into this world." Meij knew him. He'd been a schoolteacher. He told Meij that eleven days ago he and a group of other Dutch prisoners had been marched northward out of Saccam and had had nothing to eat but a bit of rice. His legs had swelled up. Unable to walk, he'd collapsed on the road, and no one had helped him up. He was still alive only because he'd managed to drink the water that pooled in wagon ruts. Meij got his overseers to load the man on a cart and take him to the next village. He died a few days later.[22]

Meij's expedition pressed forward, marking off mile by mile, until finally Koxinga ordered the party to return. Meij was relieved. "There was no human way we could have kept going another eight days, or we would have become sick and maybe even met our death, and so we turned back with joy."[23] He was lucky he'd been sent to the north. After he returned, he spoke to a surveyor who'd been sent to the south. The six thousand Chinese troops Koxinga had sent there had met stiff resistance from the natives, so they and their Dutch prisoners had had to live in stockade forts in the middle of open fields. Without indigenous support, they were starving, and nearly everyone was ill. The surveyor said he couldn't bear to talk about the things he'd seen.[24] He died a few days later.[25]

Meij was also lucky to have been recalled to the Eastern Capital, because farther north Koxinga's troops met disaster. The lands in north central Taiwan were part of an aboriginal kingdom ruled by a man called the Prince of the Middag (*Vorst van de Middagh*). Scholars today have little idea who he was and what his kingdom was like.[26] What seems clear is that when the Dutch ruled Taiwan, he was independent but at peace with them. Koxinga sent Chen Ze, the man who'd defeated Thomas Pedel, to end the prince's independence.[27]

The brilliant Chen Ze met his match. The Chinese chronicle describes the episode tersely, saying only that Chen Ze and his men "met with a violent cataclysm" when the natives revolted. European sources have more detail, particularly an account by soldier-artist Albrecht Herport, who learned from an escaped Dutch prisoner that when the Chinese first approached the prince, his people pretended to be friendly, giving the Chinese everything they wanted. Lulled into lassitude, Chen Ze's troops set their weapons down and went to bed. The natives attacked, killing fifteen hundred or so. The survivors fled into the sugar fields. The prince's troops smoked them out and killed them.[28]

This was the worst of several native attacks. The second worst occurred in southern Taiwan, when forces loyal to an indigenous ruler killed seven hundred.[29]

Still, Koxinga was more worried about starvation than natives. The potatoes wouldn't be ready for months, so he tightened the rations: only thirty pounds of rice per soldier per month.[30] That's around 1,750 calories, not enough to support the grueling work. And rice alone isn't enough to nourish a body. Soldiers needed other food, which wasn't easy to find. Venison was no longer available, and other types of meat, like pork, were extremely expensive.[31] Worst of all, it seems that these meager rations had to be shared with wives, children, and servants.

Why didn't Koxinga just order more rice from China? He tried. He ordered his minister of finance, Zheng Tai, who happened to be his adoptive brother, to send rice.[32] But, according to Yang Ying, "The minister of finance's grain ships did not arrive and the officers and men suffered from privation, and in each county the price for rice surged to four or five grams of gold per hectoliter."[33] Koxinga blamed Zheng Tai, and historians have tended to follow this judgment.[34] Indeed, Zheng Tai later did have disagreements with Koxinga and deliberately kept rice junks from going to Taiwan.

But the problem in the summer of 1661 was weather. An old scholar who lived in Jinmen and Xiamen during the war wrote a series of poems called *Anguished Cries from the Islands.* One poem is called "Windstorm":

The windstorm blows,
roiling the ocean,
churning the clouds like cotton.
The huge ships
filled with a thousand tons of rice
are turned back by towering waves
and can't go east.
The officers and men
in Taiwan are starving,
nearly at the point of death.
They look westward,
but the rice ships never arrive.

Turned back
by windstorms again
several times.
Our people may be as dead
as dried fish in the market.
Oh woe! Human life
is so tragic and cruel
one might as well starve.
The people of the coast
know what it is to live lives
brutish and sorrowful.
Today the troops in Taiwan
must be learning
how cruel life is along the shores.[35]

Would a Dutch yacht have been able to make headway against contrary winds like that? Was part of the problem of supplying Taiwan a technical one, which might have been resolved by deeper hulls and European-style rigging? It's quite possible. As we'll see, Dutch ships' ability to sail against prevailing winds provided a key advantage in the war.

In any case, as the summer stretched on, Koxinga's people began to starve. He put aside his scruples about not harassing the natives and ordered troops to gather provisions among the people: rice, fruit, taro, and sweet potatoes.[36] He forced farmers to hand over all their rice, barley, and sugar, letting them keep only a tenth of what they had.[37] Even so, his people starved. Even officials struggled. Hanging in the stores of the Eastern Capital were silk robes, which officials had pawned for rice money.[38]

It began to seem possible that Koxinga, despite his overwhelming numerical advantage, might lose this war. On the other hand, the Dutch had their own problems.

LIFE IN WARTIME

There were seventeen hundred and thirty-three people living in Zeelandia Castle: nine hundred and five soldiers and officers, sixty-three married men, two hundred and eighteen women and children, and five hundred and forty-seven slaves and children-of-slaves.[39] Everyone was crowded into quarters designed to hold a third as many. It was dirty and smelly.

It was also unsanitary. Outside the lower castle, wooden outhouses jutted over the Channel, but it was a long way to go for a piss.[40] Wealthier people had slaves or servants to carry chamber pots, but many people did their business in gutters or against the sides of buildings.[41] In the spring, rains washed the filth away, but in the high summer there was little rain, and the thick heat intensified the stench.

The worst smells came from the warehouse that had once contained pepper and cloves and fragrant woods but was now used as a hospital. The sick and injured who lay in the heat on the floor there couldn't make it to an outhouse, and many doubtless had trouble positioning themselves over chamber pots. It stank brutally.[42] It's no surprise that illness raged.

Exacerbating the problem was malnutrition. The storehouses in the lower castle held enough food to last a year if strictly rationed, and not just rice.[43] Taiwan had been a major producer of venison, and there was plenty in stock.[44] As a result, the basic ration for a Dutch soldier was considerably better than that for one of Koxinga's men: a daily portion of rice and a half-pound of dried venison. Still, venison was tough and salty, gamey and lean. Other preserved meats—like bacon and preserved pork—were more desirable, but although there were barrels of them in the warehouses, they were reserved for officers, officials, and sick people. It was possible to buy food, but the soldiers no longer received food money as they had before the war. Unless you had independent means or were an officer you could only count on rice and venison.

A diet of rice and venison doesn't provide the vitamins and micronutrients a body needs. Some people found that their gums started to bleed, their teeth started wobbling, and their breath started to reek like rotten meat. This meant that they weren't getting enough vitamin C and had come down with scurvy. For those who didn't find vitamin C, the disease progressed rapidly: their gums started growing over their teeth, making it painful to eat. Old wounds opened up, they got too tired to walk, and their skin got blotchy and dry, like paper splashed with blots of ink. Eventually they died.[45]

Others came down with beriberi, caused by eating rice unsupplemented by meat, fruit, and vegetables. That's the disease that killed the Dutch schoolteacher Meij found lying in the mud. The first thing the man would have noticed was a loss of sensation in his feet and a sense of fatigue. He'd have started to lose his appetite. His face would have gotten puffy. Then, his ankles would have swollen up and become rigid and painful, and the swelling would have spread up his legs. That was when he'd have lost the ability to walk. The further course of the disease affected one's nerves: emotional and sensory disturbances. The heart would begin pounding uncontrollably. When it reached that point, a patient was as good as dead.[46]

The besieged knew they had to supplement their diets. They thought that one of the most important supplements was alcohol. Arak, or rice wine, was cheap and popular in good times, and workers had brought five vats of it into the castle just before Koxinga captured Zeelandia City, for which Coyet felt very thankful.[47] The sick needed it most, "to strengthen them," but arak actually wasn't nutritious. Red wine, which was available in very small amounts and was usually reserved for the sick, did have small amounts of B vitamins, which would have helped with beriberi, and Dutch beer, also available in small amounts, had some minor nutritional benefits, but arak had almost no vitamins at all.

In any case, to conserve supplies, common soldiers no longer received daily rations of arak, and even officials and officers had their arak rations halved.[48] The lack of alcohol was difficult for alcoholics, of whom, it seems, there were many. "It seems to us," Coyet wrote, "that the lack of arak, which our people usually had available in great surfeit, is causing troubles among some of these drunkards, and there's nothing we can do to cure them."[49]

Some people managed to supplement their rations outside the castle. Those who could walk and who could obtain permission to go beyond the walls could find fresh food, although they had to be careful.

Along the inner beach of the bay, near the abandoned hospital, were oysters. The water there was shallow, and one could wade a long way out, pulling oysters up from the rocky sand. But it was dangerous. The enemy could shoot from the windows of the marketplace near Zeelandia

City, and Koxinga had trained a deadly new force of musketmen.[50] He didn't use many muskets in China, but he'd collected scores of them from the Dutch prisoners and the battlefield where Pedel fell. He gave them to slaves he'd liberated from the Dutch. They proved willing to fight against their former masters.[51] They were young, referred to in Dutch sources as "black boys,"[52] and they were quite effective.

If you didn't feel like wading you could try your luck in the abandoned vegetable gardens that lay on the plain between the castle and the city, although this was even more dangerous, because the young musketeers had many hiding places: up in the houses, behind the tollhouse, behind the graveyard walls. One day a group of soldiers were picking greens below the castle and showed a bit too much of themselves. A soldier was shot in the thigh. His comrades dragged him inside, which Coyet felt was "a most sad episode."[53] The same day another soldier was plucking vegetables between the castle and the redoubt and was struck in the left side of his chest, but he was lucky. The bullet lost its force and left only a blue bruise.[54]

Watermelons plumped up from the early summer rains grew on the plain between the castle and Zeelandia City, but the best ones were closest to the houses that hid enemy soldiers. One intrepid sailor brought some in from all the way near the City Hall Building.[55] There were also melons near the dunes to the south, although the enemy frequently patrolled there.

If you were good with a gun, you could hunt. Pigs that had belonged to Chinese residents rooted in abandoned gardens, but catching them was hard. Sometimes the hunts were so adventurous that they were recorded in Coyet's official dairy, as when a pig wandered near a Chinese cannon position near the Municipal Scales. One of the castle's dogs felled it and a sailor sneaked over, picked it up, and ran back to the castle. Another time a soldier shot at a pig near the ruins of the hospital that stood at the foot of the dunes where the redoubt was, but the pig ran toward enemy musketeers hiding in the market. It would have been wise to let the pig go, but the soldier chased it, shot again, and brought it down. Enemy soldiers emerged and tried to take it for themselves. He ducked their arrows, grabbed his prey, and dragged it back to the castle in triumph.[56]

Seabirds made a tasty meal, if you were skillful enough to bag one, or if you could find someone who'd bag one for you. One day a Dutch woman asked a soldier to go shoot a bird for her. He borrowed a musket, blew into it to make sure it wasn't loaded, and then playfully pointed at her, saying, "I'll shoot you instead!" The gun was loaded after all. It went off and struck her. As she lay dying, she begged the man's officer to go easy on him, saying it had been a mistake. She died an hour later and her killer was taken into prison, eventually sentenced to a bullet over the head (a symbolic execution) and five years' hard labor in chains.[57]

There was no way hunting and gathering could provide enough fresh food for the people trapped in the castle. Babies and young children were particularly vulnerable, falling ill "from a lack of fresh food and other common necessities."[58] More and more adults succumbed, too. By mid-June, the castle's chief preacher, Minister Kruyf, was too sick to give the evening sermon. The two assistant ministers were also ill, so the nightly sermon had to be delivered by a civilian. Sick bodies spread out over the floor of the warehouse-hospital, so Coyet ordered new cases taken to the church, which stood in the lower castle near the main gate to the pier. Now the sermons had to be delivered in the Great Room of the governor's mansion.[59]

By the end of June, people were falling ill with startling frequency, including soldiers, who'd generally been healthier than the others, thanks to their youth and their ability to shoot or gather their own food.[60] They died not just of nutritional diseases like scurvy and beriberi, but also of the so-called land-disease (*landziekte*), a fever that records don't describe in any detail, but which was often fatal.[61]

As the miserable summer stretched on, the two enemies—Dutch and Chinese—desperately needed fresh supplies. Koxinga's troops had planted rice and potatoes, but the harvests wouldn't come in time to save them. The Dutch had lots of provisions in their warehouses, but no sizable gardens.

Both sides needed succor from outside Taiwan. Who would receive help first? And would it be enough? The war would turn on these questions.

Relief from the Sea

In the age of sail, ships followed seasonal rhythms as surely as migratory birds. This was particularly true in Asian waters, where winds and currents were highly cyclical. For our antagonists on Taiwan, the cycle was north versus south. In the winter the wind blew cold and dry from the north. In the summer it blew hot and wet from the south. This meant that summer was when ships arrived from Batavia filled with supplies, personnel, and trade goods. Koxinga and Coyet both knew they'd soon spot Dutch sails on the horizon. But how many would there be? And would the ships carry sandalwood or soldiers?

The answer to these questions hinged on another question: Did Coyet's superiors in Batavia know about the war? Koxinga was feeling secure because by the time his fleet had arrived in late April, the winds were already blowing from the south. He believed that the Dutch couldn't defy those winds to ask for help.

He was wrong. One Dutch ship had sailed against the wind. It had been one of the three Dutch ships anchored in Taiwan when Koxinga had arrived. We've seen how those three ships fought against Koxinga's junks and how their flagship, the mighty *Hector,* somehow ignited its own powder and exploded, after which the other two ships retreated to deeper waters. They cruised for several days, until they saw smoke rising above Fort Zeelandia and presumed, correctly, that Zeelandia City was on fire. At that point, Cornelius Clawson, captain of the smaller vessel, a yacht called the *Maria*, rowed over to confer with the captain of the other ship.

There was no way to communicate with Coyet, so Clawson and his colleague knew they were on their own. The other captain said they should stay near Taiwan to warn any Dutch ships about the situation. Clawson disagreed. Instead, he said, they should sail south against the winds to warn Batavia and try to bring back reinforcements. It was an unproven route, through dangerous seas. The other captain said no. If Clawson wanted to try he was on his own.

Without another word, Clawson walked out of the meeting and rowed back to the *Maria*.[1] Why was he so upset? It's likely that the *Maria* wasn't prepared for such a risky voyage and he'd hoped that they might form a convoy, or that he'd at least be offered supplies or men. But he got nothing from his colleague, who simply recorded in his log that Clawson "set his course toward Batavia without speaking to us again."[2]

Later, the captain who remained behind managed to tell Coyet about Clawson's decision. Coyet was happy but of course had no idea whether the *Maria* would make it to Batavia.

Koxinga knew nothing about the *Maria*. Dutch envoys had told him early in the war that Batavia would be sending a big reinforcement fleet, but Koxinga knew that this was bluster. As Sun Zi writes: *An enemy brags when weak and speaks modestly when strong*. Still, Koxinga was curious about what Coyet knew about a possible relief fleet. That may be why, after ignoring Zeelandia Castle for months, he and his officers suddenly started writing letters again.

On a cloudy evening in late June, a Chinese soldier emerged from behind the tollhouse with a white flag, walked halfway across the stone path that led to the castle, and worked into the sand a bamboo stalk affixed to a letter. It was the first official communication between the Chinese and the Dutch since the Battle of Zeelandia in late May. Here and there insults had been yelled, as when a soldier on Koxinga's side had called some Dutch workers "Dog" in Portuguese and they'd replied "Dog!" in Chinese. But otherwise nothing.

Coyet and his councilors had the letter translated and read it together out loud.[3] It was from general Ma Xin, the man who commanded the forces in Zeelandia City, and this is what it said:

> My lord Koxinga has come with so many officials and soldiers to improve this island with cities, and all you have left is that little

> fortress, which is like a little musket ball when compared to the great expanses around it. My lord is righteous and good. He does not want to destroy your castle and ruin it with violence, and so he has ordered me and my soldiers to stay here in Zeelandia City and wait. Our people have great appreciation for the castle. Even if we can't open it for ten years, we'll still wait. We'll wait a hundred years if necessary, keeping you trapped within.[4]

After this pleasant thought, Ma Xin brought up the possibility of aid from Batavia:

> You are doubtless thinking that you will wait for the arrival of more ships. But you saw how we burnt your ships before when they came out to fight us. So now if new ships come, there will not be many of them, and they will just have goods for sale and will be easy for us to overcome. . . . Maybe next year your masters in Batavia will send a fleet, but even if they send more than ten ships with one or two thousand soldiers, and even if they were to make it onto land, that would be nothing to us, but in any case they would not be able to make it onto land.[5]

Ma Xin closed with the usual threats, saying that if he decided to attack the castle from four directions he'd be able to capture it that very day, and he invited Coyet to surrender, admonishing him not to wait too long.

What was Ma Xin's aim? It's possible that he hoped things had gotten bad enough for Coyet to give up, but that's doubtful. Previous demands for surrender had done little good, and they'd been made when Koxinga's entire army surrounded Zeelandia Castle. It's intriguing that Ma Xin's letter harped on the issue of reinforcements. Was he trying to find out whether Coyet expected help from Batavia? It would certainly make sense. We do know that Koxinga was very curious. Right around this time, a kidnapped Chinese soldier told Coyet that Koxinga and his officers were "greatly anticipating the arrival here of our ships from Batavia, to see who would gain the upper hand in this war . . . because the outcome hung on this matter."[6]

Ma Xin didn't get any information. As Coyet and his councilors finished reading the letter, lightning flashed and thunder clapped,[7] so no response was sent that night. The next day was Sunday, when one shouldn't bother with pagans. Then, on Monday morning, Ma Xin made Coyet mad. Anxious for a response, Ma Xin sent two Chinese soldiers out across the plain. A Dutchman met them halfway. The soldiers said Ma Xin was waiting for a letter, and they also asked whether any of the sick soldiers in the castle might want some fresh pork and some arak. We have plenty, they lied, and Ma Xin would be happy to share. When Coyet learned what they'd said, he was indignant: "These heathens certainly aren't worried about our welfare. This is an insulting way of speaking, intended to mock us."[8]

So he had his secretary write a terse letter: "We have no idea who you are, Ma Xin, and you don't seem to understand who our governor is or the situation here within our castle. You don't even seem to have any authority to write to us, so His Excellency the governor has felt it unnecessary to write back to you."[9] Ma Xin tried sending another letter, saying he was important, but Coyet thought it was a "very poor letter, broken in meaning, and vague and insinuating,"[10] and so the secretary wrote back again, saying that Coyet would correspond only with Koxinga.

So Koxinga sent a letter of his own. It, too, focused on the question of reinforcements:

> Ma Xin tells me that you want correspondence only from me. . . . I've sent many letters to you, but Your Excellency has never properly answered them. You've always tried to buy time until the arrival of your ships. But now your ships won't dare to come. And even if they do come, they'll just be ships filled with trading goods. They'll only seek their own destruction, and there's nothing you can do about it, so you'll have to wait until next year to see if you can be helped. This entire island is under my command—all the natives and their villages—so what difference does one little fortress make? I've not even thought about trying to break through that fortress, but we trust that no one can come out, and if they can't come out, how can they expect to last for so long in there, until next year, when the ships come? You know it as well as I do.[11]

What was Koxinga's intent? Again, it's doubtful that he thought his letter would persuade Coyet to hand over the fortress, although he closed it with the usual demands and threats. It's more likely that crafty Koxinga wanted to incite Coyet to reveal information, to find out what kind of fleet Coyet himself expected to arrive.

If so, the gambit worked. Coyet, who was always quick to take offense, found Koxinga's tone unforgivably arrogant: "Your ships won't dare to come. And even if they did come, they'd just be ships filled with trading goods. They'd be only seeking their own destruction." Coyet wrote a furious response.

He called Koxinga a liar for pretending peace before the war and then suddenly invading Taiwan, "acting not like a true righteous warrior but rather, attacking in a treacherous way so suddenly without any warning against all human laws." He accused Koxinga of dishonor again for attacking during peace negotiations the previous month: "We were holding talks with your envoy on 24 May, under the white flag of peace, and while we were busy answering his letter, Your Highness acted against all customs of war and attacked us with the greatest violence." By this point, a paragraph into the letter, Coyet had worked himself up: "From all of this a reasonable person—yes, even a child—could understand that such words and deeds do not proceed from a true righteous and upright soul. It's clear what trust one should place in Your Highness's words and promises."[12]

Coyet began a Calvinist rant:

> The one true God, shaper of Heaven and earth, Who guides everything with His power, so that nothing happens against His implacable will, Whom alone we worship, fear, and trust, but Who is unknown to Your Highness, has seen fit to equip us with this powerful castle with strong and courageous men and plenty of weapons and supplies, so that we can hold ourselves here protected against Your Highness, either from powerful attacks or from another year of blockade.[13]

In his anger, Coyet tipped his hand:

> We soon expect to see ships arriving from Batavia for our relief. They'll bring much more than just trade goods. . . . A little ship that fought against your Highness's junks here near the Channel will provide information [to Batavia] much clearer than

> what you were hoping. Will the ships not dare to come here, as your Highness arrogantly suspects? Time will tell, and we trust that you'll soon be surprised.[14]

This is probably just what Koxinga had been angling for, but unfortunately for him, the Dutch love meetings. Before sending the letter over, Coyet showed it to his councilors to vote on. They liked most of it, but they urged him to leave out the part about reinforcements. They said there was no reason to reveal this information, because if Koxinga thought that there might be reinforcements he might try to attack the castle right away, before the ships could arrive. And supposing that the *Maria* hadn't completed its difficult voyage, writing about the *Maria* would give Koxinga an opportunity to mock the Dutch later if aid didn't arrive. Most importantly, they pointed out that if the *Maria* had managed to complete its journey, and if Batavia did send a large reinforcement fleet, it would be much better if Koxinga were caught by surprise, because "it might cause him much more fright and astonishment (so we hope) by dint of being sudden and unexpected."[15]

By majority vote, Coyet's council decided to excise the bits about reinforcements and instead write this cagey sentence:

> As for whether the ships we expect from Batavia will be filled with trade goods and too weak to provide us any help, only time will tell, and if our beloved God, Who is great and controls everything, sees fit to send us more difficulties first, we are nonetheless certain that He will avenge himself by means of the Dutch state for your unjust and violent destruction of His church, for your spilling of Christian blood, and for your plunder of our goods.[16]

Coyet's councilors had saved him from indiscretion. Koxinga didn't get any new information.

PHANTOM SAILS, PARANOIA

But had the *Maria* made it? Would there be aid from Batavia? Everyone was eager to spot sails. One evening in early July, a soldier ran over from the redoubt, which had a panoramic sea view from its tall hill, and said he'd seen three ships on the horizon. Coyet and his councilors rushed up the stairs and peered out at the sea. They couldn't see anything. Was the soldier sure? Yes, he said, he and his comrades had seen them so clearly that they could even make out the mizzen sails.[17] But the following morning there was nothing there, "so it seems that the purported ships have changed into clouds, which has happened so many other times."[18]

They prayed. "God has seen fit," Coyet's secretary wrote, to level the sword of his judgment at Taiwan by sending this horde of Chinese enemies to rip apart the hard-won Christian church and kill and imprison so many of our friends and compatriots.[19] All of this the Dutch had brought down on themselves by their many sins. Now there was nothing to do but appeal to the merciful God.

Coyet and his council resolved to hold a special fast and prayer day. The vigil fell on a lovely July day. Everyone was supposed to pray with an upright heart and deep zeal in the fear of God. No one was allowed to work, not even the pagan Chinese in their chains. There was no gambling or lighthearted singing or games, or any other kind of earthly pleasure. They prayed to Almighty God that they would find mercy in His eyes and He would remove from them the heat of His righteous fury. They prayed that He would obstruct the heathen enemies in their evil plans and give His blessing to Dutch weapons. They prayed that He would provide health to the hundreds of sick bodies. Most important of all, they prayed that He would protect the ships from Batavia so that they'd arrive safely in Taiwan.[20]

A lewd spectacle interrupted their devotions. Across the plain, a man stood up on a sandbasket by the graveyard, smacked his ass with his hand, and yelled out in Dutch: "You bastards! We'll be coming over to get you soon enough!" He was a Swiss Catholic who'd been a soldier for the Dutch but had run away from Zeelandia the previous week. Dutch musketeers ended his ass-smacking, causing him to dive to safety, but Coyet was alarmed. The man's former comrades said that before he ran away he'd talked about how the enemy didn't yet understand the best way to attack the castle because all they needed to do was put a strong battery near the City Hall, fill it with cannons, and then start shooting. That way they'd be able to keep the Dutch from firing back from the bastions because the shots would keep them away from the cannons planted up there. Coyet had been worried "that there might be other rascals like this."[21]

So prayers gave way to paranoia. When a group of Chinese soldiers was seen marching toward the city in the Pineapples, Coyet "had a strange thought." The deserter had been seen near some Chinese in the city waving his hat at the castle, as though making a sign. Maybe he'd sent a signal to conspirers within the castle. Maybe there was a plot. There were other Catholics among the Dutch forces. What if they were planning to rise up from within? Coyet thought this was quite possible, "since we seem to have a group of faithless and vile and evil-minded soldiers here within the castle."[22]

He thought he found corroboration in the actions of Chinese soldiers, who'd been unusually active, marching around and digging trenches. Three days after the ass-smacking incident, one of the company's drummers came running into the castle "nearly overcome with fear and entirely beside himself."[23] He'd been picking vegetables near the execution grounds when he heard knocking sounds coming from beneath his feet. He'd picked up a stone and clopped the ground. The knocking stopped, but a moment later he heard it again.[24] Coyet had learned that Koxinga sometimes dug holes under walls to undermine them, and a mound of earth was piled up on the other side of the plain, where the enemy was digging trenches. Several people were sent out to put their ears to the ground, but no one heard anything. Coyet and his councilors decided to dig a trench all along the east side of the castle just in case, offering extra pay and a half a cup of arak each day.[25]

Nerves were on edge. Where were the sails?

SOME VERY BAD NEWS

On a windy afternoon at the end of July, a single ship was spotted. Coyet raised the red flag so its skipper would know there was danger. When darkness came he put a lamp up on the flagpole and fired three cannonshots, a warning to stay away. Dawn showed the ship anchored in a misty and unsettled sea. Below the main flag flew a special banner, a sign that someone important was aboard. Coyet dispatched a sampan to the anchorage. It was nearly swamped by a wave but eventually made it to the heaving ship.[26]

It returned with bad news: the ship carried barely enough rice and supplies for its own crew. Batavia hadn't heard about Koxinga's invasion. Worst of all, the ship brought new orders for Coyet and the rest of the leadership on Taiwan: they were all to be fired and sent back to Batavia to be tried and punished for their crimes. What crimes? Mistreating the Chinese and exaggerating the threat of a possible invasion by Koxinga.[27]

The previous year, 1660, when Coyet had warned Batavia of an invasion by Koxinga, and Batavia had sent admiral Jan van der Laan with a reinforcement fleet, and van der Laan and Coyet had quarreled, van der Laan had left Taiwan in a huff, furious at Coyet. The admiral had arrived in Batavia and begun accusing Coyet of cowardice and paranoia.

He'd found a receptive audience because Coyet had another enemy in Batavia, a man named Nicholas Verburg. From 1649 to 1653, Verburg had been governor of Taiwan and Coyet had been his number two. The two men had feuded bitterly, becoming heads of two warring factions that accused each other of "abuses and misdeeds so scandalous and so unchristian" as to be unmentionable in letters.[28] Batavia had ultimately sided with Coyet and rebuked Verburg, who'd resigned his position as governor. After returning to Batavia, Verburg managed to get himself promoted higher and higher, eventually becoming a member of the High Council of the Indies. Once van der Laan arrived in Batavia and told everyone that Coyet was dangerously paranoid, Verburg saw a chance for revenge.

What Verburg seized on were Coyet's actions vis-à-vis the Chinese merchants and entrepreneurs on Taiwan. Coyet had arrested them and brought them in for questioning, trying to find out what they knew about a possible invasion.[29] He'd searched their houses, detained their wives, confiscated their grain and venison and horses.[30] He'd ordered Chinese colonists to move out of their farms because "the wide dispersion of Chinese causes difficulties for us, since we have too few people to keep proper surveillance over all of them."[31] He'd brought Chinese farmers to Saccam by force.[32] He'd forbidden Chinese to fish, arresting crews and confiscating boats.

Coyet had justified his actions by saying that they were necessary in the context of Koxinga's imminent invasion, but when Jan van der

Laan said there was no invasion, Verburg was able to accuse his enemy of causing material harm to the company. Verburg had long argued that the Chinese colonists of Taiwan must be favored and nurtured and protected. The Chinese, he wrote, "are the only bees on Taiwan that give honey."[33] It was a vision he'd laid out just after resigning his post as governor of Taiwan, in a treatise he'd written to recover his reputation.[34] "For years," he wrote, "we have seen the utility and profit that have resulted from the company's efforts to establish a Chinese colony on Taiwan, which has not only allowed agriculture to flourish, but has also brought the entire republic prosperity and well-being, such that the Chinese are the soul and spirit of Taiwan's body. Without them Taiwan would be dead and inert."[35] In order to make Taiwan prosper, he'd written, "we must do our best to tenderly cherish and nurture this Chinese colony and encourage the Chinese to establish themselves in Taiwan."[36] Verburg felt that Coyet was ruining Taiwan by unjustly—and unnecessarily—harming its Chinese inhabitants.

The High Council of the Indies decided that Verburg was right and that Coyet's fears of an attack had been "from beginning to end nothing more than a bunch of false and frivolous fantasies propagated by a few evil Chinese."[37] The High Councilors declared that Coyet had acted rashly in persecuting the Chinese. "The poor [Chinese] peasants have seen their grain sheds razed, and . . . their rice burned. . . . Coyet had all the elders and other powerful Chinese . . . imprisoned. . . . [T]hey have been in detention for eight months now, and their assets, which mostly consisted in agriculture, have fallen into ruin."[38]

The High Council and the Governor-General composed a letter to Coyet. Now, on this hot night in July, 1661, one of Coyet's colleagues read it out loud. It wasn't nice. "You are weak-hearted and lacking in the spirit of bravery that should distinguish one occupying your position." "We've been very much disappointed in the confidence we'd placed in you." "You are the cause of Formosa's ruin."[39]

It even contained sentences that Coyet probably recognized had been authored by Verburg himself:

> The Chinese colony, which has been planted there at so much cost and trouble, is the only means through which that island has been brought to fruitfulness, and from which the company thus

> yearly derives such rich incomes . . . and therefore the correct maxim has always been to nurture the Chinese there. You, however, have oppressed them with such a hard hand that they are more inclined to leave Formosa than to live under such a restless and punishing government.[40]

The letter said that Coyet and his top advisors were hereby dismissed from their posts. Even worse, they were ordered to return to Batavia immediately for trial and punishment. There was a special irony in what the letter said about how Coyet's replacement, the man who sat aboard the ship, should fix things: apologize to Koxinga for any insult or offense Coyet might have given because, the letter stated, "we shall gain more from Koxinga by love than by war."[41]

After the letter had been read, Coyet quipped to his councilors that he'd like nothing more than for the new governor to come ashore right away and take up his duties, but the new governor was already running away.[42] The lone ship was supposed to wait for a decision about whether it would dock or not, but the following morning it was gone.[43]

Officially, Coyet expressed hope. The ship's pilot had told a crewmember of the sampan that a Dutch vessel had been spotted sailing to the west of Tioman Island, not far from Batavia. Coyet and his advisors prayed. "Please God, let that ship have been the *Maria*, let it have arrived in Batavia early enough so that we can get the help we so need this year!"[44]

But the rest of the besieged were devastated. As Albrecht Herport wrote, "without hope of succor, we had no courage left."[45] By now more than four hundred men were sick.[46] The stench from the hospitals wafted over the whole castle, barely to be endured, and there were more corpses to bury each day.[47] Morale plummeted.

Then, on a beautiful sunny day in August, twelve Dutch ships appeared. Coyet's prayers seemed to have been answered: "God Almighty has seen fit to let us view today an imposing fleet of Dutch ships . . . sent, so it seems, from Batavia for our relief. May His holy name be forever praised!"[48]

The sight brought joy to the Dutch and terror to the Chinese, who were caught entirely by surprise.

THREE

The Fleet

Koxinga's Eastern Capital flew into panic. Chinese officials ran through the streets without their servants or parasols, talking in anxious loud voices.[1] One could just glimpse the ships anchored outside the bay, flags flying. Chinese officials asked the Dutch prisoners over and over again ("as though," wrote Philip Meij, "they were losing their minds") how many soldiers might be on each one and whether they would come attack right away.

The Eastern Capital was undefended. More than twenty thousand men had come from China to Taiwan, but already thousands had died of hunger and thousands more were too sick to fight. The rest had been sent out to plant and forage. Only a few hundred remained to protect the officials and their families here in the capital.

Koxinga sent for his highest-ranking Dutch prisoner, the Dutch magistrate Jacob Valentine. He'd had little interest in Valentine the past couple months, ever since he'd realized that Valentine wouldn't be able to get Coyet to surrender. Recently, when Valentine had tried getting Koxinga to sign letters authorizing new food supplies for the prisoners, he hadn't even been able to obtain an audience. Lower officials kept him running from one person to another, a bureaucratic maze, and at each turn he'd had to bribe them.[2]

Now, with twelve Dutch warships offshore, there was a knock at Valentine's door. Chinese soldiers said Koxinga wished to invite him for a meal, something that had never happened before. They conducted him politely from his residence toward the fortress he'd once commanded but that now served as Koxinga's headquarters. The building was in the midst of renovations. Koxinga had added a new gate and a stone wall all the way around, which was nearly finished.[3] The botanical garden in the back had been neglected, although it was said that Koxinga still used the garden's guesthouse to play with his concubines.[4] (There was certainly some playing going on at this time, because genealogical records indicate that nine months later, there was a little Koxinga baby boom: three of his ten male children were born shortly after his death in 1662, which means that they were most likely conceived in the summer and fall of 1661 or the early part of 1662.[5])

In the past, when Dutch prisoners had been summoned, they'd had to approach Koxinga between rows of guards in full armor, with saber-staves and flashing helmets, and when they reached Koxinga they'd been forced to bow low. But Koxinga greeted Valentine at the door and walked him in to a table, seating him across and to the left.[6] As the meal was served, he asked Valentine what kind of fleet this was. Did the company ever send out this many ships at once for trade?[7]

The Chinese have a saying: *To serve a prince is to serve a tiger*. Valentine had witnessed executions: generals and colonels who'd failed in battle, farmhands who'd stolen food, ordinary soldiers who'd been disobedient or cowardly. Recently a soldier was executed along with six of his comrades for eating a beef dinner offered by his brother, a farmer he hadn't seen for years. He'd butchered one of his cows to celebrate their reunion, but Koxinga had gotten furious because all livestock now belonged to Koxinga himself.[8] Valentine had often heard the drums and horns that announced the executioner, watched him march toward the execution ground with his great black flag, his victim stripped to the underwear, thumbs bound together behind the back, a length of bamboo shoved in the mouth and tied to the ears. The executioner would push his prisoner down and then, without any further ceremony, drive his sword through the neck. He'd pick up the head by the hair and show it to the audience, holding his bloody sword behind his back.

Valentine had witnessed executions of Dutchmen, too. The most heartbreaking incident was when two men had been accused of inciting the natives to revolt. They said they were innocent, but Koxinga ordered them crucified. Valentine and other Dutch prisoners had been forced to watch the procedure. The victims were forced to lie on planks. Their hands were drawn up over their heads and crossed at the palms. A nail was driven through both hands and then nails were driven through each arm, through each leg above the knee, and through each heel, near the Achilles' tendon. Seven nails per body. The crucifixes were raised in front of Valentine's house. The victims screamed and cried, but Koxinga ordered Valentine to make sure that no one brought them anything to eat or drink or helped them commit suicide. Valentine got permission for Minister Hambroek to pray for them. All night long his prayers mingled with the men's moans and shrieks. The next day the men, still nailed up, were loaded into an oxen cart and paraded bumping and rolling through the villages near the Eastern Capital until they died.[9]

So Valentine, sitting across from Koxinga, spoke carefully. He said that sometimes this many ships did come in a given year to trade, but never all at once. It must be a war fleet, sent to attack the company's enemies. You could tell by the three flags that flew above it: one for the admiral, one for the vice admiral, and one for the rear admiral.

As the translator relayed these words, Koxinga's face darkened.[10] He said he didn't believe that Batavia could have known about the war because Coyet couldn't have sent a ship against the monsoon winds. So whom, he asked, had the fleet come to fight?

Valentine said he had no idea. Maybe, he said, it was aimed at the Portuguese in Macau.

Koxinga was genuinely nonplussed. Coyet's councilors had acted wisely in advising him to temper his angry letter to Koxinga the previous month so Koxinga would feel that much more "fright and astonishment" if a fleet arrived.[11] If Coyet's letter had been sent as originally written, Koxinga wouldn't have left his capital undefended. Now his troops were spread throughout Taiwan, and it would take weeks to recall them.

Valentine was allowed to return to his residence. Koxinga turned his wrath on someone else: He Bin. The translator had been wrong too many times. He'd assured Koxinga that Taiwan had plenty of rice,

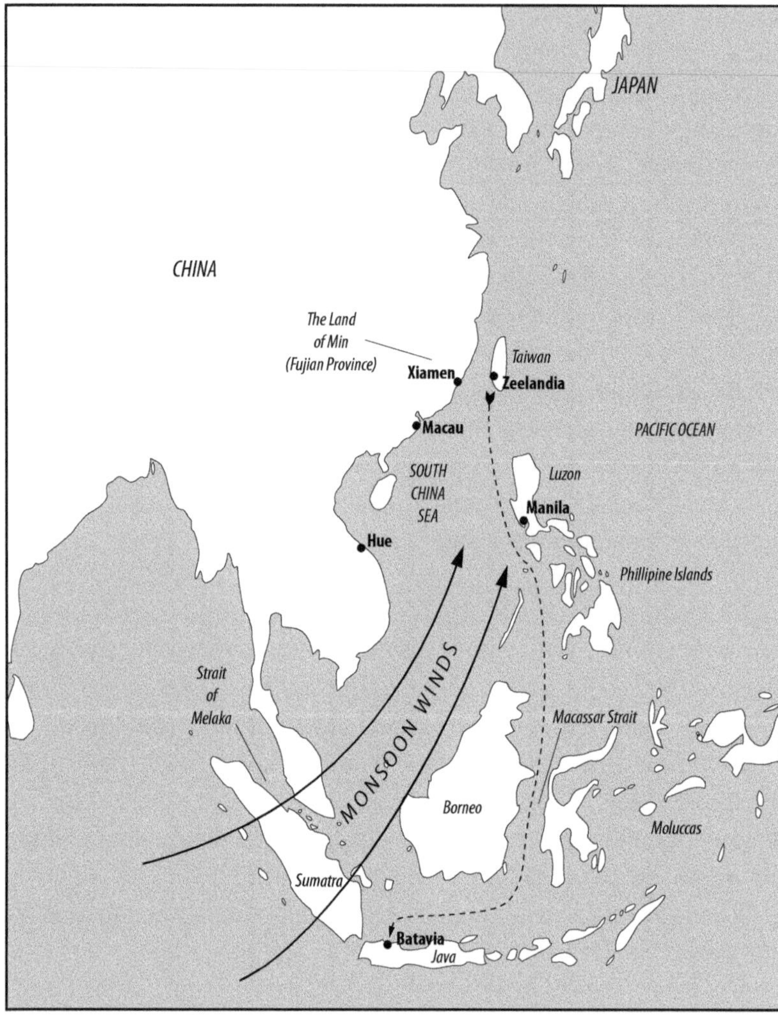

Figure 22. The voyage of the *Maria*, 6 May to 24 June 1661. The small yacht *Maria*, captained by Cornelius Clawson, sailed southward against monsoon winds to bring the news of Koxinga's invasion to the company's Asian headquarters in Batavia. This brave feat of navigation nearly turned the tide of the war, because Koxinga didn't expect the Dutch to be able to communicate with Batavia against the monsoon winds.

that the Hollanders were weak, and that the conquest would be over in a matter of days. But the invasion was turning into a fiasco. Koxinga ordered He Bin banned from his presence and confined to a small shack. He would have been executed, but Koxinga realized he might have more need for him later.

There was little else to do but send messengers out to recall the troops and trust in the Will of Heaven.

THE WILL OF HEAVEN

In the fortress, Coyet and rest were ecstatic. "Even the sick," wrote Coyet's secretary, "jumped out of their bedding with joy."[12] The besieged flocked to the walls to have a look at the fleet. Swollen-legged and bloody-gummed, they were desperate for fresh supplies.

Coyet sent the loading boat out to the anchorage. Under the best of conditions, navigating the Channel was difficult (see figure 14). Its sandbars shifted with each tide. And it was too shallow. Four decades ago, when the Dutch had first arrived in Taiwan, it had been deeper, but since then silt had filled it in, so by 1661, most Dutch ships had trouble sailing into the bay. They usually stayed anchored outside the bay, at a place called the Southern Anchorage, and the loading boat was sent through the Channel to unload them, a tedious and time-consuming process. On days when the weather was windy or stormy, even the loading boat's experienced pilot found the short trip dangerous.

This was one of those days. It was blustery, with mad whitecap waves. People had died in conditions like this, and they hadn't had to contend with the Chinese junks that were now swarming just out of cannon range, waiting for an opportunity.

The pilot managed to make it out to the fleet and back, bringing a few officials and some letters. Coyet learned how the *Maria* made it to Batavia. Because it was sailing against the seasonal winds, it couldn't sail directly southwest, as was usually done, so instead it had set a course due south to the Philippines, and then sailed through the Celebes Sea, passing Borneo via the Makassar Strait, and thence westward to Batavia (figure 22).[13] It's a testament to Dutch navigation techniques that the *Maria* reached its goal, and if this war needs heroes, then the Maria's captain, Cornelius Clawson, and his navigator, would fit the role. They arrived at the Dutch headquarters in Batavia only seven weeks after leaving Taiwan. When they said Koxinga had attacked with a huge fleet and massive army, the whole city went into action. Porters and slaves worked day and night to muster soldiers and load ammunition and supplies.[14] The city held a special fast day to pray for a speedy voyage. Indeed, the voyage proved remarkably smooth, facilitated by "the most agreeable weather and wind as has ever been experienced."[15]

But now the weather wasn't looking good. It took the loading boat all day to make one more trip to the ships. It only returned late at night, bringing the first load of supplies: twenty-five fresh troops, two thousand pounds of gunpowder, and a few crates of food. When it tried going out the following day, it couldn't make it past the Channel mouth. And the next days were worse: dark and wet and windy, with the seas getting rougher and rougher.

So the fleet with its beer and wine, pork and olives, and, most desired of all, beans and arak, heaved at anchor right out of reach.[16] Coyet was anxious to confer with the admiral and military officers, but no one could go out and no one could come in.[17]

It was at this point that a naked man swam across the bay from the Eastern Capital. His name was Hendrik Robertson. He was a musketeer's drummer who'd been captured early in the war and held captive on one of Koxinga's junks, which was anchored in front of Koxinga's headquarters in the Bay of Taiwan. He told Coyet that yesterday a friend of his—another Dutch soldier—had told him that Philip Meij and Jacob Valentine had seen the fleet and were fomenting a prisoner's uprising and needed a good swimmer to go tell Coyet about their plans so they could coordinate a joint attack. Robertson had waited until late last night, when all the Chinese on board his junk seemed to be sleeping, crept to the side, and slipped into the water. He'd swum through the rain and waded ashore through the oyster beds in the Pineapples.

His message was simple and urgent: The Chinese were terrified, and Koxinga's headquarters were unprotected. If Coyet could send just seven hundred soldiers to attack the Eastern Capital, the enemy could be defeated and the Dutch prisoners freed. Meij and some of the other Dutch prisoners had managed to keep their guns and were determined to attack the Chinese from within, barricading themselves in Valentine's house or the old City Hall Building.

Coyet was delighted. He gave the man money and clothes. "From all of this," Coyet wrote, "it seems that Almighty God is trying to cheer us, to rouse us with these tidings, to fortify us and encourage us.

Yea! He is even showing us the way to attack our enemy! May He grant His blessing in all things."[18]

But in the evening somber clouds massed. Bursts of rain pelted the tile roofs. The following morning the wind howled and dark clouds spat rain. The angry surf hurled itself against the sand.

This was typhoon weather. It was time to shutter the windows, secure the boats, and make sure every man woman and child was accounted for. Most important, it was time to move the fleet out to safer waters.

The flagship fired a cannon and signaled with its flags to raise anchors. People watched from the fortress as the ships sailed into the gloom. As the soldier Albrecht Herport noted in his diary, "We were so terribly depressed to have had such a beautiful fleet before our eyes and then have it disappear from our sight."[19]

Something even more discouraging happened that evening. The enemy called out through the rain and gloated that one of the new ships had already been captured. Driven before the wind, it had smashed against a sandbar a short distance northward, in aboriginal territory. Natives captured and killed its crew, keeping their heads for a celebration, as was their custom. They spared a few men and sent them to the Eastern Capital for questioning.[20] These crewmembers revealed that the great Dutch fleet carried only seven hundred troops, not nearly as many as Koxinga and his advisors had feared. The captives were tied to a long piece of bamboo and drowned in a creek.[21]

The weather cleared the next day and Coyet thought the fleet would return, but it didn't. A week passed. Chinese reinforcements poured into Zeelandia City and aimed their cannons at the castle. Another week passed. More enemy troops arrived, digging trenches and building new barricades. Another week passed. Chinese workers dug a trench right through the graveyard, a sign, Coyet felt, "of how afraid they are of us attacking, being willing even to dig through the dead."[22]

But the Dutch ships didn't come back for three weeks. Instead of returning directly to Taiwan, they cruised around Penghu raiding for cows. Maybe judgments were impaired because the water ration had been replaced by an arak ration. In any case, by the time they returned, Coyet had lost the advantage of surprise.

IDEAS FROM BEHIND ENEMY LINES

Once the fleet was safely re-anchored beyond the dunes, swaying in the bright fall sun, the inhabitants of Zeelandia burst into activity. The loading boat sailed in and out, fighting off junks and loading olives and beans.

Coyet considered his next move. The time for a direct assault on the Eastern Capital had passed because Koxinga had had time to reinforce his positions, but there was no shortage of ideas. The best ones were coming from the other side, from Chinese defectors.

In the first months of the war, from Koxinga's invasion until mid-August, if you were on Koxinga's side there wasn't much point in running over to the Dutch because they seemed likely to lose the war. The only defector during that time went the other way, the ass-slapper from Switzerland who fled to Koxinga in July.

The fleet changed the equation. The night after the ships first anchored near Zeelandia, two little bamboo rafts detached themselves from the piers of Zeelandia City and floated through the Channel toward the castle. Three fugitives made it inside: two African slaves and a Chinese boy. These were the first defectors. They were followed by many more. The most important was a Chinese farmer named Sait.

While the Dutch were lowering cows into boats, Sait was in his home village saying goodbye to his wife and children. Koxinga had ordered all the farmers to contribute bamboo to the war effort. So Sait brought his load to the Eastern Capital and piled it near the bayshore as instructed. There was a big stack of the stuff, which was being woven into firerafts to burn up the new Dutch ships.

Afterward, he walked around the Eastern Capital and observed its martial bustle: the soldiers guarding Koxinga's headquarters, the warjunks anchored in the bay, the watchmen patrolling the old ferry port. He ran into surveyor Philip Meij, and they talked about the lack of food and how people were beginning to starve. Maybe he tarried near the shops, running his finger over the silk robes that Koxinga's officials were pawning to buy food.

Then, instead of going home to his family, he walked south down the coast, past where the salt pans were drying under the cloudy sky, to the Narrow. He waited until the tide was low and waded across. Then he made his way through dunes overgrown with pandanus trees and abandoned melon patches, mindful of Chinese patrols, until he finally came to the end of the long narrow island where Zeelandia Castle's huge gray-stone bastions rose up over sea and sand.[23]

Early the next morning, as he looked out from his hiding place at the walls bristling with cannons, he must have considered the wisdom of what he was about to do. He was Chinese; they were Dutch. You crossed sides at your peril. The Dutch might torture him, or slap him into irons, or kill him. Or Koxinga's people might find out and harm his family. But he had ideas and advice for how to use the fleet, and he knew that Coyet would be interested in what was happening behind enemy lines. He also seems to have personally disliked Koxinga, who had, he would later say, mistreated him when he still lived in China.[24]

So he stepped out and showed himself to the Dutch sentries. He was brought through the archway into the fort, and a while later he found himself standing in a room of Dutchmen. Coyet and the other members of the Council of Formosa might have been familiar to him, since he'd lived in Taiwan before the war, but there new faces, people who'd come with the ships. The most important was Jacob Cauw, the fleet's admiral.

Cauw had been welcomed on land a couple days before by rows of soldiers in their best clothes. They'd fired three musket salvoes and five cannonades "in joy and salutation."[25] Cauw had shaken Coyet's hand and walked with him into the castle, saddened by what he witnessed:

> It's heartbreaking to see how the company's people, who had until now been so healthy and sound, as well as the soldiers, who had been regarded the healthiest of all the garrisons in the Indies, now have swollen legs and bloated bodies. It was crowded in the fortress, since everyone who lived in Zeelandia City had been brought inside the walls. It was extremely full of people, particularly blacks. The church, and also the great sugar warehouse right across from it, are used as hospitals, and they are already so full that there is no space left, which causes in the area beneath the fortress such a terrible stench that it was not to be borne.[26]

Admiral Cauw had spent a couple days touring the ramparts with Coyet, making suggestions about where they might build new batteries and how they might strengthen their defenses, but it wasn't clear yet what role he'd play and how he'd get along with Coyet. Now he sat with the others and listened.

A secretary dipped pen in ink. They asked Sait a question: Who was he, and why had he come? He said his name was Sait and he'd come because he couldn't stand it any more, the way Koxinga and his soldiers persecuted him and the other Chinese farmers. Koxinga's soldiers pressed them constantly for money. They forced them to chop bamboo and bring it to his headquarters. They demanded all the stockpiles of rice and sugar without paying anything and even made them bring it themselves and load it on Koxinga's ships. He and the other farmers had given up working their fields, knowing that whatever they harvested this year would be stolen from them. Now the worms were eating through the rice stalks even as Koxinga's soldiers and the poorer Chinese starved. This year's harvest would be terrible, he said, the worst he'd ever seen.[27]

He said he had urgent military news. When he'd brought his bamboo to the Eastern Capital he'd seen huge piles of flammable materials, not just bamboo but also dry grass and tree-bark skirts requisitioned from the natives. Koxinga was planning to make firejunks and firerafts to attack the Dutch fleet. Seven rafts were ready to send out under the next dark moon. Pilots had been chosen and had received their rewards in advance: fifty ounces of gold for those who dared to steer the rafts, and fifty ounces of silver for those who piloted the boats.

But Sait felt that the Dutch could still win the war. Koxinga was faltering because of a severe lack of food. He'd ordered thousands of his troops to start their own farms on Taiwan, but they were too weak from hunger to work the fields. Food was so scarce that they were even starting to slaughter the plow oxen. Only the soldiers were well enough to fight, and most of them were scattered through the countryside. He said many other Chinese agreed with him that the Dutch could win. In fact, those who'd lived here before Koxinga's invasion were keeping their Dutch residence permits so that if the Dutch won they could prove their loyalty.

And how might the Dutch win? Sait admitted that it might be possible to attack the Eastern Capital, or to attack Chinese positions in Zeelandia City, but he thought the best strategy would be not to attack at all. He'd noticed that Coyet had started bringing a few ships in through the canal and docking them at the pier in front of the castle. This was a mistake, he said. Instead of bringing the fleet into the bay, where the deep-drawing European vessels would be at a disadvantage,[28] he thought Coyet should use the fleet to block Chinese shipping from China. If the Dutch could cordon Taiwan off and prevent rice junks from arriving, Koxinga's troops would keep dying. Hunger might lead them to rebellion, and Koxinga himself might have to return to China. Sait said he wasn't the only one who believed in such a strategy. The other farmers thought the same thing. Indeed, he said, Koxinga himself was most afraid of a blockade.

Coyet was pleased with Sait's information. He didn't throw him into chains as he'd done with some of the other Chinese defectors. He let him live in the governor's mansion and ensured that he was treated well.

But he ignored Sait's advice. Right after the interrogation, he called a huge meeting. All his advisors were there, as well as Commander Cauw and the officials who'd come with his fleet, and also all the military men in the castle and fleet—captains, lieutenants, and skippers. He asked what they thought should be done with this fleet to best harm the enemy. We don't have the detailed minutes of this meeting (very few such minutes have survived), but we do have three different accounts of it. In none of them is there any indication that Coyet or anyone else even raised the possibility of following Sait's advice and mounting a blockade to keep Koxinga from receiving rice supplies. Instead, they resolved to attack Koxinga.

It was a stupid decision.

A Foolish Attack

The plan was straightforward on paper. The five largest ships would sail into the bay, anchor behind the enemy's fortifications in Zeelandia City, and fire broadsides down the streets, catching the enemy by surprise. Meanwhile, a flotilla of smaller vessels—skiffs, galleys, and ship's launches—would sail toward the Eastern Capital to attack the dozens of Chinese junks that were anchored in the bay.

Commander Cauw felt he should lead the attack. After all, he was the man who'd brought the fleet and all its men. But he and Coyet weren't getting along.

The trouble had started a couple days after Cauw's arrival. He'd been up on top of a bastion studying Chinese positions in the city and had noticed that the enemy was building something near the tollhouse. He ordered the gunner to fire three cannon shots. Immediately, a messenger arrived: Coyet ordered him to stop shooting.

Cauw went straight to Coyet's office and asked why.

"Because I don't want a single shot fired without my express order," said Coyet.

"If," Cauw said, "I'm not even allowed to shoot a cannon at the enemy when I can see right before my nose that he can be fruitfully attacked, then maybe I should just leave the fort and go back to my ships."

Coyet didn't reply.[1]

Cauw felt humiliated. "The governor," he would later write, "doesn't seem to think much of me."[2] He was right. Coyet felt that

Cauw was useless, having no other experience in matters of war than when he was a student in Leiden and ran his sword through people's windows. Coyet found him annoying in person, too, writing that he was "a person so defective in speech that you almost needed an interpreter to understand his words, which were all spoken through his nose."[3]

So Coyet refused Cauw's offer to lead the attack and oversaw the preparations himself. The most difficult task was to bring the ships from their deepwater anchorage to the piers in front of the fortress. Five warships were to comprise the main force, led by a great warship called the *Koukercken*. These big vessels sailed low in the water and had to be unloaded to get through the Channel into the bay. Workers even had to take out many of the cannon. Two days it took to bring them in and moor them in front of the fortress in an area sheltered from Chinese guns.

The morning of the attack was sunny. The ships' pennants flapped gently, showing a nice westerly breeze.[4] It was perfect weather.

Soldiers and officers marched onto the beach below the walls and lined up before Coyet and Cauw and the other officials. Everyone listened as Minister Kruyf gave a fiery sermon: "May His Holy Majesty bless this exploit we undertake, so that we may achieve victory over this heathenish horde."[5] Then Coyet spoke. Everyone, he said, should trust in God to deliver a glorious victory and should conduct themselves like brave and true soldiers, attacking the enemy with the utmost courage. He urged them to kill as many Chinese as possible. This was a decision he and his advisors had made when planning the attack: "In the fury of battle, none of the enemy is to be spared. Everyone is to be killed without distinction."[6] The soldiers and sailors cheered. For so long they'd been inactive, trapped in the fort. Their excitement increased when Coyet said they'd be given large cash prizes for every junk captured.

The ships opened their sails and glided toward their positions, firing cannons. The flotilla of smaller vessels followed, propelled by sails and oars.

The big ships were meant to anchor in a line just offshore of Zeelandia City so they could focus their fire on the cannons the enemy had placed in the streets. The enemy's sandbasket barricades were oriented to protect against attacks from Zeelandia Castle, so Coyet's strategy was to strike the Chinese positions from behind.

But something was wrong. "To our complete surprise," Coyet's secretary wrote, "we found the bay to be only twelve feet deep. In addition, the current was coming strongly from the south, which caused us considerable dismay."[7] Perhaps the sands had shifted during the last storm. The ships couldn't line up as planned. They clustered together behind the mighty flagship, *Koukercken*.

They let loose a thunderous barrage, seconded by guns from the fortress. Coyet noticed that the ships' cannonballs were flying way too high, over the castle itself. Some were even landing within the walls.

He ordered that someone row out and tell them to re-aim but was astounded to learn that there were no boats to row. Every vessel was already in action.

He offered a reward to anyone willing to swim out with the message. A volunteer swam alone through the maelstrom, reached the ship, and was pulled aboard. But just as he was relaying his message a cannonball ripped through his legs. The message got through, but to no avail. The gunners couldn't aim any lower because the water was too shallow.

In the meantime, the Chinese soldiers had re-aimed their cannons and were firing at the ships with startling accuracy. "It is incredible," wrote Coyet's secretary, "that the enemy in his batteries is able to handle his cannon so effectively. . . . They put our own men to shame."[8] Since the Dutch ships couldn't spread out to draw fire, the enemy's cannonfire focused on the *Koukercken*. Its crew began to panic. One of its gunners misloaded his cannon. It exploded, killing nine Dutch soldiers and wounding many others. The hull began to leak.

Things weren't going any better for the smaller vessels, which had targeted a group of Chinese junks. At first, the junks had fled toward the Eastern Capital, apparently in fear. The flotilla had chased behind, gaining with each oar-stroke.

But suddenly the Chinese turned around and rowed right toward them, yelling and shooting. Having lured the flotilla away from the large ships, they could now attack without worrying about Dutch broadsides. The man in charge of these junks was Chen Ze, the brilliant tactician who'd defeated Thomas Pedel.[9] Once again, he outfoxed the Dutch. The results were devastating.

The Dutch soldiers shot at the approaching junks with muskets, but the Chinese kept closing. The Dutch threw hand grenades, but Chinese soldiers calmly caught them with bamboo mats and threw them back.

One Dutch crew managed to board a junk and was slaughtering its crew, ignoring their pleas for mercy, but then another junk came to its aid and the Dutch had to abandon their prize.[10]

Another Dutch boat drew up alongside a Chinese commander's junk, braving a rain of arrows, and its crew was preparing to board and capture it. But this was a trap too. The Chinese leapt into the boat with bloodcurdling cries, brandishing their weapons. They killed all the crew who didn't jump overboard and rowed their prize to shore. Another Dutch boat fell to a similar attack. A third one ran aground on a sandbar. Its crew jumped overboard and tried to swim away but was overrun by small Chinese boats, whose crewmembers stabbed the swimmers dead in the water with pikes.[11]

The wind had died, so the Dutch soldiers in their boats couldn't use sails and had to paddle constantly, exhausting work that left little energy for fighting. The stillness also meant that the large ships, which were supposed to back them up and rip the Chinese junks like paper with their powerful cannon, sat limp-sailed and useless. There was nothing to do but row back to the castle.

Cauw, who had watched the whole battle from the castle, mused that "this attack was carried out with much more courage than caution, and if the enemy had kept up his fake retreat any longer and lured our vessels closer to the Eastern Capital and farther from the ships, then it's certain that not a single one of them would have survived."[12]

Coyet signaled a general retreat, but the big ships still couldn't move because there was no wind. The enemy cannons kept firing. The *Koukercken*, which was bearing the brunt of the attack, began listing in the water.

As the sun started to go down, a slight breeze arose, and the ships finally began moving slowly toward safety. Then the breeze died and the battered *Koukercken* drifted toward shore. It ran aground in front of an enemy cannon placement.

In the ship's hold sat a Dutch deacon.[13] He'd spent the battle belowdecks, next to the musket chest, and for some reason he'd brought his eight-year-old son. Maybe he thought they'd be safe in this, the largest warship. When they felt the ship run aground, father and son climbed up on deck. Bodies were strewn around, burnt, bleeding, screaming for help. The captain was gone. Those who could walk were leaping overboard.

As the two picked their way toward the side of the ship, they heard yelling in Chinese coming from the other side. The deacon was a talented linguist, able to speak several languages, including Chinese. He understood that officers were shouting at their men to board the ship. He gripped his boy's hand and prepared to jump. Then he saw a boat rowing out from the fortress. In it he recognized the ship's captain, returning with fresh men. He stood for a few seconds with his son, undecided.

An explosion ripped the air. He was hurled into the sky. When he came up for air, there was smoke and fire and debris, but his son was gone. Maybe he'd already swum to shore? It was impossible to see anything this low in the water. He swam toward the castle. A few minutes later he reached safety, but his son never made it.

The flagship was now just a burning prow sticking out of the water. Five naked men clung to it, waving their hands and calling out for help. Coyet ordered a boat to row out and rescue them, promising a rich reward, but the enemy shot so accurately it had to turn back. As Coyet and his men watched, Chinese soldiers rowed a sampan out to the flaming wreck and used their saber-staves to smite three of the men into the water and the other two into the pyre.

While the *Koukercken* sank, the four other large ships limped toward the castle. Two made it, but the other two ran into trouble. One lodged on a sandbar far enough away from Chinese cannons to be relatively safe. It would remain there until the morning tide freed it. The other ran aground near Zeelandia City. It struggled to get loose for hours while Chinese cannons pummeled it. Its crew and captain abandoned ship, leaving a sergeant and six soldiers trapped aboard. They didn't know how to swim or sail, so they just fought off sampans and fireboats, hoping the captain would return with reinforcements and a dredge-anchor to work the ship free.[14] Eventually they stopped shooting and waited quietly until a Chinese sampan approached, hiding so the enemy would think the ship was empty. When they heard the Chinese step on deck, they rushed out, commandeered the sampan, and rowed to the castle. They were safe, but the ship was lost.

With darkness came a tense peace. The wounded were brought to the church and the old warehouse, where room was made for them on the floor. Between the wails of the wounded, Chinese crews could be heard working in the abandoned city.

The next morning, the Chinese cannon placements had been rebuilt stronger than before.[15]

Bodies washed up on the bayshore below the castle walls. Some were found without arms and legs, others with noses cut off, others bound together in pairs, arm to arm, thumb to thumb, hair to hair.[16] Some had nails hammered into them in various places.[17] Worst of all were those whose genitals had been cut off and stuffed into their mouths. The Chinese had used the tide to deliver the corpses right to the castle, grisly symbols of defeat.[18] The Dutch spent the day fishing them out and burying them.

In the evening Chinese horns and drums and flutes played triumphantly in Zeelandia City. From the castle ramparts Coyet and his comrades saw fires burning in the city and groups of Chinese soldiers burning offerings and incense to thank the gods for their victory.

The Dutch also turned to a higher power. They decided to hold a day of fasting and prayer, begging the Almighty to please lighten up on the righteous wrath and instead show forgiveness and mercy.[19]

THE AFTERMATH OF THE FOOLISH ATTACK

Coyet should have listened to the Chinese farmer Sait. The attack cost him two ships and three smaller vessels, and most of the others were damaged. One hundred and thirty-one men were lost, some killed and others taken prisoner, although judging from the bodies that kept washing ashore over the next days, most captives ended up dead.

Among the saddest losses was Cornelius Clawson, the captain who'd sailed the *Maria* to Batavia. He'd asked "most earnestly" to take part in the attack, and this had been allowed, despite the fact that he was disabled from an old injury. He'd captained one of the small vessels that were lured into the Chinese trap. His boat had overturned and he'd sat astride it, drifting, until he was captured by the Chinese.[20] What happened to him next is unknown. Maybe he was one of the mutilated bodies.

Coyet wondered whether the attack had any effect on the Chinese. He turned to Sait to find out. The farmer said he'd be willing to return to Koxinga's Eastern Capital as a spy, to determine how things stood in the aftermath of the attack, how many new troops and ships Koxinga had received, whether any new rice supplies had arrived from China, and what Koxinga planned to do next.[21] He said he'd come back in a few days.

Although Coyet was ready to agree to the plan, others were more skeptical. Commander Cauw, who had his own secretary and kept his own log of events, was particularly frustrated with Coyet, whose failures of leadership in the recent attack were clear. It was, Cauw wrote, "a sad and truly blameworthy affair."[22]

Cauw felt that that failure was only the most recent of a long sequence of mistakes. Coyet and his advisors had let the gunpowder spoil and the cannons rust and the water run out in Fort Provintia. They'd given up Fort Provintia without a fight, trusting Koxinga's false promises about how he'd treat the Dutch prisoners. They'd abandoned Zeelandia City and allowed the Chinese to occupy it, when they should have burned it down and taken all of its supplies. "Some of the high officials here," Cauw complained later in a letter to Batavia, "were so preoccupied with understanding the philosophical books of Descartes that they found it impossible to pay attention to these little details."[23] Cauw felt himself to be a simple man of unstylized letters, but one who knew his business, which, for now, was fighting. One shouldn't be too trusting of these heathen Chinese.

Coyet was inclined to let Sait go, feeling that the farmer could do little harm even if he did go over to Koxinga. Sait had lived in the governor's mansion, true, but although he could hear the constant sounds of Dutch activities outside in the courtyards of the fort, he wouldn't have been able to learn anything important about the number of dead or wounded or sick, or about food supplies and gunpowder stores.

So Coyet and his council decided to engage the farmer as a spy. They offered him thirty silver reals for the trouble, a great deal of money, and found it encouraging when he said he'd accept only ten reals now and pick up the rest when he came back, because if he were discovered with too much money outside, he might be killed. The council also promised that when everything was peaceful and the Dutch were once again in control of Taiwan, he and his descendants would never have to pay taxes again on their land.[24]

The night sentries watched him disappear into the dunes. He came back a while later, saying he'd walked all the way to the narrow part of the bay, where the salt pans were, but couldn't get across because the water was too high.[25] A couple days later, when the tide was low, he set out again.[26] This time he managed to get across. He slept on the opposite shore and then, traveling in the dark, went to the Eastern Capital and then to his farm to see his family.[27]

Cauw expected never to see him again. It would have been better for Sait if that had been the case. But several days later he was back, and he brought welcome news. Although the foolish attack hadn't hurt Koxinga at all, the warlord's forces were suffering from a more serious problem: starvation. Sait heard some of Koxinga's watchmen complaining that if the siege lasted much longer, hunger would force them to mutiny. He learned also that Koxinga had recalled his troops from the frontiers, but many of them had died. Of the thousand Chinese troops who'd been sent to the south of Taiwan, only two hundred came back alive, and these men were sick and on crutches, no use in battle. Sait said that things wouldn't improve because the harvest would provide only two months of food. People were so malnourished that if they got a cut on their legs, even a little cut, it wouldn't heal. It would grow and grow until they couldn't walk. He said he'd heard that Koxinga was even sending his wives back to China, and there were rumors that he would soon follow himself, particularly because there were reports that a great force of Koxinga's other enemies, the Manchus, was attacking his base in China.[28]

Coyet's secretary recorded Sait's report without comment, but Cauw's secretary reported something suspicious. Cauw, who had little else to do, had been inspecting troops and talking with soldiers. He'd learned that the night before his return, Sait had been spotted standing behind the ruins of the hospital in the field between the fortress and the city, in full view of Chinese sentinels. Watchmen told Cauw that there was no way Sait could have been there without the consent of Chinese troops. Even more problematic, they said, was the fact that the next morning, when Sait had come over to the fort, he'd walked over not from behind the dunes, like the first time, but from Zeelandia City itself, which was controlled by the Chinese. Cauw suspected foul play.[29]

Sait tried to explain. He said he'd been forced to come back a different way this time because Koxinga's troops were keeping a stricter watch along the shore on the other side of the bay, for miles in either direction, and when he'd tried to follow his previous route they'd shot at him with arrows. So instead of walking through the Pineapple dunes he'd gone right through the abandoned city. He'd gotten there yesterday afternoon but couldn't find a safe time to come over until morning.[30]

Cauw wasn't persuaded. "It seems," his secretary wrote, "that this scoundrel wasn't the right man for the job."[31] Confronted with this evidence, Coyet turned against Sait. When the farmer asked to go home, Coyet said no. Sait was taken out through the rain to the pier and rowed to one of the ships.[32] The cold, rough waters were as effective as prison walls, and there was plenty of work to be done on board.

Sait might have survived the war by swabbing decks or carrying water or washing dishes. Instead he ended up dead in a stolen boat. The events leading up to his demise were sparked by other defectors, of whom there were many. Although most were sincere, some were not, and those spelled trouble.

The Defectors

From the beginning of the war all through that summer of 1661, only four defectors had come from the Chinese side. In the fall, defectors began pouring to the Dutch side: seventeen of them in September and October (figure 23). Dutch secretaries were so busy transcribing their stories of sickness and starvation that they neglected their other work, the constant copying, recopying, collating, and organizing that filled their days. As a result, Dutch records get increasingly haphazard as the war progresses.[1]

The Dutch encouraged this flow of turncoats. They brought Chinese defectors out onto the castle ramparts and had them call out to their former comrades in Zeelandia City. "You Chinese soldiers," the defectors cried. "Why don't you come here? Things are good here. We have food, drink, and clothing in abundance. If you stay there you'll die of starvation. Governor Coyet has promised to take us home to our own country with his ships. You're crazy if you don't come to the Dutch, because you'll never outlast them. Whoever of you comes over here and brings the head of your commander Ma Xin will be richly taken care of for life."[2]

The explicit response from Chinese troops in the city was predictable enough: "We'll get you, you bitches! Instead of staying loyal to your lords as you should have, you ran away like maggots to the enemy."[3]

But the defectors kept coming because the alternative was starvation. Some said that Koxinga's soldiers were receiving only twenty

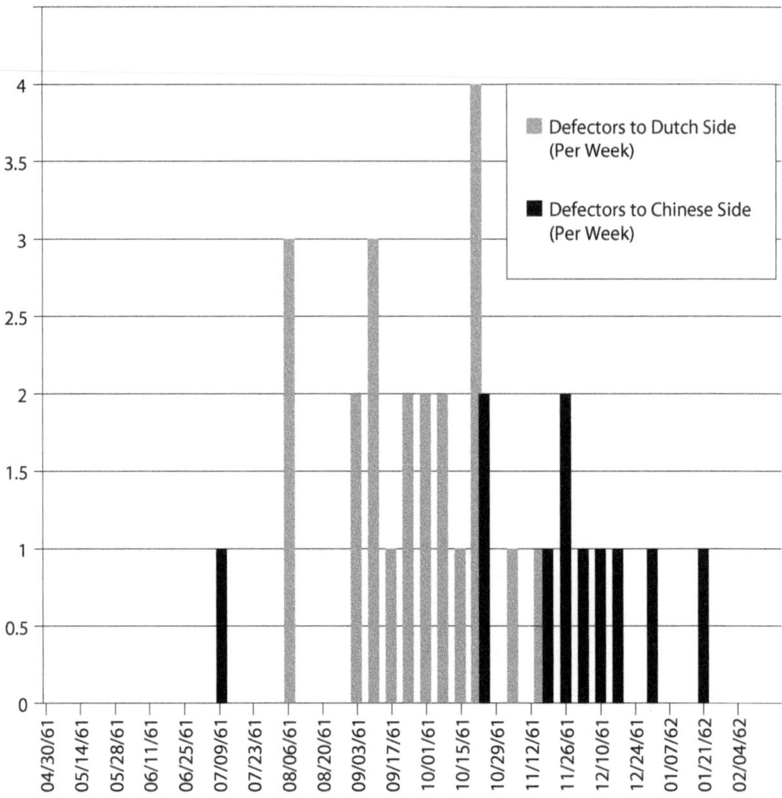

Figure 23. Defectors in the Sino-Dutch War, 1661 and 1662. This chart illustrates the changing fortunes of war. Starting in the late summer of 1661, when Cauw's fleet arrived with fresh supplies and troops, defectors began flowing from the Chinese side to the Dutch side. This continued all through the fall, a time when starvation ravaged Koxinga's troops. But the defector vector reversed in the winter, as conditions in Zeelandia Castle worsened and its inhabitants lost hope for further reinforcements from Batavia.

pounds (two gantangs) of rice per month, "and nothing else besides that, and no wages, either, and with this one had to feed wives, children, and servants."[4] This meant that each soldier and his dependents got a bit more than a thousand calories per day.[5] Others noted higher figures. A Chinese boy who'd run away from his soldier-master because he'd stolen rice from him said that the soldiers "are suffering intense hunger, and must make do with a tenth of a gantang per meal, which they have to share with their wives."[6] A tenth of a gantang is about a pound of rice, dry weight, or about 1,750 calories. Shared with others, it wasn't enough to survive on. The boy did say that the soldiers he knew received fifteen catties of beef per month.[7] Other defectors didn't mention rations other than rice, but even so, a Chinese catty was only about a half a pound,[8] meaning that the soldiers in his unit might have received at most a quarter pound of meat per day, which would have helped nutritionally, providing protein and nutrients, but wasn't enough to satisfy caloric needs.[9]

Defectors said starvation was rampant. One brought news that in one of Koxinga's encampments, at a place called Bockenburgh, which stood on a dune near the Narrow, two or three soldiers were dying each day, out of a total garrison of about six hundred.[10] Another said that several people died each day just in Zeelandia City.[11] Another said that in the Eastern Capital, sometimes seventy or eighty people died in one day, "for which reason Koxinga's strength has severely dwindled, and many of his people are running away, and others have refused to follow his orders."[12] Another noted that the Saccam area was full of fresh graves.[13] The Chinese boy who'd stolen rice from his master said that of the thousand or so troops stationed in Zeelandia City, only three or four men out of every ten were healthy.[14] In fact, he said, even officers and officials were dying—four minor officials or officers were sick from lack of food because their rations were no greater than those of the common soldiers.[15]

The defectors feared that the upcoming harvest wouldn't help much. Rice in the water fields was being devoured by worms. There might be lots of potatoes, but they wouldn't be ready for a long time.[16] Desperate people raided the fields, so Koxinga passed laws to protect the crops. Anyone caught picking sugarcane would have his hand chopped off.[17] Same for plucking potato greens.[18] Koxinga's troops had already ravaged the countryside and forced the aborigines and the Chinese settlers to hand over their food stores.[19] There wasn't much more to raid.

It's possible that the defectors were exaggerating to curry favor with the Dutch, yet Chinese sources corroborate their accounts. Yang Ying's chronicle notes that in the second half of September and the first half of October (the period during which defectors were streaming to the Dutch side), starvation among Koxinga's men was rampant, to the point that Koxinga and his officials were "daily worried about incidents of desertion and unrest."[20] Conditions were especially bad in the frontier settlements. In mid-October, Koxinga sent Yang Ying to take rice to the desperate troops stationed in the north, but it wasn't nearly enough. "The soldiers eat only two times a day," wrote Yang, "and are dying of illnesses. Their hearts cry out in anguish."[21] The chronicler tried buying up all the rice and grains in the native villages, but that provided only ten days' rations. At this point, Yang Ying himself got so sick that he stopped writing for several months, the only major gap in his decade-plus record.

A poet detailed the plight of Koxinga's poor soldiers, working away on empty stomachs in the last days of summer:

Brush blocks their sight.
Vines trip their steps.
Branches hide hanging snakes.
The grass shelters rats and foxes.
Poisonous bugs share their sleeping quarters.
They draw water for rice from malarial pools.
Four or five men of every ten are sick.
Their wailing and groaning assaults the ears.
Everyone's suffering from an empty stomach.
They're so weak—who can lift his shovel?
And summer's giving way to fall,
yet the task of reclamation for this tiny territory
still remains far from complete.[22]

Chinese sources thus corroborate the defectors' testimony.

Except that there were some false turncoats.

THE AFRICAN BOYS

The two African boys arrived at Zeelandia Castle toward the end of October, creeping through the high grass and showing themselves to the watchmen. Before the war, the older one had belonged to a Dutch official. The younger one was a freeborn, son of a Dutch soldier and an African slave. They said they'd been captured by Koxinga and given to the Chinese general Ma Xin, the man who commanded the troops in Zeelandia City.[23]

They brought bad news about Koxinga's Dutch captives. As starvation increased, the Chinese had started to see the prisoners as a waste of food. The boys said they'd watched as Koxinga, angry at Coyet's recent attack, treated a large group of Dutch prisoners to a good meal and then had them beheaded. Even schoolteachers and preachers. That's how Hambroek met his end.

The boys said that only the girls and women had been spared. They were given to Chinese officials as concubines. One of Hambroek's daughters was forced to serve Koxinga himself, living in his women's palace.[24] It seemed that some of them, such as a sixteen-year-old sister-in-law of one of the Dutch preachers, now wore Chinese clothes and bound their feet.

Coyet welcomed the boys, seeing that they were fed and giving them full run of the castle, but Cauw got suspicious. Some Chinese defectors said they'd known the boys on the Chinese side and that their Chinese master, Ma Xin, had favored them, letting them live in his own house and eat the best food from his table. Cauw began to suspect that Ma Xin had sent them over as spies. Some Dutch soldiers told Cauw they'd seen the older boy measuring the mouths of cannons with a stick and heard him asking unusual questions, such as how heavy a cannonball the large bronze cannons could shoot, or how many of those special cannons the Dutch had that could shoot cannonballs so high up in the air, meaning, surmised the soldiers, the mortars that had killed and maimed so many of the enemy. The younger boy was seen walking through the warehouse and the church, which served as hospitals, and it seemed like he was counting the ill and wounded. He'd also been asking people how many soldiers had arrived with Cauw's fleet.[25]

Confronted with these reports, Coyet ordered the boys taken to cells in the upper castle. The next day, soldiers led them to the rack.[26] At first the boys held to their story, saying they'd fled from the heathen Chinese so they could be with Christians again, since the Dutch had always treated them well and kept their bellies full and didn't hit them and beat them like the Chinese. The Dutch decided to "press the truth" out of them.[27]

The younger boy was the cleverer of the two and seemed to be the leader, probably because, Dutch officials surmised, his father was a

Hollander. But the older boy succumbed quickly. It was all true, he said. Their new master, Ma Xin, had sent them here to find out everything they could about the fortress, what the Dutch did each day, how many cannons there were in the bastions, how many sick people there were. Hearing this, the clever one gave in, "realizing that it might soon be his turn." He said Ma Xin had ordered him to measure the height of the walls of the fortress with pieces of rope and to determine how much gunpowder the Dutch had. In fact, he said, they were planning to escape this very evening to make their report.

The boys said there were other spies. Coyet and Cauw listened closely. Recent defectors had been sent out to the fleet to keep them out of the way. The boys said that some of those men were false defectors. Dutch soldiers rowed out and rounded them up.

Sait was out on the fleet, too, ever since Cauw had learned about the suspicious way he'd come over the second time. When Sait heard that defectors were taken back to the castle for questioning, he got scared. That night was cold, with a bitter wind. He crept to the side of the ship, lowered himself into the rowboat, and used a knife to saw through the mooring rope. He pushed off.

As he rowed away, sailors discovered he was gone. Shots were fired, but they missed. He'd taken the only launch available for that ship, and it would take them a long time to raise the anchor. He used his head start to try to steer toward the dunes behind Zeelandia Castle, hoping to run away into the high grass, but the night current carried him out toward the rest of the fleet. In between the ships he drifted.

Above him the sailors had been awakened by the gunfire. They called down and asked if he wanted to come aboard, thinking maybe the shots had been a warning of some sort, maybe the Chinese were attacking, maybe this man in a rowboat had information. In the darkness they couldn't tell he was Chinese and not Dutch.

Each time they asked he answered "Neen," one word so they couldn't hear his accent, and kept rowing. A group of them began chasing him in a sloop. They shot from behind with their muskets but missed as he paddled zigzag through the waves. There was a bump as the sloop struck the little boat. The sailors were lashing the two vessels together. Their commander was about to come on board. Sait drew his knife.[28]

Cauw's secretary described in vivid terms what happened next:

> Just as the skipper was about to step into the little boat, the evil scoundrel rushed toward him and would have given him his end, as they say, with a knife, if it hadn't been for a brave sailor, who grabbed him and held him fast. Then the Chinaman, seeing that he'd fallen again into our hands, raised the same knife against himself and sliced his throat clean open with a single swipe, putting an end to his traitorous life.[29]

How could Sait, who was being held tight, have been able to wield a knife well enough to kill himself? Cauw didn't address this question.

Maybe Coyet, that fan of Descartes, was considered more skeptical, because his secretary recorded a more consistent report: when the Dutch soldiers stepped into the little boat, Sait had already slashed his throat, and "they found the heathen lying there smothered in his own blood."[30]

Maybe the Dutch soldiers killed him themselves and then reported the death as a suicide. It's possible. They were certainly in the mood for revenge. That morning, ten of their comrades had staggered one after the other to the fortress. They were in terrible pain, their faces and arms streaming with blood. Their right hands had been chopped off and tied to their waists with loops of string around the thumb, swaying as they walked. Their faces and heads were bloody because the ears and nose had been cut off.[31] This was a method Koxinga used when particularly frustrated with his enemies.[32]

The noseless soldiers had told how they were captured in a fight and then tied together thumb to thumb, toe to toe, and forced to stand that way for hours and hours. They'd been taken to Koxinga, who'd asked them questions about the fleet and how many cannons were on the ships. When they'd said that the large ones had thirty-five or thirty-eight or forty cannons and the small ones had twenty or twenty-four or twenty-six, he'd shaken his head.

Then Koxinga had sent them across the bay to Ma Xin, who'd forced them to kneel with their faces in the dirt while he ate a leisurely lunch, perhaps happy for vengeance because his own son had been killed by a Dutch grenade. After an hour in this position, they'd been fed, their

Chinese hosts shoving fish and rice and alcohol into their mouths because they couldn't move their hands. Finally they'd been brought out into a square in the ruined town. Their captors bent their right arms behind them and tied each man's thumb to a rope around his waist. Then they'd sliced off the noses. Then the ears. Then the right hands. The men were released still bleeding and told to go tell the other Dutch that this is how all of them would be treated when the castle was captured.[33]

So it's conceivable that Sait was killed by vengeful soldiers. But suicide is also possible. In fact, slitting one's throat was not uncommon in this period, as a way to avoid capture or torture or to show one's loyalty.[34] Once, when Koxinga's troops were fighting in China, they'd encountered an enemy general so loyal that he'd slit his own throat and thrown himself into a river to avoid capture. Koxinga, who prized such devotion, even when shown to his enemies, ordered the man brought in and cured by his own doctors and then appointed him to a high office.[35] Was Sait making a similar act of loyalty, perhaps to Koxinga, avoiding capture so he wouldn't reveal anything under torture? It's impossible to know. In fact, we don't know whether he was really a spy for Koxinga at all. Maybe he was just scared.

He certainly had good reason to be. Several days before, a Dutch surgeon had vivisected a Chinese prisoner. It happened on one of the ships that stood at anchor, although not the one Sait was on. While sailors and soldiers looked on, the surgeon, with permission from the ship's captain, began by demonstrating how one might remove a cataract, taking a needle to the victim's eyes. Then he drilled a hole in the man's head. Then he made incisions on either side of the man's groin, explaining, as he went, various medical points. He cut off the right leg below the knee, the left hand, and the top of the head. Finally, he cut open the chest and stomach so the audience could see the heart and the lungs in action. Afterward, he'd thrown the body into the ocean.[36] Sait probably heard about this gruesome experiment. Fleeing might have seemed the safest course of action.

As for whether he was spying for Koxinga, there's no way to know. Certainly it doesn't seem to have been the case the first time he arrived. His idea about how to defeat Koxinga—to blockade Taiwan—was right on, and it was repeated by many other defectors. And the anger he'd expressed about Koxinga corroborates other evidence about how much the people of Taiwan were chafing under Koxinga's rule. Koxinga's desperation for food led him to seize crops and belongings from Chinese inhabitants on Taiwan, costing him their trust and cooperation. Many people—especially the Chinese farmers who'd done so well under Dutch rule—might have wished that the Dutch were still in power. Taxation had been clear and calculable. Hard work had resulted in profits. Food had been plentiful. Maybe Sait was different from them only in his willingness to act.

Still, his behavior when he arrived the second time—coming from the Chinese encampment in view of the sentries—was suspicious. Maybe something happened when he left the fortress as a spy for the Dutch. Maybe he was captured by Chinese soldiers as he crept through the reeds. Maybe he found soldiers waiting in his house when he got back home. Maybe Koxinga forced him to return as a spy, keeping his family hostage. Maybe he'd even met the two African boys when he'd been in Zeelandia City waiting to come back to Zeelandia Castle.

All we know is that the Dutch crew pulled his body up out of the blood, threw it into the waves, and brought the rowboat back where it belonged.[37] Sait was not mentioned again.

Two days later, the boys were brought before Coyet and Cauw and the other Dutch officials for a test. As they stood there in their chains, eight Chinese men were brought out and arranged in a line facing forward. The boys were told to pick out the men they'd accused of being false defectors. They didn't know that four of the Chinese in the lineup were wealthy merchants, friends of the Dutch who'd been asked to put on dirty clothes and muss their hair so they looked like common Chinese.[38]

The boys pointed out two of these merchants and said they'd worked in the same house with them and that their master Ma Xin had sent them here to spy. Are you sure? Coyet asked. Yes, the boys said. Concluding that the boys were liars, Coyet sent them away in chains.

Sait had died for nothing.

IGNORING ADVICE

Sait had urged Coyet not to launch his naval attack in the Bay of Taiwan, saying that Coyet should instead mount a blockade of the island.

Coyet had ignored that advice. But other defectors were urging the same thing. As one defector noted, Koxinga's soldiers are "dependent on supplies from China . . . which we [the Dutch] must try to intercept. In this way, by just sitting here doing nothing but keeping the rice from coming to Taiwan, we'd starve them out, indeed, they'd not be able to survive, and in addition, if news of such a blockade reached China then everyone there would be too afraid to come here."[39] Another defector said that this was the general opinion and that nearly everyone agreed "that if [the Dutch] can shut off the supply from outside, [Koxinga's troops] would all have to die from hunger."[40] Coyet had rejected the idea before. He continued rejecting it now.

Why did Coyet and his comrades fail to mount a serious blockade? Perhaps their fleet had been too weakened by defeat. They'd lost two ships and others were damaged. But that still left eight ships, which would seem to be enough to spread a net and intercept rice junks sailing toward the Bay of Taiwan. Indeed, as defectors pointed out, the mere fact that the Dutch were mounting a blockade would scare merchants, make them unlikely to brave the difficult and dangerous voyage, because Dutch ships were renowned for being deadly interceptors on the high seas.

Chinese sources make this clear, noting how the Dutch sat up in their crow's nests scanning the horizons. One, published by Koxinga's own clan, notes that the Dutch sit atop their tall masts, where they're able to keep a strong watch (see figure 7).[41] A later account describes how "several people sit on the peak of the mast, set up a telescope, and survey the four directions. Even if a merchant ship is a hundred *li* away, they see it and immediately turn their rudder for pursuit, and no one can escape them."[42] Another source notes that "one man would sit at the top of the mast with a telescope, looking out at the distance in the four directions. If there was a merchant ship, then they'd lower five or six of its small launches, with each boat having six or seven people, waiting for the merchant ship to arrive, and then surrounding and trapping them. . . . Those on the oceans greatly feared encountering them."[43]

The Chinese attributed Dutch interception abilities to the odd rigging of Dutch ships. The early Zheng clan account describes "rigging that is all tangled, forming something that resembles silkworm's silk or a spider web."[44] This rigging contrasted greatly with the simple rigging of Chinese sails, and Chinese observers felt it conferred on Dutch ships an ability to sail against the wind much more effectively than Chinese junks: "They have sails that spiral like a spider's web, receiving wind from eight directions, so there's nowhere they go that is not favorable. Compare this with Chinese sails and masts. When they encounter a contrary wind, they must bend over to the left and then to the right, leaning dangerously, and thus, winding and wending, they must slowly make their way dangerously forward. The two kinds of ships are as different as Heaven and earth."[45]

So the Chinese defectors, who shared a respect for Dutch ships and their lethal abilities, must have thought it obvious that Coyet would want to deploy his tall, far-seeing ships to mount a deadly blockade.

But it wasn't so easy. European ships often had a hard time catching junks. The same Chinese writer who wrote about the spider web rigging's ability to sail into the wind, also noted that his friend, a junk captain, knew ways to outrun Dutch ships:

> Although [Dutch] sails are clever, the cleverness is limited to contrary winds. In favorable winds they are not so good. A thing cannot be ingenious in all aspects—this is simply a principle of nature. If a Chinese ship runs swiftly with favorable winds, [the Dutch ship] will fall behind. So when being pursued by a red-hair's ship, one should simply turn the rudder and run with the wind and thus one can outrun them. Against the wind, however, their ships seldom lose.[46]

Coyet and his advisors knew that Koxinga's rice junks could sail faster in some conditions. Maybe they felt that a blockade wouldn't work. On the other hand, that was their best remaining option.

Eventually they did begin discussing the idea. When Coyet heard from a defector that rice junks were on their way, he sent a mini-flotilla—just three ships—to cruise between Penghu and Taiwan, advising the captain to look out for rice junks and try to prevent them from landing.[47] But another defector later said that the Chinese captains learned about the interceptors and decided to take other routes.

After this, Coyet and his advisors began talking about a more systematic blockade, considering the idea of preventing Koxinga's ships from sailing into the Deer's Ear Gap.[48] They asked the captains of the ships that remained at anchor whether that might be possible and received a positive reply.[49]

By then it was too late. That very day, twenty-three Chinese junks sailed right into the Deer's Ear Gap and anchored in front of the Eastern Capital.

Did the junks carry rice? The ass-slapping Swissman had the answer. He called out from the covered market across the plain.

"Hey sentries!" he said, "Lick my ass!"

That got their attention.

"Did you dogs see the junks that came today?" he said. "You Dutch won't be doing any more torturing or burning!"

"Wait 'til we get our hands on you, you Godforsaken!" said the watchmen.

"Shit on your God!" said the Swissman. "I dare you to come over here! You'll all be hanged. I'll deflower all the Dutch women, wives and maids alike. Soon I'll be drinking samsoe in your little fort and holding court, and your governor will have to bow before me. Why don't you shoot? Shit on your gunner! You're all out of gunpowder!"

They fired a cannon at him.

"Ha! Lick my ass! Go ahead and shoot again! Are you hungry? Tired of eating rotten meat? All out of arak? I've got plenty right here. Want some?"

He continued in this vein, using words that, alas, weren't recorded because they were considered "so foul that decency does not allow them to be put on paper."[50] Then he spat on the ground and disappeared behind a wall.[51]

A few days later, a Chinese prisoner confirmed that twenty of the newly arrived junks carried rice for Koxinga's troops.[52] Koxinga had survived another crisis, helped, once again, by good fortune or, as he saw it, the Will of Heaven. He ordered his generals to prepare a new assault on Zeelandia Castle.

Koxinga Closes In

If you visit the ruins of Zeelandia Castle today in Tainan City, you might park near a hill of Chinese graves a hundred meters to the southwest. If you climb that hill, picking your way through the dense tombs, you'll find yourself looking down at black-haired tourists posing for photographs in front of the old walls. Clearly, this hill, or one like it, would be just where you'd want to put your cannons if you wanted to attack the fortress. Beneath your feet, between the graves, you might find old red bricks with bits of seashell mortar stuck to them. These bricks may once have belonged to a little redoubt that the Dutch built to protect the large fortress below. It was called the Redoubt Utrecht.

Koxinga knew that if he could capture the redoubt and place his cannons on the hill, the main castle below would be at his mercy. But how to get close? On top and thrusting through gaps in the redoubt's stone wall were huge cannons that commanded a wide swath of area. He would have to be careful picking a place, or his cannons would be hit twice as hard from above as they could strike from below.

He and his officers studied the area. On the outskirts of Zeelandia City, just across the plain from Zeelandia Castle, stood the covered market that his African musketeers had been using as a sniper's nest. Just south of it, behind what had once been a lumberyard, lay an empty lot that offered a clear view of the redoubt. Cannons placed there could easily strike it, and although the redoubt would be able to fire back, the position had the advantage of being protected from the cannons of the main castle. Koxinga's commanders decided to attack the redoubt from this lot. It seems that one of them was so sure of success that he bet his life he could capture the redoubt with a thousand cannonballs and forty bales of powder.[1]

It was a sunny morning at the end of September when Koxinga tried this for the first time. The attack took the Dutch by surprise—not just its audacity but also its effectiveness. There were three cannons in the redoubt that could target the new Chinese battery: two on the roof and one inside. But Koxinga's battery had three large cannons and several smaller ones. They opened fire all at once, aiming at the places where Dutch cannon muzzles showed.[2] The Dutch garrison couldn't come close to matching their rate of fire. And the Chinese gunners were accurate. "The enemy," wrote Coyet's secretary, "was so good at aiming, that none of our men dared to show himself up above."[3]

The two cannons on top of the redoubt were soon rendered useless, blasted from their wheels. The Dutch couldn't man the cannon below either, because the corner in the wall from which it poked out was only two stones thick and cannonballs were smashing right through it, blasting the Dutch gunners with stone and shrapnel.[4] "If we do not do something soon," wrote Coyet's secretary, "they'll breach the redoubt. We cannot hit their battery from here [i.e., from the main castle], so they are free to just keep on shooting easily and constantly, destroying the whole rampart on that side, so that no one can last up above."[5]

By nightfall, the redoubt's walls were already weakening.[6] A Chinese defector who arrived the next day had bad news. He said that the order to fire on the redoubt had come directly from Koxinga, who was planning to build more batteries even closer to the redoubt. He intended to blast the redoubt to the ground and build a battery on its hill to aim down at the castle.[7] Sure enough, the Dutch noticed that the Chinese were hauling cannons from Zeelandia City.[8]

What could Coyet do? It wasn't enough to just reinforce the redoubt, although he did order soldiers and workers to go out at night and restore the ramparts thicker than before. There just wasn't enough firepower in the redoubt to counter the new Chinese battery.

Coyet's military officers advised building a new fortification at the base of the redoubt, on the same tall hill, large enough for six cannons, with sand-filled walls nine feet thick.[9] This, they assured him, would "silence the enemy's guns."[10] Coyet sent eight carpenters to oversee the work and a hundred soldiers to help dig and haul, but it was clear that Koxinga's cannons could destroy faster than the workers could build.[11]

Coyet wondered whether Dutch musketeers could even the playing field. So far, musketeers had lost every direct engagement they'd had with Koxinga's soldiers, who proved much more disciplined. But Coyet decided to use them as snipers. Since they'd be hidden, discipline wouldn't be such an issue. He ordered fifty of them to find nests behind the crumbling walls of the abandoned hospital, which lay to the south of Zeelandia Castle near the oyster banks, just between the redoubt and the new Chinese cannon placement, and shoot at Chinese gunners through the holes where Chinese cannon muzzles thrust through.

It worked. "Praise God," wrote Cauw's secretary, "this was so successful that none of the enemy had the heart to get near their cannons, even though our men could hear their officers trying to drive them to their positions with beatings and thrashings."[12]

All day, Dutch muskets kept the Chinese gunners from their cannons. But when night fell the musketeers left, and Koxinga's men dug all night long to prepare a nasty surprise. They buried five huge bales of gunpowder where the musketeers had been hiding and laid down a long subterranean fuse: bamboo pipes filled with gunpowder that stretched all the way to Zeelandia City.

Then they waited. Koxinga had used landmines for years in China. When they worked they were devastating, but you had to wait until just the right time to set them off.[13] In the Battle of Haicheng in 1653, the most important battle in Koxinga's life, his troops had gotten the timing just right. Qing troops were crossing the river and massing on the bank, unaware that they were standing on hundreds of pounds of buried powder. Koxinga's gunpowder specialists waited until nearly all the Manchus were on shore and only then set off the mines. The enemy "was completely burned to death, their abandoned bodies filling the water."[14]

Koxinga hoped to replicate that success here on Taiwan. In the morning, as Coyet's musketeers marched back toward their hiding place, Koxinga's gunpowder experts stood ready to ignite the fuse. But the musketeers hadn't quite reached their sniper nests when it went off and the ground erupted, blast after blast, in a line heading from Zeelandia City toward the old hospital. At the end came a tremendous explosion, with mud and sand blasting into the air. The musketeers might all have been killed if it had gone off at the right time. They speculated that maybe the fuses had gone off by mistake, that perhaps a spark from a Chinese cannon had landed on the detonation line.[15] They thanked God and began shooting.

By evening, the workers had finished the new fortification beneath the redoubt. "It's a large and beautiful piece of work," Cauw's secretary wrote, "built up against the redoubt itself, reinforced with crates filled with sand on the corners and where the shooting holes are."[16] How well would it hold against Koxinga's cannons? Just fine. A Chinese cannonball struck it and didn't even go halfway in.[17]

And that was that. Koxinga and his officers couldn't think of a way to get around the new Dutch battery.

They tried a different angle.

KOXINGA FORTIFIES BAXEMBOY

If he couldn't capture the castle directly, Koxinga thought he could at least cut it off more effectively. The Dutch were landing supplies with maddening impunity. Not only had they received provisions from Cauw's fleet, but they'd begun sending raiding missions out to bring back firewood, coconuts, vegetables, and livestock.[18] Dutch ships were too powerful to attack directly, so Koxinga decided to try to keep the loading boats from sailing back and forth between the stone pier in front of the lower fortress and the ships' anchorage outside the bay. All he needed to do was to place cannons on the other side of the Channel, on the southern shore of Baxemboy Island.

Small groups of Chinese officials began landing there. Coyet and his officials watched them, deducing from the parasols held over their heads that some were of high rank. From beneath their sunshades they stared at the castle, pointing and gesticulating.[19] Chinese sampans took soundings in the Channel, determining where it was deep and where it was shallow.[20] Chinese troops began disembarking near the ruins of the Dutch fort that had been destroyed in the Extreme and Terrifying Storm of 1656. There hadn't been this much Chinese activity on Baxemboy since the beginning of the war, when Chen Ze had killed Thomas Pedel.

Coyet wanted to lay an ambush for the Chinese officials who were overseeing the activities, but Cauw said that was impractical.[21] So Koxinga's men kept working, and one morning in late October the Dutch awoke to an unpleasant surprise: "At dawn," wrote Cauw's secretary, "we saw to our amazement that the previous night the enemy had completed a new fortification on Baxemboy right across from the castle. When they place their cannons there, they'll be able to hit all of the houses standing along the side of the lower castle's courtyard. This is truly a nasty and troubling turn of events, especially because all of our vessels are anchored, loaded, and unloaded right in front of this gate. This, needless to say, can no longer occur."[22]

How could the Dutch respond? Cauw and Coyet and the other officials agreed that they must launch an attack to destroy the fort before the Chinese could install their cannons. So under the midday sun, a hundred and seventy Dutch soldiers were rowed across the Channel to Baxemboy, while Dutch cannons fired from the castle. But the grass on the banks was high and Koxinga's soldiers were so numerous with their helmets and flags that the Dutch soldiers couldn't get ashore. The Dutch galiot the *Red Fox* fired at the nearest Chinese force, but they all suddenly dropped to the ground like modern Marines and waited for orders. A signal was given and they at once rose up again and ran for cover, hiding in the grass.[23] The Dutch troops turned back.

The new works got bigger and more elaborate. Koxinga himself arrived on Baxemboy to oversee operations. His tent—blue linen with white stripes—appeared in a new encampment on Baxemboy Island, pitched on a dune.[24] Through telescopes, the Dutch watched his troops muster before him, marching around the hill in their armor.[25] Under his supervision the fort began to take the form of a European one, with thrusting angles reminiscent of renaissance forts.[26] Had he learned from his attack of Zeelandia Castle? Had the foulmouthed Swiss defector helped him?

Cannons were installed, twenty in all. Several pointed out toward the sea to control the entrance to the Channel, but the rest were aimed at the castle. Among them were guns so powerful that Koxinga's men worshipped them. They were known as Spirit Cannons, and they had a divine origin, or so the story goes.[27]

Once upon a time Koxinga's uncle Zheng Hongkui was garrisoned at a place called Jieyang Bay in southern China. Late at night he saw a glow coming from beneath the water's surface. He thought maybe he was hallucinating, but the next night it was there again. He sent divers to investigate. "It's a luminous entity," they said, "around ten feet long. It has two handles, but it's hard to say how heavy it might be." He sent them back out, and they returned again with more information: "It's two massive cannons with handles in the shape of dragons." He had them dredged up. They were found to be brass guns weighing ten thousand pounds each. He tried them out. They shot cannonballs of twenty-four pounds, and were miraculously accurate. "If one prayed and shot there was nothing they wouldn't hit."[28] They were even said to be able to hit targets two or three kilometers away. The cannons' first test in warfare was a resounding success. They blasted to bits the walls of an enemy fortress, whose defenders immediately surrendered, "saying that these were supernatural items."[29]

The story sounds like pure fabrication, but it may have a historical basis. In the late Ming period, officials in southern China made a practice of salvaging artillery from European wrecks.[30] In one Ming source, an official describes personally overseeing a salvage operation, rowing out in a boat to the wooden sea platform he'd had constructed and supervising divers as they fastened ropes around the handles to hold them in place while they carefully removed rock and sand. Eventually the cannons were free enough to be winched up with a huge wooden crane. The official exulted when the two massive guns were finally on shore: "The cannons gleamed bright and brilliant, sparkling, so that the people around found them to be rare and marvelous objects."[31] This passage—with its description of the gleaming cannons—is strikingly similar to the story of the discovery of the Spirit Cannons. It's also intriguing that uncle Hongkui was said to have dredged the Spirit Cannons up in the far south of China, not far from where the historical cannons were salvaged. There's a good chance that these Spirit Cannons came from Dutch or British wrecks.

However he got them, uncle Hongkui gave them to Koxinga, who used them in his campaigns. At one point they were nearly lost. In 1658, when Koxinga's loud soldiers woke the blind dragons and aroused a typhoon, the Spirit Cannons sank. He executed the man who'd been in charge of them and ordered that they be recovered. They were dredged up a second time.[32]

Now, it seemed, these monstrous cannons were pointed at Zeelandia Castle. The Dutch watched from the castle as Koxinga's men held a special ceremony. First they burned offerings. Then a gong sounded. Then the new fort's small cannons started shooting blank shots. Then, all at once, the huge pieces spewed forth. It wasn't an attack—just a bravade or initiation, done, in Cauw's words, "as though in play."[33] The cannonballs flew over the castle, causing no damage.

The damage came later. The besieged in Zeelandia used to spend a lot of time on the stone docks, washing, doing laundry, or just going to the wooden outhouses that hung out over the Channel. But when Koxinga's troops started aiming their cannons in earnest, these activities became lethal. A servant girl doing the wash was hit in the leg and died.[34] A slave woman was struck so hard that a chunk of her flesh flew over the wall and landed in the fortress. She died too.[35] A Dutchman trying to bring firewood in by boat was struck in the nether regions, the cannonball "taking away most of the flesh in that region, including one testicle, but without hitting the legs themselves."[36] These people were all outside the walls, but the cannons could also strike targets within the castle, as when one shot pierced the wall of the governor's office, setting off a blizzard of fine white plaster dust, so that "the clerks working there looked more like flour millers than men of the pen."[37]

More importantly, the fort was achieving Koxinga's aim of sealing Zeelandia Castle off from the sea. It wasn't so much that the cannons could hit Dutch vessels directly, although they did do this, striking the loading boat and shooting off its rudder.[38] It was that the fort extended the range of Koxinga's own navy. Under its cover his vessels could now navigate the Channel.

The Channel itself was a narrow band of deepwater bordered on each side by sandy shallows, with tricky bends and turns that changed with each storm. These were conditions ideally suited to Koxinga's deadly shallow-water attack boats, a unit of his navy that had been developed for river warfare. One of Koxinga's generals, a man named Huang An[39] who'd once served under the genius admiral Shi Lang, systematized this shallow-warfare unit, and this is how he is said to have described the vessels to Koxinga in seeking his approval for them:

> In the high seas, naval forces must use huge ships, using the wind to attack and press forward, but now we must fight on the rivers, where the wind is slight and the currents intense and where our great ships can't tack forward fast enough. I propose that we pair a dozen or so huge cannon ships with specialized little boats. Each boat will use two long sculling poles, one on each side, as well as eight lighter oars. In front of each of these lighter oars will be mounted a cannon, and at the front of each little boat will be a larger cannon. When encountering the enemy, each little boat will first fire the large cannon and then use its oars to spin around so the right side can fire its guns. Then, when the right side has fired, the boat will spin round again so the left side can fire. . . . In this way, all our boats will come flying in and attacking the enemy, leaving none of his ships undamaged.[40]

Koxinga was impressed with this proposal and adopted it at once. The little vessels proved effective against Qing forces in China.

Now the new battery on Baxemboy allowed Koxinga to deploy them in the Channel. When the Dutch loading boat ventured out from the pier, the little boats swarmed in and attacked, while the new fort provided covering fire. Cauw was astonished by the speed and agility of these boats. "They're so fast, quick, and light, that they can venture easily into the shallowest waters, even two and a half or three feet deep. On each side they have two heavy oars, and one behind to serve as a rudder, and they use them to great effect, spinning and twirling like a top, so fast and able that they're a wonder to behold."[41]

Compared to these agile vessels, the Dutch loading boat was slow and ponderous. It hung up on a sandbar, and the oared boats pressed in, "astonishingly full of people."[42] The Dutch crew fled. The Chinese climbed aboard, stealing pots and pans and capturing a Dutch carpenter who'd stayed behind trying to recover money from his sea chest. The Dutch warships raised their anchors and tried to sail in closer to fire their cannons. The Chinese boarders abandoned their prize, but the Dutch couldn't think of a way to safely reclaim it. They decided it would be better to sacrifice the loading boat than have it fall into Chinese hands permanently. So a few Dutchmen went aboard to set a fuse to its powder stores, piling mattresses nearby to catch flame. They rowed away and watched as the Chinese boats came up alongside again.

There was an explosion, and thick clouds of smoke piled above the deck. They thought they'd "let the red rooster in," as Cauw's secretary put it, using a proverb for arson.[43] But no. The explosion just jarred the loading boat free from the sandbar and sent it drifting toward the other Dutch ships. It was aflame, "with no sailors and only the Almighty as its steerman."[44] A brave Dutch skipper leapt aboard and threw the burning mattresses overboard. He managed to extinguish the flames.

The Dutch managed to recover the loading boat, but the battle left them shaken. Zeelandia Castle depended on supplies from outside. Koxinga's new coastal fort, combined with these frightful attack boats, gave the Chinese control over the Channel. Zeelandia Castle was cut off. It couldn't even communicate with the fleet that lay just offshore.

What else could Coyet do? He'd tried attacking the fort. That hadn't worked. He'd tried using the powerful Dutch ships to cover the Channel. That hadn't worked. He and his colleagues tried a succession of other measures. They armed each of the loading boats, filling them with firebombs and grenades, cannons and musketeers, and only let them venture in or out of the Channel when the tide and current were right, and then only in convoys, threatening with death any sailor who might disobey this order.[45] That didn't work. They tried building a new cannon placement in front of the castle, pointing out toward Baxemboy. That at least protected the inhabitants of Zeelandia Castle from attack as they washed or went to the bathroom, since it had a blind that "stretched out to the—to put it delicately—public conveniences that stand there on the waterside."[46]

But the basic problem remained: Koxinga's ships could sail deep into the Channel, and Dutch cannonfire had no effect. As Cauw's secretary wrote, "they're completely cutting off our boats from sailing in or out, putting this castle into the greatest danger."[47]

RENAISSANCE ARCHITECTURE TO THE RESCUE

In exasperation, Coyet called a meeting with his military commanders. "Although," he said, "we've tried shooting at the junks with the new battery on the shore beneath the castle, and also from the ships outside the Channel, they just sit there, unharmed."[48] What, he asked, should they do?

The officers proposed a new fort. A hundred yards west of the castle, behind the redoubt, a sandy beach flanked the entrance to the Channel. They believed that a fort placed there would be able to keep the attack boats at bay. They sketched out plans for a small renaissance fort, with two diamond-shaped bastions that met in the middle, forming what would look from above a bit like a bowtie. It would hold six large cannons and several smaller ones, with wood-encased earthen walls ten feet thick.[49] The bastions would afford a wide field of fire, but most guns would aim along the length of the Channel to target the attack boats.

Workers, motivated by extra wages, made quick progress. Soon Cauw was supervising the movement of huge bronze cannons, a job he undertook at night so the Chinese couldn't see and, as he wrote, so that "when the enemy shows himself in the Channel again we can give him a nice morning surprise."[50]

An opportune morning soon arrived. When a small convoy of Dutch boats detached themselves from the stone pier in front of the castle and sailed slowly out toward the anchorage, a flotilla of attack boats raced out after them, followed by ten larger cannon junks. Dutch gunners waited until the boats had nearly reached the Dutch vessels and then opened fire from their new fort. Cannons in the castle and the anchored warships also roared forth. The attack boats were beset by cannonballs, their crews strafed repeatedly with shrapnel. They retreated. The Dutch convoy got through.[51]

The next day, when another Dutch convoy sailed through the Channel, the attack boats didn't even make an attempt. "It seems clear," wrote Cauw's secretary, "that yesterday the enemy was hosted and entertained in such a way that he no longer has a desire to set sail or any interest in showing himself, but rather prefers to stay moored. He is still shooting a lot from his huge fort on Baxemboy, firing at our boats and at the castle, but for the most part without causing any damage."[52] From that point, the Channel was safe for Dutch ships.[53]

The Dutch, masters of renaissance fortification, had checked Koxinga again, but the victory didn't bring much peace to Coyet. The castle was running out of firewood and fresh food. Illness was increasing again, even as the nights got colder.

Then two leaky Dutch ships arrived at anchor with miraculous news. Their commander, David Harthouwer, had made contact with the Manchus, who wanted to ally with the Dutch against Koxinga.

The Accidental Embassy

When David Harthouwer's leaky ship sailed into an unknown bay, he had no intention of opening one of the most unlikely alliances in world history, between the Calvinist merchants of Holland and the Buddhist Qing Dynasty. It was a potential turning point in the Taiwan War, and it was pure happenstance.

In fact, Harthouwer hadn't wanted to command any expedition at all. He'd been begging Coyet to let him resign his post as senior merchant in Taiwan, saying that his wife and kids were in a "situation of complete desolation" and asking for permission to take them back to Batavia. Coyet had said no because he needed Harthouwer's help. In the far north of Taiwan, two Dutch forts still perched on the edge of the ocean. They needed rescuing, and Coyet felt Harthouwer was the only man fit for the job. In the fall of 1661 he ordered him to sail north at once to save the people, take the cannons, and salvage the doors, planks, and windows,[1] and then blow up the walls so Koxinga wouldn't be able to use them.[2]

The usual route to northern Taiwan followed the treacherous western coast of Taiwan, where shoals and sandbars stretched invisibly under the sea, shifting with each storm. If you ran aground, the natives might cut off your head and use it to decorate one of their men's lodges, and Koxinga's junks would certainly be hiding in coves and inlets. But most worrisome of all was the weather. It was autumn, and the southern monsoon was nearly over. Once the northern winds started it would be hard to make headway. Worst of all, it was typhoon season, and the deadliest storms spin in September and October, just when Harthouwer was embarking.

Harthouwer's three-ship flotilla labored up the Taiwan coast, and, sure enough, the winds began blowing hard from the north. He'd been allowed to choose his flagship and had made a bad choice, picking a large war-yacht called the *Hasselt* that had a tendency to tip to the side.[3] The other two ships weren't much better, having been damaged in Coyet's foolish attack in the bay. All three were short of rigging, ropes, and anchors.

They were making no progress, and conditions were getting worse. Waves swamped the deck. Harthouwer decided to turn back to Zeelandia Castle, arriving there after a harrowing sail—water leaking into the hold, sailors pumping and bailing to stay afloat (figure 24).

Coyet didn't even let him come ashore. A letter was rowed out to the anchorage saying that Harthouwer must leave again at once. This time, Coyet wrote, Harthouwer should take a different route, northward along the Chinese coast, using "land winds" to make headway against the northerlies.[4] Coyet's official records pitch a note of confidence about the expedition, but Coyet's disgruntled rival, Admiral Cauw, was more candid, musing that Coyet and his advisors actually didn't have much hope that Harthouwer would complete the journey.[5]

En route to the Chinese coast, Harthouwer stopped in the Penghu Islands to fill the *Hasselt* with ballast stone, hoping to make it more stable, but his bad luck continued. As a group of sailors and slaves started loading the hold, a group of his crewmembers went ashore to steal food from Chinese farmers. They ran into a Chinese patrol. There were sixty Dutchmen and only thirty Chinese soldiers, who were accompanied by a group of armed Chinese peasants. It should at least have been a balanced fight, but when the Dutch musketeers began shooting in volleys, the Chinese held formation, seven banners waving. "In no time at all," Harthouwer wrote, "our men lost all order and ran for the water, where tall waves swamped them one after the other." Thirty-six men were drowned, captured, or killed. It was one of the costliest battles in the war, and Harthouwer blamed it squarely on cowardice: "When our soldiers saw the enemy's bright swords and

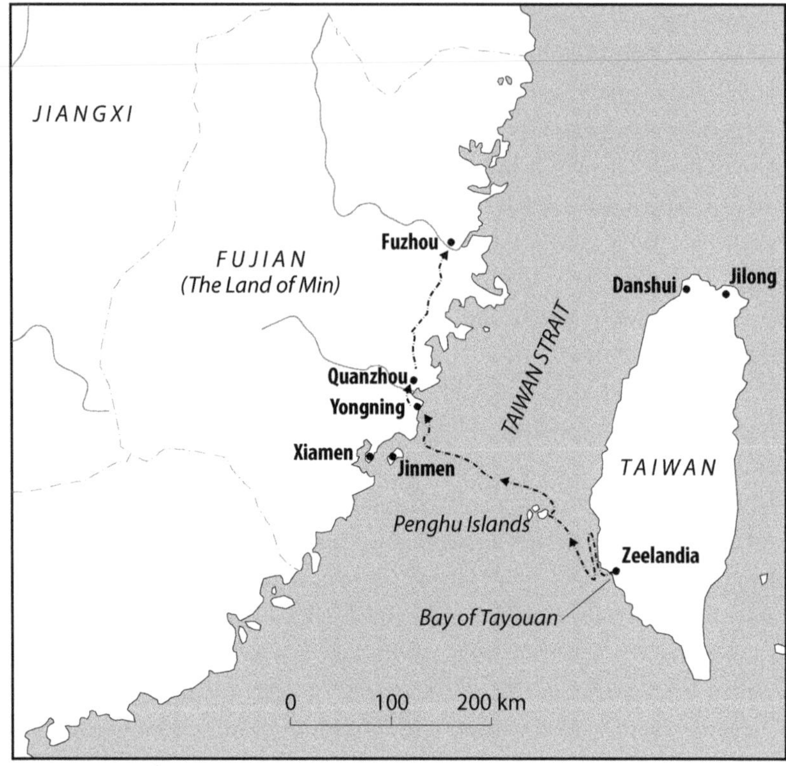

Figure 24. Hurt and Clewerck's harrowing voyage, October and November 1661.

helmets flashing in the sun, their faces became as white as death. They couldn't even use their guns."[6] The Dutch troops, for all their vaunted musket discipline, didn't maintain their ranks. Once again, European muskets lost the field to Koxinga's troops with their bows and arrows and lances and swords.

There was no time for grief. Harthouwer set sail again, unhappy to find that a hull full of stone didn't keep the *Hasselt* from leaking and listing.[7] As they approached the Chinese coast and pointed their prows northward, the weather got worse. Gusts of wind pelted them with rain. Swells smashed against the sides of the ships, rolling them up and down.

Harthouwer wasn't just worried about the weather. These were contested waters. Koxinga's junks might attack. And who knew what the Manchus might do if they spotted a foreign fleet so close to their shores in a time of war?

THE BAY

The clouds made it impossible for Harthouwer to check his latitude, so he didn't know where he was, but when the wind worked itself into a rainy gale, he gave the order to find shelter. The three ships sailed into a small semicircle of a bay, three or four kilometers across and ringed with a long sandy beach. Some fishing boats bobbed in the water.[8] On the northern side, near the bay's wide mouth, stood a fortified town. As they cast anchor, crowds of people gathered on the walls and began waving. They didn't seem hostile, but it was impossible to talk to them because the water was too wild to send out a ship's launch.

In the age of sail, when any plan could be dashed by a strong wind, a good manager planned thoroughly and pessimistically. Coyet might have lacked people skills, but he was methodical and meticulous. The detailed orders he prepared for Harthouwer read like a flow chart, plotting responses to every contingency he could imagine. Consulting his orders, Harthouwer knew that if he were forced to call in Manchu territory, he should try to make contact and buy provisions for Zeelandia Castle. Coyet had provided Harthouwer with a secret weapon: four Qing refugees.

The foursome had been rescued months before from a derelict junk Cauw's fleet had found drifting in the open sea. Although most of the passengers on the wreck had had long hair, indentifying them as subjects of Koxinga, these four men had had shaven heads with long Qing-style braids.[9] They said they'd been captured by Koxinga and imprisoned on this junk, which had then been attacked by pirates, lit on fire, and set adrift. So Cauw had taken special care of the men. The other Chinese on the wreck were used as slaves and thrown overboard when they got "filthy sick,"[10] but these four men were fed and clothed and taken back to Taiwan. Just before Harthouwer had left, they'd been transferred to his flagship, so that he could use them to open communication with the Manchus, if the occasion arose, sending them ashore as "happy evidence of our good intentions."[11]

The refugees told Harthouwer that they recognized this bay. In fact, their homes were near here. The town with the castle, they said, was called Yongning.[12] It was under Qing control, and they said they even knew the names of the castle's commanders. Harthouwer decided that there was no way to send them ashore now, because the wind was too high and the sea too rough, and, in any case, his first duty was to complete his mission and rescue the Netherlanders in northern Taiwan, who might be starving to death. So he noted the events in his log and then gave the order to set sail.

But it seemed like the elements wanted him to stay. The wind blew harder and forced him back into the bay. This time he found thirty warjunks there, and as he sailed in, one of them pulled up alongside his flagship. Its crew made threatening gestures, yelling that he must leave at once. He complied.

Yet for a third time, the wind drove him into the bay. This time, as though he'd accepted that fate wanted him to stay, he sailed resolutely in, anchored where the waters were calmer, and dispatched the ship's launch toward the town with two of the shaven-headed refugees. As the little boat approached the beach, a crowd gathered. They seemed to be welcoming the men joyously.

Not everyone was so happy. A group of junks sailed out from a cove and advanced toward Harthouwer's ships. Two small vessels rowed right up close. They were filled with people, who began grabbing ropes hanging over the sides as though they were going to climb aboard. They claimed they wanted to trade, but Harthouwer found their eagerness unnerving. When he realized that they had long hair, he warned them to back off. They let go and rowed back, saying they'd come back to trade later. They didn't.

Shortly afterward, a wobbly boat see-sawed through the waves. The two refugees were back and had brought Qing envoys, who said that the commander of Yongning was delighted and would love to meet with the Dutch. The envoys warned Harthouwer that the junks in the bay belonged to Koxinga and had been raiding and robbing.

Harthouwer sent two Dutchmen ashore. Their names were Melchior Hurt and Jacob Clewerck. Hurt was an assistant merchant, the lowest rank of management in the Dutch East India Company, and

Clewerck was an accountant. They thought this assignment would be quick, that they'd be back at their normal jobs by nightfall. Instead, they were swept up on a journey deep into Manchu China, voyaging laboriously from one town to the next, until finally they found themselves bowing before one of the most powerful men in China, the Viceroy of Fujian, Prince Geng Jimao.[13] By that point they feared they might never return.

YONGNING

Their adventure started with a bang. As they got ready to row to shore, a fleet of Koxinga's junks sailed out to block their way. Harthouwer opened fire. It was no grand battle, but the powerful broadsides drove the vessels away and made an impression on the Qing commander, who had no ability to control the waters just outside his walls. Hurt and Clewerck's launch rowed through the choppy waves.

As the two men stepped onto the sand with their translator and white flag, horsemen dismounted and welcomed them. They offered their mounts for the ride to town. Hurt and Clewerck demurred politely, but the men insisted, so the Dutchmen climbed into the strange saddles and were led along the beach toward the town walls.[14]

By Chinese standards this was a small town, a minor outpost, but to the Dutchmen it was large and imposing.[15] The fortifications were extensive, with impressive battlements and shooting holes big enough for a man to stand up in. Outside the walls, fishermen's huts and farmers' shacks rose in clusters, and beyond the town, sweet potato fields stretched for miles inland.

They rode through a dilapidated gate and into rundown streets. Women stared from doorways, children in their arms, and the townsmen seemed poor—dirty and foul-smelling, their hair worn Manchu-style, shaved in the front. The houses were strange, made from a mixture of stone and clay with odd elements mortared in: shards of floor tiles and rough rocks. In some streets, half the buildings were in shambles, walls collapsing, red-tiled roofs caved in. It seemed that the town had been fought over, and the fighting must have gone street to street. Hurt and Clewerck didn't realize it, but this town had been the site of a notorious massacre in 1647, when Manchus had stormed through and slaughtered thousands of people.[16] There wasn't much sign of commerce—a few vegetable stands and fish stalls—which was disappointing, because the Dutchmen would have liked to use this opportunity to lay the groundwork for regular trade in staples and, eventually, Chinese silk and porcelain.

The commander's residence stood deep within the walls and was grander than the rest of the town. Its main receiving hall had tables arrayed for guests, and there were tall stone statues with weapons arrayed in front, an exotic but pleasing exhibit.[17] The commander invited them to sit in chairs to his right, which they were told was an honor extended only to grandees and friends from afar. Tea was served and drunk, and Hurt and Clewerck presented some gifts: stacks of linens from Guinea, cloth from India, and an ivory chest that held a sundial, a compass, and a bottle of fine Spanish wine.[18]

Their translator wasn't very good, but they managed to thank their host for letting them shelter in his bay and say that it would be helpful if they could call regularly in Qing ports to buy supplies. This would help them fight Koxinga, their common enemy. Already, Hurt said, Koxinga had been weakened by Dutch victories in Taiwan and his force was half of what it had been. Perhaps the Dutch and Qing could work together. With one strong strike on the Chinese coast, Koxinga could be defeated for good.[19]

The effect of this suggestion was immediate. The commander got out a brush and some paper and began writing an urgent letter to his superior, who was based in the prefectural capital of Quanzhou, several hours away. Once he finished, he asked Hurt and Clewerck to sign their names. They did. Then he had the idea of asking them to write a letter of their own. They did.[20]

They dined together, with thirty or so servants bringing food and drink. It was probably the best meal Hurt and Clewerck had had in months, but it ended in worry, because when they asked to go back to their ship, their host shook his head. This had been a mere snack. His servants were even now working to prepare a suitable dinner, with wine and entertainment so they could "be happy together." They must stay the night, he said. He insisted on it. They could go back tomorrow morning, once he'd received a reply from his superiors in Quanzhou.

Hurt and Clewerck explained that Harthouwer had been very clear in his instructions: they were supposed to return to their ship that afternoon so the expedition could get under way again before the northern winds got any stronger.

But, their host said, the feast had already been paid for. He'd put it together just for them. It would be impolite to leave. And, he said, if they left they might not come back, and he'd get in trouble with his superiors, who would think the Dutch had only come to spy.

He laid it on pretty thick. The two Dutchmen assented, writing a nervous little letter to Harthouwer: "We tried demurring time after time, politely, but ultimately, for the good of the Honorable Company, we felt we couldn't turn him down, and so we expect we'll see you tomorrow."[21]

Their enjoyment of the evening—when alcohol and food flowed freer than they'd had it for five months—was marred by the letter Harthouwer sent back: "We weren't at all pleased to hear that you've stayed on land, because we don't know what might happen to us in this bay, there being lots of junks that might attack."[22]

They awoke at dawn the next day to unsettling news: the "Great Mandarin of Quanzhou" insisted on their coming to see him at once. There were fast conferrals with Harthouwer, who reluctantly agreed that they must go. But, he said, you must make sure you're back on board tomorrow evening.[23] The Manchus said that that wouldn't be a problem, and so the two clerks found themselves part of a procession, trotting out of the town gates accompanied by twenty horsemen in fine dress, with a richly-garbed official to guide them.[24]

QUANZHOU

The party made its way through fields of potato farms and miles of rice paddies interspersed with villages. At dusk they came to the Jin River, wide and shallow, which they crossed via a long, ancient bridge made of huge slabs of stone, each piece twenty or thirty feet long.[25] When they reached the city, the gates were closed. They spent the night in a guesthouse so exposed to the north wind that they couldn't sleep.

Early the next morning, their arrival in Quanzhou became a parade. Throngs of people followed along, vying for a glimpse. Deep within the city was the magistrate's palace. They were led through various rooms into a hall where a man sat cross-legged on a velvet cushion, a line of advisors sitting in like fashion on his left. They bowed before him European-style and stood for a moment. A mat was spread on the ground and they were told to sit. They sat. People seemed to be waiting for something. Music played, announcing the arrival of a man they were told was the second-in-command. He made a grand entrance, with a large coterie and much pomp and circumstance.

The interview started. Hurt and Clewerck said they'd sailed into the Yongning Bay to bring home four Qing subjects whom the Dutch had rescued from Koxinga's claws, and they decided while they were here that they might as well try to enter into friendship with the Manchus, to see whether it might be possible to buy provisions in Manchu ports and perhaps coordinate in the war against Koxinga, attacking him from two sides at once. Really, they said, this was just an initial query. They had to get back to their ship so they could go rescue their compatriots.

To their consternation, the man said they couldn't go back, that they must instead proceed at once to the City of Fuzhou to see his superior, the Viceroy of Fujian Province. They protested, saying they had no authorization to go any farther, that they were expected back that very evening. They weren't prepared for a visit to such an august personage as the viceroy. We don't, they said, even have enough clothes to "beautify our naked bodies."[26] The man tried to calm them, saying that it was just three day's journey. They kept protesting, but he stopped listening.

They were led to a large house where, they were told, grandees took their pleasure, and where they'd be spending the night. But there was no repose. Word had spread and everyone wanted to see them, to talk to them, to touch and poke and prod them. "There was such a ridiculous amount of pulling and grabbing at our clothes that we thought we'd have nothing intact left to wear."[27]

The poking was interrupted by military officials who grilled them about Koxinga's forces: the size of his navy, the condition of his troops. How many ships did the Dutch have in Taiwan, and how many would be sent from Japan, from Batavia, and when would those ships arrive, and how many Dutch soldiers were on Taiwan, and how many cannons were in Zeelandia Castle? Hurt and Clewerck exaggerated Dutch troop strengths and inflated Dutch victories. When the officials got out a piece of paper and asked them to sketch a picture of Zeelandia Castle, they took a brush and drew it as best they could.

After the military men went away, the grabbers returned, pressing so close that, Hurt wrote, "we had trouble even breathing."[28] Hurt and Clewerck closed the door. The crowds broke through. They retreated into another room. The crowds pressed in, clutching and tearing at their clothes. "This unpleasant visiting continued well into the night, and even then we weren't left alone by our bodyguards and translator and caretakers, and for dinner we were given very little to eat, which we blame only on the servants, because Their Excellencies had commanded otherwise."[29]

The next morning they were told to get ready for the long trip to Fuzhou. Special conveyances had been prepared—covered palanquins—so they could sit in comfort and be carried by four men. Of course, their guides said, if they'd prefer to go on horseback, they were welcome to. Horses would have been faster, but Hurt and Clewerck said they didn't want to create any difficulties and it was all the same to them so whatever their hosts would like would be fine. After a series of delays, their palanquins were bobbing through the streets of Quanzhou.

Hurt and Clewerck were impressed by the roads, which were smooth and well-maintained, but they still made slow progress. They received invitations to dine and drink tea, and they felt they couldn't refuse. "The treated us with extraordinarily great friendship, and we couldn't repay them except with our thanks."[30] Sometimes they were forced to undergo long, grand receptions. In one town they were welcomed by a company of soldiers standing at attention with pennants and weapons.[31] The top official invited them into his residence. They demurred. He insisted. He seated them up on his dais next to him and gave them tea and food. After two hours with him the tired Dutchmen were invited to the home of the second-in-command, and the invitation was proffered with such enthusiasm that they couldn't refuse. He was keen to drink, "a business that these people are extraordinarily fond of,"[32] and filled their cups again and again. "It all went to our head, and we could barely see out of our eyes."[33] The party lasted until at least midnight, but eventually their host showed them to their cots, giving them "nice blankets and covers," so that finally, heads reeling, they lay down to sleep, "which, honestly, we'd much rather have done than drink cup after cup of their bad drink."[34]

But they liked the Manchus. "They're a kind and sociable people," wrote Hurt, "moderate in drink except when playing host."[35] "They wear thick robes buttoned under the arms and on the right breast. For a hat they wear a colored silk cap with a silk or fur decoration on top. Their heads are shaven bare except for the back, where they have a braid, which they roll up and fasten with a little pin. They wear their swords backward, with the hilt in back, whereas we wear ours with the hilt in front."[36]

Still, Hurt and Clewerck tried to hurry things along, relieved when there was no socializing to do, as when a local official was too sick in bed to greet them. They crossed over beautiful creeks and streams and cut through a land filled with rice paddies. They were impressed by the diligence of the farmers, who left no corner of land untended, although they were puzzled that a land this rich had so little livestock. The Dutch countryside was full of pigs and sheep and cows. Here they saw just oxen to pull plows and lots and lots of geese and chickens.

On the sixth day of this journey they'd been told would last three days, they arrived at the Min River. On the other side they could see the huge city of Fuzhou, nestled against green mountains and surrounded by massive walls.

FUZHOU

Crossing the river by ferry, they passed through a stone gate with forts on either side, and they thought they'd entered Fuzhou, but they were told, to their wonderment and consternation, that they weren't even in the main city yet.[37] On and on they were carried, along a straight and busy road that was so long that, Hurt wrote, "we felt we'd never get to the end."[38] This was the commercial district called Nantai, which stretched out below Fuzhou proper.

Eventually they arrived at another river, which they called the lower river, on the other side of which rose the walls of Fuzhou proper. A huge fleet of warjunks was moored below, sixty or so of them, some very large. They were told that this fleet was being prepared to attack Koxinga in conjunction with a large land force. Perhaps the Dutch would join in this attack with their powerful ocean ships.

As they were borne across a stone bridge, Hurt and Clewerck mused hopefully about Fuzhou's potential for commerce. "The river's very deep where we crossed it, and it runs out to sea, about 11 Dutch miles or so [75 kilometers]. We believe that our ships would be able to enter it, because the junks we saw there are also quite large and are able to sail all the way out to sea."[39]

They were carried through one gate and then across a plaza and through another gate. They were impressed. "It is," wrote Hurt, "a beautiful, huge, pleasant city, with elegant buildings and extraordinary shops selling all kinds of goods and wares."[40] It was also thickly populated. Crowds of "onlookers and clothes-pluckers" formed around them.

It was evening when they were finally led into a large, dark hall in a huge complex. A man sat cross-legged in a raised chair against one wall. He was Li Shuaitai, the Governor-General of Fujian Province. To his left, a row of advisors sat on the ground. The Dutchmen doffed their hats and kowtowed three times.[41] Li told them to put their hats back on and approach him.

He looked at them carefully. Then he gave an order. His advisors stood, gathered their robes about them, and moved to his other side. Servants spread a rug where they'd been sitting, and the Dutchmen were told to sit down. A table was brought and set in front of Li, who began eating alone. When he finished, more tables were brought in and he invited the guests to eat. Hurt and Clewerck must have looked self-conscious with their chopsticks, because Li told them not to be embarrassed, to eat according to their own fashion.[42]

After dinner he brought out a model of a European ship and asked if that was the type of ship the Dutch had. Yes, they said. And then, "for fun or because he wanted to see if we spoke out of one mouth, as it were," he called for an African[43] jester who spoke good Portuguese. The jester asked Hurt and Clewerck what nation they were from and why they'd come, to which Hurt and Clewerck replied that they'd already told His Excellency and didn't see any need to repeat themselves.

Then Governor-General Li signaled that the interview was over. Tomorrow, he said, they'd meet the Viceroy. That's when they'd be able to discuss trade.[44] Hurt and Clewerck were led to a horse stable, which they were told was to serve as their quarters for the night, and then, when they protested, to a room with no walls and then, after more protests, to a room "which was tiny, but had the advantage of freeing us from the press of curious crowds."[45]

The next morning they were awoken early and told to hurry and dress for their audience with His Highness the Viceroy of Fujian.[46] They hurried to get ready and then went outside to meet their escorts, who would soon convey them to His Highness's palace. They were kept waiting. Soon they were surrounded by an assertive crowd that began undoing their preparations: "Our hats were taken off our heads. They grabbed at our daggers, shirts, stockings, shoes—everything that was attached to us, no matter how small. They would have taken everything we had if we hadn't prevented it with force. They kept at it, pulling and tearing, and our clothes became so threadbare that you could barely recognize the fabric."[47]

They were left "in this wolves' mouth"[48] for an hour, and when they finally got under way again, they were waylaid by mounted warriors in splendid costume who shrieked in terrifying voices that everyone must clear the streets. Hurt and Clewerck's escorts rushed them into a nearby house, from which they watched a scene of incredible ostentation: silk flags, golden staves dragging and beating against the ground, umbrellas held high aloft, calligraphic signs with incomprehensible admonitions, loud instruments wailing and crying. At the center of the procession moved a beautiful covered palanquin bearing a mysterious personage. No one dared say anything until the whole procession was gone, but then they were told that it was the third most powerful person in the empire.[49] Hurt and Clewerck provide no Chinese or Manchu names for most of the people they met, so it's impossible to know for certain who the person in the palanquin was.

Finally they arrived at the viceroy's palace and were led through room after room to a beautiful hall where His Highness sat alone on a golden chair. Ten similar chairs stood empty to his right. The man on the throne was one of the most august personages in the empire, the

Jingnan Prince Geng Jimao, a man whose family was one of the first Chinese families to join the Manchus and which had fought against the Ming for decades. Now he was stationed in Fujian, with orders to work together with Li Shuaitai to root out Koxinga.

Hurt and Clewerck were late. They had no gifts or letters. Their clothes were in tatters. They kowtowed three times and were told to approach and sit on the bare floor below the throne.

The prince spoke. The translator translated: You are Dutch, are you not? Yes, replied Hurt and Clewerck. I know you're speaking the truth, he said, because I've met your nation before—when I was stationed in Tonkin. Have either of you been in Tonkin? Your nation was there five years, is that not so? And who were the Dutchmen in charge there at that time?

This was a strange line of questioning. Tonkin, a region we now call northern Vietnam, wasn't Qing territory, and the Dutch had only had a marginal trading presence there. No one, to their knowledge, had ever met any Qing officials there. It was odd, but Qing officials had been asking about Tonkin repeatedly, and each time the Dutchmen's answers seemed to confuse their hosts. In Quanzhou they'd been told, through their translator, that once, years before, white men had come through that city on their way to Beijing and that those white men had come from Tonkin.[50] It had seemed strange that their hosts identified them with white men from Tonkin.

Hurt and Clewerck did their best to answer the prince. They said they'd never been to Tonkin themselves, but as far as they knew the Dutch had traded there for ten or twelve years. They tried to remember the names of some of the Dutchmen who'd run the trading post there: Keijser, de Voogt, and Baron. The prince didn't seem satisfied with their answers.

What they didn't know is that their interpreter was mistranslating the term Tonkin. The officials were really asking about Guangzhou, one of China's most important seaports. The Dutch had sent a diplomatic mission to the Qing government in Guangdong six years before, when both Prince Geng and Li Shuaitai had been stationed there. Since foreigners were hard to tell apart and always engaging in tricky schemes, he and his comrades wanted assurances that Hurt and

Clewerck were from the same nation that had traded in Guangzhou. Hurt and Clewerck realized the mistake only after they'd returned and written up their report of the mission. We find it noted in the margin of their account, added after it had already been composed and copied at least once.[51]

Despite the fact that their translator consistently mistranslated Guangzhou as Tonkin, the embassy was ending on a promising note: Prince Geng proposed a grand alliance between the Qing Dynasty and the Netherlands. He told them about the great assault he and his generals were planning against Koxinga and said he hoped the Dutch could coordinate a joint action by sea.

Hurt and Clewerck said they were sure that their lord the governor of Taiwan would be delighted to because naturally he wanted to do everything possible to reduce that scoundrel Koxinga to nothing. "Our ships," they said, "are already cruising on his coasts to destroy everything of Koxinga's that they can find, and Their Excellencies in Batavia will also doubtless send a large new fleet this coming year."[52]

Hurt and Clewerck asked His Highness to send a letter to Coyet. He said he would and so would Governor-General Li Shuaitai.

Then tea was served from a golden dispenser. After it was drunk His Highness signaled that the audience was over.

They'd done it. Despite having no gifts, despite their frayed (and probably smelly) clothes, despite having a translator who couldn't tell the difference between Vietnam and China, they'd laid the groundwork for a momentous agreement.

Now they just had to get back before Harthouwer left them behind.

TAKING LEAVE

They were desperate to depart. Harthouwer had ordered them to stay on land for only one day and said he might have to leave them behind if they were late. Since then, a whole week had passed, and they didn't like the idea of being stuck in this land of clothes-pluckers.

They were shocked to hear, soon after taking leave of the viceroy, that he expected them to stay in Fuzhou until he himself was ready to go south to strike against Koxinga. This was distressing news. Their escorts tried to reassure them by saying that the viceroy would be leaving in several days, but, Hurt wrote, "we knew well how such a journey would go—it couldn't be completed easily even in a month."[53] They passed an anxious night.

The next morning, they were relieved to find that the idea of their waiting longer in Fuzhou had been just a rumor. Li Shuaitai saw them off, serving them warm tea and giving them each a Manchu robe, which he urged them to put them on right away. They did, although they later complained that the robes were "of poor quality."[54] A little boy came out, Li Shuaitai's son. Hurt and Clewerck gave him some silver coins, saying they wished they had more. Li Shuaitai gave them letters—one from him and one from Prince Geng. Then they said thank you and goodbye.

The trip back was less festive than the trip there. Li Shuaitai had promised fancy new covered palanquins to bear them back, but they never arrived, "sold," Hurt mused, "by his servants for their own profit."[55] They climbed into their old ones and started their voyage. On the way up they hadn't had to pay for anything. Now nothing was free, "and our hosts weren't nearly as liberal with the drink and food."[56] Sometimes the men who were supposed to host them hid from them instead, "afraid," wrote Hurt, "that we'd want a gift from them, as is their custom, because they'd promised us big presents when we passed through the first time, even though we'd said that we didn't want any gifts because all we really wanted was to have a good audience with His Highness the Viceroy."[57] Each time they stopped for the evening their embarrassed guides would take them from house to house, only to be told at each doorway that no one was home. "But this didn't make us too sad," wrote Hurt, "because then we could keep on traveling like we wanted."[58]

As a result they made good time, and by the fifth day of their journey they crossed the famous Luoyang Bridge back into Quanzhou, where they ran into the man who'd started the whole adventure, the commander of Yongning. "As soon as he saw us, he raised his hat to us in the Dutch way, although from much farther away, and he greeted us so warmly that it was like we were family."[59] He said he'd come to Quanzhou to find out what was wrong and why they'd been gone so long, worried that maybe they'd been attacked by Koxinga's pirates or by tigers. He said David Harthouwer had been asking about them every day and was getting increasingly frustrated. Hurt and Clewerck were relieved to hear that Harthouwer hadn't left yet and that they'd be able to see him the following day.

The next morning they were fetched from their lodgings and taken on horseback to a building on the outer wall of Quanzhou, where the commander had some business to finish. They found him yelling at a group of advisors. After the yelling stopped, he turned to them and hung silver medals round their necks inscribed in Manchu. They later complained that the medals "were so thin that they bent in the wind,"[60] but they were happy to know that they'd soon be back in Yongning, just a few hours away by horse.

Their joy vanished when a messenger came and said Harthouwer's ships had left the bay. Harthouwer had sent a letter ashore before he left:

> Honorable Sirs, we've been waiting with great longing for your return, but we see no sign of you nor any indication of an end to our waiting . . . and so duty compels us to end our long sojourn here and take up our journey again. . . . We may be back, if forced by hard winds, but if not, you must stay here in this place . . . until the situation allows you to be picked up. Behave yourselves well and honorably so that no shame or trouble comes to our country or to the company.[61]

The letter was accompanied by a chest with some money, although not much, so Harthouwer's letter instructed them to rely on Manchu hospitality and keep track of their expenses so the company could reimburse their hosts later, adding that they should "live in moderation so that the costs do not add up too high."[62] He signed off with "your devoted friend," noting that he was writing from the yacht *Hasselt*, lying "sail-ready before the City of Yongning."[63]

Hurt and Clewerck were just hours away from Yongning when they heard the bad news. It was, as Hurt put it laconically, "not at all pleasing."[64] But then another messenger arrived. A single Dutch ship had returned and anchored in the bay. There was still hope.

They rode fast through the bitter cold. As they approached Yongning, they passed people carrying packs and bundles, who explained that they were leaving because Prince Geng's army would be arriving soon and they were afraid the troops would occupy their homes and steal their things and rape their wives. The people of the coastal areas had suffered tremendously in this long war.[65]

The Dutchmen reached the bay at dusk. There was Harthouwer's flagship, its pennants stiff in the wind. The sight, Hurt wrote, "brought us no little joy."[66] The waters were too rough to row out, so they passed an uneasy night, still worried that the *Hasselt* might leave.

But it was there in the morning. They rowed out through the surf, along with an increasingly queasy Qing official who'd accompanied them from Fuzhou. Harthouwer fired the cannons three times in salute as the man—now quite green in the face—handed Harthouwer the letters from Prince Geng and Li Shuaitai.[67] After this the man expressed an earnest desire to leave, so he was given a gift of a telescope and some fine cloth and rowed back to shore.[68]

Hurt and Clewerck showed their comrades their thin robes and tinny medals. They told their stories, excusing themselves for not providing more details about the land and the people. They didn't have any pen or paper with them, they said, and had only been able to scrounge a few scraps of Chinese paper here and there for notes.[69]

The accidental embassy had ended well. "We thanked God," wrote Hurt, "that . . . despite the fact that we appeared there in such a humble state everything turned out in the end to such a desirable result."[70] None of it would have happened if bad weather hadn't forced their ship ashore, and they wouldn't have been able to report on it if bad weather hadn't forced Harthouwer to return to the bay, because he didn't return for them. He came back only because the wind was too stiff and the waves too strong to continue northward.

The ship nearly capsized on its way back to Taiwan,[71] but it arrived safely, and the inhabitants of Zeelandia Castle were overjoyed by the "delightful and unexpected news."[72]

Coyet read the letter from Prince Geng with excitement:

> It is known throughout the world what magnificent deeds the Hollanders have achieved in warfare. In helping destroy and

> extirpate this villainous pirate, your achievement will be written of in the histories for all time and your people will be even more famous. In the near future my captain-general Pou-I [Shuaitai] and I will enter the pirate's land to attack and destroy him wherever possible, which I tell you now so that you can send your navy by sea to launch a coordinated attack. Thus with one blow we can end this war.[73]

This was heady stuff. If the Dutch could cooperate effectively with the Qing, they might be able to turn the war around and defeat Koxinga. And successful cooperation might bring material benefits: "Once we've won this battle together, we will tout [the Dutch] role above our own, and you will be celebrated by the emperor himself and richly rewarded."

You'd think that Coyet and his colleagues would have done everything they could to pursue it. You'd be wrong. Coyet and his colleagues were so mired in the misery of their life under siege, so divided against each other, that they squabbled their time away.

Acrimony

> Disturbance in the enemy's camp means his generals have lost their prestige and authority. . . . When lower officers become irritable, they have become weary of war.[1]
>
> —Sun Zi, *Art of War*

When reading official Dutch records, you usually can go for hundreds of pages and gain an impression of calm deliberation. But in the winter of 1661, spite and rancor poured from the secretaries' quills.

We read that Coyet slapped one of his top military commanders in the face, angry, he said, because the man had given him an arrogant answer. We read about an old and respected officer named Captain Herman van Oudhorn fulminating against Coyet in the public square of the lower castle. The military people in this fort, he yelled, were being oppressed! The ration supervisor was giving the sailors anything they wanted, while the soldiers, who worked so hard, were being discriminated against! Why should sailors get as much arak as they wanted, while soldiers got nothing? It shouldn't be like that. And what's more, it's all Coyet's fault, and he shouldn't have slapped Captain van Aldorp like that either. That kind of thing just isn't right. Just let Coyet try doing that to him. He wouldn't stand for it. He'd get his dagger out and stick it right up against Coyet's nose, he would.

The tirade was touched off by alcohol, by the fact that the ration supervisor[2] had refused to fill Outhorn's cup. Drunken rants were common in those days, when alcohol was considered safer to drink than water, but this one was threatening. Oudhorn was the highest ranking military commander in the fort, and he yelled so loudly that nearly everyone could hear, especially the sick and wounded people who filled the church and the warehouse. Coyet was understandably shaken. He ordered Oudhorn banned from the Council of Formosa and prosecuted.[3]

Put a bunch of people in a small space that smells like shit and piss, feed them bad food, interrupt their sleep for months and months with cannon shots and alarms, and they'll get testy. By the time the leaky *Hasselt* returned to Taiwan, the situation in Zeelandia Castle had become hellish.

It had been a cold winter, and firewood was so scarce that the soldiers sometimes couldn't even boil their rice.[4] There were no vegetables to be scavenged, so nearly everyone suffered the bleeding gums of scurvy or swollen limbs of beriberi. The sailors in the ships at anchor were so afflicted they could barely wind the anchor cranks.[5] About one in seven inhabitants of Zeelandia Castle was confined to bed—or actually to floor, since there were few beds in the warehouse and church that served as hospitals.[6] People were dying at such a rate that Coyet and his colleagues had to streamline the testament procedure.[7]

Even going to the bathroom was dangerous because the main outhouses were located outside the castle walls. With Koxinga shooting at them from Baxemboy and with the cold weather, people just dropped their drawers or raised their dress and peed in the nearest corner, despite heavy fines designed to abolish such "pisshooks."[8] Sometimes people didn't have time to make it to the bathroom or even the chamber pot—diarrhea was rampant. All kinds of illness were rampant.

"Everything is scarce here," wrote Coyet's secretary, "and very expensive."[9] Soldiers and company employees still received their basic rations of rice and venison, and higher-ups a bit more—perhaps some wine and bacon. But nearly everyone had to buy food to supplement rations, and staples like butter and sugar had gotten so scarce that people stopped selling them altogether.[10] "The war," wrote Coyet's secretary, "has brought this entire community into utter poverty and extreme want. Most people can barely eke out their daily needs."[11]

Even those who'd once been rich were ruined. The widow of Thomas Pedel had been wealthy, but, like most upper-class citizens, her money had been tied up in ventures with Chinese businessmen. She and her husband had had extensive dealings with He Bin, the man who'd started the whole war by giving Koxinga a map of Taiwan and leading him here. She had a lien on his properties—two large stone houses in Zeelandia City and extensive fields near Saccam—but the houses were occupied by Chinese troops and the lands were being planted by Koxinga's homesteading soldiers. Her vast wealth was gone and she couldn't pay her creditors.[12]

The thick web of credit that had helped the colony prosper had been torn to pieces. Coyet and his councilors had declared an interest holiday: all interest that had accrued since the beginning of the war had been zeroed out, and no one was allowed to add more interest to accounts or demand its payment.[13] But they couldn't do anything about the basic problem: the colony's wealth had been destroyed by war, and the people in the castle were hungry, malnourished, and sick.

Most people couldn't even have a drink. Alcohol had gotten so expensive that soldiers were known to pay fourteen or fifteen shillings for a jug of the worst-quality arak, about half a month's wages for an ordinary sailor.[14] (A jug was about a liter and a half.) That's like paying five hundred dollars for a six-pack.

The besieged had expected more supplies to come in the annual fleet from the company's office in Japan, but they were disappointed. There was almost no wood on the ships because the shogun was buying up supplies of lumber for a new palace. The ships brought rice, wheat, hardbreads, sugar, preserved fish, grapefruits, and vegetables, but in small amounts.[15] And there was no sake, "for which we'd had tremendous hope."[16] As a result, even the small daily ration of arak was abrogated.[17]

Coyet tried sending out provisioning expeditions to gather food and firewood, and these provided some relief, but they were also costly and dangerous. On one expedition, the deacon Daniel Hendrickson, the man who'd lost his son to the explosion during Coyet's foolish attack, ventured onto an offshore island to try to purchase supplies from some natives, since he was a talented linguist and spoke their language. "He was attacked by multitudes of armed natives and killed. They took his head, his arms, his legs, his other parts, and yes, even his entrails to hold a victory celebration, leaving the torso lying on the ground."[18]

GETTING OUT

Everyone in Zeelandia was trying to find a way to leave "this difficult and miserable Taiwan," but there were few good escape routes.[19]

One could run to the enemy, but it wasn't easy. Before winter, only one company employee had fled to Koxinga's side, the foulmouthed Swissman who'd defected in July, and after his flight, Coyet had established mounted patrols south of the castle. To beating drums, a town crier had proclaimed that there were now limit poles around the castle, and anyone who passed them without permission would be considered a runaway and punished for treason. No one else from the Dutch side went over to the Chinese all summer long. Defections went the other way instead.

But on a cold, windy day at the end of October, the defection gradient reversed. Two company employees ran over a sand dune and past the old hospital to a Chinese sentry post. They were fed and clothed and taken to see Koxinga himself. A couple days later, these two men reappeared across from the castle wearing costly golden robes and trying to tempt their former comrades to join them. We're being treated wonderfully, they called out, and anyone else who wants to come over will have fresh meat and as much arak as they can drink. And if you don't come, we'll come see you soon enough and collect the rest of our belongings.[20]

Some of their comrades accepted the invitation: a Dane from Copenhagen, a German from Westphalia, a Walloon from Tournai, Dutchmen from The Hague and Amsterdam, sneaking away through the grass.[21] Cauw was convinced that these men were rabble: "They are defecting for no reason more than dice and gambling and drinking, activities which have become so endemic here in the castle . . . that it's a wonder to see and hear. Many soldiers wager a day's pay, or even many months' pay . . . on a single throw of the dice and lose it all."[22] He didn't think defectors like this would be useful to Koxinga and noticed that Koxinga hadn't even bothered to dress the latest defectors up in silk robes and display them in front of the castle "to mock and insult us," as he'd done with those who'd gone before, probably, he surmised, "because he mistrusted them, suspecting that they hadn't gone over to him for any other reason [than the gambling and drunkenness]."[23]

But it was a dangerous trend. Each defector might bring information to the enemy, and it was at least certain that Koxinga knew how desperate things were getting in Zeelandia Castle.

The "rabble" might be able to run away, but others had to find other ways to leave. Women and children, widows, and "unproductive slaves" were encouraged to depart, loaded onto ships to be sent to Batavia.[24] Even many Chinese were sent to Batavia, such as defectors who'd come during the summer, although not the Chinese prisoners from before the war. They were rich men who'd been imprisoned on suspicions of having contact with Koxinga, and they owed too much money to the Dutch to be allowed to go.[25] A few company managers were permitted to leave, such as an assistant merchant named Michael Baly, who was sick and whose wife was pregnant.[26]

But most people who asked to go were denied. Cauw, for example, made the request, saying that he wasn't asking out of his own self-interest but only for the greater good of the company and the Netherlands. After all, Coyet hadn't let him lead any battles, and Cauw felt he could do more service for the company in Batavia than in Taiwan. He said he always put the company before anything else, including his own self, and he promised that when he arrived in Batavia he'd explain in detail how things stood in Taiwan and get them to send help. Coyet probably knew that Cauw wouldn't say flattering things about his leadership and denied his request.[27] But Cauw didn't give up. He claimed that he had secret orders that required him to go back to Batavia. When Coyet demanded to see them, Cauw said it wasn't Coyet's place to see his secret orders, that he knew what orders he had or didn't have, and that he wasn't required—nor did he intend—to show or talk about them.[28] This response didn't get him any closer to leaving Taiwan.

THE MANCHU OPPORTUNITY

When Coyet and his councilors resolved to send a mission to the Manchus, many people jumped at the chance to volunteer. They'd heard Hurt and Clewerck's stories about Manchu hospitality and seen the robes and medals they brought back. A battle with Koxinga might bring glory. At the very least, there might be fresh food.

Cauw immediately offered to command the ships, and Coyet and the others saw no reasonable way to deny him. Cauw's friend, a man named Jacob Casembroot, volunteered to serve as ambassador. He was of high rank, having originally been intended to replace Jacob Valentine as chief magistrate of Taiwan, and since he'd volunteered first and there were few others of his stature who were healthy, he was selected.[29]

But a few days later the arguing started. Casembroot told Coyet he'd need at least four soldiers in his honor guard, "in order to have suitable grandeur when meeting the worthies of that land, because these heathens seem to set so much store by such things."[30] Coyet said Casembroot could have no more than two. Casembroot said that in that case he'd be nothing more than a glorified mailman and Coyet might as well select someone of lower rank. The meeting exploded into yelling and cursing.

David Harthouwer was particularly incensed. He already had a reservoir of resentment. He'd been asking Coyet to let him leave Taiwan for months, and he reminded the governor that the last time he'd asked Coyet had instead ordered him to sail a leaky ship during typhoon season. Harthouwer thought perhaps his services in obtaining the good news from China might persuade Coyet to finally let him go, but Coyet refused his request again.

Harthouwer decided that if he couldn't take his family back to Batavia, he should at least be allowed to head up the mission to China and was furious that Casembroot had been chosen instead. "You know how long I've been wanting to leave this difficult and miserable Taiwan. You've kept me hanging, feeding me with hope that next time my request will be granted. This dreadful war has harmed me so much that I'm now determined to leave in order to protect and preserve my family."[31] He asked Coyet once again for permission to leave Taiwan. "If,"

Harthouwer warned, "you decide that my staying here is necessary, then I am compelled to protest against the irregular choice of Casembroot as ambassador to Fuzhou. He's an unruly man, something I've determined after many obstacles and much trouble, thanks to God's help. So if you decide that I cannot go to Batavia, then it's only reasonable that the embassy to the Tartars [i.e. Manchus] be entrusted to me."[32]

Harthouwer's insinuation that the selection of Casembroot was "irregular" infuriated Casembroot and Cauw, who demanded that their feelings about the matter be written into the records so Harthouwer could be disciplined later. Coyet, for his part, disliked Cauw, was furious with Casembroot, and had his differences with Harthouwer.

Coyet ordered Harthouwer and Casembroot both to leave the meeting. Then he and the remaining council members decided that neither would go to China. Instead, they'd select a "smaller person."[33] The person they chose—after a long meeting "with lots of caviling"[34]—was the secretary of Formosa. It was an astonishing decision, as though the United States decided to send a midlevel diplomatic attaché to an important meeting with the foreign minister of China.

Equally damaging, infighting cost time. Coyet and the others let several weeks elapse between the arrival of the Manchu letter and the final selection of personnel, and after that there were still concrete preparations to see to. They had to search through the warehouses for gifts: tropical luxury goods like fine red wool, cloves, sandalwood, fine Indian cottons.[35] The Manchus liked Dutch guns, so they added to the list a fine rifle and two pistols. His Highness the Viceroy of Fujian had expressed interest in a Dutch saddle, and there weren't any new ones in Taiwan, so the council decided to buy one from Casembroot for seventy-five reals, twice the annual salary of a Dutch sailor.[36] Perhaps this was a way to compensate Casembroot for not letting him be envoy.

Coyet and the others also had to prepare detailed shopping lists of supplies to buy in China, and we can see from those lists how many things the people of Zeelandia lacked: fifty casks of arak, a hundred iron pots and pans, three hundred porcelain dishes, five hundred plates, five hundred medium bowls, ten rice mills, a hundred leather hides of finished leather for shoes, fifty catties of cobblers' laces, a thousand pairs of cotton socks of correct size, thirty picols of writing paper, wood, little nails, chickens, geese, pigs, grapefruits, garlic, radishes, onions, iron.[37]

Most important of all, they needed to compose official letters to the viceroy that conveyed the right tone of confidence and optimism:

> We were delighted to learn that Your Highness is about to launch a great expedition to attack that pirate Koxinga, and here in Taiwan we're working every day to harm him in every way possible, so that he's already been weakened, which your Highness must have already noted to your contentment there in China. We expect that within a few months we'll have driven him from here and be able to pursue him to his own lands, if he even has any of those left and has not meanwhile been driven from them by Your Excellencies.[38]

SAILING FOR CHINA

When Cauw finally rowed out to his flagship it was a beautiful, cold, clear morning. It's too bad Cauw hadn't set out earlier (the weather had been ideal for two weeks), because that afternoon, as workers were loading the last of the cargo, the sky darkened and the wind began gusting.[39] The fleet had to lie at anchor for several days until the risk of departure was judged acceptable, but then, as soon as it got out of sight, the weather turned.[40] Coyet and the others prayed that "The Highest Navigator guide our ships and give them a safe journey."[41]

But the Highest Navigator was in the mood for a storm. "The wind began to increase hand over hand," Cauw wrote in his logbook, "so strongly that it began blowing our mainsails to tatters."[42] The sea became "angry and unsettled."[43] He anchored in the Penghu Islands, hoping for conditions to improve, but the wind raged. Then the heavens "burst out into a true storm."[44] The sea became a range of whitetop mountains, "terrifying to see,"[45] and it was so bitterly cold that the crew, whose berths were equipped with only thin blankets, became sick.

One, two, three ships were torn away from their anchors and disappeared into the darkness. Cauw's flagship began leaking.[46] Cables snapped and anchors were lost. The crew struggled to keep their anchorage, knowing that if they started to drift the ship would be blown far to the south and wouldn't be able to fight its way to the Chinese coast. But the waves got so high that the ship was in danger of being dragged under by its own anchors. The crew was exhausted, more and more of them falling ill. Cauw decided that "it was no use to fight against Heaven, weather, and wind any longer."[47] He gave the order to turn back to Taiwan.

Instead of making it to Taiwan, the ship was driven far, far to the southwest, with four feet of water sloshing in the hold. His navigator said there'd be no way to reach Taiwan.[48] "Thus," wrote Cauw's secretary, "our grand undertaking to go to the coast of China has come to nothing and had to be abandoned, to the great detriment of the company and the besieged in Taiwan."[49]

Cauw blamed the weather, but others blamed Cauw. Coyet would later write that Cauw had "betrayed his mission," that Cauw had always wanted to go back to Batavia and merely found a convenient excuse in the weather.[50] Cauw's superiors in Batavia, who liked to blame everything on everyone but themselves, would adopt a similar opinion: "It doesn't seem that necessity compelled him to abandon his mission to the coast of China."[51] And it's true that two of the ships in Cauw's five-ship fleet did make it to China, anchoring in Yongning Bay for six days before finally giving up and sailing back to Taiwan. Historians have not been kind to Cauw. They take their cue from Coyet, calling him "faithless" and accusing him of abandoning his mission on purpose.[52]

In any case, Cauw sailed through calm, warm seas toward Batavia to request urgent reinforcements for Taiwan and complain about Coyet's leadership. But it was too late. Koxinga was shooting the castle's most important defenses to smithereens, thanks to the help of a German alcoholic.

The Last Battle

German sergeant Hans Radis decided to betray his comrades on a cold December afternoon. Waking up from a drunken nap, he grabbed his gun and said to his roommate, "Put on some hot water. I'm going out for fresh meat."

"Good," the man said, "Shoot well."

Radis shouldered his gun and walked out past the abandoned hospital to the bayshore, but he didn't stop to shoot seabirds. He kept going through the bitter wind, past the oyster beds, past where the old graveyard used to be, and past the first empty fishing village. It wasn't until he reached the place where the second fishing village used to be, where there was now a Chinese sentry-hill, that his comrades realized his intent. They sent riders out to catch him, but it was too late. He made it to Koxinga's camp.

Coyet felt that Radis's treason lost the war:

> Radis directed Koxinga's attention to the hilltop redoubt behind the castle and pointed out the vulnerable castle walls beneath it. Those walls were so low that you could watch the soldiers inside from the redoubt. So it stood to reason that if Koxinga could capture the redoubt and take possession of the hill on which it stood, not a single soul in the walls could protect himself, or even remain within them. . . . And having once gained possession of the hill, the Chinese would be able to hide in the redoubt and

> fortify themselves there, protected from the castle's cannons and muskets but very close to the walls of the upper castle. These and many other suggestions were given to the heathen Koxinga by this blasphemous and treacherous man, suggestions which brought death to so many Christians and ruin to the territory of Taiwan.[1]

Historians have taken Coyet's word for it.[2] But are we really to believe that Koxinga and his generals, who were masters of terrain-based warfare, who had reduced scores of fortified cities in China, needed a drunk German to tell them about the hilltop redoubt? No. We've already seen that Koxinga recognized the importance of the redoubt and tried to destroy it well before Radis's defection. Perhaps Coyet exaggerated Radis's role on purpose, to help shift blame for the loss of Taiwan from himself. After all, a traitor makes a good story.

But Coyet wasn't the only one in Zeelandia Castle who blamed Radis. Swiss soldier Albrecht Herport independently wrote: "At this time a sergeant of ours, along with three other soldiers, ran over to the enemy, telling them how they could attack the redoubt first."[3] Herport was an ordinary soldier, someone who probably had little direct contact with Coyet or the other Dutch leaders. The fact that he came to a similar conclusion suggests that Radis's defection was commonly seen as a turning point in the war.

Radis wasn't like the other defectors who'd run to the Chinese, the rabble who irked Admiral Cauw. He was a sergeant, one of the highest ranks in the castle. He didn't give Koxinga the idea of capturing the redoubt, but as we'll see, he helped Koxinga achieve the goal.

What motivated him to betray his comrades? Facts about him are maddeningly sparse. We know he was from Stuttgart. We know he was a seasoned commander, who had fought in Europe before arriving in Asia. Most intriguing, we have a few descriptions of him as a drunken, grandiose personality, although these descriptions were written by a man who hated him, a man whom he tried to have killed and who returned the favor.

That man was Philip Meij, the surveyor who'd spent the war helping Koxinga measure coastlines and assess rice paddies. By this point, nearly all the other prisoners had starved or been executed, but he and a couple others had survived because of their professional skills. They were living in the Eastern Capital, hungry and frightened to ask their captors for food, since the last time they'd begged for rice, their warden hadn't even granted an audience. He'd just sent his manservant to the door with seven sour lemons.[4]

Radis showed up at Meij's house not long after defecting. Clad in silk, purse full of silver, he claimed that he was a double agent, that Coyet had secretly sent him over to "take Koxinga's head" and free Meij and the other Dutch captives. He said eighty more men would soon follow, two or three at a time, to help bring Koxinga down from within. To demonstrate his sincerity, he gave Meij some pieces of eight.

But soon Meij learned that Radis was plotting against him. Some old Portuguese men from Macau—probably Chinese mestiços—had befriended Meij, having served Koxinga for years but become exhausted from heavy labor in the gardens, work they weren't used to. "These poor people," wrote Meij, "were inclined to our side because of discussions about the Dutch religion, wondering at the notion that we were also Christians and had the Old and New Testaments, and had the Our Father just as they did, and so almost nothing happened that they did not tell us about."[5] They said Radis had stood up at a dinner with Koxinga and declared that Meij was dangerous and should be executed immediately. Fortunately, Koxinga had just laughed and replied that Meij was too insignificant to worry about.

This wasn't the first time Meij had been threatened by a defector. A couple months before, another defector had tried to tell Koxinga that Meij had fomented a secret plot. In that case the defector was right. When Cauw's fleet had arrived, Meij had sent sent a messenger—the naked swimmer we met before—to Zeelandia to tell Coyet how to attack the Eastern Capital. Yet the Portuguese translators refused to translate the defector's words to Koxinga, so Meij was safe. Meij had been terrified that the defector might tell someone else and wondered if he should try to talk to Koxinga directly and discredit the man, saying that any talk of swimmers and plots was a lie. No! said the Portuguese. If Koxinga heard one word about this sort of thing, either from Meij or someone else, he'd crucify Meij on the spot.[6]

Now Radis was scheming against him, and he was even more dangerous.

Meij schemed back. Although Meij's account is reticent about the details, it seems he tried to undermine Radis by telling people—so that they'd tell Koxinga—that Radis had told him he had come to the Eastern Capital to cut off Koxinga's head.

Neither man managed to get the other killed, but Radis won a larger victory. A month after defecting, he came to Meij's door, drunk. Referring to Koxinga as his king, he said: "You're a clever bird, you are. I've tried many times to catch you in your maneuverings,[7] but I never could do it. You know it's all lies, what you said about my king's head. But it's too late now. I've brought the Hollanders to the point that they have to give up the castle and throw themselves on my king's mercy."[8]

It was true. By this point Coyet and his colleagues were on the point of surrender. How did they reach that point? And was Radis justified in claiming responsibility?

PREPARING AN ATTACK

According to Meij, in December of 1661, most people in the Eastern Capital believed that Koxinga had no immediate plans to attack Zeelandia Castle. Instead, he was planning to use the rest of the winter—the dry season in southern Taiwan—to march against the Prince of the Middag, the native ruler who'd massacred hundreds of his troops. A final assault against Zeelandia Castle would wait until the wet season began in the spring.

But Koxinga changed his mind because some new arrivals from China said that "David Harthouwer had been to see the Tartars and had brought them ten chests of gold, twenty-four pieces of Dutch fine woolens, and other rarities as a present, and had also asked for help with soldiers, which the Tartar agreed to provide, promising seven thousand men, who now stood ready to be sent by ship."[9] Koxinga couldn't have known that the news was false, that although Harthouwer had made contact the Manchus hadn't promised any troops.

So Koxinga summoned his advisors. For two days they talked and planned, and immediately afterward Chinese were ordered to fell trees and haul beams to the Eastern Capital, where they were sawed and hammered into carriages for forty-three cannons that had arrived a few weeks ago from China. They were massive guns. Meij saw the cannonballs piled beside them and estimated that some weighted twenty-four pounds, some twenty-eight pounds, and some even more. They were as large as anything the Dutch had in Zeelandia Castle. Meij asked where they were from and was told that Koxinga's father had had them forged by the Portuguese in Macau in 1644.

While farmers and carpenters made cannon carriages, natives hauled bamboo to the Eastern Capital to weave into sandbasket barricades. People were ordered to gather all the iron they could find to cast it into cannonballs and shrapnel.[10]

On the other side of the bay, Coyet and comrades saw enemy soldiers moving their cannons out of Baxemboy and loading them onto junks. They watched the cannons ferried to Zeelandia City and rolled down the streets to point at the castle.[11] On an overcast day eight hundred Chinese soldiers marched from the Narrow to the place the Dutch still called the Second Fishery, even though the fishermen had long fled and their huts had been swept away by storms. The soldiers unfurled their flags in the cold wind and put up tents. Some of the Dutch thought they caught a glimpse of cannons.[12] "There's no doubt," Coyet's secretary wrote, "that they're planning something."[13] A Chinese defector confirmed that Koxinga was planning to storm the castle.[14]

On a bright January day, Koxinga himself rode southward from his capital along the coast. It was a dazzling sight. Forty horsemen and a personal honor guard of sixty surrounded him, and four hundred and fifty more specially selected troops—the very best of the men that were left—marched along.[15] The host forded the Narrow and trotted northward to join the new encampment.[16]

Raftloads of bamboo were poled across the bay, following the old ferry route to Zeelandia City.[17] The bamboo was fashioned into storm ladders and sandbaskets. The sandbaskets were piled up into barricades. At first they were placed where Koxinga had put them the last time he'd tried storming Dutch positions: in the field south of the market, behind the company's old lumberyard. This wasn't too worrisome, since the Dutch had fended off an assault from there before.

But on a windy morning the Dutch awoke to find that a new battery had appeared on a dune a hundred yards southwest of the redoubt. It wasn't quite as high as the redoubt's dune, but it was still a threatening vantage point. Coyet's secretary described it as "right under the redoubt."[18]

More disquieting was how the new work was designed. Built with "unbelievable speed," it was what military engineers called a "demi-lune," a self-contained bastion in the form of a crescent. This was a hallmark of renaissance fortification.

Coyet sent riders galloping out to investigate. Hidden behind the new work they saw hundreds of Chinese. On top they saw Hans Radis.[19]

So the German defector was playing a role not as a strategist but as a tactician and engineer. The last time Koxinga had tried capturing the redoubt he'd been stymied by Dutch engineers, who built a new battery to counteract his cannons. Koxinga had given up. A Dutch commander would have persevered. European siege warfare was characterized by a long, slow dance of fortification and counterfortification. European commanders knew that capturing a renaissance fortress required siegeworks nearly as extensive as the fort they were trying to capture. Instead, Koxinga had followed Sun Zi's dictum: *Military tactics are like flowing water. Just as water flows from high to low, military tactics always avoid the enemy's strong points and attack his weak points.*[20] He'd turned to another strategy, trying to seal off the castle by establishing control over the Channel. That failed, too, when the Dutch countered him by building the new fortress on the beach.

But now Radis was helping design European-style siegeworks. The new demi-lune couldn't be hit by the main castle, and when filled with cannon it would concentrate fire directly at the redoubt.

"There's no other conclusion," Coyet told his nervous councilors, "than that Koxinga has resolved to finally carry out what he's threatened to do for so long."[21] He asked his officers for advice.[22] Perhaps we could storm the new battery? No, they said. We'd need four or five hundred men, which wouldn't leave us enough to man the castle.[23] Perhaps we could destroy the battery with a preemptive barrage? No, they said, because gunpowder supplies are too low, and it's necessary to keep plenty of powder on hand to defend against an enemy assault.[24] Perhaps we could bombard the battery from the sea, anchoring on the other side of the dunes and lobbing cannonballs? No, the ships' commander said. Sandy flats stretch out from the beach just where we would need to place our ships, so we can't get even half as close as we would need to in order to hit the battery, even with our heaviest cannons.[25]

There was nothing to do but shore up the defenses. He ordered the last of the women and children rowed out to the ships.[26] He considered moving the company's treasures out to the fleet but decided not to because it would cause worry among the soldiers.[27] He sent four months' worth of provisions to the redoubt, in case communication between it and the castle were cut off.[28] He ordered workers to construct spikes out of nails and wood and place them in the trenches and in front of the redoubt and the wooden fort on the beach.[29] He tried boosting morale by telling the garrisons of the redoubt and the new fortification on the beach that if they resisted valiantly the officers would get promotions and the soldiers would get extra wages.[30]

The Chinese kept working, "swarming over their new works like ants."[31] They worked in the evening, while "bastard defectors" cursed with filthy words from the town, the yelling and screaming lasting well after dark.[32] They worked at night, the Dutch having trouble sleeping because "the whole night through we heard the enemy bustling loudly and making a tumult outside."[33]

Each morning the Dutch awoke to find the positions had crept closer. Cannon batteries stretched out in front of the graveyard and the old market, seventeen feet thick and twelve feet high.[34] The sandbaskets that comprised them were said to contain bones from the graves.[35] Some cannon positions rose higher than the walls of the marketplace.[36] Junks and sampans sailed into the Channel, "cheerfully adorned with flags," and moored in front of the Chinese fort at Baxemboy, while Chinese soldiers sat on the ground with their swords and bows and saber-staves, staring at the castle.[37]

THE ASSAULT

The last battle started on 25 January 1662. The morning sun illuminated hundreds of Chinese flags snapping in the wind. They flew over the town, over the barricades, from the masts of ships and sampans, but there was no time to admire the spectacle.

The assault came from all sides at once. Junks attacked from the Channel, coming right under the walls. The Dutch cannoneers couldn't drive them away because the best gunners were needed on the other side of the castle to answer a thundering barrage. Yet Koxinga's siegeworks were so well-placed that the castle's guns couldn't reach them. The Chinese fired with impunity from the graveyard, from the market, from the area near the lumberyard.

Most devastating of all was the demi-lune that Hans Radis had helped build. The entire dune roared with cannonfire.[38]

Most of Koxinga's cannons were aimed at the redoubt. The barrage flayed the white mortar that covered its ten-foot-thick walls, exposing the brick beneath. "So strong and sustained were the cannonades," wrote Meij, who was watching from the Eastern Capital, "that the redoubt quickly lost the whiteness of the mortar and showed itself very red."[39] The main Dutch gun emplacements on the top of the redoubt were rendered useless, the crenellations blasted away so that no one could even go up there.

Coyet couldn't do anything to stop it. "From the castle," he wrote, "we couldn't shoot the enemy anywhere, and so he happily thundered on by himself, and we watched with sadness and grief as our redoubt was destroyed."[40]

The redoubt's garrison stopped shooting back. Two Chinese soldiers emerged from behind their barricades, snuck up the hill, and fired arrows into the gunports to see if anyone was alive inside. Musket muzzles appeared and shot. The bowmen retreated. The cannons started up again.

They blasted holes in the walls. The roof caved in.

The cannons stopped again. Chinese troops came with pikes and ladders to breach the walls. The redoubt's garrison threw hand grenades and stinkpots and drove the assailants away with pikes and swords. Two times the Chinese stormed, putting their ladders against the walls, and two times the defenders—perhaps eager for their promotions and extra wages, but more likely just scared to death—drove them back.

The cannons started for a third time. The amount of firepower concentrated on the redoubt was astounding. Philip Meij wrote that the Chinese fired seventeen hundred cannon shots that day; Coyet's secretary estimated that twenty-five hundred cannonballs were fired. Some of these balls were huge, thirty pounds or more. Most struck the redoubt.[41] Modern researchers share Coyet and Meij's dismay about the ferocity of Koxinga's cannon attack. "For so many shots to be fired in one day was an earthshaking[42] phenomenon," writes Taiwanese scholar Jiang Shusheng. "Although by today's artillery technological standards, shooting twenty-five hundred shots in one day is not that strange, by the technological standards of three hundred years ago, Koxinga's ability to fire twenty-five hundred shots in one day cannot help but leave one astonished at his army's modernization."[43]

By late afternoon, the redoubt was entirely silent. Coyet sent a lieutenant named de Roer out with thirty soldiers to investigate. They found seven Chinese dead on the ground and most of the Dutch garrison inside wounded, including some of its top officers and its chief gunner. De Roer helped repair the most dangerous breach in the walls with a support beam, but the enemy just blew new holes.

By evening the redoubt had been blasted open on the north, east, and south walls. Coyet sent a master builder to inspect it. He reported that the structure was about to collapse even as the enemy kept trying to storm. It would be too dangerous to try to hold the redoubt into the night.

BOOM

Coyet and his councilors decided to abandon the redoubt, but they ordered Lieutenant de Roer to leave a surprise. He and some men climbed down to the redoubt's powder cellar, arranged shrapnel in and around four barrels of gunpowder, and lit three long fuses. They closed the cellar door behind them and nailed it shut.

Minutes later Chinese soldiers congregated around the redoubt. A few went in, and then more. Finding no one inside, they fired flaming arrows into the sky to signal their gunners to stop firing. Some of Koxinga's top officers went inside, including Ma Xin, the general who'd kept the Dutch pinned down since early in the summer. While they were looking around they received a summons that saved their lives: Koxinga wanted them to come to camp to celebrate the victory.[44] The redoubt exploded just after they left.

When the last sand filtered to the ground, all that was left was a bit of wall.

In the castle, Dutch gunners passed the night aiming at grunts and digging sounds. When the sun came up they saw that the Chinese had already constructed fortifications on the ruins of the redoubt and all the way down the dune, and still the enemy kept building, all day and into the following night. "All night long," Coyet's secretary wrote, "we heard sounds from the enemy on all sides, although we couldn't tell what they were doing."[45]

Coyet held meetings. Should they bombard Koxinga's new siege-works from the castle? No, his officers said. The works were already too thick, and there was so little powder left that it wasn't worth it to try.[46] What about launching an infantry assault? The officers said there was no point. The Chinese were too numerous: "Even if the enemy lost a thousand men, he wouldn't give up, but for us even a much smaller number of dead and wounded would be devastating."[47]

While the men with expensive hats talked, slaves and soldiers "warmed themselves with labor." Zeelandia Castle had been designed to withstand an assault from the sea or town but not from the dunes. Its walls were weak on that side. At one place—where the lower castle joined up with the upper castle—the wall was only a couple feet thick.[48] Coyet ordered everyone out of the houses that backed up against this wall so that the workers and soldiers could remove their roofs and fill them with sand, effectively thickening the wall.[49] They gutted other houses, scavenging planks and boards, which they used to build wooden retaining walls that could be filled with sand.[50] Other laborers were ordered to build barricades on top of the wall using wooden crates filled with dirt.

But the soldiers and slaves had lost morale. Their supervisors said they were lazy.[51] When they were promised arak as a reward, they said they'd be happy to give their supervisors arak in exchange for rest.[52] "We've constantly experienced laziness among our people," wrote Coyet's secretary, "but never like this, which is perhaps to be explained by the fact that they've just seen the powerful redoubt, with its ten-foot-thick walls, destroyed and flattened to the ground."[53] Coyet and the others prayed: "Almighty God grant our people bravery and manliness."[54]

But the next morning he, too, decided to forego manliness. That's because the winter sun glinted from cannon muzzles all around. The Chinese had built a new battery in the field near the castle, between the demolished hospital and the market. The dunetop where the redoubt had stood also bristled with cannons, which thrust out toward the weak walls. "On that hill," Coyet's secretary wrote, "they can see the soles of our feet. They can dominate the entire castle, so nobody inside will be able to find any refuge."[55]

Coyet called together all the "qualified people." As they began to stream into the room—bureaucrats, clerks, and military men—a messenger brought disturbing news: The commander of the Dutch fleet was saying that if he saw the Chinese get too close he would raise anchor and sail away, "thus putting us in an extreme position so that we would be less likely to surrender the castle."[56] Coyet sent David Harthouwer out to investigate.

Coyet opened the meeting. There was a bit of manliness at first. Some people pointed out that the enemy had used so much powder in his barrage that he probably didn't have much left, so it was doubtful that he would really be able to shoot from all sides at once, as his cannons were poised to do. Instead, he'd probably have to focus on one place, and even if he created a breach the Dutch could easily keep the Chinese from storming through it. They might still hold Koxinga off for a while, and reinforcements might arrive from Batavia. The warehouses still held four or five months of provisions.

But most people weren't feeling so brave. People pointed out that the warehouses had been damaged and the provisions would soon spoil, that Batavia wasn't likely to be sending reinforcements now, that Koxinga probably had plenty of powder, and that in any case there was no way to keep him from blowing holes in the weak walls. If they chose to fight, people would be killed by stones and splinters blown from shattered walls, which was senseless, because defeat was inevitable.[57]

After deliberating at length, they prayed and took a vote. It was unanimous. They would send a little letter to Koxinga saying they were ready to surrender.[58]

Koxinga didn't like the note.

Surrender

A Dutch soldier emerged from the castle with a white flag. Chinese soldiers were so excited that they jumped up behind their barricades. Hundreds of eyes watched as he walked along the stone pathway, stopped well before their trenches, and worked a bamboo stalk with a letter attached into the sandy ground. Only when he was back in the castle did a Chinese soldier run out and grab the message.

It was terse:

> Your Majesty:
> If your Excellency wishes to enter into an Honest Treaty concerning this fortress, please be so good as to send a letter in the Dutch language as an answer and place it in the middle of the stone path, so long as you henceforth also cease the use of weapons and the building of hostile works, both in water and on land, and keep all of your men within their fortifications without allowing them to approach us, or otherwise they will be greeted as enemies.
>
> Signed Frederick Coyett, Governor of Formosa
> —Zeelandia, 27 January 1661[1]

Koxinga thought Coyet's tone wasn't abject enough. He summoned Philip Meij.

The knock sounded at Meij's door in the Eastern Capital late at night. A summons like this was terrifying to the few Dutch who remained, people who'd seen their friends crucified or beheaded by Koxinga's soldiers. "Each time any one of us left," Meij wrote, "we supposed he was going to his death," and whenever a summoned person managed to return he was greeted "with such happiness . . . that we didn't know what to do with our joy."[2]

Meij was led into the windy night, through the narrow streets of the Eastern Capital, and onto a sampan at the old ferry port, which conveyed him to Koxinga's fly-infested camp.[3] The warlord showed him Coyet's note and said that he wanted help writing out a response in Dutch.

This is how Meij's translation turned out:

> The Great Ming Rebel-Quelling Supreme Commander Koxinga sends this letter to Governor Coyet and his Advisors: I've received your letter but it is of so few words that I cannot make out its meaning, and so I find no satisfaction in it. If you have something you want to say, you may send a person of authority to tell me. If not, it does not matter to me. My weapons will remain silent until noon, by which time you must let me know your intent. I have had Philip Meij write this in Dutch so you can understand it better.[4]

The letter was checked by the defectors to make sure Meij hadn't included any secret messages and then planted on the stone path for the Dutch to find in the morning.[5]

When the sun came up, Meij was summoned again. He found Koxinga standing in the grassy dunes, bow in hand. The Sea King was in the mood to show off. Koxinga shot three arrows out over the hills toward the ocean.

"How far did that last one fly?" he asked Meij.

"About one hundred and twenty paces," said the surveyor.

"You've guessed well," said Koxinga. He mounted his horse and trotted into the dunes. Meij followed on foot with a retinue of guards and servants. Koxinga was waiting for them on a long, flat beach.

One of Koxinga's servants got out three short staves of wood, each of which had a ring the size of a large coin on one end. These rings had been pasted over carefully with red paper. The servant ran out and planted the staves in a straight line along the strand, a hundred feet apart.

Koxinga pulled three arrows from a quiver and placed them in his belt behind his back. He spurred his horse and cantered down the beach until he was a small figure. Then he galloped toward them. He pulled an arrow from his belt, quickly fitted it to his bowstring, and shot the first stalk through the ring. Then the second. Then the third. He did it all in one pass, without slowing down.

He dismounted in front of Meij and said, "Have you ever seen such a thing done? Could you do it yourself?"

Meij said he couldn't.

Then Koxinga told one of his military men to show Meij a trick. Galloping at full speed, the man drew one leg out of the stirrup, pulled it over the horse's back, and, with one hand holding the reigns, stood up straight and bowed low to Koxinga as the horse thundered past. He came past again upside-down with both feet in the air.

Then, show over, Koxinga dismissed Meij and rode back to his tent.

When Koxinga summoned Meij in the afternoon, he was in a bad mood. He hadn't slept well the night before because of the sand flies. Now the noon deadline had passed and Coyet hadn't sent a response. He yelled that Coyet was trying to trick him, that Coyet just wanted to slow him down until he'd dug himself in. Meij tried to calm him down, saying that the Dutch would certainly soon send envoys and couldn't he please wait just a bit.

But it was evening when two Dutchmen finally trotted out of the fortress with a white flag. Koxinga refused to meet them on principle, and the letter they brought just made him angrier because Coyet was demanding to take the castle's treasure back to Batavia.

Koxinga wrote a firm reply:

> When I came here with my powerful army, I asked you to hand over your castle and did not demand any of your goods. . . . You did not accept that offer, which I repeated several times. Now you have been under siege for nine months, and you have only yourself to blame for this situation. . . . Nine months of wages and immense amounts of gunpowder I have had to expend to keep my huge army here and to blast

> your redoubt into smithereens, not to mention numerous other costs and outlays. Why should I now content myself with an empty fort?[6]

He sent the letter to Coyet and ordered Meij to accompany him back to the Eastern Capital, saying he wanted to get away from the sand flies. As the boat glided through the darkness, he asked Meij about the Netherlands, but Meij felt that Koxinga didn't always believe his answers, like when he said that sometimes a thousand or more ships left a Dutch harbor for sea in one day, going to nearly all the countries of the world to trade and traffic, and even after they'd left, the harbor would still be filled with innumerable ships, like a forest.

Koxinga asked him how much treasure was in the castle. Meij said he thought Coyet had probably already removed most it to the ships, but Koxinga disagreed. The soldiers, he said, would never have allowed that, because they would have felt abandoned. Moreover, Koxinga said, if there was nothing left in the castle, why would Coyet have spent so much effort defending it, enduring the horrible conditions the defectors had told him about?

Meij was relieved to get home. Then Hans Radis came to see him, drunk. He gloated about how he'd brought the Dutch to their knees and said that after Coyet gave up the castle, Koxinga wouldn't stop there. "It won't be long," he said "before my king comes to pay a visit to you Dutch in the Malaccas."[7]

The next day, back in the fly-infested camp, Koxinga prepared a forceful letter to Coyet:

> If you wish to give me the fortress and everything in it, that is good. You can do this with a single word. If not, that is also fine, and you can do that with one word, too. . . . But if you are sincerely interested in reaching an agreement, then be a good man and stop expressing one thought at one time and another thought at another. My goal is to capture your fort and break it into pieces. Yours is to preserve it. But you can always come to me later for an agreement after I start shooting, with no fear. I just wanted to let you know all this.[8]

The warlord also wrote out a direct appeal to Dutch soldiers and officers, ordering Meij to copy out a statement in large block letters, like a placard:

> I am beginning to make strong preparations to overcome your fort and capture it. What is the origin of this latest disagreement? Coyet and his advisors are refusing to give me the company's treasures. . . . But that is not your fault. Lower officers and common soldiers cannot be held responsible for it. I have made huge expenditures on powder and cannonballs and on maintaining my army here, and the company must recompense me with its treasures. Coyet's treasures, as well as those of the other top leaders, will be given to my soldiers as booty, because that is how Heaven punishes those who do evil. But you captains, lieutenants, ensigns, sergeants, corporals, and soldiers bear no guilt in all this, so your belongings will not be harmed, not a single bit. All of you will be allowed to keep everything you have. . . . Coyet and your leaders have been more interested in money and goods than in saving your lives. Is that proper? Are they good people or evil people?[9]

Koxinga ordered Meij to sit at his feet in the dirt and read the placard out loud so the Dutch defectors could make sure it was correct. Then copies of the sign were placed on different sides of the castle where they could be viewed from the walls. It was a clever gambit. The soldiers in Zeelandia Castle were restive, resisting orders to work, stealing, and vandalizing things.[10] Those on the ships were getting mutinous.[11]

But Coyet continued to procrastinate, and when Koxinga summoned Meij the next time, he was in a white hot fury. It was a misty day. Koxinga was standing on top of a sand dune. As soon as Meij crested the hill, Koxinga turned and began shrieking at him, his face contorted in rage: Coyet was trying to trick him! He should have sent an answer by now! Koxinga slammed his fists together. He jumped up and down on both feet. He yelled, spit flying from his mouth. He screamed that was going to start shooting. He yelled for his executioners. Meij heard them come marching up the hill behind him. He didn't dare turn around, but he felt them standing there, five or six of them, while Koxinga kept spitting and yelling. Meij expected a sword to slice through his neck.

Two horses galloped from Zeelandia City lathered in sweat. Ma Xin and another high official dismounted and bowed until their heads were in the sand, their entire bodies bent over. You're worthless! Koxinga yelled. You're stinking dogs! They endured the tirade, foreheads resting on the ground. Finally Koxinga turned and stalked down to his tent. Ma Xin got up and followed. Meij saw him direct a few words into the darkness within and then heard shrill laughter: "Philip! Philip!" Koxinga called out, "Your nation is good and honest!"[12] Coyet had finally sent a letter with a properly meek tone: "We agree to hand over to Your Highness this castle and the company's money and goods."[13] The executioners marched down the dune and left Meij shaken but alive.

There were more details to be attended to—what exactly was meant by the company's money and goods, how much Coyet and the high officials could take with them, what parts of the company's records would be copied. But a few days later, evening on the first day of February 1662, the final contract was signed by the Dutch and sealed by the Chinese in an open-air ceremony in the City of Zeelandia, each side swearing by solemn oath "in the manner of their country" to abide faithfully by its provisions.[14]

Hostages were exchanged to ensure that the terms were carried out properly. Poor David Harthouwer was chosen, and he was instructed to try to locate wives and children of Dutchmen and persuade them to return to Batavia. He found that many Formosa-born wives didn't want to leave. When they insisted, he told them that Koxinga was cruel and tended to kill his prisoners and subjects. These reasonings didn't seem to help. One wife, for example, said she'd rather die in Taiwan than sail to Batavia, and if Harthouwer was so worried about a half-Dutch child he was welcome to take the baby even though it was still nursing. When Harthouwer told Coyet, the governor replied, "That she could make this kind of offer shows clearly how little interest she has in her own children, and this makes it easier for us to leave her behind."[15] Maybe Coyet felt bad for everything he'd put Harthouwer through, because he sent him a bottle "of good stuff." "I hope," Coyet wrote to him, "that you've been able to use some of that drink and have already consumed a good amount of it for your good health."[16]

Koxinga held on to Philip Meij. At first the warlord had promised him his freedom and Meij had thanked God, finding it miraculous that he'd been "one of the only three men who'd lived when three hundred others had been killed. God Almighty be always praised and thanked for this, Who has helped me through all this adversity so mercifully and protected me so miraculously from all these evils and delivered me to freedom."[17]

But when Meij went to the Eastern Capital to collect his wife and family, Hans Radis came over, drunk, and said Meij shouldn't be so confident, because until the Dutch prisoners were on the ship everything could still go wrong. And, Radis said, even if you do make it to Batavia, you shouldn't stay there long, because Koxinga will soon come knocking just as he knocked on the door of the redoubt. "I paid no attention," Meij wrote, "to this bastard's drunken words and filthy blather."[18]

Radis was right that things could still go wrong. Koxinga got furious again because Coyet was refusing to vacate the castle until Koxinga had given back all the slaves he'd captured during the war. Koxinga roared to Meij that there was nothing in the contract about slaves, and that if there was, someone had put it there without his knowledge, and whoever did it should be killed right away! Since Meij had been involved in the translation of the document, he was understandably rattled. So he begged Coyet to reconsider his position. Coyet refused. Meij begged Coyet to let him stay in the castle, because he was sure Koxinga would kill him, but then he remembered his wife. So he went back to the Eastern Capital, where he managed, with the help of some Chinese officials, to calm Koxinga.[19] Coyet ended up renouncing his demand for the slaves.[20]

Finally Meij's wife and their household were loaded into a boat and rowed through an intense wind to Zeelandia. Meij was already in the castle, helping He Bin inventory the warehouses: eighty-six barrels of bacon, five barrels of butter, and so on. By the time they finished it was late at night. He found to his shock that the little boat with his things was still moored in front of the castle. No one had bothered to unload it, and it was too dark to do it now. The next morning he and his wife awoke to find the boat dashed to pieces and their things gone. Just a few items were washed up on the sand.

On the morning of 9 February, the ground still wet with rain from days of stormy weather, drums began beating in Zeelandia Castle. Chinese soldiers watched warily as the Dutch soldiers marched out, company after company, flags flying, drums beating, musket fuses burning, a bullet in each mouth. They marched out onto the stone pier and then embarked onto the waiting boats. Coyet stood on shore with a group of advisors and handed the keys to a Chinese official. Then he boarded a boat and watched Zeelandia Castle float away.

Koxinga rode down from the destroyed redoubt and toured the castle, but he didn't stay long, worried that Coyet might have left a mine. He insisted that a few Dutchmen stay inside the castle for several days, ostensibly to count and recount the gold and silver. Hans Radis advised him to torture them to make sure there was no bomb, but Koxinga didn't. He seemed to believe the Dutchmen when they promised with a solemn oath that there was no hidden powder. "Our words," they wrote, "seem to have more verity with His Highness than those of the defector."[21]

Two weeks later, the fleet set sail.

"And thus," wrote Philip Meij, "we had to leave our castle Zeelandia and all of the Island Formosa, to the shame of our nation in these Indian lands, to the great detriment of our lords and masters, and to the utter ruin and destruction of my family."[22] The Beautiful Island, an "earthly paradise,"[23] and "one of the most beautiful pearls in the crown"[24] of the Dutch empire, was gone.

A Mad Death

The end of the siege brought little peace to Koxinga. The warehouses of Zeelandia Castle were given to him full of treasure and provisions, but the amounts did little to feed his starving men. He was desperate for rice, and none was coming from China. He was having a disagreement with his brother Zheng Tai, who served in Xiamen as his minister of finance. Zheng Tai had never agreed with the Taiwan adventure, and now, to make the point, he was refusing to send grain. Koxinga was furious and declared that "the Minister of Finance has failed in his command and must be declared guilty."[1] When Zheng Tai continued defying him, Koxinga ordered him and others still in China to send their families and dependents to the Eastern Capital. They refused. As a result, one Chinese source notes, Taiwan was completely cut off from China, and not a single junk sailed to Taiwan.[2]

One junk must have made the crossing, however, because a tall and frightened Dominican father named Victorio Riccio sailed from Xiamen to Taiwan in early 1662.[3] Riccio had been tending his small flock of Chinese Christians in Koxinga's mainland base and trying unsuccessfully to keep Koxinga's son from taking away his church and property when suddenly Koxinga had sent for him with no explanation. Koxinga's deadly rages were well-known to his subjects, so when Riccio parted from a crying congregation, he thought he was being "called to his death."[4] He arrived safely in Taiwan and waited for an audience, readying his soul for death and observing the terrifying tumult of the place. One midnight, for example, someone knocked on his door to summon one of the people he lived with, who was needed in connection with one of Koxinga's orders: to throw some women from Koxinga's palace into the sea.

Eventually Riccio learned why he'd been summoned. Koxinga wanted him to go to the Philippines and demand tribute from the Spaniards. Koxinga gave him a letter to take to the Spanish governor:

> It has been the practice since antiquity and is still the custom today that every foreign nation recognize celebrated princes chosen by Heaven and pay them tribute. . . . I am sending this father to persuade you to submit yourselves to the Will of Heaven and . . . humbly come each year to pay me homage. . . . If you do not comply, my fleet will immediately attack you. It will burn and destroy your forts, your cities, your warehouses, and everything else.[5]

The letter warned the Spanish not to make the same mistake the Dutch had. "If they had come to humbly salute me and pay tribute, I would perhaps have been appeased and they wouldn't be so miserable now."[6]

Riccio felt that Koxinga's demand was "a barbaric and insane move."[7] The Spanish would never submit. Koxinga would be forced to go to war to "destroy those islands with fire and blood, leaving no stone that is not reduced to ashes."[8]

Sure enough, when Riccio arrived in the Philippines, accompanied by some grandly dressed Chinese officials, the Spanish were defiant. The city of Manila erupted into uproar. Mobs formed and began threatening to massacre the tens of thousands of Chinese who lived outside the thick walls. Chinese formed militias to defend themselves, killing some Africans and Spaniards and attacking the city gate. There were skirmishes, cannon shots, drownings.

Riccio and the Spanish governor worked hard to avoid a slaughter, remembering that in 1603 and again in 1639 tens of thousands of Chinese settlers had been hunted down and killed by Spanish and Philipino forces. Riccio liked the Chinese. He didn't want anything to happen to them, so he went outside the walls into Chinatown to talk to Chinese leaders with his excellent Chinese.

He and another priest addressed a mob of thousands and asked them to lay down their arms. Most agreed, but some remained hostile. His companion was killed. He himself was nearly killed but, "pallid in face," made it back to the city and persuaded the governor and the Spanish military commanders that the Chinese should be deported rather than killed. They were loaded onto junks, which "departed so full of Chinese—much like a cargo of coal or firewood—that there was no place to stand. All were squeezed together like sheep in a pen, and there was scarcely enough room to manage the sails."[9] The Spanish governor wrote a proud letter, and Riccio offered to take it back to Taiwan even though Koxinga had said he'd kill him if the Spanish refused. Riccio said he was ready for martyrdom. He embarked on the last Chinese junk out of Manila.

It was a terrifying voyage. Directly out of port the craft was thrashed by a terrible storm. Its passengers were forced ashore in the northern Philippines, where they were attacked by local villagers. When they re-embarked, they were blown off course and had to sail, hull leaking, along Taiwan's dangerous east coast. At this point the Chinese sailors decided the bearded friar was bad luck and tried to persuade the few Chinese Christians on board to throw him overboard. Another storm tore away the mast and rudder. The junk was driven before the wind and rain. Riccio prayed with a candle, while the Chinese "sounded their drums and called upon their gods to help them, but the gods couldn't help them and the tempest got stronger."[10] Riccio felt that his own prayers worked, because the ship was miraculously blown to Jinmen Island.

Jinmen was still under the control of Koxinga's brother Zheng Tai. Riccio was seized and sentenced to death by throat slashing, but he was saved by two things. First, people attested to his role in protecting the Chinese in the Philippines. Second, Koxinga died a mad death.

According to Riccio's Chinese informants, Koxinga's death occurred after he'd learned that the Spaniards were on the point of killing thousands of Chinese in the Philippines. He'd flown into a rage and ordered his forces to prepare to attack Manila. Riccio wrote:

> But God looked down with providence at the Catholic Islands of the Philippines . . . and, heeding the prayers of the people of

> Manila . . . , sent the angel of justice . . . to punish the blasphemous tyrant. Koxinga was struck by a violent sunstroke. He was so overcome with rage and pain that he bit his fingers and clawed at his face and five days later gave up his soul to the devil. He committed horrible actions until the end, beating and kicking anyone who tried to attend to him, ordering executions left and right, and he died with a horrifying look on his face.[11]

What are we to make of this description of Koxinga's death? Riccio is a credible source. He was keyed into events in Koxinga's court, thanks to a network of Catholic Chinese who lived in Taiwan and China. And the image of Koxinga dying in a mad rage jibes with Meij's descriptions of Koxinga's foaming-at-the-mouth tantrums.

Most importantly, various Chinese sources also say that Koxinga's life ended in madness. One of his earliest biographies puts it simply: "He went crazy and died."[12] Other accounts provide a reason for his madness. In the late spring of 1662, they say, Koxinga learned that his son and heir apparent Zheng Jing had slept with his younger brother's wet nurse.[13] According to Koxinga, this was incest. He flew into a rage. He ordered his son executed, and the mother, and the baby, and even his own number-one wife, who he felt should have kept better order in the family.[14] His brother Zheng Tai had the baby and the wet nurse killed but declined to execute the son and wife. Koxinga was furious. He sent renewed execution orders and vowed to kill his generals and officials in Xiamen if they didn't comply. Zheng Tai and the others began defying him openly, preparing to recognize Koxinga's son Zheng Jing as their leader. According to the *Official Qing History*, all this emotional tumult undid Koxinga: "The hate welled up in him so intensely that he went crazy and died gnawing his fingers."[15]

Other Chinese accounts suggest that Koxinga died of a fever—perhaps malaria—although in these sources, too, there are hints of madness. One of the most authoritative describes how he threw his medicine on the floor and exclaimed, "I've failed in both loyalty and filiality, dying with unfinished business. Oh Heaven! Oh Heaven! How could you let me come to this?" after which he died stamping his feet, yelling, and pounding his chest.[16] Another early Chinese account says he died clawing at his eyes and face, crying, "I'm too ashamed to face the late emperor (in Heaven)!"[17]

One intriguing possibility to explain Koxinga's end-of-life madness is that he had syphilis. In 1654, a Dutch surgeon named Christian Beyer was sent to Xiamen to help treat Koxinga. It was a good will gesture, when Koxinga and the company were still getting along, and the Beyer looked at "a few lumps on his left arm, which according to Koxinga felt had been caused by cold and wind, but about which Beyer himself had a different opinion."[18] It's possible that the Dutch writer's reticence about the true cause indicates that Beyer suspected it was syphilis, which in earlier stages can cause rashes and lesions on skin and in later stages can cause psychosis.[19] The idea that as he was dying he scratched his eyes and face might perhaps fit a diagnosis of tertiary syphilis, in which gummas form on the face. On the other hand, it's notoriously difficult to diagnose syphilis, which doctors have referred to as "the great imposter."

To Europeans, this mad death was God's justice. An account by a Belgian priest spins a story of Koxinga seeing ghosts of his victims. Standing on the ramparts of Zeelandia Castle, he suddenly screams and orders his retainers to "take away those decapitated bodies! Don't you see them? Over there! Lying on the ground! Can't you hear them? They're looking for me, saying I killed them and they were innocent!" He falls down and lies ill for three days. Then, gnawing his fingers, he dies.[20]

A Dutch poem published in 1670 makes this sense of divine justice explicit:

His horrible mouth bites desperately
Into his very own flesh
That's how God's justice works:
He who chopped off others' hands
Now bites off his own.[21]

Koxinga's passing ended the threat for the Philippines, but Victorio Riccio's trials continued. He was captured by Qing soldiers, who stripped off his silk robe and dragged him barefoot through burrs and stones and thorns so he "bathed the path in blood." He was loaded into a boat, whose captain beat him and made him sit in the prow with the rest of the garbage. A servant boy made him trade underwear, so Riccio ended up with a set that "was soiled, torn, and smaller in size." The Qing transferred him to a Dutch ship, whose crew swore at him and threw him in the brig. He shivered in his dirty underwear until the Dutch admiral learned who he was and freed him.[22]

In the meantime, Coyet was undergoing his own tribulations. When he and the rest of the besieged arrived in Batavia after a stormy month at sea, they were forbidden to go ashore.[23] Men came aboard and searched their luggage and unloaded the ships while keeping an eye on them, "so that nothing might be sent ashore without their knowledge."[24] Coyet was allowed to land but was confined to his house while his chests, boxes, and valuables were impounded.[25] They wouldn't let him meet with the Governor-General or the High Council of the Indies to report on the siege.

The Governor-General and the councilors felt that the surrender was fishy, particularly the fact that the leaders of Formosa had decided to give Koxinga all the capital in Zeelandia Castle. They were in a punitive mood. All the soldiers, officers, and officials who were in Zeelandia Castle when it surrendered were fined six months of pay.[26] Coyet was stripped of his rank and privileges. He was ordered to move from his spacious house in Batavia to an old house in Batavia Castle, and when he refused on the grounds that it was too small and dirty, they retaliated by confining him to the front hall of his house.[27] They tried to prevent him from reading his letters and diaries or writing letters to the Netherlands. They forced him to sit at a table with the man who was prosecuting him and sign papers and records that, in the confusion of the war, had remained unsigned. He resisted doggedly and increasingly vehemently, using "heavy words," and saying that what was being done to him was "nothing more than pure violence and tyranny," vowing to avenge himself and demonstrate before the entire world that he was an honorable man and a true servant of the company.[28]

After years of exile, he was released on special order of the Prince of Orange and returned to Holland, but his promising career was over, and in the meantime, his enemy Nicholas Verburg, the man who had intrigued against him for so long, had become one of the richest men of Holland.[29]

Coyet got his revenge. His book *Neglected Formosa* portrayed Verburg and Cauw and the rest of the company leadership as selfish fools, saying that they were responsible for the loss of Formosa because they failed to listen to his advice and provide proper defenses and adequate reinforcements.

But was he right? Could the Dutch have staved off Koxinga's massive invasion?

CLOSING

Epilogues and Conclusions

When I started this book I was firmly in the revisionist camp. I believed that Europe held little if any technological lead over developed parts of Asia during the sixteenth and seventeenth centuries. The Sino-Dutch War offers much to corroborate that view. Dutch cannons provided no advantage against Koxinga, who fielded artillery every bit as good. When Swiss soldier Albrecht Herport reminisced about the war, he expressed a common opinion in saying that the Chinese "know how to make very effective guns and cannons, so that it's scarcely possible to find their equal elsewhere."[1]

Those cannons were adopted from European models, but of course the Chinese had invented cannons first, and copying is part of war. The French and Italians and Dutch and Spanish had been imitating each other's designs for decades. Herport goes on to note that the Chinese were especially good at this process of adoption: "Anything they see even one time they can produce themselves quickly."[2]

Yet their ability to make good cannons was no accident. A century before the war, the Ming had established a special bureau to study western cannons.[3] They used them against the Japanese in the Korean War of 1592–1598 to devastating effect. The Japanese, who possessed advanced guns of their own, became so wary that they avoided Ming artillery for the rest of the war.

Ming officials were so intrigued by European cannons that, as we've seen, they even dredged them up from shipwrecks. In the

1620s, at least forty-two Dutch and British pieces were salvaged in southern China and shipped to Beijing, a distance nearly equivalent to the distance between Paris and Moscow. The operations were massive, with derricks and cranes and chains of steel.[4] To reverse-engineer the cannons, Beijing sought artisans from the Land of Min, whose people were renowned throughout China as forgers and casters, having learned about advanced cannon designs from the westerners themselves.[5] "These days," a Chinese writer noted, "the westerners are floating around the seas of southern China, and there's no shortage of people consorting with them. The people of Min have already learned from them the craft of forging powerful cannons."[6] Beijing was soon making what they called Red Barbarian Cannons. Thus, by the time the Sino-Dutch War started, Chinese cannon technology was highly advanced, particularly in Koxinga's home province.

Of course, it's one thing to make good guns and another to use them. Scholars have argued that a hallmark of European modernization was a precocious focus on measurement, the application of mathematical principles to practical purposes, particularly to warfare.[7] In the sixteenth and seventeenth centuries, scientists like Nicholas Tartaglia and Galileo Galilei developed targeting tools that helped gunners aim and load their cannons, improving accuracy (figure 25). The Chinese seem to have adopted these tools.[8] We have no direct evidence about Koxinga's own use of them, but we do know that his artillery teams were swift and accurate, so much so that a frustrated Coyet wrote, "They are able to handle their cannons so effectively . . . [that] [t]hey put our own soldiers to shame."[9]

What about handguns? Muskets were known in East Asia long before the Taiwan War. The Japanese pointed them at the Chinese in the 1590s. The Ming studied them. They also studied the advanced muskets that Europeans brought in the early seventeenth century. They appear in the *Jing guo xiong lüe*, the military manual and strategy guide published by Koxinga's father in 1645, which describes how accuracy increased as boring practices improved and gives advice about unifying muzzle sizes and pellet weights.[10] It noted that although advanced muskets, referred to as "bird guns," were "quick and accurate," they were also "weak and ineffective in defending against large

Figure 25. Gunners using instruments to measure a cannon, 1618. This plate depicts gunners using what was known as a "geometrical gunnery instrument" to measure a gun and its ladle (a ladle is a long-handled scoop to load powder). Although Chinese literati were aware of such measuring devices (they appear in various Chinese treatises), it's not clear how widely they were actually employed in Chinese warfare. Whether or not Koxinga's gunners made use of such instruments, they easily matched their Dutch counterparts in expertise. Illustration from Leonhard Zubler, *Nova geometrica pyrobolia*, 1618. Used by permission of Anne S. K. Brown Military Collection, Brown University Library, Providence, Rhode Island.

armies, insufficient for defending strategic places or extending military might."[11]

Koxinga did experiment with muskets—his African musketeers proved lethal against the Dutch—but he preferred larger and more powerful handguns and bows and arrows, a decision that didn't hurt him in the Taiwan War. Dutch musketry companies, so famous in Europe, proved useless against his soldiers. When Thomas Pedel marched out on the second day of the war, confident that the ancient-looking Chinese troops would scatter at the first taste of lead, it was his own men who panicked and ran. A few other musket skirmishes, such as the one on Penghu when Harthouwer's soldiers were overwhelmed by a small Chinese detachment, also show no advantage for Dutch muskets against Koxinga's saber-staves and bows and arrows.

That's because Koxinga's troops were extremely well disciplined, which leads us to reject another common argument about European warfare. Partisans of the Military Revolution Theory argue that a key part of the Military Revolution was a new emphasis on drills and tactics, new ways of organizing bodies and instilling discipline. This book should make us cautious about the idea that such a disciplinary regime was unique to Europe or lay behind Europeans' success overseas. Koxinga's soldiers proved far more disciplined and effective on the battlefield than the Dutch, despite the fact that the Dutch were renowned throughout Europe for their drill officers and military manuals.

This is an important issue, because it draws us into wider theories about European society, such as the work of Michel Foucault, whose writings have had a seminal influence. One of the key examples Foucault uses to illustrate the great transformation he sees in European society, from social control by spectacle to social control by surveillance and discipline, is military drill. For him, these new drilling regimens represent a decisive moment in the development of modern modes of social control. It's striking that the progenitor of the Military Revolution Model, historian Michael Roberts, and Foucault use precisely the same example to make their cases: a medal struck by Louis XIV that shows the king conducting a military parade with all his soldiers in lockstep. There's no evidence that they read each other.

This notion of western discipline shows up in arguments about a so-called western way of war, the idea that westerners were better killers because of a unique host of factors: "organization, discipline, morale, initiative, flexibility, and command."[12] This list is from a book by Victor Davis Hanson, who argues that westerners have proven the most effective soldiers for thousands of years because of a cohesive military tradition. Yet he barely mentions China, and many of his contentions about the uniqueness of western warfare would be contradicted by data from East Asia. He argues, for example, that "infantrymen, fighting en masse, who take and hold ground and fight face-to-face are a uniquely Western specialty—the product of a long tradition of a middling landholding citizenry who expresses unease with both landless peasants and mounted aristocrats."[13] Of course, in China, the infantry was often the core of Chinese armed forces, especially in the south, and the entire implied schema of historical development that lurks beneath his analysis—the "middling landholding citizenry," the "mounted aristocrats"—is so clearly based on Europe that it can't be stretched over the Chinese experience.

One of Hanson's key arguments is that westerners were more disciplined than nonwesterners. "Warriors," he writes, "are not necessarily soldiers. Both types of killers can be brave, but disciplined troops value the group over the single hero and can be taught to march in order, to stab, thrust, or shoot en masse and on command, and to advance and retreat in unison—something impossible for the bravest of Aztecs, Zulus, or Persians."[14] We've seen here that Koxinga's soldiers were more disciplined than the Dutch soldiers they faced. This emphasis on drill was an ancient Chinese heritage, one that was considerably elaborated and systematized in the Ming and early Qing period. I don't intend here to argue against Hanson's views wholesale.[15] My point is merely that Hanson shows how we need more research into military history, particularly nonwestern military history.

Fortunately, there are signs of life on this front, the small but growing group of historians whom I refer to as the Chinese Military Revolution School.[16] Their findings are overturning core ideas about European military history. For example, Sun Laichen has shown convincingly that the Chinese were the first to develop volley fire. The standard view has been that the practice emerged in Japan and Europe at the end of the sixteenth century, but Sun finds it described in Ming sources in 1387.[17] Similarly, most military historians, who have tended to focus on Europe, would be surprised to learn that in the late sixteenth and early seventeenth centuries, at precisely the time that the military manual was spreading so rapidly in Europe, there was a surge in military manual production in China, Korea, and Japan.

These manuals seem to share with European ones a focus on repetitive drilling and the use of illustrations to describe formations.[18] Hanson may be right that there's a western way of war, but we'll never know so long as our knowledge of nonwestern war remains so rudimentary.

The more we learn, the more we'll understand what truly made European warfare unique.

Cannons and muskets and military discipline provided no discernable edge to Dutch forces, but there were two areas in which the the Dutch did hold an advantage: the broadside sailing ship and the renaissance fortress.

SHIPS

Chinese observers weren't reticent about judging European ships superior in deepwater combat, and it's clear from the naval battles in this book that Dutch ships could stand up to far larger numbers of Chinese warjunks. Of course, superior leadership could undo this advantage, as in 1633, when Zheng Zhilong defeated a Dutch fleet at Liaoluo Bay by disguising fireships as warships. Similarly, the Dutch could squander their advantage, as when Coyet insisted, against the advice of Chinese defectors, on bringing his deep sailing ships into the Bay of Taiwan for a foolish attack.

But at sea and under strong leadership, Dutch ships were masterful. This is especially clear in a naval battle that occurred after the surrender of Zeelandia Castle. The day after Koxinga's mad death, a Dutch admiral named Balthasar Bort led a fleet to China to avenge the loss of Taiwan.[19] Many of the men who sailed under him had been in Taiwan during the war. In fact, the skipper of Bort's flagship was the man who had allowed a Dutch surgeon to vivisect a Chinese prisoner and had watched the procedure with his one good eye.[20]

Admiral Bort got to the Chinese coast and learned that Koxinga had died and that his son Zheng Jing—the one who'd slept with a wet nurse—was vying for control over the organization. It was a good opportunity, and he urged Qing leaders to strike quickly. The Qing were slow, and the two allies couldn't get things together until the following year, 1663, but when they did they achieved a magnificent victory.

Prince Geng Jimao, the man whom Hurt and Clewerck had voyaged so far to see when driven ashore in 1661, devised the basic plan: jointly attack the Zheng bases of Xiamen and Jinmen (see figure 9). In the past, the Qing could never defeat the Zheng navy. At one point, a Qing fleet was beaten so badly its commander committed suicide.[21] Prince Geng believed that Dutch ships could tip the balance.

He wasn't the only one. When November winds brought Bort's fleet to Jinmen Island in 1663, the "Koxingers," as the Dutch had begun calling Koxinga's heirs, got worried. Zheng Jing had hundreds of powerful junks, whereas the Dutch fleet had fifteen ships, but his commanders sent panicked letters to Bort: "We cannot with our ships fight against your ships."[22] They begged him to switch sides or at least choose neutrality: "Please, we ask that you and your ships not support the Manchus against us but sail to another place, and if you . . . can't meet our request, then please let us know right away, or sail with your fifteen ships to Liaoluo Bay and watch us fight against the Manchus, and you'll see that they will flee."[23]

The letters promised and pleaded and threatened. They said the Dutch could have ports on Taiwan. They said the Manchus were deceptive.[24] They said the waterways had "dry spots, and reefs, and hidden rocks, and so I warn you not to run aground in all your going back and forth and thus suffer shipwreck."[25] They threatened to burn his fleet with two hundred fireships. They reminded him that there were Dutch prisoners in Taiwan. They had one prisoner write a letter begging Bort to keep his ships to the side, or fire empty cannons, or just tell the Manchus that his ships lacked water and couldn't participate. Please, the prisoner said, think of him and the others and, for the love of God, end their captivity. Bort ordered his secretary to commend the man to God's protection and sent him three pieces of bacon and some cheese.[26]

It was a lovely day when Bort and the Qing attacked. The water was calm. A perfect wind was blowing. Bort led eight ships around one side of Jinmen, and his rear admiral led seven around the other side. Trapped between them in a narrow passage were a hundred Zheng junks. Bort's squadron sailed right in. Our ships, Bort wrote, "were spewing such powerful fire and flame against them that they didn't dare stand up against us."[27]

Yet the junks managed a dazzling escape. Some sailed into the shallows along the shore. Others ran before the wind, zigzagging. Their path was blocked by the rear admiral. Somehow they evaded him and headed straight toward a huge Qing fleet. It dwarfed the Dutch fleet: four hundred junks. The Koxingers were heavily outnumbered, but to Bort's surprise the Qing fled, seeking shelter near Dutch ships and blocking Dutch cannons.[28] The Koxingers captured two flagships and killed the chief commander of the fleet, a man named Ma Degong, one of the Qing side's most illustrated generals. All but three Zheng ships managed to escape.[29]

It was stunning seamanship. The Koxingers, Bort wrote, "conducted themselves as behooved magnificent soldiers."[30] He was less impressed by the Qing:

> Now we can see what kind of cowardly people the Manchus are. They didn't even dare with their entire armada to fight against seven or eight enemy junks but instead came and tried to save themselves under our cannons, leaving their own people in the lurch. Indeed, they left behind their own admiral Ma Degong as well as another top commander, . . . both of whom were killed there. What kind of help we might expect to receive from them in a time of need we can clearly see here.[31]

The next day the Qing and Dutch cooperated better. Bort attacked a Zheng fleet that was trying to prevent the Qing from landing forces on Xiamen. He drove the Zheng away and the Qing succeeded in capturing Xiamen. Soon Jinmen fell too. The Koxingers fled.

Thus Dutch ships again proved their superiority in an open firefight. After the battle Bort received a letter from Qing commander Li Shuaitai: "I watched your ships from a mountain top and rejoiced to see how with their thundering cannon they made the rebel ships flee. . . . I shall not delay to inform the emperor quickly, by special post, of the services you have done for the Empire, and that the Hollanders are brave and daring in their attacks on our enemy and theirs."[32]

Bort sent a less flattering report to Batavia: "the cowardice of our friends [the Manchus] was so great that we can truthfully say that the enemy would have defeated and destroyed their entire fleet if we hadn't protected them."[33] He complained that he couldn't count on the Qing for much help, but it didn't matter, because "on water . . .

our own power is (with God's help) sufficient enough to withstand the entire enemy fleet."[34]

It wasn't idle arrogance. Victorio Riccio—clothed, one hopes, in better underwear—watched the naval battle from a Dutch ship and wrote that "the Dutch ships equaled all the rest in strength, because the smallest Dutch vessel bore thirty-six pieces of heavy artillery."[35] Contemporaries—Chinese, Manchu, and Dutch—all agreed. Bort's fifteen ships were capable of standing up to Zheng Jing's entire navy.

But a question remains: Were Dutch vessels better at sailing into prevailing winds? No sailing ship can sail directly upwind, of course, but some can sail at closer angles. Chinese sources suggest that European ships were great at this, but we know next to nothing about traditional Chinese vessels.[36]

Evidence suggests that Ming junks had a difficult time sailing into the wind. I corresponded with a crewmember of a replica of a Ming junk that completed a round-trip from Taiwan to California in 2008–2009. I should say "nearly completed," because his vessel was rammed by an oil tanker less than a hundred miles from the finish line. He said Chinese junks can only sail downwind. "I can," he said, "personally vouch to this from experience."[37] His point is cautiously supported by other experts.[38]

Certainly, evidence from Sino-Dutch conflicts corroborates it. In 1633, in the battle of Liaoluo Bay, when Hans Putmans's fleet was defeated by Zheng Zhilong's disguised fireships, Zhilong wrote in his official report that he'd tried chasing the Dutch ships with his junks but couldn't catch them because "the barbarian ships tacked against the wind toward the outer seas and . . . the more we chased them the farther they got away."[39] Similarly, in the summer of 1661, Koxinga was shocked when he found, against all expectation, that the Dutch had been able to send a ship southward against monsoon winds to warn Batavia of his invasion (see figure 22). The idea of arriving in Taiwan after the monsoon winds changed had been a key part of his strategy, and he wouldn't have put so much stock in it if he hadn't expected it to work.

It's no surprise that European ships might have been better at sailing close to the wind because they were designed for different conditions than Chinese junks—or indeed Asian vessels in general. Maritime Asia had monsoons, and although there were local variations, they generally blew one direction in spring and another in fall. You could cover large distances by sailing with the wind. But the Atlantic Ocean had complicated patterns. To get up and down the coasts of western Europe and, especially, to navigate around Africa, you contended with bewildering and complex winds and currents.[40] European vessels and navigation techniques thus evolved to suit a great many different conditions.[41] Chinese junks—like most Asian vessels—simply didn't need to sail close to the wind as effectively as European ships.

Yet even more important than Dutch maritime technology was Dutch military engineering.

FORTS

Evidence from the Taiwan War shows that the renaissance fort deserves its reputation as a key technology of European colonial expansion and that Jeremy Black is too quick to cast aspersions on this idea by quipping, in an eminently quotable line (this is the second time I quote it), that non-Europeans were able to capture such fortresses relatively easily because they "had not read some of the literature on military revolution and did not know that European artillery forces were supposed to prevail with some sort of technological superiority over non-Europeans."[42]

Koxinga, who led one of the most powerful armies in the world, was stymied by Zeelandia Castle. He eventually managed to capture it, but it took him four separate attempts. The first time, his storming troops were shredded by Dutch cannons, and his officers were so shocked that they pleaded with Dutch prisoners to run out and tell their compatriots to stop shooting. The prisoners wisely demurred. The second time, he established a clever cannon position and tried to capture the dunetop redoubt that stood behind Zeelandia, but the Dutch merely built a new fortification that could provide counterfire. The third time, he tried from Baxemboy Island, personally overseeing the construction of an elaborate coastal fort with elements of European fortress design. This attempt, too, nearly succeeded, allowing his attack boats to cut the castle off by sea. But once again, the Dutch built a counterfortification and neutralized the threat.

The fourth and last time, he was helped by a high-ranking European officer, the drunkard Hans Radis. It was he who showed Koxinga that to capture a renaissance fortress you needed an elaborate set of siege-works. Those counterfortifications did the trick, but by then more than nine months had passed and Koxinga's army had been decimated by battle, starvation, and disease. As many as half his men had died.

In 1666, four years after Coyet's surrender, Koxinga's heirs had another chance to capture a renaissance fort. In 1664, the Dutch decided to establish a new colony on Taiwan, in the island's far north, on an offshore islet called Jilong. It was unhealthy and isolated, surrounded by ambivalent natives. But the Dutch began building a renaissance fortress there on the ruins of one they'd abandoned in 1661. Work was slow, because it rained constantly. One Dutchman complained in verse:

Why, oh Heaven, why?
Must you cry and cry?
For how long will this rain
Maintain its sodden reign?
How long, oh Lord, how long
Will this soaking keep enduring?
Please stop this constant wet
From pouring pouring pouring![43]

The garrison worked in the wet to finish a large, squat, four-sided renaissance fortress.[44] Two bastions jutted out over the sea. The other two faced flat fields that stretched to a green mountain, on the peak of which they built a redoubt, just as, forty years before, other Dutchmen had built the dunetop redoubt that protected Zeelandia Castle.

The Koxingers attacked in May of 1666. Forty junks sailed around Jilong Island and disembarked three thousand troops on the beach behind the mountain, out of reach of Dutch cannons. They marched around the base of the mountain and then waited, sheltering themselves in the dense brush and peering out over the field. A small company of Dutch musketeers stood near some sparse vegetable gardens.

The musketeers fired. The Chinese shot back. The musketeers retreated. The Chinese pursued.

But the Dutch commanders were taking a page right out of Koxinga's own playbook: *feign weakness and lure.* It was a convincing performance. "We got them to the point," wrote the Dutch official in charge of the garrison, "that they were following and chasing after our little fleeing group, coming within range of our cannons in the fort. . . . It was beautifully done, because just when they thought they would come running into our fortress in their shoes and stockings, they were stopped by cannonfire and attacks by our soldiers."[45]

Chinese soldiers fell. Their commander was struck in the head. They retreated, pursued by musketmen, who drove them back behind the mountain. "And all this," the Dutch commander exulted, "with such few people! It seemed that the enemy was so shocked and frightened that we could have defeated them if we'd had fifty or sixty more men. If we'd had a hundred or a hundred and fifty more, we could have driven them from the island altogether."[46]

The next day thousands more Chinese troops arrived. There were perhaps six thousand of them against just three hundred Europeans. Instead of attacking the main fortress they focused on the mountaintop redoubt, which had just twenty defenders. At three in the morning they stormed, two thousand strong, trying to set up ladders and scale the walls. The defenders fired cannons and muskets, threw hand grenades and vats of cloddy gunpowder with fuses, one of which exploded before it could be hurled, burning four defenders.

The Chinese tried again the following night. "But," wrote the Dutch commander, "the Great Almighty War Hero fought on our side, so that the enemy could not overpower the redoubt but was driven away with great courage. Many of their side were killed and many wounded. We could hear from our fortress the wailing of the enemies."[47]

Having failed to storm the redoubt, they built a fort along a foothill below the mountain and placed four cannons in it. Protected from Dutch counterfire, they shot a hundred and nine shots at the redoubt. (The Dutch kept careful count.) Nearly all missed. A Dutch soldier was killed, but no damage was done to the walls.

Then, nine days after arriving, they left. The Dutch commander claimed to be disappointed: "We thought they'd try to attack the main fort again, and we even greatly desired this, so we could play a nice game with them again. All our people, including the least among them, were full of courage, determined to fight with zeal against our enemies, those evil heathens. But the enemy didn't dare attempt it. They didn't even have the courage to come out from behind the mountain."[48] They boarded their junks and sailed away, "to their great shame and God's great glory."[49]

He was perplexed by the way the Koxingers went about the attack, bringing so few cannons and not even trying to build proper siegeworks. "They didn't have more than four pieces of artillery. . . . It seemed that they didn't think it was worth the trouble to do anything but try to take the fortress by storm."[50] He believed that if they'd mounted a proper siege, or a blockade, or if they'd merely stayed longer, they would have won. His assessment is worth quoting:

> We must not take credit for this victory, because God the Great Warrior is the only one to whom honor can be given. It was He who defeated our enemy and drove them away, because if the Chinese had used proper means of warfare, then they would have had us. . . . By creating a little more alarm for us in the fortress, they would have exhausted all of our people and it wouldn't have taken more than a few days for us to use up all our lead, of which we had very little. I won't even mention that if they had fired at us with cannons out of batteries we would have quickly run out of cannonballs, because most of our cannons were three or four pounders, for which we had very little ammunition or schrapnel in our armory.[51]

Why didn't the Chinese use "proper means of warfare"?

They must have forgotten the lessons learned in Zeelandia. Hans Radis was still alive, but he evidently wasn't consulted. They approached the fort as they might have approached a Chinese wall, one without bastions and defended by few cannons, and they were surprised by its deadly firepower. The Dutch commander felt he'd been lucky—or, rather, felt he'd been helped by God—because the Chinese should by all rights have won. They would have if they'd used proper means of warfare.

So the renaissance fortress deserves its reputation as a key technology behind European expansion. Traditional walls—even the massive walls of China—could be stormed. Once you shot away the battlements and the defenders were no longer able to shoot or, as they sometimes did, hurl rocks and dead dogs and human excrement, you could scale the walls. Or, if you preferred, you could batter down a gate. But to take a renaissance fort you needed extensive siegeworks, and you had to expect that the enemy would build his own counterfortifications. You had to respond with new siegeworks, and so on. It was tedious, time-consuming, and expensive.[52] Koxinga figured it out in the end, thanks to Hans Radis's help, but it seems that the knowledge wasn't passed on. His heirs failed to capture the Jilong fort. Fortunately for them, the Dutch eventually abandoned it, blowing up its walls so that "nothing was left for the enemy but a pile of dust."[53]

The Koxingers were lucky in another way, too: the Dutch abandoned their alliance with the Qing and their plans to recapture Taiwan. The partnership had been tense from the start, but in 1664, the disgruntlements broke into the open. Bort and a Qing admiral named Shi Lang, whom you might remember as a talented general who ran from Koxinga's side to escape execution, were working together to recapture Zeelandia Castle, and Prince Geng had promised that the Dutch would get to keep Taiwan.[54] At first things went well. Bort's ships rendezvoused with Shi Lang's fleet at Liaoluo Bay, the place where Zheng Zhilong had defeated Hans Putmans and where Koxinga had embarked for his invasion of Taiwan. They set sail on Christmas Eve of 1664 under strong winds. But suddenly Bort heard three shots fired from Shi Lang's flagship and saw the whole Qing fleet—three hundred vessels—turn back. Bort was furious. Shi Lang said it was too dangerous to sail. Bort disagreed. Shi Lang retorted that he'd try again in the spring and if Bort didn't want to help out that was fine, because he could do it himself. He taunted the Dutch for having lost Taiwan in the first place.[55] Bort sailed for Batavia.

He didn't come back, and those who replaced him couldn't fix the alliance. The Dutch were indignant at "Tartar Perfidy." Prince Geng and Li Shuaitai, the men who'd welcomed Hurt and Clewerck in 1661, became angrier and angrier. There were disputes about trading and debts. There was yelling. There were accidents. A Dutch soldier killed a Qing subject. Dutch soldiers raided a Buddhist shrine. The alliance collapsed. Taiwan remained in Zheng hands.[56]

The Qing tried reviving the pact in the late 1670s, but Dutch leaders were still bitter and said no. In 1683 Shi Lang conquered Taiwan. By then the idea of letting the Dutch have the island had long been forgotten, and the Dutch weren't interested anyway. The Qing installed their own government, and the following year they allowed Europeans to trade in China itself, which is what the Dutch had always wanted.

WAYS OF WAR

Today, a Chinese regime rules Taiwan, a situation not so different from the way the Zheng family ruled it for twenty-two years in opposition to the Qing. It's not clear what the future holds, although the People's Republic of China is rapidly developing new missiles, submarines, destroyers, and aircraft carriers, which worries many western experts.[57] There are reports that it has nicknamed one of its aircraft carriers the *Shi Lang,* after the man who captured Taiwan from Koxinga's heirs. This is a signal—one of many—that it doesn't intend to let Taiwan maintain independence.

The United States has pledged to defend Taiwan, so there may someday be a war between the two giants. If so, does the Sino-Dutch War of 1661–1668 hold any lessons? After all, the balance of technological power today resembles that of the seventeenth century more than that of the Opium Wars, the Boxer War, or the Korean War of 1950–1953.

One lesson is that technology alone doesn't win wars. In the Sino-Dutch conflict, leadership was key, and Dutch leadership was poor. Foolish Thomas Pedel let himself be outmaneuvered by Koxinga's commander Chen Ze. Jacob Valentine failed to keep Fort Provintia stocked with food and water and gunpowder. Coyet was constantly feuding with his colleagues. He and Admiral Jan van der Laan argued in 1660, leading the admiral to abscond with the best ships and officers. He quarreled with Jacob Cauw, the leader of the relief fleet of 1661, describing him as a ninny with a speech defect. He had a long-standing feud with Nicholas Verburg, who sat on the High Council of the Indies in Batavia.

Coyet derided these men in his book, and historians have adopted his caricatures, but maybe Coyet was the source of the trouble. He seems like a difficult man, indignant, quick to avenge perceived slights. He slapped an underling for failing to show respect and then launched an investigation into the underling's comrade, who said some unfortunate things in a drunken tirade. By the end of 1661 he was quarreling so intensely with Harthouwer and Casembroot and Cauw that they failed to take full advantage of the Manchu alliance. And his feud with his enemies in Batavia affected the colony's interactions with superiors.

In contrast, Koxinga and his commanders were strong leaders. This was evident on the very first day of the invasion, when they avoided the main channel and sailed into Taiwan through the Deer's Ear Gap, taking advantage of a high tide. Koxinga's chronicler ascribed that tide to the Will of Heaven, but Koxinga timed his invasion carefully to coincide with the tide, so he could avoid Zeelandia Castle and land his troops before Coyet could even react. Within days he'd established control over much of mainland Taiwan and achieved the surrender of Fort Provintia. His commander Chen Ze achieved victories on land against the overconfident Thomas Pedel and at sea against three Dutch ships. Later, when Coyet made his foolish naval attack in the Bay of Taiwan, Chen Ze lured the Dutch into a trap, thoroughly routing them. In nearly every engagement during the nine-month siege of Zeelandia, Koxinga's troops outfought and Koxinga's officers outfoxed the Dutch.

Of course Koxinga's leadership wasn't perfect. His own side was affected by discord, as when his adoptive brother Zheng Tai refused to send rice to Taiwan. And Koxinga could be overconfident. When Zhang Huangyan urged him to attack Nanjing right away, saying armies shouldn't sit still because mistakes can happen, he foolishly ignored the advice because he was so sure Nanjing would soon give in. He was similarly overconfident the first time he attacked Zeelandia

Castle, and after he failed to capture it, overconfidence once again led him to send almost all his troops into Taiwan's frontiers, leaving his new capital undefended. He was sure the Dutch wouldn't be able to send for reinforcements against the winds and was shocked when the relief fleet arrived.

Despite such lapses, Koxinga and his officers displayed superior leadership, and some Chinese historians have argued that they benefited from China's deep legacy of military thought.[58] It's a compelling idea. Maxims and stratagems from Sun Zi and other sources pepper Koxinga and his father's sources. When Zhilong was preparing to assault Hans Putmans's fleet with fireships in 1633, he told his commanders that *a warrior prizes speed above all else*, a famous line found in Sun Zi. Similarly, when Koxinga was learning to be a general in Southern China in the late 1640s, he and his commanders uttered maxims like *geography is the root of strategy* and *always use local guides.* In all his campaigns, he explicitly used tactics right out of the Chinese military tradition: *feign weakness and lure, cut the tail off from the head, use leisure to await the enemy's exhaustion.*

Many of these maxims involve deception. Indeed, the first substantive dictum in the *Art of War* of Sun Zi is *War is the art of deception*, and the principle underlies much of the rest of the treatise. It also underlies nearly all of the ancient military maxims that Sinologist Harro von Senger has devoted his life to studying: the so-called Thirty-Six Stratagems.[59]

All military traditions have stories of generals who trick their foes, but the theme runs especially deep in China, whose most celebrated military mastermind, famous in history and fiction, is the trickster figure Zhuge Liang. In the famous Battle of the Red Cliffs, he pretends to attack across the Yangtze River. It's foggy. The enemy can't see that the soldiers on the boats are figures made of straw. He orders his men to beat wardrums and shout to complete the illusion and then sips wine while the enemy wastes his arrows, which are gathered up and used to counterattack. In another famous story, Zhuge Liang tricks an adversary by opening his city gate and calmly drinking wine on the parapets while children play nearby. The enemy suspects a trap, turns around, and leads his troops away, leaving Zhuge Liang safe in his stronghold, which is actually devoid of troops. Ruse is a central trope of traditional Chinese war stories.

Of course we mustn't overstate the differences between western and Chinese warfare. Both traditions are complex, multilayered, and comprised of many varying strands. The most famous western war story is a trick so famous it's still part of everyday speech: the Trojan Horse. And open valor on the battlefield—the kind of fighting that was so esteemed among the warrior-aristocracies of Europe—was also highly valued in China, whose warrior heroes, such as those of the famous book *The Water Margin,* bear a resemblance to characters from the chivalric romances of feudal Europe.[60] Indeed, in many ways Koxinga's own public persona embodied a lordly ideal quite similar to that of a European knight: righteous and fiercely loyal to his sovereign.

Yet the understanding of war as deception thoroughly marked Koxinga's leadership, as he himself made clear. In 1660, when a Dutch envoy asked him whether he intended to attack Taiwan, he replied, "I'll often circulate a rumor that I'm moving west when I'm really intending to move east."[61] This is one of the most famous of the Thirty-Six Stratagems: *feign east, attack west* (*sheng dong ji xi* 聲東擊西). And indeed, as we've seen, Koxinga employed ruse whenever possible. *Feign weakness and lure* worked for him again and again.

In fact, he drilled ruse into his troops. Although we still know little about his Five Plum-Flower method, evidence suggests that it included formations for false retreats.[62] A wonderful description of the Battle of Zhenjiang of 1659 shows such a formation in action. His troops were clashing directly with a Qing force when suddenly, in the center of his ranks, a white flag waved and his men began falling back.

> It looked as though they were withdrawing. There were some who didn't move fast enough, and they fell to the ground. The Qing troops, seeing this, thought it was a retreat. They pressed their advantage and attacked, quickly rushing forward on their horses and bursting through to the front. But unexpectedly, from within Koxinga's ranks, huge cannons fired out, killing more than a thousand. The [Qing] troops got frightened and were routed. Koxinga's troops rushed forward, severing the

> forward five teams of cavalry troops, surrounding them, and attacking heavily.[63]

It was a decisive victory.

Chen Ze defeated Pedel with a ruse, sneaking around behind him and hiding troops in the pandanus trees. Later he defeated Coyet's foolish attack in the bay with another ruse, pretending to retreat and luring the Dutch vessels away from safety before turning around and attacking. In fact, the only Dutch victory on land against Chinese forces occurred when the Dutch themselves employed a ruse—in 1666, when the commander of the rain-soaked garrison of Jilong faked a retreat and lured the enemy into cannon range.

Thus, clever leadership, informed by a rich military tradition, helped Koxinga win the war, but another factor was equally important: Koxinga's adaptibility. He transformed himself from a samurai boy whose mother tongue was Japanese into a Chinese student so promising that the most famous scholar of the day lauded his abilities. When war came, his first forays failed but he kept learning, parlaying a band of dozens into an army of thousands. Yang Ying's chronicle shows how he got better week to week, month to month, testing himself against the fortified villages of southern China and then against the Qing, building an army and organization that grew steadily. His defeat in Nanjing might have devastated a less flexible commander, but he regrouped and adapted, launching a huge invasion across the risky Taiwan Straits, in defiance of his generals' judgments.

His first assault against Zeelandia Castle failed, so he nimbly switched to a strategy of blockade. The arrival of the Dutch relief fleet prompted him to shift his strategy again. First he tried to capture the dunetop redoubt behind Zeelandia Castle with a new cannon battery. When the Dutch countered by building a new fortification, he withdrew and built a renaissance-style fortress of his own on Baxemboy Island, whose cannons allowed his sandboats to cut off Dutch shipping. The Dutch responded by building another fort, and he adapted again, building powerful siegeworks following European models. These allowed him to capture the dunetop redoubt and force Coyet to surrender.

Within a nine-month span, he learned siege tactics that had taken Europeans centuries to perfect. Of course, he had help from European defectors, most notably the German Hans Radis. But this doesn't detract from his achievement. His willingness to listen was a sign of adaptability.

Coyet, in contrast, didn't listen. When the Chinese farmer Sait suggested that he use the newly arrived fleet to blockade Taiwan, he instead launched a foolish assault. Afterward, Chinese defectors kept advising him to mount a blockade and he kept ignoring them. Of course, there were reasons why a blockade would have been difficult—the winds were high, the seas were unsettled, the coastal areas were shallow, junks had an advantage sailing with the wind—but it was his best remaining option. Koxinga's troops were starving and desperate for rice. The Dutch wouldn't have been able to catch all the supply junks, but, as Chinese defectors noted, fear of Dutch ships would have dissuaded many Chinese captains from undertaking the crossing in the first place. In fact, defectors said Koxinga and his officers were terrified about the prospect of a Dutch cordon. If Coyet had listened he might have kept away the huge rice shipment that saved Koxinga's men from starvation.

Perhaps Koxinga's adaptability was a reflection of his multicultural heritage. His mother was Japanese and his Chinese father was a Portuguese-speaking Catholic. The family fortune came from international trade, which was carried in Chinese junks that incorporated elements of European design. His father employed an African honor guard. Koxinga copied him, creating a force of African soldiers who used Dutch muskets under the command of a Chinese commander who, it seems, enjoyed dressing in European fashions.[64] Similarly, Koxinga's famous Iron Men wore armor and used tactics influenced by Japanese warfare.[65] It's no surprise that his final victory over the Dutch was aided by a German sergeant.

Which leads us to the deepest lesson of this book: Modernization itself was a process of interadoption. The Military Revolution began in China. It spread to Europe. Then it spread back. This sort of borrowing had been going on for millennia, but it reached a new threshold in the seventeenth century, when, as historian Timothy Brook writes, "more people were in motion over longer distances and sojourning away from home for longer periods of time than at any other time in human history."[66] Commodities and technologies and ideas flowed farther and faster than ever.

The Chinese adopted European guns, but the Dutch were wearing silk from China, sweetening Javanese coffee with Brazilian sugar, grinding Indian pepper onto American potatoes served on Japanese porcelain. Dutch Delftware, which is considered to be as Dutch as wooden shoes and Gouda cheese, was a copy of Chinese white-blue porcelain. There are hints of Chinese influence on the paintings of Vermeer, even as Chinese painting was being transformed by trends from Europe.[67]

Europe, which increasingly found itself at the center of global trading networks, has been seen as the epicenter of modernity, and the orthodox model of world history holds that Europeans' conquests overseas were enabled by superior technology. Yet Koxinga easily adapted European cannons, his disciplined soldiers routed Dutch musketmen, and his siege armies conquered the renaissance fortress. Doesn't his adaptability argue for caution when it comes to arguments about European technological superiority?

Yes, but it does seem that the technological balance during the Sino-Dutch War favored the Dutch. Revisionists might find this conclusion objectionable, but most Chinese historians wouldn't. One Sinophone scholar even argues that the superiority of European military technology was rooted in science, showing that European targeting techniques, based on mathematical and physical understandings of ballistics, were more advanced than Chinese techniques and provided a key advantage to European arms.[68]

At the same time, orthodox models need to adapt. For too long, Asia has been viewed as stagnant and the west as dynamic. Yet processes associated with European modernity—commercialization, financial innovation, long-distance trade, medical advances, demographic expansion, agricultural productivity, and military modernization—were also occurring in Asia.[69] We must broaden our understanding of modernity and our search for its deep causes. Historians have long viewed the gun as one of the key drivers of Europe's precocious modernization.[70] Yet that invention occurred in China, which also first saw the rapid changes that flowed from the gun. The history of modernity becomes a history less of European dominance than of increasingly rapid diffusion. Europe's own contributions—particularly in science and its application to technology—were vital and mustn't be minimized, but they must be placed within a global context. It was the unprecedented movement of people and goods and ideas that have truly marked modernity.

Today the process of transculturation is stronger than ever. My eldest daughter's favorite movie is the Japanese anime classic *Nausicaa and the Valley of the Wind*, whose author, Hayao Miyazaki, loves myths and stories from around the world. The film's heroine, Princess Nausicaa, is a global amalgam, based partly on a Homeric princess and partly on a Japanese folk character. One day my daughter was humming the movie theme and her art teacher overheard her and was delighted because she herself had loved the movie as a girl in Japan. Such connections surprise us less and less today. We're more and more aware that we're part of a global family. The seventeenth century was when we first really began to recognize our interdependence.

Yet the people of the seventeenth century recognized something that eludes many of us today: the fact that Heaven is the supreme determinant of human affairs. I don't mean by this God or any supernatural entity. I mean simply that we are all—regardless of our technology—at the mercy of nature.

Koxinga and Coyet both knew this. How could they not? Again and again, weather destroyed their plans. In 1658 Koxinga was ready to sail up the Yangtze and attack Nanjing, and his timing was perfect because the largest Qing armies were in China's far southwest. But when he anchored his fleet at Sheep Island, a typhoon scattered ships and drowned troops. The following year, when he did manage to penetrate the Yangtze, a large Manchu force was returning from its southwestern adventures and helped defeat him. If that storm hadn't struck, Koxinga might have taken Nanjing in 1658. He might have turned the tide against the Qing. He might never have invaded Taiwan.

Similarly, a storm blew Cauw's fleet away before Coyet had time to land its troops and launch an attack against Koxinga's Eastern Capital. Another storm blew Harthouwer to the coast of China, where he made contact with the Qing, potentially changing the war again. And yet another storm prevented Cauw from reaching China to pursue that alliance.

Indeed, it was weather that set in motion the whole train of events. The climate change that occurred in the middle of the seventeenth century—volcanoes and dwindling sunspots—caused droughts and floods that destabilized not just the mighty Ming but also many other governments, making the seventeenth century arguably the most warlike and tumultuous in human history.

That episode of climate change was nothing compared to what we're likely to see in the twenty-first century. We moderns are about to learn a lesson in humility.

Acknowledgments

It's impossible to thank all the people who made this book possible, but the best place to start is with my colleagues at Emory. Kristin Mann, chair of the history department; Bobby Paul, former dean of the college; Robin Forman, current dean of the college; and Lisa Tedesco, dean of the graduate school, provided support of all kinds, from help arranging leave time to financial support for travel, reproductions, permissions, maps, and indexing.

Colleagues in the history department created an unusually collegial environment. Mark Ravina, Phil Rosenberg, and Jen Tierny provided fellowship and conversations about writing. Conversations with Jeffrey Lesser helped me conceive of this project and move it along. Clifton Crais gave perhaps the best advice about writing I've ever heard. When I asked how he writes so much, he responded, "Paragraph by paragraph." I smiled dully, expecting more, but he just said, "I'm serious." Patrick Allitt introduced me to Trollope's autobiography, which helped me adopt a no-nonsense approach. I can't say I write with a watch in front of me and "require from myself 250 words every quarter of an hour" (nor do I hold a full-time job as a postal inspector), but I found his perspective refreshing: there's nothing mysterious about writing. You sit down and do it.

Students in Emory's wonderful SIRE (Scholarly Inquiry and Research at Emory) program inspired and enlivened my work, most notably Christina Welsch and Matt Zorn. Kirsten Cooper provided detailed comments on a draft. But most of all I must thank my talented research assistants—Saul Arvizu, Jackson Harris, Shirley Yang, and Hannah Kim—who helped find, scan, collate, copy, format, and proofread. Without their help this book would have taken far longer to complete.

Friends played a role as well. Hee-Kyung Kim and her son Alex helped translate obscure blog posts in Korean. Playwright Jen Barclay and her novelist husband, Andrew Newsham, invited my wife and me and our one-year-old daughter to share their honeymoon in Puerto Rico when I was at an early stage of research, and conversations with them about dramatic structure and theme were much more useful and formative for me than they probably imagine. Another influence was Andrew Leonard, who read the book proposal with enthusiasm and has inspired me daily with his wonderful blog at Salon.com.

Archivists and librarians are a researcher's best friends. Yale University's Sterling Library generously agreed to lend out its collection of microfilms, for which I particularly thank Susanne Roberts, May Robertson, and Carol L. Jones. Princeton University Library's Ming Specialist, Martin Heijdra, helped with questions about rare military manuals. Harvard's Yenching Library provided access to the *Jing guo xiong lüe,* a rare strategy manual published by Koxinga's family, and generously gave permission to reprint plates from it.

Emory's Woodruff Library has an extraordinary staff. Marie Hansen and her colleagues Margaret Ellingson, Sarah Ward, and Anne Nicolson in Interlibrary Loan managed to find and obtain huge numbers of esoteric sources, often with only incomplete citations. Chinese subject librarian Guo-Hua Wang obtained scores of specialized—and expensive—Chinese books, as well as access to scholarly databases. History librarian Alan St. Pierre built up a mirror site of parts of the Dutch East India Company Collection of the National Archives of the Netherlands. The resulting collection of microfilms makes Woodruff Library one of the best places in North America to conduct research into the seventeenth-century Dutch empire.

Frans Paul van der Putten at *Itinerario*, Kevin Haggerty at *The Canadian Journal of Sociology*, and Jerry Bentley at *The Journal of World History* accepted portions of three different chapters of this book for publication, which were strengthened by the review and editorial process in each case. They also generously provided permission for those portions to appear here.

This book might never have existed at all if it weren't for the insight and enthusiasm of Dan O'Connell, my erstwhile agent. He glimpsed the promise of the topic from an early article I published. When I finally came around to the idea of writing it, he helped me think the project through and put together a book proposal. Remarkably, the book ended up much as originally envisioned.

Princeton University Press has been wonderful. Brigitta van Rheinberg and Clara Platter's enthusiasm kept me motivated, and her matter of fact prodding kept me on deadline. Sara Lerner's thorough production management was a paragon of efficiency. Dimitri Karetnikov made the illustrations look beautiful, Michael Alexander did the maps, Jennifer Harris did the copyediting, David Luljak did the indexing, and Jason Alejandro designed the beautiful cover. Princeton's crack marketing team came up with the title, and Clara helped me overcome my scholar's discomfort with it, assuring me that it would attract more readers than any of the other titles I suggested. Since I feel we academics should try to reach as wide a public as possible, I agreed to let them run with it.

I must also thank the reviewers at Princeton University Press, particularly Jack Wills, who waived anonymity and worked closely with me on revisions. His books and articles are so deeply influential that it's impossible to acknowledge them fully. He's a model scholar, careful, deeply informed, and, most importantly, generous, always willing to share his wisdom and knowledge. This book wouldn't have been possible without him, not just because of his unstinting help, but also because he's a giant in the field of Ming-Qing history. His work is foundational.

Another foundational figure is Lynn Struve, whose deeply researched and wonderfully written work laid the groundwork for our current understanding of the Southern Ming. She, too, provided concrete guidance for this project. She may not agree with everything I say here, but I am deeply grateful for her help.

Leonard Blussé's engaging and intimidatingly well-researched work has had such a deep influence on my own that it's impossible to acknowledge him enough. A short article he wrote on Chinese victories over the Dutch ("De Chinese nachtmerrie") prefigures the arguments of this book in key ways. He also generously read and commented on a draft of this book.

Geoffrey Parker has influenced me directly as a mentor and indirectly as a scholar. He has a gift for taking large issues—the Military Revolution, the Global Crisis—and treating them empirically and with nuance. This book might be seen as a branch of the Parker tree, if he'll forgive the metaphor. He, too, read a draft and provided comments that have strengthened it considerably.

Others who read and commented on the manuscript are Pol Heyns, Dahpon Ho, Xing Hang, and Peter Silver. All of them provided insights and advice that have improved the work, but Peter's advice was particularly useful, helping me to reconceive the conclusion and make some important adjustments to the text. It goes without saying that none of those who helped with the manuscript are in any way responsible for any errors of fact or judgment or interpretation that might be found herein.

My greatest debt is to my family. My wife, Andrea Artuso Andrade, shouldered the heavy burdens of primary parenting and the running of a household with two young children. She unstintingly protected my writing time. I couldn't have done this without her. My eldest daughter, Amalia, also helped. I told her stories almost daily and learned that what most kept her attention wasn't plot or excitement but emotion. I dedicate this book to her, because she helped me learn to tell good stories.

Notes

ABBREVIATIONS

BZDSJL	Zhang Huangyan, *Bei zheng de shi ji lüe*
DRB	Bort, Daghregister
DRC	Cauw, Daghregister
DZ	Dagregisters Zeelandia, see Blussé, Leonard, *De Dagregisters van het Kasteel Zeelandia*
FJHYJS	Zou Weilian, "Feng jiao Hong yi jie shu"
HCCA	Hurt, Melchior, and Jacob Clewerk, "Corte aanteijkening"
HJJY	Xia Lin, *Hai ji ji yao*
HSJWL	Ruan Minxi, *Hai shang jian wen lu*
JHZ	Peng Sunyi, *Jing Hai Zhi*
MHJY	Xia Lin, *Min hai ji yao*
MSRJ	Jiang Shusheng, *Meij shi ri ji*
Resolution	Resolutions of the Council of Formosa
TWWJ	Jiang Risheng, *Taiwan wai ji*
TWWXCK	*Taiwan wen xian cong kan*
VOC	Dutch East India Company Collection, National Archive of the Netherlands, The Hague. Please note that "VOC" also refers to the Dutch East India Company itself (Verenigde Oost-Indische Compagnie) and appears in this sense in some titles of books and articles I cite.

XWSL	Yang Ying, *Xian wang shi lu*
ZCGZ	Zheng Yizou, *Zheng Chenggong Zhuan*

AN EXECUTION

1. My image of early modern Batavia is drawn from many sources, of which the most important is Valentijn, *Oud en Nieuw*, 229–239. The painting *View of Batavia*, by Andries Beeckman, is a wonderful source, discussed in Zandvliet, *Dutch Encounter*, 34–35. Travelers' accounts supply additional details, the most important being Wintergerst, *Reisen*, pt. 2, 122–128; Herport, *Reise*, 28–30; Schouten, *Oost-Indische*. 48–49.

2. Coyet to Governor General Carel Hartsinck, 12 April 1662, in "Resolutions of the Grand Council of the Indies, Batavia, 13 April 1662," VOC 678: 73–74.

3. Criminele sententie van de Hr Frederick Coyet dato den 12 Januarij 1666, Kopie-criminele sententiën van de Raad van Justitie in Batavia, VOC 9335 (unfoliated).

4. Coyet, *Verwaerloosde*. A good English translation is Coyet, *Neglected*.

5. Jack Wills, one of the world's foremost authorities on China's relations with maritime Europeans, writes, "Nothing [the Dutch] could have done . . . would have enabled them to withstand the large and well-disciplined army with which [Koxinga] . . . landed on Taiwan." Jack Wills, "Relations," 373. See also Mostert, "Chain of Command," 109.

6. Diamond, *Guns*.

7. The term "revisionist" is used in various places, including Flynn and Giráldez, "Cycles"; Landes, "Why Europe"; and in Bryant, "West and the Rest." Jack Goldstone, one of the revisionists, happily accepts the label in a response to Bryant: Goldstone, "Capitalist Origins." I discuss the historiography of this age-of-parity argument in detail in Andrade, "Beyond Guns."

8. Frank, *ReOrient*; Goldstone, "Rise of the West"; Goody, *Capitalism*; Pomeranz, *Great Divergence*; Wong, *China Tranformed*.

9. Bryant, "West and the Rest," 403 and 418. Bryant, of course, is not the only one critical of the revisionists. Similar counter-revisionist positions are staked out in Mokyr, *Enlightened Economy*; Landes,

"Why Europe"; and Maddison, *World Economy* (esp. 249–251). See also Duchesne, "Peer Vries"; Vries, "Is California"; and Broadberry and Gupta, "Early Modern."

10. Andrade, *How Taiwan*.

11. I was, of course, not the first one to argue along these lines. See Wills, "Maritime," and Wills, "Was There?" Sanjay Subrahmanyam has also published a brilliant article pointing out other cases of Asian maritime expansion: Subrahmanyam, "Of Imârat."

12. Bryant, "West and the Rest," 435, footnote 29.

13. Black's arguments against Geoffrey Parker can be found in various places in his voluminous oeuvre. Most important is perhaps Black, "War." See also Parker, "Military Revolutions," and Black, "On Diversity."

14. Sun, "Ming-Southeast," 31.

15. Sun, "Ming-Southeast," 75.

16. Sun, "Military," 516.

17. The most important figures are Kenneth Swope, Peter Lorge, and Kenneth Chase.

18. Needham argues that the idea of a European origin for gunpowder "continued to hold its ground" until World War II. Needham, *Science*, pt. 7, 51–65, esp. 62.

19. Chase, *Firearms*, xiii.

20. Chase, *Firearms*, 32.

21. Swope, "Crouching," 20.

22. Huang Yi-long, "Ou zhou."

23. There were previous conflagrations between European and Chinese Forces, most notably two battles in 1521 and 1522, in which Portuguese fleets were defeated by Chinese naval forces. But those were mere skirmishes compared to the Sino-Dutch War. I date the ending of the Sino-Dutch War as 1668, because that's when the Dutch finally gave up on Taiwan. Sporadic hostilities continued, particularly in Southeast Asia. An upcoming dissertation by Taiwanese scholar Cheng Wei-chung details this continuing conflict. (The dissertation, still untitled, is scheduled to be completed in 2011 or 2012 at Leiden University, under the direction of Leonard Blussé.) Tristan Mostert argues that the war didn't involve the Netherlands as such, since it was fought by the Dutch East

India Company (Mostert, "Chain of Command," 13). I take Mostert's point, but I believe that given the close ties between the company and the Dutch government, and given that the company was authorized to conduct war and make treaties on behalf of the United Provinces, it is reasonable to call this a Sino-Dutch war.

24. Goldstone, "Capitalist," 127.

25. Jiang Shusheng, *Zheng Chenggong,* 42.

26. The first such use of the technique is attested in a Chinese battle of the mid-1300s. Sun, "Military," 500.

27. See Platt, "Chinese Sail."

28. Leonard Blussé's work, written with panache and attention to both Chinese and European sources, is the vital taking-off point: Blussé, "Chinese nachtmerrie," and "Verzuymd." Indeed, his analysis has prefigured in important ways the arguments of this book. Also noteworthy is Jiang Shusheng, *Zheng Chenggong*. Many other studies and accounts are less detailed but still very useful. The most important of these are Boxer, "Siege"; Lu Jianrong, *Ru qin,* 20–89; Tang Yunxuan, *Chenggong*; Deng Kongzhao, "Zheng Chenggong shou fu"; Mostert, "Chain"; and Yang Yanjie, *He ju*. Of older accounts there are many, including Dickens, "Formosa"; Kalff, "De val"; and "Kort en bondigh verhael." The best place to start for understanding the war in terms of primary sources are Struve, *Voices*; and *Zheng Chenggong shou fu Taiwan shi liao xuan bian*.

29. The botanist's name is Wolfgang Stuppy, of the Royal Botanic Gardens, Kew.

30. Zurndorfer, "What Is the Meaning," 90.

31. Hanson, *Carnage*, 5.

32. Zhang and Sun, "Zhongguo chuan tong."

33. Schouten, *Oost-Indische*, 171.

DESTINIES ENTWINED

1. I've adapted this story from various versions: Liu Xianting, *Guang yang za ji*; JHZ, 1; Lin Shidui, *He cha cong tan*, 155; and Lu Qi, *Xian yan*.

2. FJHYJS. The Zou Weilian letter is 34–42, quoted on 40. The phrase I translate as "entwined destinies" (情緣) might be better

glossed as "karmic affinities" or "predestined affinities." I use the term "entwined destinies" because it seems clearer to an English-speaking readership.

3. Zhang Linbai, "Ping guo," 370–371.

4. Ji Liuqi, *Ming ji*, 518. Liu Xianting, *Guang yang za ji* also indicates that he slept with his stepmother: Liu, *Guang yang*, 34–35. Historian Chen Bisheng doubts the stories on the grounds that Zhilong's father was too poor for a concubine. Chen Bisheng, "Ming dai mo qi," 77.

5. The detail about the stick comes from JHZ, 1, and is also contained in Ji Liuqi, *Ming ji nan lüe*, 518.

6. Chang, "Chinese Maritime Trade"; Wills, "Relations"; Ng, *Trade*; Chang, "Maritime Trade," 63–82; Ren-Chuan Lin, "Fukien's Private," 163–216; and Ng, "South Fukienese," 297–316.

7. 聖母踏龍頭.

8. Palafox, *Conquest*, cited in Boxer, "Rise and Fall," 427–428.

9. Iwao, "Li Tan," 76.

10. Clulow, "Global Entrepôt."

11. Zhang Linbai, "Ping guo," 371. Zhang's account gives the name Li Xi, not Li Dan. It's likely but not certain that they are one and the same person. See Chen Zhiping, "Zheng shi," 374.

12. De Fu, *Min zheng ling yao*, cited in Chen Zhiping, "Zheng shi," 372–373.

13. Scholars are more certain of the surname Tagawa (田川) than the given name Matsu (松). In Chinese sources she's referred to with the surname Weng (翁氏).

14. Blussé, "Dutch Occupation."

15. Gerrit Fredricxz. De Witt to Governor-General Pieter de Carpentier, 15 November, 1626, VOC 1090: 196–206, fol. 202.

16. De Jong, "*Staat van Oorlog*."

17. These were terms written into the company's charter itself. A good English translation can be found online at the Australian Hydrographic Society's website: http://www.australiaonthemap.org.au/content/view/50/59 (accessed 17 July 2010).

18. Iwao, "Li Tan," 51–52.

19. Some Dutch sources say he ran away without bothering to resign. Hamel, "Verhaal," 105. Also cited in Iwao, "Li Tan," 77.

20. TWWJ, 5.

21. See Andrade, *How Taiwan*, 2: 1–6.

22. Governor Gerrit Fredericxz. De Witt to Governor-General Pieter de Carpentier, 4 March 1626, VOC 1090: 176–181, fol. 179. See also Resolutions, 26 June 1627, VOC 1093: 385v–386.

23. H. Brouwer, P. Vlack, and J. van der Burch, Batavia, to the Heren XVII in Amsterdam, 1 December 1632 (Cheng, "De VOC en Formosa," 105). See also Blussé, "Minnan-jen," 255. These were just the official tallies. Blussé suggests that many proceeds weren't reported to Batavia. Blussé, "VOC as Sorcerer's," 99.

24. Commandeur Cornelis Reijersz. to Gouverneur General, 20 February 1624, in Groeneveldt, *Nederlanders,* 482.

25. Generale Missiven, 6 Jan. 1628, in Hamel, *Verhaal,* 105. Also cited in Iwao, "Li Tan," 78.

26. *Zheng shi shi liao chu bian*, 1. I've adopted Wong's interpretation of the phrase 製自外番 (Wong, "Security," 124), which can also be interpreted as "copied from foreign barbarians."

27. *Ming shi lu Min hai guan xi shi liao*, 154.

28. *Zheng shi shi liao chu bian,* 1.

29. Kawaguchi, *Taiwan*, 5.

30. See Wong, "Security," 125.

31. JHZ, 3. Other Ming documents confirm that Zheng cultivated an image of benevolence. See, for example, Cao Lütai, *Jing hai ji lüe*, 3–4.

32. Memorial by Board of War's Minister of Military Affairs (兵部尚書), Liao Tingdong (梁廷棟), *Ming shi lu Min hai guan xi shi liao,* 154.

33. Cited in Tang Jintai, *Kai qi,* 123.

34. Dong Yingju, *Chong xiang ji xuan lu,* cited in Chen Bisheng, "Ming dai mo qi," 82.

35. These words are attributed to the defender of Quanzhou, a man by the name of Wang You. See Lin Shidui, *He cha cong tan,* 155. Modern scholars, too, feel that Zhilong was looking for recruitment from an early period. Chen Bisheng, "Ming dai mo qi," 84.

36. Memorial by Board of War's Minister of Military Affairs (兵部尚書), Liao Tingdong (梁廷棟), *Ming shi lu Min hai guan xi shi liao,* 154.

37. Memorial by Board of War's Minister of Military Affairs (兵部尚書), Liao Tingdong (梁廷棟), *Ming shi lu Min hai guan xi shi liao,* 154.

38. JHZ, 3.

39. DZ 1, A: 394.

40. DZ 1, A: 394.

41. 鍾斌.

42. This, at any rate, is what a Chinese man told the Dutch. DZ 1, A: 395.

43. DZ 1, A: 399.

44. Putmans to Specx, 5 October 1630, VOC 1101: 412–423, fol. 422; Putmans to Coen, 10 March 1630, VOC 1101: 408–411.

45. Memorial by Board of War's Minister of Military Affairs (兵部尚書), Liao Tingdong (梁廷棟), *Ming shi lu Min hai guan xi shi liao,* 153–154.

46. FJHYJS, 40.

47. FJHYJS, 40.

48. FJHYJS, 40.

49. Huang Zongxi, *Ci xing shi mo*, 1.

50. FJHYJS, 40.

51. Putmans to Specx, 9 November 1632, VOC 1109: 195–197.

52. DZ 1, B: 591–592.

53. Putmans didn't refer to Zhilong as Zhilong. For the sake of consistency and reader accessibility, I've altered the names in my translations. Putmans to Specx, 5 October 1630, VOC 1101: 412–423, fol. 416.

54. Putmans to Specx, 5 October 1630, VOC 1101: 412–423, fol. 416. As so often, I'm indebted to Leonard Blussé for calling attention to this passage in his scholarship.

55. A Dutch sailor earned around eight gulden per month, which equates to around 3.5 taels per month, or 42 taels per year. *Uytrekening,* 12.

56. Generale Missive, H. Brouwer, A. van Diemen, P. Vlack, Philips Lucasz., en J. van der Burch, Batavia, 15 August 1633, in Cheng "De VOC," 108–112.

PIRATE WAR

1. Dewald, *Europe.*

2. Parker, Military Revolution, 104–113. The classic statement of the position is less nuanced: Cipolla, *Guns.*

3. Marshall, "Western Arms."

4. Andrade, "Asian Expansions"; Chaudhuri, *Trade and Civilisation*, esp. 63–79; Pearson, *Indian Ocean*; Newitt, *A History* (although Newitt suggests that the military variable has been overlooked in recent work); Ringrose, *Expansion*, 149–160; Glete, *Warfare*, 76–77; Darwin, *Tamerlane*. A brilliant counterpoint is Subrahmanyam, "Of *Imârat*."

5. But see Guilmartin, *Gunpowder*.

6. Anthills is 垤. This quote is from the 中丞南公祖來視閩師, excerpted in Su, *Taiwan shi yanjiu ji*, 60.

7. Zheng Dayu, *Jing guo xiong lüe*. The quote is from the section entitled *Wu bei kao* 武備考, juan no. 8, fols. 22–22v.

8. *Xin jiao ben Ming shi*, 8437.

9. FJHYJS, 40.

10. TWWJ, 43.

11. *Xin jiao ben Ming shi*, 8437.

12. Putmans to Specx, 5 October 1630, VOC 1101: 412–430, fol. 416.

13. Some sources say that there were only fifteen of these massive warjunks. See Chen Bisheng, "Ming dai mo qi," 88.

14. Parker, *Military Revolution*, 94–96.

15. Putmans to Brouwer, 30 September 1633, VOC 1113: 776–787, fol. 777v.

16. A Chinese source indicates that the ships were being cleaned (燂洗). Cited in Yang Xuxian "Zheng Zhilong," 301.

17. Riccio, "Hechos," cited in Busquets, "Los Frailes," 404.

18. My description of the battle is culled from three different Dutch sources, each of which emphasizes different details: DZ 1, F: 16; Putmans to Brouwer, 30 September 1633, VOC 1113: 776–787, fols. 777–778; and Putmans to the Kamer Amsterdam, 30 September 1633, VOC 1109: 227–234, fol. 229.

19. The attack cost him more than the fleet: he was also demoted. Yang Xuxian "Zheng Zhilong," 301.

20. Iquan (Zheng Zhilong) to Putmans, 24 July 1633, VOC 1113: 548–549.

21. Iquan to Putmans, 24 July 1633, VOC 1113: 548–549, fol. 549v. I've changed the order of the phrases, putting "you've behaved like a pirate" at the beginning. Also, the phrase I've translated as "Are you

proud of yourself?" might more literally be translated as "Do you think you've done well?"

22. Report by Shi Bangyao (施邦曜), excerpted in Yang Xuxian, "Zheng Zhilong," 301.

23. The demands were laid out in various letters to Chinese officials. See, for example, Putmans to the Haijto van Chincheuw, 29 July 1633, VOC 1113: 564–566.

24. Putmans to Brouwer, 30 September 1633, VOC 1113: 776–787, fol. 786v.

25. Putmans to Brouwer, 30 September 1633, VOC 1113: 776–787, fol. 786v.

26. Generale Missiven, H. Brouwer, A. van Diemen, P. Vlack, J. van der Burch, and Antonio van den Heuvel, Batavia, 15 December, 1633, in Cheng, "De VOC," 116.

27. Putmans to Brouwer, 30 September 1633, VOC 1113: 776–787, fol. 786v.

28. Putmans to Brouwer, 30 September 1633, VOC 1113: 776–787, fol. 787.

29. Putmans to Brouwer, 30 September 1633, VOC 1113: 776–787, fol. 787.

30. See Yang Xuxian, "Zheng Zhilong," 299–300, which excerpts a confused but nonetheless revealing section from a Xiamen Gazeteer (Zhou kai, *Xiamen zhi*), which in turn quotes the *Donglin Annals* (東林傳), giving us a sense of the flavor of their disagreement. Yang also lists some other sources on the Zou Weilian case (p. 300).

31. Report from Zheng Zhilong to Zou Weilian, Chongzhen 6, 9th month, 22nd day (24 October 1633), in FJHYJS, 35. Dutch sources note the huge retinue, which Batavian officials seem to have learned about from Chinese merchants who'd sailed from China. Generale Missive, H. Brouwer, A. van Diemen, P. Vlack, J. van der Burch, and Antonio van den Heuvel, 15 December 1633, in Cheng, "De VOC," 118.

32. There are seven separate inventories of money and goods pillaged and declared "a rightful prize of war" during this time, which can be found in the VOC archives: VOC 1109: 240–242.

33. Blussé, "Chinese nachtmerrie," 223.

34. DZ 1, F: 34.

35. DZ 1, F: 33. See also Putmans to the Kamer Amsterdam, 28 October 1634, VOC 1114: 1–14, fol. 1.

36. DZ 1, F: 33. A nearly identical account is found in Extract van het dachregister in het jacht Bredamme gehouden over het verongelucken van het jacht Catwijk, 13 October 1633, VOC 1113: 705–706. I took some liberties with this translation. "Schier buijten hoope" I translated as "we had little hope." I'm also not certain that Putmans himself was writing, although he certainly had to approve everything written.

37. Putmans to the Kamer Amsterdam, 28 October 1634, VOC 1114: 1–14, fol. 1.

38. DZ 1, F: 33.

39. DZ 1, F: 34. Blussé thinks the news was false. "Chinese nachtmerrie," 223.

WAR IS THE ART OF DECEPTION

1. 兵者詭道也, Sun Zi, *The Art of War.*

2. DZ 1, F: 35. I've altered the translation slightly. The literal translation would be "How can a dog be permitted to lay its head on the pillow of one of the emperor's resting places?" In the seventeenth century, "dog" was one of the worst insults you could muster, but nowadays the insult sounds silly, so I added "bitch," to put forth the force of Zhilong's words.

3. Blussé, "VOC as Sorcerer's," esp. 102–104.

4. Putmans to the Chitoo, VOC 1113: 569v–570 (summarized in DZ 1, F: 25).

5. DZ 1, F: 35–36.

6. Putmans to Kamer Amsterdam, 28 October 1634, VOC 1114: 1–14, fol. 1. DZ 1, F: 35 discusses the blue pennants. In the extant Dutch descriptions of the battle of Liaoluo Bay, the pirates are barely mentioned. We know they were there from Chinese sources and from one Dutch source that says they all fled. Generale Missive, H. Brouwer, A. van Diemen, P. Vlack, and J. van der Burch, Batavia, 20 February 1634, in Cheng, "De VOC," 125.

7. Report from Zheng Zhilong to Zou Weilian, Chongzhen 6, 9th month, 22nd day (24 October 1633), in FJHYJS, 35.

8. TWWJ has the battle taking place in 1639, but I've concluded, along with other scholars, that it is describing the battle of 1633. See Yang Xuxian, "Zheng Zhilong," 304–305.

9. TWWJ, 43–44.

10. TWWJ, 43–44.

11. Shen Yun, *Taiwan Zheng shi*, 6.

12. DZ 1, F: 36.

13. Putmans to Kamer Amsterdam, 28 October 1634, VOC 1114: 1–14, fols. 1v–2.

14. The detail about yelling is from Generale Missive, H. Brouwer, A. van Diemen, P. Vlack, and J. van der Burch, Batavia, 20 February 1634, in Cheng, "De VOC," 124.

15. Report of canjiang Deng Shu to Zou Weilian, Chongzhen 6, 9th month, 22nd day (24 October 1633), in FJHYJS, 39.

16. Report by Quannan youji Zhang Yongchan to Zou Weilian, Chongzhen 6, 9th month, 22nd day (24 October 1633), in FJHYJS, 38.

17. DZ 1, F: 36.

18. Report from vice-general (fuzong) Gao Yingqiu to Zou Weilian, received 22nd day of the 9th month of Chongzhen 6 (24 October 1633), in FJHYJS, 37.

19. DZ 1, F: 36–37.

20. Putmans to Kamer Amsterdam, 28 October 1634, VOC 1114: 1–14, fol. 2.

21. Report from vice general (fuzong) Gao Yingqiu to Zou Weilian, received 22nd day of the 9th month of Chongzhen 6 (24 October 1633), in FJHYJS, 37.

22. Zheng Zhilong, "Report," 36.

23. DZ 1, F: 36.

24. Putmans to Kamer Amsterdam, 28 October 1634, VOC 1114: 1–14, fol. 1.

25. Zheng Zhilong, "Report," 35.

26. Zheng Zhilong, "Report," 35.

27. Zheng Zhilong, "Report," 36.

28. Zheng Zhilong, "Report," 36.

29. Zheng Zhilong, "Report," 36.

30. Monsterrol van het jacht Broeckerhaven, fol. 769; and Monsterrol van het jacht Sloterdijck, fol. 768.

31. Bazhu was 吧哇, which in Southern Min is pronounced "pa-tsoo," which certainly referred to Antonij Paets, the highest ranking man the Dutch lost. Monsterrol van het jacht Broeckerhaven, 769; and Monsterrol van het jacht Sloterdijck, 768. Paets was on the *Broeckerhaven,* which was the ship that sank early in the battle.

32. Report by Quannan youji Zhang Yongchan to Zou Weilian, Chongzhen 6, 9th month, 22nd day (24 October 1633), in FJHYJS, 38.

33. *Zheng shi shi liao chu bian,* 88–90 and 94–95, cited in Wong, "Security," 128.

34. FJHYJS, 42.

35. Zheng Zhilong, "Report," 36.

36. Colenbrander, ed., *Dagh-register*, 1631–1634, 253.

37. DZ 1, F: 37.

38. Generale Missive, H. Brouwer, A. van Diemen, P. Vlack, and J. van der Burch, Batavia, 15 August 1634, in Cheng "De VOC," 132.

39. According to the Mingshi, Zou was slandered by people from Min, which allowed his enemies to get him removed from power. *Xin jiao ben Ming shi,* 6138.

40. I took liberties when translating the last part of this passage because the original Chinese contains esoteric references: "I must be like Wang (and) Meng, the way that Wang (and) Meng treated Zheng Qiang, writing to ask for glorious promotions in order to reward miraculous achievements." So I changed the specifics to generals in order to make the meaning clear. FJHYJS, 40.

41. "Zou Weilian," Baike [Chinese Wikipedia] entry on Zou Weixian, available at http://baike.baidu.com/view/222016.htm (accessed 25 November 2009).

42. Su Tongbing, *Taiwan shi yanjiu ji,* 64.

43. Andrade, *How Taiwan*, chs. 3, 6, 7, and 8.

44. Lin Shidui, *He cha cong tan,* 156; and ZCGZ, 3. These sources use the term "jin" (金), which in the Ming and Qing periods was often used as a stand in for "tael."

45. From 1627 to 1640, company revenues averaged 2.7 million florins yearly. De Korte, *De Jaarlijkse,* 31. See also Gaastra, *Dutch*, 132. At a rate of 3.5 taels per florin, that would be on the order of nine or ten million taels. See *Uytrekening*, 12. The exchange rate fluctuated

considerably through the seventeenth century, as did bimetallic ratios in general. Flynn and Giraldez, "Arbitrage."

46. One careful estimate from a later period is that the Zheng clan brought in around twenty-five million taels of silver per year from its overseas trade. Figures for the 1630s and 1640s may have been significantly higher. Yang Yanjie, "Yi liu wu ling," 231–233. See also Han Zhenhua "Zai lun."

47. This is corroborated by a similar comparision for a later date: Hang, "Between Trade," 102–109.

48. Lu Qi, *Xian yan*, section on Zheng Zhilong. Victorio Riccio, a reliable source, concurs with this assessment. Riccio, "Hechos," cited in Busquets, "Los Frailes," 398.

49. Lin Shidui, *He cha cong tan*, 156.

50. Lin Shidui, *He cha cong tan*, 156; and ZCGZ, 3.

51. JHZ, 6.

52. Lu Qi, *Xian yan*, section on Zheng Zhilong.

53. Wong, "Security," 129.

54. ZCGZ, 3.

55. Lin Shidui, *He cha cong tan*, 156.

THE WRATH OF HEAVEN

1. Parker, "Crisis and Catastrophe," 1053.

2. Parker, "Crisis and Catastrophe," 1056.

3. For recent controversies on Chinese demographic history, see Marks, "China's Population."

4. Magisa, *Svcceso raro*, cited in Parker, "Global Crisis."

5. William S. Atwell shows that the years 1640–1643 saw thick dust veils in the northern hemisphere, which correlated with high sulfate acid levels in ice cores. Atwell, "Volcanism," 62–63.

6. Parker, "Crisis and Catastrophe," 1067–1068.

7. Parker, "Crisis and Catastrophe," 1069.

8. Parker, who cites Buisman, *Duizend Jaar weer*, IV, 469–470.

9. Geoffrey Parker, "Global Crisis."

10. Parker, "Global Crisis."

11. Cited in Parker, "Global Crisis," section on China. Parker in turn cites Des Forges, *Cultural Centrality*, 62.

12. Ye Shaoyuan, cited in Michael Marmé, "Locating Linkages," 1083. See also Atwell, "Volcanism," 67–68. I changed the wording ever so slightly, from "in the days of my life" to "in my lifetime."

13. Atwell, "Volcanism," 66 and 68.

14. Chan, *Glory and Fall,* 333.

15. Spence, *Search,* 25.

16. Dorgon to Wu Sangui, cited in Cheng, Lestz, and Spence, *Search,* 26. I've made a couple of small changes to the translation.

17. Struve, *Southern Ming,* 77.

18. Deng Kongzhao, "Zheng Zhilong de yi sheng," 179–180.

19. Deng Kongzhao, "Zheng Zhilong de yi sheng," 181.

20. One of the best descriptions is JHZ. A longer and more detailed examination, which is surprisingly more favorable to Zheng Zhilong, is Chen Yanyi, *Si wen da ji.*

THE SAMURAI

1. This story is taken from the delightful *Taiwan wai ji*, a book that's a maddening mix of the verifiable and the fanciful. This story falls into the latter category. TWWJ, 8.

2. See Andrade, *How Taiwan*, ch. 10, note 6 (p. 222).

3. Keene, *Battles*, 44.

4. Keene, *Battles*, 44.

5. Wu Zhenglong 吳正龍, suggests that Koxinga's loyalism has been exaggerated. See Wu, *Zheng Chenggong*. Deng Kongzhao calls him a courageous, loyal hero. Deng, "Lun Zheng," 19–37. Wong Young-tsu portrays him as fanatically loyal. Wong, "Security," 133. Ralph Crozier, surveying the evidence, raises questions about Koxinga's loyalty but ultimately sees the question as unresolvable. Crozier, *Koxinga,* 20–23. See also Yang Jinlin, "Lun Zheng," 290–302. Xing Hang offers a nuanced and compelling portrayal, which tends to portray Koxinga as pragmatic more than fanatic, describing him as similar to a "shrewd company executive," a "shrewd businessman," someone who "diversified his political risks." Hang, "Between Trade," 128.

6. Coyet, *Verwaerloosde,* 90

7. Mysterious discoveries keep rolling in, as, for example, when a new scroll in Koxinga's calligraphy was discovered in Japan in the mid-1990s. It seems to have been composed after he left Japan, however. See Xia Ming, "Riben."

8. Carioti, *Zheng.* The evidence stems from the fact that Koxinga's half brother Tagawa Shichizaemon was an *ashigara*.

9. Hang, "Between Trade," 72, note 31.

10. Many stories and anecdotes are told about Koxinga in Japan, which is little surprise given his fame there. As one Chinese scholar suggests, Koxinga, by virtue perhaps of his Japanese birth, is one of the three most famous Chinese figures in Japan, along with Zhuge Liang and Yue Fei. Gao Zhihua "Ri ren," 367–368.

11. The title Koxinga was not used, but rather Koxinga's boyhood name, Zheng Sen. Cited in Mao Yibo, *Nan Ming shi tan*, 153.

12. Mao Yibo, *Nan Ming shi tan*, 154.

13. Wong, "Security," 133.

14. XWSL, 62.

15. See Chen Zhiping, "Zheng shi," 384. For more evidence about the provincial stage, see Li Guohong, "Xin jin," 319–320.

16. ZCGZ, 3.

17. Wakeman, "Romantics," 637.

18. How Qian's decision haunted his poetry is discussed in Yim, *Poet-Historian*. See also Huang, *Negotiating*, 77–78.

19. MHJY, 2.

20. Longwu referred to him as guo xing Chenggong (國姓成功). Chen Yanyi, *Si wen da ji*. (For memorials from Longwu himself referring to Koxinga this way, see pp. 59 and 94.)

21. Chen Yanyi, *Si wen da ji*, 31. There's also evidence in Zheng clan genealogies. *Zheng shi zong pu* 鄭氏宗譜, cited in Zhang Zongqia, "Zheng Chenggong jia shi," 145.

22. 招討大將軍.

23. 征夷大将軍.

24. MHJY, 3. See also ZCGZ, 4.

25. MHJY, 3.

26. MHJY, 3.

27. MHJY, 3.

28. MHJY, 3.

29. There's ample evidence of Koxinga receiving military orders in Longwu's chronicle, Chen Yanyi, *Si wen da ji*. See also Chen Bisheng, "Zheng Chenggong fen ru fu," 108–110.

30. Ji Liuqi, *Ming ji nan lüe*, 317. This is not a primary source, but it is one of the earliest accounts and generally reliable.

31. MHJY, 4.

32. MHJY, 4.

33. ZCGZ, 5. The phrase "idealism of youth" might more literally be translated as "youngsters look on this with repugnance." Thanks to Lynn Struve for her views on this passage.

34. Alas, we know little about this force, or about Africans in China at all. It would make a great research project. Perhaps the best place to start is Boxer, "Rise and Fall," 437.

35. ZCGZ, 5.

36. Ruan Minxi, *Hai shang,* 3.

37. Boxer, "Rise and Fall," 437, note 42.

38. JHZ, 14. A similar account is found in Huang Zongxi, *Ci xing shi mo*, 2. Another version, composed quite early, skips the cleansing of the bowels and instead notes that after she was siezed and "disgraced," Zhilong, who'd not yet been taken under house arrest, paid to ransom her, but when she was released she hanged herself. Chen Zhiping, "Zheng shi shi liao ji bu," 370–388.

39. ZCGZ, 5.

40. ZCGZ, 5.

41. See Wills, *Mountain,* 225. Compare to Chen Bisheng, "Zheng Chenggong fen ru fu," 107–116.

THE GENERAL

1. Riccio says he had just one sampan, Riccio, "Hechos," cited in Busquets, "Los Frailes," 401.

2. Riccio, cited in Busquets, "Los Frailes," 401.

3. ZCGZ, 5.

4. The Chinese term is 紙上談兵.

5. Precisely where Koxinga and his comrades swore their vow is disputed. See Chen Bisheng "Zheng Chenggong fen ru fu," 111–112, and Chen Bisheng, "Cong 'Hui'an,'" 120.

6. Huang Zongxi, *Ci xing shi mo*, 2.

7. Wang Zhongxiao notes how after Longwu's death he and others raised righteous armies, coordinating with each other across the province. Wang Zhongxiao, "Zi zhuang," in Wang, *Wang Zhongxiao,* and excerpted in Li Guohong, "Xin jin," 325–327.

8. This number is from JHZ, 15, and HSJWL, 5.

9. HSJWL, 5; JHZ, 15.

10. HJJY, 6. *Hai shang jian wen lu*, 6.

11. Another partial copy was found in 1961. Both were used to create XWSL.

12. XWSL, 1.

13. XWSL, 10–11.

14. XWSL, 9.

15. XWSL, 12.

16. XWSL, 15.

17. The phrase is, literally, "The kingly not dying" (王者不死). The help of Heaven is implied. I took the liberty of making it explicit. Yang Ying, 17.

18. Technically, Zheng Lian, the "uncle" who controlled Xiamen, wasn't Koxinga's uncle but a distant cousin who was elder. See Zhang Zongqia, "Zheng Chenggong zai Xiamen," 177. I took the liberty of changing the term to "uncle" because western—at least modern anglophone—kinship terms are much less precise than Chinese ones. An elder male relative is often referred to as "uncle" in the United States, even if that person is technically a cousin twice removed.

19. ZCGZ, 15.

20. Li Guohong, "Xin jin," 326–328.

21. HJJY, 7.

22. ZCGZ, 15. The Chinese text uses the term "elder brother" instead of "uncle," which is technically more accurate (see note 18, earlier).

23. Compare to Zhang Zongqia, "Zheng Chenggong zai Xiamen," 176–177.

24. Yang Ying doesn't record such stories, stating merely that Koxinga went to Xiamen and issued an order dissolving his relatives' military authority, and that one complied and the other fled. XWSL, 17.

25. XWSL, 24.

26. XWSL, 24–25.

27. ZCGZ, 9.

28. XWSL, 25.

29. His silence is noted in HJJY, 8, and in JHZ, 21.

30. XWSL, 26.

31. Zhiwan is Zheng Zhilong's cousin, according to Chen Bisheng.

32. Ruan Minxi, *Hai shang jian wen lu,* 10.

33. XWSL, 28.

34. XWSL, 28.

35. XWSL, 16.

36. XWSL, 16–17.

37. This information, which comes from a letter Koxinga wrote to his father, might be exaggerated. XWSL, 63.

38. XWSL, 16.

39. XWSL, 33.

40. 以逸待勞; 以飽待饑.

41. XWSL, 35.

42. XWSL, 37–39.

43. XWSL, 40. See also HJJY, 11; HSJWL, 11.

44. There are various versions of this story. I used the one in the *Dong guan Han ji*. For a brief English account, see "Wang Ba," Giles, *Chinese Biographical*, 833–834.

45. XWSL, 43.

46. XWSL, 43–44.

47. XWSL, 47.

48. ZCGZ, 10. He's referring to a single poem, and says "who can bear to read it?"

49. JHZ, 27.

50. HSJWL, 13; JHZ, 27.

51. HSJWL, 13; JHZ, 27.

52. ZCGZ, 10.

53. ZCGZ, 10.
54. HSJWL, 13; JHZ, 27.
55. 河溝.
56. XWSL, 54.
57. XWSL, 55.
58. XWSL, 55.
59. XWSL, 55.
60. XWSL, 55. Koxinga doesn't actually say "show it to them," but I felt in the translation that it was important to make that point explicitly.
61. XWSL, 55.
62. XWSL, 55.
63. XWSL, 55.
64. XWSL, 56.
65. XWSL, 56.
66. XWSL, 56.
67. XWSL, 57.
68. XWSL, 56.
69. Decree of Shunzhi to Koxinga, in XWSL, 69–70.
70. Confucius, *Analects*, 13.18.
71. "箇中事未易未易." XWSL, 83–84.
72. Wu Zhenglong, *Zheng Chenggong yu Qing*, 182.
73. "Fanatical" is Wong Young-tsu's word. Wong, "Security and Warfare," 133. Compare to Deng Kongzhao, "Lun Zheng Chenggong dui Zheng Zhilong," 19–37.
74. According to Yang Ying, it was an explicit strategy. XWSL, 62.
75. XWSL, 75–76.
76. See Gao Zhihua, "Ri ren," 368–369.
77. XWSL, 25.
78. XWSL, 28.
79. XWSL, 62.
80. 總督部院陳錦.
81. HJJY, 11.
82. XWSL, 39, for example.
83. XWSL, 87.
84. XWSL, 87.

85. HJJY, 18.

86. HJJY, 19. See also p. 12.

THE SEA KING

1. ZCGZ, 12.

2. Koxinga had permission from Yongli to establish this mirror site and make appointments to a certain rank. HJJY, 13.

3. On these academies, see Lü and Ye, "Zheng Chenggong zai Xiamen," 133–134.

4. HJJY, 13.

5. HJJY, 14.

6. On the location of the Drilling Field, see Zhang Zongqia, "Zheng Chenggong zai Xiamen," 177–178; and Lü and Ye, "Zheng Chenggong zai Xiamen," 154–155.

7. XWSL, 112–116.

8. XWSL, 119.

9. XWSL, 119.

10. XWSL, 120 or 121.

11. XWSL, 121 or 121.

12. Riccio, "Hechos," 590.

13. Navarrete, *Tratados* cited in Busquets, "Los Frailes," 410. On Japanese stories about Koxinga, see Gao Zhihua, "Ri ren," 367–368.

14. Riccio, "Hechos," 590.

15. The Su Mao and Huang Wu incident is found in XWSL, 20–22.

16. XWSL, 21.

17. JHZ, 36.

18. See especially Nan Qi, "Taiwan Zheng shi," 194–208.

19. See Wu Mei, "Lun Huang Wu," 182–199.

20. XWSL, 127.

21. XWSL, 127.

22. Cheng Xunchang, "Zheng Chenggong," 93–94.

23. Struve, *Southern Ming*, 181.

24. XWSL, 123.

25. The best account of the northern expedition is still Liao Hanchen, "Yan ping wang bei zheng." (There are two versions. The 1964 version is more detailed.)

26. XWSL, 154.
27. ZCGZ, 14.
28. Chen Bisheng, "1657," 1–2.
29. Riccio, "Hechos," cited in Busquets, "Los Frailes."
30. Yang Ying wasn't the only one. Versions of this story occur in various Chinese sources. My telling (which leaves out a few bits of Koxinga's speech) is taken from XWSL, 176–177, and JHZ, 42.
31. Perhaps a better translation would be "Chief Harbor Guide." The Chinese is 引港都督.
32. Liao, "Yan ping wang," 96.
33. Some of these concubines and sons managed to survive. See Zhang Zongqia, "Zheng shi wen wu," 210–212; and Guo Rong "Guo xing," 300–302.
34. Liao Hanchen reviews the evidence carefully. Liao "Yan ping wang," 95–96.
35. Qing veritable records, cited in Liao "Yan ping wang," 95.
36. The bitter laugh is found in XWSL, 177.
37. BZDSJL, 1.
38. Liao Hanchen argues that Koxinga was in a hurry to reach Nanjing before reinforcements arrived from the far southwest and that his preoocupation with those reinforcements explains much of his behavior during the 1659 campaign. Liao, "Yan ping wang," 108.
39. BZDSJL, 1.
40. BZDSJL, 1.
41. XWSL, 197.
42. XWSL, 198.
43. Literally "pound on the Guanyin Gate," BZDSJL, 2.
44. BZDSJL, 2.
45. BZDSJL, 2.
46. BZDSJL, 2.
47. XWSL, 201–202. Blood in the ditches comes from ZCGZ, 16.
48. JHZ, 48.
49. JHZ, 48.
50. XWSL, 202–203.
51. JHZ, 48.
52. XWSL, 199.
53. BZDSJL, 3.

54. BZDSJL, 3.

55. 兵貴先聲. ZCGZ, 17.

56. XWSL, 203.

57. Most historians blame Koxinga for ignoring Gan Hui and Zhang's advice but don't take into account his attempt to march by land. Going by water may have been the better choice under the circumstances. Yang Ying notes that the marchers weren't meeting their distance goals because of the rain. XWSL, 204. A notable exception is Liao Hanchen, "Yan ping wang," 104–105, although Liao does blame Koxinga for tarrying too long at Zhenjiang.

58. BZDSJL, 2.

59. BZDSJL, 3.

60. XWSL, 204.

61. Struve, *Southern*, 187.

62. BZDSJL, 4.

63. XWSL, 208.

64. XWSL, 208.

65. XWSL, 208.

66. XWSL, 208.

67. XWSL, 208.

68. XWSL, 210.

69. XWSL, 210.

70. XWSL, 212.

71. BZDSJL, 4.

72. BZDSJL, 4.

73. An Shuangcheng, "Qing Zheng," 122–124.

74. BZDSJL, 4.

75. BZDSJL, 4.

76. ZCGZ, 17.

77. JHZ, 50.

78. JHZ, 49–50.

79. ZCGZ, 17.

80. The most trustworthy version of the story of Yu Xin is XWSL, 210–212.

81. In Nanjing lore, the story is told about the Xingzhong Gate 興中門 (originally called the Yifeng Gate 儀鳳門), but according to the JHZ, the Qing attack came through the Shen Ce Gate 神策門. JHZ is

reliable, and is based on Qing sources as well as Zheng sources. JHZ, 50. XWSL provides corroboration: Yu Xin had the Fengyi Gate well guarded, because he expected the attack to come from there. XWSL, 211.

82. JHZ, 50.

83. Jiangjun Mountain 將軍山, which in those days was called Guanyin Mountain 觀音山.

84. JHZ, 50.

85. Zongdu.

86. JHZ, 51.

87. XWSL, 216.

88. BZDSJL, 4–5.

89. BZDSJL, 5.

90. The scholar's name was Luo Zimu (羅子木). The incident is recounted in at least two accounts: the *Dong nan ji shi* and the *Ye Luo er ke zhuan*. Cited in Liao Hanchen, "Yan ping wang," 101.

HEAVEN HAS NOT TIRED OF CHAOS ON EARTH

1. XWSL, 244.

2. XWSL, 244.

3. The phrase "expressions of reluctance" (難色) appears in two of the most reliable accounts of this meeting: XWSL, 244, and JHZ, 56.

4. Teng, *Taiwan's*.

5. Yang Ying. XWSL, 244. For more on the resistance Koxinga received from his officers, see Chen Bisheng, "Zheng Chenggong zai shou fu," 55–56.

6. XWSL, 244; JHZ, 56.

7. Many Chinese historians portray He Bin as a hero. Chen Bisheng, for example, even defends him from early Chinese sources that speak of him fleeing from Taiwan because of debts and embezzlement, going so far as to hail him as "a man of tremendous merit and achievement." Chen Bisheng, "He Bin," 106.

8. Andrade, "Chinese," 10–11.

9. Andrade, "Chinese," 11–13.

10. Vertoogh van de voornaemste Chineesen in Tayouan over de onhebbelijckheden gepleecht door den tolck Pincqua, 15 November 1654, VOC 1207: 550–552.

11. Vertoogh van de voornaemste Chineesen in Tayouan over de onhebbelijckheden gepleecht door den tolck Pincqua, 15 November 1654, VOC 1207: 550–552.

12. Letter from Batavia to Formosa, 14 May 1655, VOC 878: 209–242, quote at 232v.

13. Letter from Batavia to the Great Mandarin Koxinga in China, 17 July 1655, VOC 879: 296–298.

14. Letter from Batavia to Taiwan, 26 July 1655, VOC 879: 413–427, esp. 416–417.

15. DZ 4, A: 249–251.

16. DZ 4, A: 266.

17. *Generale Missiven,* vol. 3 (1655–1674), Maetsuyker, Hartzinck, Cunaeus, Van Oudtshoorn, et al., XIII, 31 January 1657, quote at 117.

18. Governor Cornelis Caesar to Governor-General Jan Maetsuycker, 27 December 1656, VOC 1218: 467–471, quote at 469.

19. DZ 4, B: 159.

20. Cited in Andrade, "Chinese," 18–19.

21. Andrade, "Chinese," 18.

22. For more about the evidence that this toll was sanctioned by Koxinga's organization, see Andrade, "Chinese," 22–23.

23. DZ 4, B: 255.

24. Coyet, *Neglected,* 19.

25. Andrade, "Chinese," 22–23.

26. Some have argued that Coyet was complicit in He Bin's scheme. Chen Bisheng "He Bin," 104. That's certainly what the zealous prosecutor of his case in Batavia argued. (Eysch en conclusie, gedaan maken, en den E. Achtbaren Raad van Justitie des Kasteels Batavia overgelevert, by ende vanwegen Mr. Louis Philibert Vernatti, advocaat fiscael van India, in Coyet, *Verwaerloosde,* 212–224. See Coyet, *Neglected,* 120–127.) Resolutions and dagregisters that Coyet and his comrades kept, however, suggest that they were legitimately shocked when they learned of He Bin's secret toll.

27. It's possible that He Bin brought the map during an earlier visit to Xiamen. See Chen Bisheng, "He Bin," 103–104.

28. XWSL, 244.

29. XWSL, 244.

30. On the plows and farm tools, see Wu and Huang "Lüe shu," 239.

31. XWSL, 245.

32. Parthesius, *Dutch,* 60.

33. 黑水溝.

34. Yu Yonghe, *Pi hai,* 6.

35. Xie Jinluan, *Xu xiu,* 31.

36. Deng Kongzhao argues that Koxinga loaded many provisions before departure. See Deng Kongzhao, "Zheng Chenggong shou fu Taiwan de zhan lüe yun chou," 7–8. That may be so, but there is strong evidence that Koxinga ran into food troubles in Penghu, a conclusion accepted by other Sinophone historians. See, e.g., Zhang Zongqia, "Zheng Chenggong shou fu," 28.

37. XWSL, 245. Yang Ying uses the unit "stone" (石), which is roughly equivalent to a hectoliter.

38. There are various versions of this story, of which the most authoritative is the *Dong guan Han ji.* See "Wang Ba," Giles, *Chinese Biographical*, 833–834.

39. XWSL, 245–246.

40. TWWJ, 194–195.

AN EXTREME AND TERRIFYING STORM

1. DZ 4, A: 285.

2. DZ 4, A: 285.

3. DZ 4, A: 286.

4. The Dutch called them pineapple trees, but they were probably pandanus (林投樹). See Guo Rong, "Guo xing," 295–296.

5. DZ 4, A: 287.

6. DZ 4, A: 298.

7. DZ 4, A: 299.

A FOGGY MORNING

1. Schouten, *Oost-Indische*, 165.

2. DZ 4, D: 506.

3. Dutch decrees tried to prevent this: DZ 4, D: 478; and Resolutions, 14 February 1661, VOC 1235: 474–475.

4. Herport, *Reise,* 50.

5. Herport, *Reise,* 51.

6. Herport, *Reise,* 50.

7. DZ 4, D: 508.

8. Herport, *Reise,* 51.

9. Coyet, *Verwaerloosde,* 85.

10. Coyet, *Verwaerloosde,* 84.

11. Coyet, *Verwaerloosde,* 87.

12. Coyet, *Verwaerloosde,* 89. I changed this from indirect to direct speech.

13. Koxinga to Coyet, Yongli 14, 10th month, 19th day, in Coyet, *Verwaerloosde,* 89–91.

14. Koxinga to Coyet, Yongli 14, 10th month, 19th day, in Coyet, *Verwaerloosde,* 89–91.

15. Koxinga to Coyet, Yongli 14, 10th month, 19th day, in Coyet, *Verwaerloosde,* 89–91.

16. XWSL, 223.

17. Yang Ying doesn't mention fog but does make a telling distinction between daybreak (黎明) and when the sun shone through at the first watch (7–9 AM). DZ notes that the weather was "still and misty" (DZ 4, K: 513), and Herport notes that there was a very thick fog: "one couldn't see far, but as soon as the fog lifted, we saw [the] ships" (Herport, *Reise*, 51.

18. XWSL, 247.

19. Zhang Zongqia suggests that Koxinga would have wanted to land on the first or sixteenth of the lunar month, when the moon was new or full and tides were high. Zhang Zongqia, "Zheng Chenggong shou fu," 28.

20. That's the interpretation of Zhang Zongqia, "Zheng Chenggong shou fu," 29.

21. The sequence of events in DZ for 30 April 1661 is out of order, due, it seems, to a transcription error that arose before the published version was created. Folio 518, in describing Dutch soldiers chasing some Chinese troops from Baxemboy, ends with the words "niet en conden achterhalen," which should be followed, I believe, by a sentence at folio 515, which begins, "Een wijl de plunderagie Chinesen vervolght hebbende." I've tried reconstructing the chronology, but whereas other places in DZ where events are out of sequence admit to

reconstruction, this time I wasn't able to find a definitive solution. My chronology is approximate.

22. These were not true pineapples, as noted earlier.

23. DZ 4, D: 516.

24. Yang Ying also mentions these little boats' reconnaissance mission. XWSL, 246–247

25. DZ 4, D: 516–517.

26. Taiwan-based scholar Guo Rong 郭荣 points out that Ma Xin was the first commander to land in the Smeerdorp area, leading his powerful cavalry. Guo Rong, "Guo xing Zheng," 286.

KOXINGA'S VICTORIES

1. The phrase is from Parker, *Military Revolution*, 17.

2. Sun, "Military Technology," 500.

3. Parker, *Military Revolution*, 140.

4. Parker, *Military Revolution*, 20–23.

5. *Generale Missiven*, 1633–1655, Reniers, Maetsuyker, Hartzinck, Cunaeus, Caesar, and Steur VII, 24 December 1652, 611; Governor Nicolaes Verburg to Batavia, 30 October 1652, VOC 1194: 121–127; Huber, "Chinese Settlers," 172–175.

6. DZ 4, D: 523; Herport, *Reise*, 54. Pedel had several children. This boy was probably young, since he was described with the diminutive (soontjen) and had a tutor. It was perhaps Abraham Pedel, baptized 17 September 1656. Indonesian National Archive, Burgerlijke Stand Collection, Taiwan Doop-en Trouwboek, Burgerlijke Stand No. 360. Thomas Pedel also had at least one other son, William Pedel, who was considerably older. He was a translator.

7. According to the official resolution records, the governor and council had already decided the previous day to send Pedel out. Resolution, 1661-04-30, VOC 1235: 352. On the other hand, in DZ that decision is given as occurring on 1 May. The confusion is worsened by the fact that the resolution manuscripts are in terrible shape, with whole passages illegible.

8. Governor Pieter Nuyts to Batavia, 15 September 1629, VOC 1098: 33–38, fol. 36.

9. 鎮.

10. XWSL, 249. A Chinese prisoner said in interrogation that "one of the four top leaders on the fleet was Zoncktisieu," which might correspond to Chen Ze. He also said that Sonihaio was "one of the top leaders on the flotilla lying outside [the bay]" (DZ 4, D: 523).

11. Coyet, *Verwaerloosde,* 104.

12. Coyet, *Neglected,* 47.

13. It is not easy to reconstruct the topography of Baxemboy Island, but this bit about first the dunes and then the little "pineapple" forest I got not just from Herport and Coyet's and the DZ's descriptions, but also from maps. The most important of these is Pascaert, waerin verthoont wort de gelegentheut van Tayouan enz., Dutch Nationaal Archief, inventarisnr, VEL0302, which notes that there was a "tweede bos" a ways down the island. Of course, this Pascaert was drawn nearly forty years before Pedel's quixotic attack.

14. Resolution of the Council of Formosa, 1661-04-30, VOC 1235: 352.

15. The polished bit comes from DZ 4, D: 525. The rest is from Herport, *Reise.*

16. Parker, *Cambridge,* 2.

17. Swope, *Dragon's Head,* 18–19, 169, 183. See also Lorge, *Asian,* 60–61 and 80–81.

18. XWSL, 112.

19. DZ 4, D: 525.

20. "Gliederweiss," is the term Herport uses. Herport, *Reise*, 56.

21. 知地利.

22. 相度地利.

23. 占得地利.

24. 地利失據.

25. Herport, *Reise*, 54.

26. XWSL, 249.

27. According to the diary of Admiral Jacob Cauw, for example, the four largest war yachts in his fleet carried 36 (9 bronze and 27 iron), 34 (4 bronze and 30 iron), 33 (4 bronze and 29 iron), and 32 (4 bronze and 28 iron) cannons, and they carried 104, 90, 90, and 86 soldiers, respectively, in addition to the crew. DRC, 13.

28. DZ 4, D: 621.

29. Dagregister gehouden bij den schipper Andries Pietersz, in the yacht 's-Gravenlande, 30 April 1661 to 5 July 1661, VOC 1237: 41–56, fol. 41.

30. According to a description in DZ, which was relayed later by one of the people in the *'s-Gravenlande*, the Chinese attackers attached themselves to the *Gravenlande*'s ship's launch, which was attached to the back by a rope. DZ 4, D: 589.

31. Dagregister gehouden bij den schipper Andries Pietersz, in the yacht 's-Gravenlande, 30 April 1661 to 5 July 1661, VOC 1237: 41–56, fol. 41v.

32. "Basisrondleiding Batavia 2006," 26. Available at www.batavia werf.nl/assets/files/Batavia_basisrondleiding.pdf (accessed 4 February 2011).

33. See for example Chen Bisheng, "Zheng Chenggong shou fu Taiwan zhan shi," 31.

34. Chen Bisheng, "Zheng Chenggong shou fu Taiwan zhan shi," 11.

35. The Dutch used the term "yacht" for a wide variety of sizes of ships, from very small to very large. See Parthesius, *Dutch Ships*, 72–80.

PARLEYS AND CAPITULATIONS

1. DZ 4, D: 530.

2. For more on the location of Koxinga's camp, with references to present-day Tainan landmarks, see Guo Rong, "Guo xing Zheng Chenggong," 286–287.

3. MSRJ, rear 5.

4. I'm not absolutely sure the woman was of Dutch birth. She doesn't appear in Taiwan Doop-en Trouwboek, Indonesian National Archive, Burgerlijke Stand Collection, Burgerlijke Stand No. 360.

5. Jacob Valentine to Frederic Coyet, 1 May 1661, VOC 1235: 881.

6. XWSL, 249.

7. Yang also misidentifies the man as Valentine's brother and the woman as Valentine's sister-in-law. XWSL, 249.

8. MSRJ, rear 4. The text of the placard is found in DZ 4, D: 521–522.

9. DZ 4, D: 520–521.

10. See the reconstruction of Provintia by Kees Zandvliet in Ran, *Shi qi*, v. 2, 82.

11. Jacob Valentine to Koxinga, 1 May 1661, VOC 1235: 908–909.

12. Koxinga to Valentine, 2 May 1661, VOC 1235: 906.

13. Koxinga to Valentine, 2 May 1661, VOC 1235: 906.

14. The stench is mentioned repeatedly in various sources, the earliest being a letter from Jacob Valentine to Coyet, 1 May 1661, VOC 1235: 882. The MSRJ also mentions it (rear p. 8), as does Resolution of the Council of Formosa, 4 May 1661, VOC 1235: 361v.

15. DZ 4, D: 535–536 says who they are: Leonard Leonardus, Thomas van Iperen, Joan van Valkenstein, Willem Pedel, and the Sergeant Hendrick Draek, along with four soldiers as bodyguards.

16. Meij, "'t Naervolgende."

17. MSRJ.

18. Resolution, 1661-05-02, VOC 1235: 356–359, fol. 358.

19. Resolution, 1661-05-02, VOC 1235: 356–359, fol. 359v. See also Iperen and Leonardis, "Mondeling verhael," fol. 917. On the drink with the governor, see DZ 4, D: 535.

20. Resolution, 1661-05-02, VOC 1235: 356–359, fol. 358.

21. Resolution, 1661-05-02, VOC 1235: 356–359, fol. 359v. The governor and council laid out the conditions that Valentine should try to get Koxinga to agree to, including provisions about the Christians of Formosa, an honorable quitting of the fort, and so on.

22. The four or six or ten men deep comes from Iperen and Leonardis, "Mondeling Verhael," fol. 914.

23. MSRJ, rear 10.

24. Ji Liuqi, *Ming ji nan lüe*, 329.

25. Iperen and Leonardis, "Mondeling verhael," fol. 914v.

26. The envoys brought a letter from Coyet to Koxinga, which also says that Coyet wanted "to understand His Highness's letters, whose meaning appears to us still unclear because of a lack of qualified translators." Coyett to Koxinga, 2 May 1661, in DZ 4, D: 534–535.

27. Iperen and Leonardis, "Mondeling verhael," fol. 915.

28. Iperen and Leonardis, "Mondeling verhael," fol. 915.

29. Iperen and Leonardis don't mention showing Koxinga the treaty in their account, but a Resolution of the Council of Formosa

notes that they put it "in front of his eyes." Resolution of the Council of Formosa, 4 May 1661, VOC 1235: 360v. It's not clear which 1630 document they might be referring to here.

30. This business about yelling and threatening the envoys doesn't appear in the envoys' official report, but it's mentioned in Philip Meij's journal, which notes that the envoys told him and Valentine about this yelling and threatening. MSRJ, rear 11.

31. Iperen and Leonardis, "Mondeling verhael," fol. 918.

32. MSRJ, 12.

33. The Resolutions of the Council of Formosa say that the flag was to be raised and lowered thrice; Meij says twice. Resolution, 1661-05-04, VOC 1235: 361v; MSRJ, rear 12.

34. MSRJ, rear 17.

35. MSRJ, 17–18.

36. 府尹. Although according to Yang Ying, he was not named Prefectural Governor until the second day of the fifth lunar month, which would correspond to the end of May 1661.

37. Yang Ying notes that Koxinga "bestowed on Valentine rich gifts of Chinese native products" (厚賜唐山土儀) (XWSL, 259). Meij provides details and one can sense him drooling down through the centuries: an official robe of black silk with gold embroidery, a blue silk sash adorned with gold, some "mandarin's socks" adorned with black velvet and gold laecken, and a hat like Koxinga's, with a little white feather in the brim.

38. Herport, *Reise*, 58.

39. Valentine to Coyet, Saccam, 7 May 1661, VOC 1235: 877–878.

40. Valentine to Coyet, Saccam, 7 May 1661, VOC 1235: 877–878.

41. Koxinga to Coyet, 2 May 1661 (Yongli 15, 4th month 4th day), in DZ 4, D: 528–529.

THE CASTLE

1. Some scholars, most notably Kelly DeVries, have offered compelling evidence that medieval walls stood up rather better to cannonfire than had once been assumed. See especially DeVries, "The Walls."

2. The classic and still authoritative account of this process is Parker, *Military Revolution*.

3. Lynn, "Trace," 169–199.

4. The best recent study about this process is Zandvliet, "Vestingbouw."

5. Black, "Western Encounter," 23.

6. DZ 1, F: 51–52.

7. DZ 1, L: 737.

8. Most of my descriptions of Zeelandia are gleaned from scattered references in the DZ and other Dutch records. The bit about the brick cobblestone streets comes from Dapper, *Gedenkwaerdig*, 41–42.

9. This incident, which is discussed in Coyet's book, seems to have left no trace in the official records.

10. DZ 4, D: 543–545.

11. This heat and sun business comes from a letter written by Valentine to Coyet on behalf of Koxinga, trying to persuade Coyet to give the fort over soon. Valentine to Coyet, 9 May 1661, VOC 1235: 879–880.

12. Valentine to Coyet, Saccam, 7 May 1661, VOC 1235: 877–878.

13. DZ 4, D: 550.

14. See, for example, the Resolution, 1661-05-14, VOC 1235: 374.

15. DZ 4, D 567.

16. DZ 4, D: 573.

17. DZ 4, D: 576.

18. Herport, *Reise*, 66. Herport has this grenade being launched toward the end of May, but he also notes it was the first grenade, and that the Chinese hadn't seen one before. Herport is great with details of incidents, but not with their sequence. I have been able to corroborate nearly everything he describes, even some things that I'd not expected to be able to, but his dates are often imprecise.

19. DZ 4, D: 603.

20. DZ 4, D: 679.

21. DZ 4, D: 760.

22. DZ 4, D: 604.

23. DZ 4, D: 587.

24. DZ 4, D: 569.

25. DZ 4, D: 538.

26. Koxinga to Coyet, 4 May 1661 (Yongli 15, 4th month 6th day), DZ 4, D: 542.

27. Valentine to Coyet, Saccam, 7 May 1661, VOC 1235: 877–878.

28. Valentine to Coyet, Saccam, 9 May 1661, VOC 1235: 879–880.

29. Valentine to Coyet, Saccam, 9 May 1661, VOC 1235: 879–880.

30. Coyet discussed this vicarious diplomacy as a conscious strategy with his advisors. Resolution, 1661-05-07, VOC 1235: 369.

31. Coyet to Valentine, 7 May 1661, VOC 1235: 876.

32. Coyet to Valentine, 7 May 1661, VOC 1235: 876.

33. Koxinga to Coyet, 2 May 1661, in DZ 4, D: 528–529.

34. Koxinga to Coyet, 3 May 1661 (Yongli 15, 4th month 5th day) in DZ 4, D: 536–537.

35. Koxinga to Coyet, 10 May 1661 (Yongli 15, 4th month 12th day), DZ 4, D: 563.

36. Koxinga to Coyet, 10 May 1661 (Yongli 15, 4th month 12th day), DZ 4, D: 563.

37. Coyet to Koxinga, 10 May 1661, DZ 4, D: 565.

AN ASSAULT

1. DZ 4, D: 581–582.

2. DZ 4, D: 588.

3. DZ 4, D: 592.

4. Koxinga to Coyet, 24 May 1661 (Yongli 15, 4th month 26th day), in DZ 4, D: 595–597. The Dutch translation, which is, alas, the only extant version of this letter (and all other letters Koxinga wrote to the Dutch), says "it is God's will." I changed the phrase to "it is the will of Heaven," because Koxinga didn't write about God. I suspect that Valentine, who made the final Dutch translation and was a rather good writer, translated "Heaven" as "God."

5. Resolution, 1661-04-24, VOC 1235: 384–385.

6. XWSL, 252. The incident occurred on 10 May (4th month 12th day). The term hujiang 壺漿 is from Mencius, in which the phrase *dan shi hu jiang, yi ying wang shi* (簞食壺漿, 以迎王師) appears. It's a phrase Koxinga liked, using it to exhort his troops to good behavior, as, for example, in XWSL, 170 and 191.

7. Andrade, "Landdag."

8. 土官.

9. Hambroek's intelligence from Koxinga's camp and Provintia is in DZ 4, D: 600–605.

10. DZ 4, D: 600; Resolution, 24 May 1661, VOC 1235: 386.

11. See Zandvliet, "Art," and Jiang Shusheng, "VOC."

12. Maybe more than just the top story. The remains of Zeelandia Castle are in poor shape today. All we have left to figure out its original structures are a few drawings and paintings and a few walls.

13. The figure "omtrent 50 zielen" is from Resolution, 25 May 1661, VOC 1235, fol. 387.

14. Resolution, 25 May 1661, VOC 1235, fol. 386. This page is damaged and difficult to read.

15. Resolution, 25 May 1661, VOC 1235: 387.

16. Resolution, 25 May 1661, VOC 1235: 388.

17. Resolution, 25 May 1661, VOC 1235: 389.

18. The sequence is from DZ 4, D: 607–608, and Herport, *Reise,* 63–65.

19. Coyet, *Neglected,* 61; Herport, *Reise,* 64–65.

20. Resolution, 25 May 1661, VOC 1235: 389.

21. Resolution, 25 May 1661, VOC 1235: 389.

22. Resolution, 25 May 1661, VOC 1235: 389.

23. Resolution, 25 May 1661, VOC 1235: 390.

24. All of these quotes are from Coyet, *Neglected*, 59–60. I've altered the translations slightly for accuracy and readability, referring to Coyet, *Verwaerloosde*, 121–123.

25. Coyet, *Neglected*, 60.

26. Mote, "Transformation."

27. Parker, *Military Revolution*, 143.

28. Lorge, *Asian*, 74.

29. Parker, *Military*, 144.

30. Sun Zi, *Art*, "Offensive Strategy," Juan 1.

31. Chen Kongli, "Zheng Chenggong shou fu," 317; Deng Kongzhao, "Zheng Chenggong shou fu Taiwan de zhan lüe," 11–13.

32. Deng Kongzhao, "Zheng Chenggong shou fu Taiwan de zhan lüe," 11–13.

33. The data are drawn solely from Koxinga's main chronicle, XWSL. Each time the chronicle records Koxinga gaining or trying

to gain a fortification—a city, town, or fort—I noted down the main means he used. These data are thus not exhaustive, and I should note some other caveats. I found fifty-three incidents that offered data, but I wasn't always able to discern a clear primary means of getting through the wall. In other cases, he tried more than one method, and I had to make a judgment about which was the main method. It's important also to note that I made no attempt to consider how long he held the place in question. The seat of Changtai County, for example, he besieged twice in the same year.

34. If we leave out the huge number of defections that came to him during the Nanjing Campaign of 1659, this percentage falls to 27%, but it still represents by far the most prevalent means by which he gained access to fortified places.

35. DZ 4, D: 539.

36. Cited in Wills, *Pepper*, 46.

37. MSRJ, rear 27.

38. Coyet, *Verwaerloosde*, 122.

39. Deng Kongzhao, "Zheng Chenggong shou fu Taiwan de zhan lüe," 12–13.

40. See Subrahmanyam and Parker, "Arms," esp. 26–28; and Needham, *Science,* vol. 4, pt. 6, 260–265.

41. Bort, Daghregister, fol. 2614.

42. This particular attack on Outing Zhai (鷗汀寨) occurred in 1657.

43. Indeed, a Chinese prisoner captured soon after the attack told Coyet that Koxinga had only used his cannons to frighten the Dutch.

44. MSRJ, rear 26.

45. DZ 4, D: 650.

46. On the other hand, there's a little scrap of evidence from a prisoner's testimony that Koxinga was very angry at Beja (who commanded the forces in Zeelandia City) for shooting so intensely against the castle. DZ 4, D: 627.

47. Coyet to Koxinga, 25 May 1661, in DZ 4, D: 597–598.

48. Herport, *Reise*, 63. Herport gets the sequence of events slightly wrong, having Hambroek leave the fortress before the attack rather than after.

49. Schouten, *Oost-Indische*, 168–169.

50. Valentijn, *Oud en Nieuw*, vol. 4/B, pt. 3, 90–92.

51. Nomsz., *Anthonius*.

52. For an example of the poetry, see Moens, "Edele zelfopoffering."

53. DZ 4, F: 754. The source is a Chinese soldier who defected to the Dutch side on 3 September 1661.

54. MSRJ, 27.

A SUMMER OF MISERY

1. DZ 4, D: 611.

2. Description from Herport, *Reise*, 70.

3. I've found no description of the Zeelandia rack, but most Dutch torture racks at the time had this gingerbread-man form.

4. DZ 4, D: 622.

5. DZ 4, D: 624.

6. In fact, Chinese sources don't even mention the cannon battle of 25 May. Yang Ying notes only that on 22 May 1661, Koxinga decided that attacking Zeelandia Castle "would result in many deaths." (Yang Ying gives the date as the twenty-fourth day of the fourth month, a date that would coincide with 22 May [XWSL, 252].) Why doesn't he mention the defeat? It certainly occurred. European sources provide a day-to-day account—sometimes an hour-to-hour account—and from multiple perspectives. Moreover, Yang Ying offers details that corroborate Dutch sources, noting that one of Koxinga's top commanders, Lin Fu (林福), was "wounded by the red-haired barbarians' cannons" right when the defeat would have taken place (XWSL, 252). This correlates with something that Ciko told Coyet, to wit, that "a mandarin named Limtouw had his arm shot off" (DZ 4, D: 622). "Lim" is the Southern Min dialectical pronunciation of the character Lin, so it seems likely that he was referring to Lin Fu. Ciko also told Coyet that people in Koxinga's army were close-lipped about the number of wounded in the attack. The fact that a small force of Dutchmen could stop his mighty army might have seemed too embarrassing for Yang Ying to acknowledge.

7. The party, which included Yang Ying, was sent out on 20 May (4th month 22nd day).

8. XWSL, 252. The chronicle indicates that Yang Ying was supposed to gather those grains stored up by the red-haired barbarians, so there might have been other stores available. But one suspects that Yang Ying and his companions would have wanted to be thorough and have a strong report on their return.

9. XWSL, 252. The term I'm translating as "hectoliter" is shi 石.

10. A cup of dry rice has around 600 calories. There are four cups per liter, so a liter of rice has around 2,500 calories. A hectoliter has 250,000 calories; 6,000 hectoliters of dry rice has 1,500,000,000 calories.

11. DZ 4, D: 613 (26 May).

12. XWSL, 252.

13. 東都明京, XWSL, 252. The Dutch learned about this renaming from Chinese captives: DZ 4, D: 655.

14. XWSL, 254.

15. XWSL, 252.

16. XWSL, 253–255.

17. Philip Meij uses the term "hour" as a unit of distance. If we use the WNT definition of an uurgaans (5,555 meters), we see that eight hours is about 45 kilometers.

18. Jiang Shusheng translates this passage incorrectly into Chinese, I think, saying that the settlements should be four hours from the coast (MSRJ, 51). Zantvliet notes that they should be "as close to the coast as possible," which I think is closer to the what Meij wrote. Zantvliet, "Contribution," 134.

19. MSRJ, rear 33.

20. MSRJ, rear 33–34.

21. Meij gives these measurements in rods (*roeden*), which I convert to feet at the rate of 10 feet per rod. MSRJ, rear 33–34.

22. MSRJ, rear 34–35.

23. MSRJ, rear 33.

24. MSRJ, rear 35–36.

25. Zandvliet, *Mapping*, 158.

26. It's possible that "Middagh" should be translated as "south," although since the kingdom was located north of the main Dutch settlement, this, too, seems problematic. The fullest reference to the

King of the Middagh comes from a now-lost account by a Scotsman named David Wright. See Campbell, *Formosa*, 6–7.

27. XWSL, 257.

28. Herport, *Reise*, 66–68. Meij's diary corroborates the outlines of Herport's account, if without the details. MSRJ, rear 37. Another account, given by a Chinese defector, is in DZ 4, F: 754–755.

29. MSRJ, rear 37.

30. DZ 4, D: 737; MSRJ, rear 32. The figure one most commonly encounters among all the reports of captured Chinese or Chinese defectors is three *gantangs* per month. A gantang differed considerably from place to place in the East Indies, but it was probably ten pounds or less. That means the soldiers were getting at most around a pound of rice a day. A gram of unenriched dry rice contains about 3.5 calories, so if we presume a 500-gram pound, then soldiers would have had 1,750 calories a day from rice. Not enough to support the grueling labor they were performing. This figure of three gantangs per month comes from two different Dutch accounts. Of course, rations might well have differed by unit and place stationed. For example, a Chinese defector revealed in September 1661 that he received four gantangs of rice per month, which he felt wasn't nearly enough, which is why he defected in the first place (DZ 4, F: 753). Accounts indicate that Koxinga's soldiers were hungry everywhere on Taiwan.

31. DZ 4, D: 737.

32. According to Zheng clan genealogies, Zheng Tai was a distant cousin—technically speaking, a third cousin (遠房族兄). Zhang Zongqia, "Zheng Chenggong," 146. But Zhilong adopted him into the family as a son, which is how he came to be Koxinga's brother. See Hang, "Between Trade," 82.

33. XWSL, 257.

34. See, for example, Chen Bisheng, "Zheng Chenggong shou fu Taiwan zhan shi," 16.

35. Lu Ruoteng 盧若騰, "Shi you feng" 石尤風, in Lu Ruoteng, *Dao*, 25. I changed the phrase "on the Eastern Expedition" to "in Taiwan." Historian Deng Kongzhao finds corroboration of unusually stormy winds in other sources of the period. See Deng Kongzhao, "Cong Lu," 62–69.

36. XWSL, 257.

37. DZ 4, D: 655. This is what a Chinese captive told Coyet on 18 June 1661.

38. DZ 4, D: 739.

39. It's not clear whether officials like Coyet himself were included in this tally, although I suspect they were. Resolution, 16 May 1661, VOC 1235: 374.

40. See DRC, 126. See also Zandvliet, *Mapping*, 143.

41. Resolution, 21 September 1661, VOC 1238: 544.

42. DRC, 76–77.

43. Resolution, 5 May 1661, VOC 1235: 365–366.

44. Andrade, *How Taiwan*, 134–136.

45. Brown, *Scurvy*, 3–4.

46. Carpenter: *Beriberi*, 2–3.

47. Resolution, 16 May 1661, VOC 1235: 375. A *legger* was around six hundred Dutch *kan* or about nine hundred liters (two hundred forty gallons). From the *Woordenboek der Nederlandsche Taal*, "Legger," definition F, no. 4, which notes that "De legger arak wordt in Batavia op 160 oude Engelsche wijngallon gerekend: dat zijn . . . 605.6 ned. kan."

48. Resolution, 16 May 1661, VOC 1235: 374–375.

49. DZ 4, D: 677.

50. One source, a Chinese soldier who defected to the Dutch side on 11 October 1661, noted that there were twenty-four of these "black boys, who knew how to use muskets," stationed in Zeelandia City (DZ 4, D: 806).

51. MSRJ, rear 31, discusses the creation of this force.

52. DZ 4, D: 661.

53. DZ 4, D: 671.

54. DZ 4, D: 671.

55. DZ 4, D: 707 (23 July 1661).

56. DZ 4, D: 634 (2 June 1661).

57. DZ 4, D: 695. His sentence is noted in DZ 4, D: 724.

58. DZ 4, D: 657.

59. DZ 4, D: 666.

60. DZ 4, D: 677.

61. DZ 4, D: 688.

RELIEF FROM THE SEA

1. This meeting is described in only one source, which was written by the other captain. Clawson himself didn't leave any documents behind. Dagregister gehouden bij den schipper Andries Pietersz int jacht 's-Gravenlande, op de Taijouanse rhede leggende, als op de Formosaens cust swervende, VOC 1237: 41–56.

2. Dagregister gehouden bij den schipper Andries Pietersz int jacht 's-Gravenlande, op de Taijouanse rhede leggende, als op de Formosaens cust swervende, VOC 1237: 41–56, fol. 42.

3. I'm assuming that he didn't read it out loud himself. Most likely his secretary, Constantine Nobel, read it.

4. Ma Xin to Coyet, 25 June 1661 (5th month 29th day), in DZ 4, D: 665–666.

5. Ma Xin to Coyet, 25 June 1661 (5th month 29th day), in DZ 4, D: 665–666.

6. DZ 4, D: 656, 20 June 1661.

7. DZ 4, D: 666.

8. DZ 4, D: 667.

9. Constantine Nobel, Secretary, to Ma Xin, 27 June 1661, DZ 4, D: 667–668.

10. Resolution, 1661-06-28, VOC 1235: 401v–402.

11. Koxinga to Coyet, 29 June 1661 (6th month 3rd day), DZ 4, D: 672–673.

12. Coyet to Koxinga, 1 July 1661, DZ 4, D: 675–677.

13. Coyet to Koxinga, 1 July 1661, DZ 4, D: 675–677. The last few lines of this resolution are water-damaged, and although I'm fairly sure I got them right, I'm not entirely sure.

14. Coyet to Koxinga, 1 July 1661, DZ 4, D: 675–677.

15. Resolution, 1 July 1661, VOC 1235: 404–405.

16. Resolution, 1 July 1661, VOC 1235: 404–405.

17. DZ 4, D: 686.

18. DZ 4, D: 686.

19. Resolution, 14 July 1661, VOC 1235: 409.

20. Resolution, 14 July 1661, VOC 1235: 409–410.

21. DZ 4, D: 690.

22. DZ 4, D: 701. The hat waving is at DZ 4, D: 699.

23. DZ 4, D: 704.

24. DZ 4, D: 704.

25. Resolution, 22 July 1661, VOC 1235: 411–412.

26. Klencke's diary says there were five sailors; the dagregister says six. It's a small detail. Journael off dagregister gehouden bij Herman Klencke van Odessen int Jacht Hoogelande, zedert 22en Junij Jongstleden dat met 'tselve . . . voor vervanger int gouverno des E Heer Gouverneur Frederik Coijet naer taijouan vertrock, tot heden dat met het jacht Hogelande in Japan voor het eijlant 'schisma behouden ten ancker koomen, VOC 1237: 11–30. DZ 4, D: 716.

27. Actually, Coyet and his councilors already knew the bad news. A Chinese ship from Batavia had gotten to Zeelandia first. In one draft of this chapter, I told the story of that ship—how it ran aground on Baxemboy and how its crew and passengers fled, trying to save their valuables, how Dutch sailors helped the merchants cross to Zeelandia Castle (stealing or being given—depending on whom you believe—money to make the effort worth their while), while the rest of the crew and passengers went to Koxinga. But I decided to excise that section to keep the word count down. Relevant sources are Herport, *Reise*, esp. p. 70; Resolution, 28 July 1661, VOC 1235: 412–413; and DZ 4, D: 710.

28. Cited in Roos, "Amalgamation," 45.

29. Coyet, *Verwaerloosde,* 194–195.

30. Coyet to Govenor-General Jan Maetsuycker, 10 March 1660, VOC 1233: 700–714, fol. 711.

31. Coyet to Governor-General Jan Maetsuycker, 11 April 1660, VOC 1233: A146–A152 (behind folio 810), fol. A149.

32. Coyet, *Verwaerloosde,* 198.

33. Governor Nicholas Verburg to Batavia, VOC 1172: 466–91, fol. 472. He was fond of this phrase and variants thereof. It appears in his Verburg, "Cort vertooch," as well, on fol. 235.

34. Verburg, "Cort vertooch."

35. Verburg, "Cort vertooch," fol. 237.

36. Verburg, "Cort vertooch," fol. 237. I substituted "in Formosa" for the word "here" for the sake of clarity.

37. *General Missiven*, 1655–1674, Maetsuyker, Hartsinck, Van Oudtshoorn, Verburch, and Steur, XXI, 26 January 1661, 361.

38. *General Missiven*, 1655–1674, Maetsuyker, Hartsinck, Van Oudtshoorn, Verburch, and Steur, XXI, 26 January 1661, 361–362.

39. Coyet, *Verwaerloosde*, 130–133. Cf. *Neglected*, 66.

40. Governor-General Jan Maetsuycker to Coyet, 21 June 1661, VOC 1234: 265–290, fol. 277v.

41. Governor-General Jan Maetsuycker to Coyet, 21 June 1661, VOC 1234: 265–290, fol. 283.

42. Resolution, 1 August 1661, VOC 1235: 519.

43. DZ 4, D: 717; Journael off dagregister gehouden bij Herman Klencke van Odessen int Jacht Hoogelande, zedert 22en Junij Jongstleden dat met 'tselve . . . voor vervanger int gouverno des E Heer Gouverneur Frederik Coijet naer taijouan vertrock, tot heden dat met het jacht Hogelande in Japan voor het eijlant 'schisma behouden ten ancker koomen, VOC 1237: 11–30, fol. 23.

44. DZ 4, D: 717.

45. Herport, *Reise*, 71.

46. DRC, 76–77.

47. Herport, *Reise*, 71.

48. Resolutions, 12 August 1661, VOC 1238: 523.

THE FLEET

1. MSRJ, rear 39.

2. MSRJ, rear 31.

3. DZ 4, D: 735.

4. This tidbit is from the testimony of Hendrick Robbertsz. van Amsterdam, who escaped to Zeelandia Castle after three months of captivity. DZ 4, D: 735.

5. Zhang Zongqia, *Zheng Chenggong zu pu*, 4–5 and 241–242.

6. This account is from MSRJ, 40. Another, third-hand report has Zheng visiting Valentine in his residence (DZ 4, D: 736). The two accounts are remarkably similar, however, in how they report the details of Valentine and Koxinga's conversation.

7. MSRJ, rear 38.

8. MSRJ, rear 29.

9. Most of the description of this crucifiction I took from MSRJ, 28–29, but the detail about its occurring in front of Valentine's house comes from DZ 4, D: 729. Another account of this incident can be found at DZ 4, D: 748–749.

10. DZ 4, D: 736.

11. Resolution, 1 July 1661, VOC 1235: 404–405.

12. DZ 4, D: 726.

13. Cauw to Coyet, 1661-08-12, in DRC, 41–42, quote from 41.

14. Schouten, *Oost-Indische*, 164.

15. DZ 4, D: 728. For more on the speed of the journey, see DRC, 37.

16. Coyet noted in a letter to Cauw, one of the few able to get through the Channel, that beans and arak were what he most wanted sent over, because Zeelandia Castle had none. DRC, 47. For more, see DZ 4, D: 746, which lists the lading of the *Domburgh*, a ship that arrived a bit later.

17. DRC, 45.

18. DZ 4, D: 740.

19. Herport, *Reise*, 72.

20. Sources for the Urk: DZ mentions a letter from a survivor named Benjamin Velthuysen (the original doesn't seem to have survived), DZ 4, D: 743, which notes that the crew was captured by the enemy. Another account, at DZ 4, D: 749, has fourteen of the forty-two crew members beheaded by the people of Sinkan. (The rest were, the teller believes, sent southward.)

21. This is the most standard story, but see also DZ 4, D: 743.

22. DZ 4, D: 751.

23. The description of the Chinese farmer's route is based on DZ 4, D: 774–776, and DRC, 79–80. Cf. Resolution, 14 September 1661, VOC 1238: 519–621, fol. 535.

24. DZ 4, D: 775.

25. DZ 4, D: 769–770.

26. The words were likely written not by Cauw himself but by his secretary, who recorded them in Cauw's official journal: DRC, 76–77.

27. What Sait said to Coyet, Cauw, and the others was taken from DZ 4, D: 774–776, and DRC, 79–80.

28. DZ 4, D: 775.

A FOOLISH ATTACK

1. DRC, 81–82.
2. DRC, 188.
3. Coyet, *Neglected*, 69. I've altered the translation slightly for readability.
4. DZ 4, D: 781.
5. DRC, 83. (See also DZ 4, D: 781.)
6. DZ 4, D: 780. The term *neder te vellen* I have translated as "to kill."
7. DZ 4, D: 781.
8. DZ 4, D: 784.
9. Chen Bisheng, "Zheng Chenggong shou fu Taiwan zhan shi," 17.
10. DZ 4, D: 783.
11. DZ 4, D: 782.
12. DRC, 86.
13. I use "deacon" to translate *krankenbezoeker.*
14. I use "dredge anchor" to translate *dregge.*
15. DZ 4, D: 785.
16. DZ 4, D: 785.
17. DRC, 93.
18. Herport, *Reise*, 73–74.
19. DRC, 93.
20. DRC, 90 and 92.
21. Resolution, 23 September 1661, VOC 1238: 545–546; DRC, 97–98; DZ 4, D: 792–793.
22. DRC, 90.
23. DRC, 184–185.
24. DRC, 97–98 (see also Resolution, 23 September 1661, 545–546, and DZ4, D: 792–793).
25. DRC, 98.
26. DZ 4, D: 792–793.
27. This itinerary is based on the perhaps suspect report that Sait gave of his spy work on 1 October 1661 in DZ 4, D: 796–798, and in DRC, 105–107.
28. DZ 4, D: 796–798; DRC, 105–107.
29. DZ 4, D: 796–798; DRC, 105–107.
30. DZ 4, D: 796–798, and DRC, 105–107.

31. DRC, 105.

32. The decision to take Sait out to the ships and Coyet's doubts about his report are absent from Coyet's dagregister (DZ 4, D: 796–798). See DRC, 107.

THE DEFECTORS

1. This is attested in Verbael gehouden bij den secretaris Pieter Marville ten overstaen van den heeren Louijs Philibert Vernattij, advocate fiscael van India, Joan Croon, ontfanger generael, en Willem van Outhoorn, gecommitteerde leden uijt den achtbaren raedt van Justitie des Casteel Batavia, door ordre van haer Ed. Ten hijse van d'E. Frederick Coyett gewesen gouverneur van het Eijlandt Formosa bij sich hebbende sijne raetspersoonen, om de resolutien bij haer lieden getrocken en alhier ongeteeckent overgebracht, te teekcenen, Batavia, 20 September 1662, VOC 1238: 799–847.

2. DZ 4, D: 796.

3. DZ 4, D: 796. The term "bitches" I've used to translate the term "dog," which in its gender neutral version doesn't sound derisive in American English. I've used the term "maggot" to translate the Dutch term *schelm,* which was one of the worst things you could be called in seventeenth-century Dutch, but if you want to understand the emotional impact in modern American English, you'd do better to resort to a gendered term like "pussy" or "twat." Odd that so many of our most powerful insults today are gendered like this. It doesn't seem to have been so true of seventeenth-century Dutch. (It's impossible, by the way, to know what Chinese term the Dutch were translating by the word *schelm.*)

4. DZ 4, D: 789 (23 September 1661); DZ 4, D: 803 (7 October).

5. Since a gantang was about 10 pounds, or 5 kilograms, and since a gram of unenriched dry rice contains about 3.5 calories, and since twice 5 kilograms makes 10,000 grams, which means 35,000 calories per month, or a bit more than 1,000 per day.

6. Arrived on 6 October, DZ 4, D: 802.

7. Arrived on 6 October, DZ 4, D: 802. Another defector said that soldiers received a half a catty of beef each day, "which was nearly useless" (DZ 4, D: 805).

8. *VOC Glossarium*, "Kati."

9. Beef contains around seven hundred calories per pound, depending on its fat content, and the oxen being slaughtered were likely lean, lean, lean, since they were plow oxen used in a time of dearth, not cattle raised for meat.

10. Arrived on 7 October, DZ 4, D: 803.

11. DZ 4, D: 805.

12. Arrived on 30 September, DZ 4, D: 795.

13. Arrived on 7 October, DZ 4, D: 803.

14. DZ 4, D: 802.

15. DZ 4, D: 802.

16. Arrived on 7 October, DZ 4, D: 803.

17. DZ 4, D: 806.

18. Arrived on 7 October, DZ 4, D: 803.

19. Arrived on 26 September, DZ 4, D: 791.

20. XWSL, 257. See Chen Bisheng, "Zheng Chenggong zai shou fu kai fa," 56.

21. XWSL, 258.

22. Lu Ruoteng 盧若騰, "Dong du xing" 東都行, excerpted in Wu and Huang, "Lüe," 246.

23. The boys used his title, Commander Ma (馬本督), which they pronounced Beebontock.

24. The information about the black boys is much more copious in Cauw's dagregister than in the Zeelandia dagregister. News of their arrival and report is found in DRC, 128–130.

25. How the African boys fell under suspicion is found in DRC, 134–135.

26. Cauw's dagregister notes that the pijnbanck would be used as a threat but does not note that it was in the same room. And later they use canes to beat the boys rather than just the rack itself. DRC, 135.

27. The description of the interrogation and torture of the two boys is taken from DRC, 135–137, and DZ 4, E: 632–634.

28. There are two accounts of the flight of Sait from the galiot *de Roode Vos* as it lay at anchor at sea near Tayouan. The fullest is DRC, 139–141. The other is DZ 4, E: 637–638.

29. DRC, 141.

30. DZ 4, E: 637–638.

31. DZ 4, E: 634–637.

32. XWSL, 134.

33. DZ 4, E: 634–637.

34. The practice was called *zi wen* 自刎.

35. XWSL, 39. In the famous Japanese puppet play about Koxinga first performed a half century after the warlord's death, this practice is taken to ridiculous extremes, with one character after another committing suicide for loyalty or honor. Chikamatsu, "Battles."

36. Resolutions of the Grand Council of the Indies, 12 April 1662, VOC 678: 71–72.

37. DZ 4, E: 637–638.

38. DRC, 142.

39. Arrived on 26 September, DZ 4, D: 791.

40. Arrived on 30 September, DZ 4, D: 795.

41. Zheng Dayu, *Jing guo*, "Wu bei kao," juan 8, fol. 22v.

42. Yu Yonghe, *Pi hai*, 64.

43. TWWJ, 42.

44. Zheng Dayu, *Jing guo*, "Wu bei kao," juan 8, fol. 22.

45. Yu Yonghe, *Pi hai*, 64. See Keliher, *Small Sea*, 192–195.

46. Yu Yonghe, *Pi hai*, 64.

47. Resolution, 1661-09-27, VOC 1238: 547; and 1661-10-03, VOC 1238: 550v. On the intelligence about the rice junks, see DZ 4, D: 801.

48. DZ 4, D: 807. Also DRC, 116.

49. DRC, 117.

50. DZ 4, D: 808.

51. This exchange is described in two sources: DZ 4, D: 808, and DRC, 117. They agree closely.

52. DZ 4, D: 810.

KOXINGA CLOSES IN

1. DZ 4, D: 798. This information comes from Sait's testimony on 1 October 1661, and so it should be taken with some skepticism.

2. DRC, 102.

3. DZ 4, D: 793.

4. Resolution, 29 September 1661, VOC 1238: 549.

5. Resolution, 29 September 1661, VOC 1238: 549.

6. DRC, 102.

7. DZ 4, D: 794–795; and DRC, 106.

8. Resolution, 29 September 1661, VOC 1238: 549.

9. DRC, 102. Cauw says nine feet; the Resolutions say seven feet. Resolution, 29 September 1661, VOC 1238: 550.

10. Resolution, 29 September 1661, VOC 1238: 549v.

11. Resolution, 29 September 1661, VOC 1238: 550.

12. DRC, 102–103.

13. XWSL, 42.

14. XWSL, 56.

15. DRC, 105.

16. DRC, 105.

17. DRC, 105.

18. DRC, 126.

19. DZ 4, D: 807.

20. DRC, 114.

21. DRC, 115.

22. DRC, 123.

23. DRC, 124–125. Cauw's is the best description of the attack, but see also Resolution, 20 October 1661, VOC 1238: 557–558; and DZ 4, D: 813.

24. DZ 4, E: 625.

25. DRC, 142.

26. DRC, 141.

27. The Chinese terms are 靈熕 and 龍熕. The term 熕 is a Southern Min word for "cannon." HSJWL, 8. That the Spirit Cannons were placed in Baxemboy we learn not from Chinese sources, which are sparse and few at this period, but from the Dutch, to whom a Chinese defector revealed the information. See DZ 4, E: 678, and DRC, 190–191.

28. XWSL, 179.

29. XWSL, 179.

30. Huang Yi-long, "Ou zhou," 573–634.

31. Deng Shiliang, *Xin yue*, cited in Huang Yi-long, "Ou zhou," 603.

32. XWSL, 179.

33. DRC, 138.

34. The incident occurred on 27 October 1661. DZ 4, E: 639.

35. DZ 4, E: 669. This incident occurred on 14 October 1661.

36. This incident occurred considerably later, on 10 January 1661. DZ 4, E: 715.

37. DZ 4, E: 648.

38. DZ 4, E: 638.

39. 黄安.

40. XWSL, 206.

41. DRC, 149–150.

42. DRC, 149.

43. DRC, 148.

44. DZ 4, E: 641.

45. Resolution, 7 November 1661, VOC 1238: 567v. Information about the death penalty we find in DRC, 166.

46. DRC, 125–126.

47. DRC, 165.

48. Resolution, 7 November 1661, VOC 1238: 568.

49. Resolution, 7 November 1661, VOC 1238: 568v.

50. DRC, 169.

51. DRC, 171.

52. DRC, 171–172.

53. DRC, 175.

THE ACCIDENTAL EMBASSY

1. Instructie voor den coopman David Harthouwer vertrekkende als commissaris naar Tamsiu en Quelang, 26 September 1661, VOC 1235: 838–841, fol. 839.

2. Resolution, 21 September 1661, VOC 1235: 542v.

3. DZ 4, D: 793 (choosing ship). Resolution, 26 November 1661, VOC 1238: 580.

4. Resolution, 1661-10-05, VOC 1238: 552; DZ 4, D: 801.

5. DRC, 109.

6. DZ 4, E: 627.

7. Harthouwer, Daghregister, fol. 941–942.

8. The presence of fishermen comes from Harthouwer, Daghregister, fol. 943.

9. DRC, 50–51.

10. DRC, 67.

11. Instructie voor den coopman David Harthouwer vertrekkende als commissaris naar Tamsiu en Quelang, 26 September 1661, VOC 1235: 838–841, fol. 840.

12. 永寧鎮. I refer to the bay as Yongning Bay, but its proper Chinese name is Shenhu Bay (深沪湾).

13. 靖南王 耿繼茂.

14. DZ 4, E: 652.

15. The following description of this town is taken from two sources, from Harthouwer's own impressions, when he visited it a week later (Harthouwer, Daghregister, 954–955), and from Hurt and Clewerk's description (HCCA, 959–962). There is also a passage in DZ 4, E: 649–651.

16. *Bie cheng fen zhi qing xi Zhang shi jia pu xu* 鰲城分支清溪張氏家譜序, cited in Li Guohong, "Xin jin," 326, footnote.

17. DZ 4, E: 650.

18. Cloth from India = *salempoeris*. The sundial (*sonwijser*) might actually have been a sextant.

19. Melchior Hurt's journal doesn't mention the precise contents of the conversation, but we can guess from the instructions that Harthouwer painstakingly wrote out for him and Clewerck: Bericht en memorie voor d Srs Melkior Hurt ende Jacob Clewerik gaande als expresse gecommitteerden aande Tartarischen Gouverneur der stadt Inglingh Thia genaemt, 16 October 1661, VOC 1235: 945–947.

20. HCCA, fol. 960v.

21. Melchior Hurt and Jacob Clewijk to David Harthouwer, 16 October 1661, VOC 1235: 947.

22. David Harthouwer to Melchior Hurt and Jacob Clewijk, 16 October 1661, VOC 1235: 947v.

23. HCCA, fol. 961v.

24. The description of the departure comes from HCCA, but the number of horsemen (twenty) comes from Harthouwer, who heard

it from the ship's surgeon, who was ashore at the time and witnessed their departure from Yongning. Harthouwer, Daghregister, fol. 949.

25. DZ 4, E: 653–654. This was probably the Shunji Bridge (順濟橋), which had been built at the beginning of the thirteenth century but was dismantled in 2006 after flooding caused a partial collapse.

26. HCCA, fol. 963.

27. HCCA, fol. 963v.

28. HCCA, 964v.

29. HCCA, fol. 964v.

30. HCCA, fol. 965v.

31. HCCA, fol. 966v. They called the town Hingoughoe, which probably corresponds to Xinghua Fu (興化府), near Putian. Thanks to Jack Wills for helping decipher the Dutch transliteration.

32. HCCA, fol. 966v.

33. HCCA, fol. 966v. I changed this to the plural. In the original it is "so that I could scarcely see out of my eyes." I'm still not sure who authored the piece, although I suspect it was Hurt.

34. HCCA, fol. 966v.

35. HCCA, fol. 966v.

36. HCCA, fol. 966v.

37. "Hebben int incomen binnen sijn muragie van wederzijden noch een fortjen affgesloten." Hurt and Clewercq, "Corte aanteijkening," fol. 967.

38. Hurt and Clewercq, "Corte aanteijkening," fol. 967.

39. Hurt and Clewercq, "Corte aanteijkening," fol. 967v.

40. HCCA, fol. 971.

41. I'm assuming that the "low bows" of the manuscript are actually kowtows, as this seems most likely.

42. The manuscript here is damaged, so I'm not sure what precisely it says. HCCA, fol. 968.

43. The man was described as a "caffer . . . die soo't scheen voor geck diende." HCCA, fol. 968v.

44. HCCA, fol. 968v.

45. HCCA, fol. 968v.

46. HCCA, fol. 968v.

47. HCCA, fol. 969.

48. HCCA, fol. 969.

49. HCCA, fol. 969–969v.

50. Letter from Melchior Hurt and Jacob Clewijk to David Harthouwer, Quanzhou, China, 16 October 1661, VOC 1235: 947.

51. Harthouwer figured out that Geng had previously been stationed in Guangzhou, so it's likely that he's the one who caught their translator's error, although by then it was too late to help Hurt and Clewerck. They didn't realize their error until they returned. Harthouwer, Daghregister, fol. 952v.

52. HCCA, fol. 970.

53. HCCA, fol. 970v.

54. HCCA, fol. 971.

55. HCCA, fol. 971v.

56. HCCA, fol. 972.

57. HCCA, fol. 972v.

58. HCCA, fol. 972v.

59. HCCA, fol. 973.

60. HCCA, fol. 973v.

61. Letter from David Harthouwer to Melchior Hurt and Jacob Clewerck, Yongning (Inglingh) Bay, 30 October 1661, Harthouwer, Daghregister, fol. 956v–957v.

62. David Harthouwer to Melchior Hurt and Jacob Clewerck, 30 October 1661, Harthouwer, Daghregister, fol. 957.

63. David Harthouwer to Melchior Hurt and Jacob Clewerck, 30 October 1661, Harthouwer, Daghregister, 957v.

64. HCCA, fol. 973.

65. Dahpon Ho details this suffering in a wonderful PhD dissertation he is working on, which should be complete sometime in 2011, at University of California, San Diego. Ho, "Sealords."

66. HCCA, fol. 974.

67. Harthouwer, Daghregister, fol. 959.

68. Harthouwer, Daghregister, fol. 959.

69. HCCA, fol. 974.

70. HCCA, fol. 974.

71. Harthouwer Daghregister, fol. 975v.

72. The quote's from DRC, 167.

73. Tsinglamongh to Coyett, in DZ 4, E: 663–664.

ACRIMONY

1. 軍擾者,將不重也。. . . 吏怒者,倦也.

2. *Dispencier*.

3. Two different accounts of this incident exist: Resolution, 1661-09-27, VOC 1238: 545v, and, better, DRC, 98.

4. DRC, 151.

5. DRC, 112.

6. There were, according to Cauw, more than three hundred people in hospital. The total population of Zeelandia Castle was around twenty-one-hundred. DRC, 133.

7. Resolution, 1661-10-17, VOC 1238: 555–555v.

8. Resolution, 1661-09-21, VOC 1238: 544.

9. Resolution, 1661-11-18, VOC 1238: 574v.

10. Resolution, 1661-12-23, VOC 1238: 594.

11. Resolution, 1661-10-28, VOC 1238: 561.

12. Resolution, 1661-10-25, VOC 1238: 559–560.

13. Resolution, 1661-10-28, VOC 1238: 561.

14. DRC, 191–192.

15. DRC, 152.

16. Resolution, 1661-11-05, VOC 1238: 566.

17. Resolution, 1661-11-05, VOC 1238: 566.

18. DRC, 175.

19. Vertoogh bij den coopman David Harthouwer aen den Edele Heere Frederick Coyet, Raat extraordinaris van India ende gouverneur over Formosas ommeslag etc., midtsgaders sijn E ord en nogh bij te voegene Heeren Raaden [29] November 1661, VOC 1238: 582–583 (contained in Resolution, 29 November 1661, VOC 1238: 582–583), fol. 582.

20. DRC, 139.

21. DRC, 190–192, and DZ 4, E: 700.

22. DRC, 191–192.

23. DRC, 191–192.

24. Resolution, 1661-10-11, VOC 1238: 553, 553v; Cauw, 112.

25. Resolution, 1661-11-05, VOC 1238: 566v.

26. Resolution, 1661-10-11, VOC 1238: 553v.

27. Resolution, 1661-11-05, VOC 1238, fols. 565–566.

28. Resolution, 1661-11-08, VOC 1238: 570–570v.

29. Resolution, 26 November 1661, VOC 1238: 579–579v.

30. Resolution, 29 November 1661, VOC 1238: 581–581v.

31. Vertoogh bij den coopman David Harthouwer aen den Edele Heere Frederick Coyet, Raat extraordinaris van India ende gouverneur over Formosas ommeslag etc., midtsgaders sijn E ord en nogh bij te voegene Heeren Raaden [29] November 1661, VOC 1238: 582–583 (contained in Resolution, 29 November 1661, VOC 1238: 582–583), fol. 582v.

32. Vertoogh bij den coopman David Harthouwer aen den Edele Heere Frederick Coyet, Raat extraordinaris van India ende gouverneur over Formosas ommeslag etc., midtsgaders sijn E ord en nogh bij te voegene Heeren Raaden [29] November 1661, VOC 1238: 582–583 (contained in Resolution, 29 November 1661, VOC 1238: 582–583), fol. 582v.

33. Resolution, 29 November 1661, VOC 1238: 583v.

34. DRC, 193.

35. Resolution, 29 November 1661, VOC 1238: 584v–585v.

36. Resolution, 29 November 1661, VOC 1238: 585.

37. Taken from two sources: DZ 4, E: 690, and DRC, 200.

38. Coyet to the Veltheer der krijsvolckeren en tweeden gebieder over 't lantschap Fuzhou, 3 December 1661, in DZ 4, E: 686v–687v, quote at E: 687. Coyet used this term "Highness" to address the general rather than for the viceroy, which is odd.

39. DZ 4, E: 680.

40. DZ 4, E: 691.

41. DZ 4, E: 691.

42. DRC, 202.

43. DRC, 202.

44. DRC, 202.

45. DRC, 202.

46. DRC, 203.

47. DRC, 203.

48. DRC, 205–206.

49. DRC, 206.

50. Coyet, *Verwaarloosde*, 148–151.

51. Resolutions of the Grand Council of the Indies, Batavia, 4 February 1662, VOC 678 (unfoliated).

52. "Faithless" is from Campbell, *Formosa*, 73; Manthorpe, Forbidden, 78–79; Mostert, "Chain." Beerens, "Formosa verwaarloosd," refers to Cauw as a "deserter" (p. 50).

THE LAST BATTLE

1. Coyet, *Neglected*, 80. I have made some changes to the translation, including substituting the phrase "hilltop redoubt behind the castle" for the name of that redoubt, "Redoubt Utrecht."

2. Mostert, "Chain"; Campbell, *Formosa*, 73; Manthorpe, *Forbidden*, 79; Le Monnier, "Vergessene," 352; Kalff, "De Val," 128–129; Boxer, "Siege." See also Blussé, *Tribuut*, 69; Yang Yanjie, *Heju*, 290–291; DZ 4, E: 614, footnote 78; Jiang Shusheng, *Zheng Chenggong*, 30; and Andrade, *How Taiwan,* ch. 11. The idea of Hans Radis as being responsible for Zheng's capture of Zeelandia has also found its way into the literature on comparative military history. See, for example, Black, *War and the World*, 83.

3. Herport, *Reise*, 75.

4. MSRJ, rear 50.

5. MSRJ, rear 49–50.

6. MSRJ, rear 48.

7. In reeden te vatten.

8. MSRJ, rear 56.

9. MSRJ, rear 52.

10. MSRJ, rear 52.

11. DZ 4, E: 715–716.

12. DZ 4, E: 716.

13. DZ 4, E: 716.

14. DZ 4, E: 717.

15. I'm assuming the flashing here, since 17 January was a bright, sunny day. DZ 4, E: 718.

16. MSRJ, rear 52.

17. DZ 4, E: 718, 719.

18. DZ 4, E: 721. In the Resolutions, the distance is given as "a short musket shot," which is around a hundred yards (Resolution, 1662-01-21, VOC 1238: 600v). Philip Meij corroborates this, saying that the

main battery was placed about twenty-five to thirty rods (*roeden*) from the redoubt. A rod was about ten feet. MSRJ, rear 53.

19. DZ 4, E: 721.

20. 夫兵形象水，水之形，避高而趨下；兵之形，避實而擊虛。水因地而制流，兵因敵而制勝 (Sun Zi, 41).

21. Resolution, 1662-01-21, VOC 1238: 600v–.

22. Resolution, 1662-01-21, VOC 1238: 601v.

23. Resolution, 1662-01-21, VOC 1238: 601.

24. Coyet to Batavia, 25 January 1662, in DZ 4, E: 728–732.

25. Michael Engelken to Coyet, 21 January 1662, in DZ 4, E: 721–722.

26. DZ 4, E: 724.

27. Resolution, 1662-01-23, VOC 1238: 605.

28. Resolution, 1662-01-21, VOC 1238: 601v.

29. DZ 4, E: 724.

30. Resolution, 1662-01-22, VOC 1238: 603.

31. DZ 4, E: 725.

32. DZ 4, E: 723–724.

33. DZ 4, E: 724.

34. MSRJ, rear 59.

35. Short report by Philip Meij, 2 February 1662, in DZ 4, E: 760.

36. I get the term "shooting hills" (*schietheuvels*) from Coyet to Batavia, 25 January 1662, in DZ 4, E: 728–732, fol. 729, but the information about the mounds of earth in the market is from DZ 4, E: 724.

37. DZ 4, E: 724.

38. Coyet to Batavia, 25 January 1662, in DZ 4, E: 728–732, esp. fols. 728–729.

39. MSRJ, rear 53.

40. Coyet to Batavia, 25 January 1662, in DZ 4, E: 728–732, esp. fols. 728–729, quote at 734.

41. The Resolutions say 2,500 (Resolution, 1662-01-26, VOC 1238: 606); Philip Meij says 1,700 (MSRJ, rear 53); Wouter Schouten also says 1,700 shots (Schouten, *Oost-Indische*, 171). Jiang Shusheng accepts the figure of 2,500 (Jiang Shusheng, *Zheng Chenggong*, 42).

42. 驚天動地.

43. Jiang Shusheng, *Zheng Chenggong,* 42.

44. This is in any case what the Dagregister says, which is usually pretty accurate, although in this case the information came to the writers indirectly, after the fact DZ 4, E: 734.

45. DZ 4, E: 736.

46. Resolution, 1662-01-26, VOC 1238: 606v.

47. Resolution, 1662-01-26, VOC 1238: 607.

48. Resolution, 1662-01-27, VOC 1238: 608.

49. Coyett, *Verwaerloosde,* in Struve, "Voices," 232. According to the Resolutions, it was a warehouse—the "new warehouse"—that had its roof removed. Resolution, 1662-01-27, VOC 1238: 608.

50. Resolution, 27 January 1662, VOC 1238: 608.

51. Resolution, 1662-01-27, VOC 1238: 608.

52. Resolution, 1662-01-27, VOC 1238: 608v.

53. Coyet to Batavia, 25 January 1662, in DZ 4, E: 728–732, esp. fols. 728–729, quote at 734.

54. Coyet to Batavia, 25 January 1662, in DZ 4, E: 728–732, esp. fols. 728–729, quote at 734.

55. Resolution, 1662-01-27, VOC 1238: 610.

56. Resolution, 1662-01-27, VOC 1238: 608v.

57. Resolution, 1662-01-27, VOC 1238: 609.

58. Resolution, 1662-01-27, VOC 1238: 610.

SURRENDER

1. DZ 4, E: 737.

2. MSRJ, rear 46.

3. MSRJ, rear 53.

4. Koxinga to Coyet, 28 January 1662 (Yongli 15, 12th month, 9th day), in DZ 4, E: 740.

5. DZ 4, E: 740. In the published version of the Zeelandia Dagregister, this first, short letter from Koxinga is preceded by another, longer letter that Koxinga wrote to the officers and soldiers of the fortress. See below, note 9.

6. Koxinga to Coyet, 28 January 1661 (Yongli 15, 12th month, 9th day), in DZ 4, E: 742–743.

7. MSRJ, rear 56.

8. Koxinga to Coyet, 29 January 1662 (Yongning 15, 12th month 16th day), in DZ 4, E: 745.

9. In the Zeelandia Dagregister, this placard to the soldiers appears in the wrong place. It's inserted in the entry for 28 January 1662, whereas Philip Meij's journal makes clear that it was actually written after this date (MSRJ, 57). To make sure of this, I went back to the original manuscript version of DZ. I could see clearly that this longer letter was inserted out of sequence (VOC 1238: 739v–741) by checking a safety mechanism in Dutch scribery. Whenever Dutch scribes reached the bottom of a page, they always wrote, below the very last line, the first word of the following page. It was clear that sometime after the original composition of the dagregister, someone moved the placard to the earlier date. Why might this person have done this? Possibly in order to cover his ass. By putting the bellicose letter first, with its threats to storm and kill, the person in question might have hoped to give the impression that the rapid decision to surrender was more warranted.

10. DZ 4, E: 742.

11. Harthouwer to Coyet, 29 January 1662, DZ 4, E: 746.

12. MSRJ, 58.

13. Coyet to Koxinga, 30 January 1662, DZ 4, E: 747–748.

14. DZ 4, E: 755, and MSRJ, 5.

15. Coyet to Joan van Oetgens and David Harthouwer, 10 February 1662, DZ 4, E: 767–769. See also Harthouwer and Oetgens van Waveren to Coyet, 9 February 1662, in DZ 4, E: 765–766.

16. Coyet to Oetgens and Harthouwer, 10 February 1662, DZ 4, E: 767–769.

17. MSRJ, rear 60.

18. MSRJ, rear 60–61.

19. MSRJ, rear 61.

20. Resolution, 1662-02-05, VOC 1238: 618v.

21. Iperen to Coyet, written in Zeelandia Castle, 11 February 1662, DZ 4, E: 771–772.

22. MSRJ, rear 63.

23. Schouten, *Oost-Indische*, 165.

24. Schouten, *Oost-Indische*, 171.

A MAD DEATH

1. XWSL, 257.

2. HSJWL, 40.

3. "Tall and pale" come from Riccio's own description of himself: Letter from Riccio to Dutch trading post in Fuzhou, 9 August 1665, VOC 1257: 1156–1158, in Borao, *Spaniards in Taiwan,* vol. 2, 631–633.

4. Riccio, "Hechos," 599.

5. Imbault-Huart, *l'Ile,* 77–78.

6. Imbault-Huart, *l'Ile,* 77–78.

7. Riccio, "Hechos," 599.

8. Riccio, "Hechos," 599.

9. Riccio, "Hechos," 607.

10. Riccio, "Hechos," 612.

11. Riccio, "Hechos," 607. This is my translation.

12. Song Zhengyu, "Zheng Chenggong," 383. The biography dates from between 1662 and 1668.

13. JHZ, 60, says that the woman Zheng Jing slept with was Koxinga's favored concubine. Other sources, such as HJJY, 30, and the *Qing shi* say that the woman Zheng Jing slept with was a wet nurse. This occurred in the fourth month of Yongli 16 (1662). "Qing shi lie zhuan, Zheng Chenggong," in *Zheng Chenggong zhuan.*

14. Wills, *Pepper*, 28.

15. "Qing shi lie zhuan, Zheng Chenggong," in *Zheng Chenggong zhuan*, 44.

16. HJJY, 30.

17. Wu Weiye, "Zheng Chenggong zhi luan" 鄭成功之亂, in Wu Weiye, *Lu qiao*, 63.

18. DZ 3, E: 444.

19. Chinese sources generally favor the explanation that Zheng Chenggong died of a cold (感冒風寒) (see MHJY, 30). Other sources, such as Wu Weiye, *Lu qiao*, indicate that as he was dying, Koxinga scratched his eyes and face, which would perhaps fit a diagnosis of tertiary syphilis, in which gummas form on the face. Some records indicate that he went mad just before dying, such as the Qing Veritable Records, which state that Chenggong "could not contain his

anger and suddenly went insane" (cited in Chen Shengkun, "Zheng Chenggong siyin," 56). See also Li Tengyue, "Zheng Chenggong," 35–44. Although both Chen Shengkun and Li Tengyue discuss Chenggong's episodes of madness, neither attributes them to syphilis. Thanks to John Hibbs, MD, for a helpful medical perspective on syphilis and its epidemiology (personal communication, October 2004).

20. Rougemont, *Historia,* 108–110, cited in Keene, *Battles*, 71. I've changed the wording slightly.

21. Cramer, *Borts*, 62.

22. Riccio, "Hechos," 619–623.

23. Resolutions of the Grand Council of the Indies, Batavia, 21 March 1662, VOC 678 (unfoliated).

24. Resolutions of the Grand Council of the Indies, Batavia, 17 March 1662, VOC 678 (unfoliated).

25. Resolutions of the Grand Council of the Indies, Batavia, 17 March 1662, VOC 678 (unfoliated).

26. Resolutions of the Grand Council of the Indies, Batavia, 19 May 1662, VOC 678 (unfoliated).

27. Resolutions of the Grand Council of the Indies, Batavia, 28 April 1662, VOC 678 (unfoliated). Vogels, *Coyet*, 36.

28. Resolutions of the Grand Council of the Indies, Batavia, 14 April 1662, VOC 678: 76.

29. See Zandvliet, *De 250*, 57 and 131–132.

EPILOGUES AND CONCLUSIONS

1. Herport, *Reise*, 84.

2. Herport, *Reise*, 84.

3. It was a division of a larger unit called the Firearms Division, which was first established in 1407. Swope, "Crouching," 21.

4. Huang Yi-long, "Ou zhou," 603.

5. Huang Yi-long, "Hong yi," 60–61.

6. Cheng Kaihu, *Chou liao*, cited in Huang Yi-long, "Ou zhou," 579.

7. Crosby, *Measure*.

8. Huang Yi-long, "Hong yi."

9. DZ 4, D: 784.

10. Zheng Dayu, *Jing guo,* "Wu bei kao," juan 6.

11. "The Bird Gun 鳥銃," Zheng Dayu, *Jing guo,* "Wu bei kao" 武備攷, juan 6, fol 3.

12. Hanson, *Carnage*, 21.

13. Hanson, *Carnage*, 445.

14. Hanson, *Carnage*, 446.

15. Lynn, *Battle*.

16. See "An Execution."

17. Sun Laichen, "Military Technology," 500.

18. Swope, *Dragon's*. See also Swope, "Crouching."

19. There's some dispute about the date of Koxinga's death, but I accept Jack Wills's dating of 23 June 1662, since he is one of the most careful scholars I know. See Wills, *Pepper*, 28. The Dutch fleet left on 24 June.

20. Wills, *Pepper*, 34.

21. This was in 1660. See HJJY, 26.

22. Letter from Summinpesiouw or Tsoubontjock to Bort, 19 November 1663 (Yongli 17, 10th month 19th day), in Daghregister gehouden in de oorlogs vloot bescheijden onder de vlagge van den heer admirael Balthasar Bort, op de cust van China, zedert 27en October anno 1663 tot 3en December daeraen volgende, VOC 1244: 2546–2624, fols. 2597v–2598v, quotation at 2598–2598v.

23. Letter from Summinpesiouw or Tsoubontjock (number two under Zheng Jing) to Bort, 19 November 1663 (Yongli 17, 10th month 19th day), in DRB, 2597v–2598v, quotation at 2598.

24. Daghregister gehouden in de oorlogs vloot bescheijden onder de vlagge van den heer admirael Balthasar Bort, op de cust van China, zedert 27en October anno 1663 tot 3en December daeraen volgende, VOC 1244: 2546–2624, 2597v.

25. Letter from Summinpesiouw or Tsoubontjock (number two under Zheng Jing) to Bort, 19 November 1663 (Yongli 17, 10th month 19th day), in DRB, 2597v–2598v, citation at 2597v.

26. DRB, fol. 2593.

27. Bort to Batavia 3 December 1663, VOC 1244: 2517–2531, fols. 2521–2522v, quote from fols. 2521v–2522.

28. Bort to Batavia, 3 December 1663, VOC 1244: 2517–2531, fols. 2521–2522v.

29. It's disappointing that a Chinese account of this battle written by Geng Jimao doesn't have more detail about the naval engagements, although this reticence in a way illustrates how little attention the Qing paid to naval affairs. Ji Liuqi, *Ming ji*.

30. DRB, fol. 2600v.

31. DRB, fols. 2601–2601v.

32. Li Shuaitai to Bort, 20 November 1663, cited in Wills, *Pepper*, 73. (Original in VOC 1244: 2604v–2605v.) (Wills's translation.)

33. Bort to Batavia, 3 December 1663, VOC 1244: 2517–2531, fol. 2524.

34. DRB, fols. 2601–2601v.

35. Riccio, "Hechos," 618. I've changed the translation ever so slightly.

36. Brian Platt, a man who sailed a junk across the Pacific Ocean in 1959, wrote that junks were pretty good at sailing to windward, although they had a tendency to slip leeward much more than deeper-hulled western vessels. This meant that they made slower progress overall. Platt, "Chinese Sail."

37. Larz Stewart, crewman on the *Princess Taiping*, personal communication, 27 April 2010. For more on Stewart, the *Princess Taiping*, and the ramming thereof by a tanker, see "Oregon Native."

38. Hans K. Van Tilburg, for example, suggests that Ming vessels, with their flat hulls, were likely less effective when sailing into the wind than pre-Ming Chinese ships, which had V-shaped hulls, although he points out that further research is needed, since so many factors can influence a ship's behavior, and since we have no replicas of earlier Chinese ship designs. Hans K. van Tilburg, personal communication, 5 May 2010.

39. Report from Zheng Zhilong to Zou Weilian, Chongzhen 6, 9th month, 22nd day (24 October 1633), in Zou Weilian, "Feng jiao," 35.

40. Thornton, *Africa,* 21–24. On the Mediterranean, see Pryor, *Geography*.

41. Seed, "Jewish."

42. Black, "Western Encounter," 23.

43. Cramer, *Bort's Voyagie*, 110, cited in Vogels, "Nieuwe," 73. I've taken *extreme* liberties with the translation to provide rhyme and meter, which is the chief attraction of the original Dutch.

44. Two of these bastions were half-moon bastions, which means they were rounded, not arrow-shaped. See Borao, "Fortress," 66–67. Compare to Vogels, "Nieuwe," 37–47.

45. Joan de Meijer to Willem Volger, 11 Augustus 1666, VOC 1258: 1487–1499, 1492.

46. Joan de Meijer to Willem Volger, 11 Augustus 1666, VOC 1258: 1487–1499, 1493.

47. Joan de Meijer to Willem Volger, 11 Augustus 1666, VOC 1258: 1487–1499, 1495.

48. Joan de Meijer to Willem Volger, 11 Augustus 1666, VOC 1258: 1487–1499, 1490–1495.

49. Joan de Meijer to Willem Volger, 11 Augustus 1666, VOC 1258: 1487–1499, 1490–1496.

50. Joan de Meijer to Willem Volger, 11 Augustus 1666, VOC 1258: 1487–1499, 1490–1493.

51. Joan de Meijer to Willem Volger, 11 Augustus 1666, VOC 1258: 1487–1499, 1502v–1503. The phrase I translate as "used proper means of warfare" is *crijghs gebruijk int werck gestelt*.

52. On the ideal European siege, see Ostwald, *Vauban*, 21–45.

53. Generale Missive, 13 December 1668, VOC 1266: 228v–229, cited in Vogels, "Nieuwe," 93.

54. See Wills, *Pepper*.

55. Wills, *Pepper*, 99.

56. All of this is described in detail in Wills, *Pepper*.

57. Wong, "Chinese Military."

58. Yun and Sun, "Zhong guo."

59. The most accessible introduction is Harro, *Book*.

60. See Liu, *Chinese Knight*, and Wan, *Green Peony*, esp. 2–3.

61. Koxinga to Coyet, Yongli 14, 10th month, 19th day, in Coyet, *Verwaerloosde*, 89–91.

62. Lü and Ye, "Zheng Chenggong zai Xiamen," 156.

63. Ji Liuqi, *Ming ji*, 329.

64. See "A Foggy Morning."

65. Hang, “Between Trade,” 70.

66. Brook, *Vermeer’s*, 19

67. Brook, *Vermeer’s*, 21–22.

68. Huang Yi-long, “Hong yi.”

69. Wong, *China*; Pomeranz, *Great Divergence*.

70. McNeil, *Pursuit*; McNeill, *Age*; Tilly, *Coercion*; Parker, *Military Revolution*.

References

Please note: Most archival records I quote in this book are cited in full in the endnotes. This references section contains only manuscript sources that I used frequently enough to warrant acronyms, to keep the book's word count at a reasonable level.

An Shuangcheng 安雙成. "Qing Zheng Nanjing zhan yi de ruo gan wen ti" 清鄭南京戰役的若干問題. In *Zheng Chenggong yan jiu guo ji xue shu hui yi lun wen ji* 鄭成功研究國際學術會議論文集, 115–131. Nanchang 南昌市: Jiangxi ren min chu ban she 江西人民出版社, 1989.

Andrade, Tonio. "Asian Expansions and European Exceptionalism: The Maritime Factor." In *Asian Expansions: The Historical Processes of Polity Expansion in Asia*, ed. Geoff Wade. London: Routledge (2011, expected).

———. "Beyond Guns, Germs, and Steel: European Expansion in Eurasian Perspective, 1400–1800." *Journal of Early Modern History* 14 (2010): 165–186.

———. "Chinese under European Rule: The Case of Sino-Dutch Mediator He Bin." *Late Imperial China* 28, no. 1 (2007): 1–32.

———. *How Taiwan Became Chinese: Dutch, Spanish, and Han Colonization in the Seventeenth Century*. New York: Columbia University Press, 2008. Available online at http://www.gutenberg-e.org/andrade/ (accessed 29 October 2010).

———. “Political Spectacle and Colonial Rule: The Landdag on Dutch Taiwan, 1629–1648.” *Itinerario* 21, no. 3 (1997): 57–93.

Atwell, William S. “Volcanism and Short-Term Climatic Change in East Asian and World History, c. 1200–1699.” *Journal of World History* 12, no. 1 (2001): 29–98.

Beerens, Jan-Jozef. “Formosa verwaarloosd: Frederick Coyett, een zondebok.” Master’s thesis, Leiden University, 1988.

Bisson, Thomas. *The Crisis of the Twelfth Century: Power, Lordship, and the Origins of European Government*. Princeton, NJ: Princeton University Press, 2008.

Black, Jeremy. “On Diversity and Military History.” In *Recent Themes in Military History: Historians in Conversation*, ed. Donald A. Yerxa, 22–25. Columbia: University of South Carolina Press, 2009.

———. *War and the World: Military Power and the Fate of Continents*. New Haven, CT: Yale University Press, 1998.

———. *War: Past, Present, and Future*. New York: St. Martin’s Press, 2000.

———. “The Western Encounter with Islam.” *Orbis* 48, no. 1 (2004): 19–28.

Blussé, Leonard. “De Chinese nachtmerrie: Een terugtocht en twee nederlagen.” In *De Verenigde Oost-Indische Compagnie tussen oorlog en diplomatie*, eds. Gerrit Knaap and Ger Teitler, 209–238. Leiden: KITLV Press, 2002.

———. “The Dutch Occupation of the Pescadores (1622–1624).” *Transactions of the International Conference of Orientalists in Japan* 18 (1973): 28–44.

———. “Minnan-jen or Cosmopolitan? The Rise of Cheng Chih-lung, alias Nicolas Iquan.” In *Development and Decline of Fukien Province in the Seventeenth and Eighteenth Centuries*, ed. E. B. Vermeer, 245–264. Leiden, Netherlands: E. J. Brill, 1990.

———. *Tribuut aan China: vier eeuwen Nederlands-Chinese betrekkingen*. Amsterdam: Otto Cramwinckel, 1989.

———. “’t Verzuymd Brazil and ’t Verwaarloost Formosa: An Investigation into the Loss of Two Dutch Colonial Settlements.” Paper delivered at the Lost Colonies Conference, Philadephia, 26–27 March 2004.

———. "The VOC as Sorcerer's Apprentice: Stereotypes and Social Engineering on the China Coast." In *Leiden Studies in Sinology*, ed. W. L. Idema, 87–105. Leiden, Netherlands: Leiden University Press, 1981.

Blussé, Leonard, Nathalie Everts, W. E. Milde, and Yung-ho Ts'ao, eds. *De Dagregisters van het Kasteel Zeelandia, Taiwan, 1629–1662*, four vols. The Hague: Instituut voor Nederlandse Geschiedenis, 1995–.

Borao, Eugenio. "The Fortress of Quelang (Jilong, Taiwan): Past, Present, and Future." *Revista de Cultura* 27 (2008): 60–77.

———. *Spaniards in Taiwan,* vol. 2. Taipei: SMC Publishing, Inc., 2002.

Bort, Balthasar. Daghregister gehouden in de oorlogs vloot bescheijden onder de vlagge van den heer admirael Balthasar Bort, op de cust van China, zedert 27en October anno 1663 tot 3en December daeraen volgende. Dutch East India Company Collection, National Archive of the Netherlands, The Hague, VOC 1244: 2546–2624.

Boxer, C. R. "The Siege of Fort Zeelandia and the Capture of Formosa from the Dutch, 1661–1662." *Transactions and Proceedings of the Japan Society of London* 24 (1926–1927): 16–47.

Broadberry, Stephen, and Bishnupriya Gupta. "The Early Modern Great Divergence: Wages, Prices, and Economic Development in Europe and Asia, 1500–1800." *Economic History Review* 59, no. 1 (2006): 2–31.

Brook, Timothy. *Vermeer's Hat: The Seventeenth Century and the Dawn of the Global World.* New York: Bloomsbury Press, 2008.

Brown, Stephen R. *Scurvy: How a Surgeon, a Mariner, and a Gentleman Solved the Greatest Medical Mystery of the Age of Sail.* New York: St. Martin's Press, 2003.

Bryant, Joseph M. "The West and the Rest Revisited: Debating Capitalist Origins, European Colonialism, and the Advent of Modernity." *The Canadian Journal of Sociology* 31, no. 4 (2006): 403–444.

Buisman, J. *Duizend Jaar weer: wind en water in de Lage Landen.* Franeker, Netherlands: Van Wijnen, 1995.

Busquets, Anna. "Los Frailes de Koxinga." In *La investigación sobre Asia-Pacífico en España. Colección Española de Investigación sobre*

Asia-Pacífico, ed. Pedro San Ginés Aguilar, 393–422. Granada: Universidad de Granada, 2007.

Campbell, William. *Formosa under the Dutch: Described from Contemporary Records, with Explanatory Notes and a Bibliography of the Island*. London: Kegan Paul, 1903.

Cao Lütai 曹履泰. *Jing hai ji lüe* 靖海紀略. *Taiwan wen xian cong kan* 臺灣文獻叢刊. No. 33. Taipei: Taiwan yin hang 臺灣銀行, 1959.

Carioti, Patrizia. *Zheng Chenggong*. Naples: Instituto Universitario Orientale Dipartimento di Studi Asiatici, 1995.

Carpenter, John. *Beriberi, White Rice, and Vitamin B: A Disease, a Cause, and a Cure.* Berkeley: University of California Press, 2000.

Cauw, Jacob. Daghregister gehouden bij den commandeur Cauw beginnende 5 Julij 1661 en eijndigende 3 Februarij 1662. Dutch East India Company Collection, National Archive of the Netherlands, The Hague,VOC 1240: 1–213.

Chan, Albert. *The Glory and Fall of the Ming Dynasty*. Norman: University of Oklahoma Press, 1982.

Chang Pin-tsun. "Chinese Maritime Trade: The Case of Sixteenth-Century Fu-chien." PhD dissertation, Princeton University, 1983.

———. "Maritime Trade and Local Economy in Late Ming Fukien," In *Development and Decline of Fukien Province in the Seventeenth and Eighteenth Centuries*, ed. E. B. Vermeer, 63–82. Leiden, Netherlands: E. J. Brill, 1990.

Chase, Kenneth. *Firearms: A Global History to 1700*. Cambridge, UK: Cambridge University Press, 2003.

Chaudhuri, Kirti N. *Trade and Civilisation in the Indian Ocean: An Economic History from the Rise of Islam to 1750*. Cambridge, UK: Cambridge University Press, 1985.

Chen Bisheng 陳碧笙. "1657–1659 nian Zheng Chenggong san ci bei shang Jiangnan zhan yi" 1657–1659 年鄭成功三次北上江南戰役. In Chen Bisheng, *Zheng Chenggong lishi yanjiu* 鄭成功歷史研究, 175–215. Beijing: Jiuzhou chu ban she 九州出版社, 2000.

———. "Cong 'Hui'an Wang Zhong xiao quan ji' de liang tiao shi liao zhong shuo ming 1646 nian Zheng Chenggong shi zen yang zai hai shang qi bing de "從"惠安王忠孝全集"的兩條史料中說明 1646年鄭成功是怎樣在海上起兵的. In Chen Bisheng, *Zheng*

Chenggong lishi yanjiu 鄭成功歷史研究, 117–120. Beijing: Jiuzhou chu ban she 九州出版社, 2000.

———. "He Bin shi ji lüe kao" 何斌事跡略考. In Chen Bisheng, *Zheng Chenggong lishi yanjiu* 鄭成功歷史研究, 99–106. Beijing: Jiuzhou chu ban she 九州出版社, 2000.

———. "Ming dai mo qi hai shang shang ye zi ben yu Zheng zhilong" 明代末期海上商業資本與鄭芝龍. In Chen Bisheng, *Zheng Chenggong lishi yanjiu* 鄭成功歷史研究, 72–98. Beijing: Jiuzhou chu ban she 九州出版社, 2000.

———. "Zheng Chenggong fen ru fu shuo zhi yi" 鄭成功焚儒服說質疑. In Chen Bisheng, *Zheng Chenggong lishi yanjiu* 鄭成功歷史研究, 107–116. Beijing: Jiuzhou chu ban she 九州出版社, 2000.

———. "Zheng Chenggong shou fu Taiwan zhan shi yan jiu" 鄭成功收復臺灣戰史研究. In Chen Bisheng, *Zheng Chenggong lishi yanjiu* 鄭成功歷史研究, 1–24. Beijing: Jiuzhou chu ban she 九州出版社, 2000.

———. "Zheng Chenggong zai shou fu kai fa Taiwan guo cheng zhong suo mian lin de fan dui he dou zheng" 鄭成功在收復開發臺灣過程中所面臨的反對和鬥爭. In Chen Bisheng, *Zheng Chenggong lishi yanjiu* 鄭成功歷史研究, 54–60. Beijing: Jiuzhou chu ban she 九州出版社, 2000.

Chen Kongli 陳孔立. "Zheng Chenggong shou fu Taiwan zhan zheng de fen xi" 鄭成功收復臺灣戰爭的分析. In *Zheng Chenggong yan jiu lun wen xuan* 鄭成功研究論文選, 304–321. Fuzhou: Fujian ren min chu ban she 福建人民出版社, 1982.

Chen Shengkun 陳勝崑. "Zheng Chenggong siyin de tanjiu" 鄭成功死因的探究. In Chen Shengkun, *Yi xue, xin li yu min su* 醫學,心理,與民俗, 52–59. Taipei: Ju jing wen hua shi ye 橘井文化事業, 1982.

Chen Yanyi 陳燕翼. *Si wen da ji* 思文大紀. *Taiwan wen xian cong kan* 臺灣文獻叢刊. No. 111. Taipei: Taiwan yin hang 臺灣銀行, 1961.

Chen Zhiping 陳支平. "Zheng shi shi liao ji bu" 鄭氏史料輯補. In *Zheng Chenggong yan jiu guo ji xue shu hui yi lun wen ji* 鄭成功研究國際學術會議論文集, 370–388. Nanchang 南昌市: Jiangxi ren min chu ban she 江西人民出版社, 1989.

Cheng Kaiyou 程開祐. *Chou liao shuo hua* 籌遼碩畫. Taipei: Tai lian guo feng chu ban she 台聯國風出版社, 1968.

Cheng Shaogang 程紹剛. "De VOC en Formosa, 1624–1662: een vergeten geschiedenis." PhD dissertation, Leiden University, 1995.

Cheng Xunchang 盛巽昌. "Zheng Chenggong de 'kong cheng ji'" 鄭成功的"空城計. *Ke ji wen cui* 科技文萃 6 (1995): 93–94.

Cheng, Pei-Kai, Michael Lestz, and Jonathan Spence, eds. *The Search for Modern China: A Documentary Collection*. New York: W. W. Norton and Company, 1999.

Cipolla, Carlo. *Guns, Sails, and Empires: Technological Innovation and the Early Phases of European Expansion, 1400–1700*. New York: Pantheon Books, 1965.

Clulow, Adam. "From Global Entrepôt to Early Modern Domain: Hirado, 1609–1641." *Monumenta Nipponica* 65, no. 1 (2010): 1–35.

Cockle, Richard. "Oregon Native Faces Death When Oil Tanker Hits Boat," *The Oregonian*. Available at http://www.oregonlive.com/news/index.ssf/2009/04/this_is_it_an_oregon_native_an.html (accessed 29 October 2010).

Colenbrander, H. T., ed. *Dagh-register gehouden int Casteel Batavia vant passerende daer ter plaetse als over geheel Nederlandts-India*. The Hague: Martinus Nijhof, 1898.

Coolhaas, W. Ph., ed. *Generale missiven van gouverneurs-generaal en raden aan Heren XVII der Verenigde Oostindische Compagnie.* The Hague: M. Nijhoff, 1960–1985.

Coyet, Frederick. *Neglected Formosa: A Translation from the Dutch of Frederic Coyett's 't Verwaerloosde Formosa*, ed. and trans. Inez de Beauclair. San Francisco: Chinese Materials Center, Inc., 1975.

———. *'t Verwaerloosde Formosa, of waerachtig verhael, hoedanigh door verwaerloosinge der Nederlanders in Oost-Indien, het Eylant Formosa, van den Chinesen Mandorijn, ende Zeeroover Coxinja, overrompelt, vermeestert, ende ontweldight is geworden*, ed. G. C. Molewijk. Zutphen, Netherlands: Walburg Pers, 1991. (Originally published in 1675.)

Cramer. Matthijs. *Borts voyagie near de kuste van China en Formosa (1662–1664)*. Amsterdam: Pieter Diercksz. Boeteman, 1670.

Crosby, Alfred W. *The Measure of Reality: Quantification and Western Society, 1250–1600*. Cambridge, UK: Cambridge University Press, 1997.

Crozier, Ralph C. *Koxinga and Chinese Nationalism: History, Myth, and the Hero*. Cambridge, MA: Harvard University Press, 1977.

Dapper, Olfert. *Gedenkwaerdig bedryf der Nederlandsche Oost-Indische Maetschappye, op de kuste en in het keizerrijk van Taising of Sina*. Amsterdam: Jacob van Meurs, 1670.

Darwin, John. *After Tamerlane: The Global History of Empire since 1405*. London: Allen Lane, 2007.

De Fu 德福. *Min zheng ling yao* 閩政領要. Beijing: Jiu zhou chu ban she 九州出版社, 2004.

De Korte, J. P. *De Jaarlijkse financiële verantwoording in de VOC*. Leiden, Netherlands: Martinus Nijhoff, 1984.

Deng Kongzhao 鄧孔昭. "Cong Lu Ruoteng shi wen kan you guan Zheng Chenggong shi" 從盧若騰詩文看有關鄭成功史. In Deng Kongzhao, *Zheng Chenggong yu Ming Zheng Taiwan shi yanjiu* 鄭成功與明鄭臺灣史研究, 62–69. Beijing: Tai hai chu ban she 台海出版社, 2000.

———. "Lun Zheng Chenggong dui Zheng Zhilong de pi pan yu ji cheng" 論鄭成功對鄭芝龍的批判與繼承. In Deng Kongzhao, *Zheng Chenggong yu Ming Zheng Taiwan shi yan jiu* 鄭成功與明鄭臺灣史研究, 19–37. Beijing: Tai hai chu ban she 台海出版社, 2000.

———. "Zheng Chenggong shou fu Taiwan de zhan lüe yun chou," 鄭成功收復臺灣的戰略運籌. In Deng Kongzhao, *Zheng Chenggong yu Ming Zheng Taiwan shi yan jiu* 鄭成功與明鄭臺灣史研究, 1–18. Beijing: Tai hai chu ban she 台海出版社, 2000.

———. "Zheng Zhilong de yi sheng" 鄭芝龍的一生. In Deng Kongzhao, *Zheng Chenggong yu Ming Zheng Taiwan shi yan jiu* 鄭成功與明鄭臺灣史研究, 176–184. Beijing: Tai hai chu ban she 台海出版社, 2000.

Deng Shiliang 鄧士亮. *Xin yue xuan gao* 心月軒稿. Beijing: Beijing chu ban she 北京出版社, 1997.

Des Forges, Roger. *Cultural Centrality and Political Change in Chinese History*. Palo Alto, CA: Stanford University Press, 2003.

DeVries, Kelly. "'The Walls Come Tumbling Down': The Myth of Fortification Vulnerability to Early Gunpowder Weapons." In *The Hundred Years War*, eds. L. J. Andrew Villalon and Donald Kagan, 429–446. Leiden: Brill, 2005.

Dewald, Jonathan. *Europe 1450–1789: Encyclopedia of the Early Modern World*. New York: Scribner, 2003.

Diamond, Jared. *Guns, Germs, and Steel: The Fates of Human Societies*. New York: W. W. Norton, 1999.

Dickens, Charles. "Formosa and the Japanese." *Charles Dickens, All the Year Round: A Weekly Journal* 33 (1875): 463–468.

Dong Yingju 董應舉. *Chong xiang ji xuan lu* 崇相集選錄. *Taiwan wen xian cong kan* 臺灣文獻叢刊. No. 237. Taipei: Taiwan yin hang 臺灣銀行, 1967.

Duchesne, Ricardo. "Peer Vries, the Great Divergence, and the California School: Who's In and Who's Out?" *World History Connected* 2, no. 2 (2005). Available online at http://worldhistoryconnected.press.illinois.edu/index.html# (accessed 29 October 2010).

Fernández Navarrete, Domingo. *Tratados historicos, politicos, ethicos, y religiosos de la monarchia de China*. Madrid: En la imprenta real, por J. García Infançon, 1676.

Flynn, Dennis O., and Arturo Giráldez. "Arbitrage, China, and World Trade in the Early Modern Period." *Journal of the Economic and Social History of the Orient* 38, no. 4 (1995): 429–448.

———. "Cycles of Silver: Global Economic Unity through the Mid-Eighteenth Century." *Journal of World History* 13, no. 2 (2002): 391–427.

Frank, Andre Gunder. *ReOrient: Global Economy in the Asian Age*. Berkeley: University of California Press, 1998.

Gaastra, Femme. *The Dutch East India Company: Expansion and Decline*. Zutphen, Netherlands: Walburg Press, 2003.

Gao Zhihua 高致華. "Ri ren guan dian zhong de Zheng Chenggong" 丑人觀點中的將成功. In *Chang gong hai tao lun Yanping: Ji nian Zheng Chenggong qu He fu Tai 340 zhou nian xue shu tao hui wen ji* 長共海濤論延平: 紀念鄭成功驅荷復台340周年學朮研討會論文集, 366–381. Shanghai: Shanghai gu ji chu ban she 上海古籍出版社, 2003.

Giles, Herbert Allen. *A Chinese Biographical Dictionary*. London: Bernard Quaritch, 1898.

Glete, Jan. *Warfare at Sea, 1500–1650: Maritime Conflicts and the Transformation of Europe*. London: Routledge, 2000.

Goldstone, Jack. "Capitalist Origins, the Advent of Modernity, and Coherent Explanation: A Response to Joseph M. Bryant." *Canadian Journal of Sociology* 33, no. 1 (2008): 119–133.

———. "The Rise of the West—or Not? A Revision to Socioeconomic History." *Sociological Theory* 18, no. 2 (2000): 173–194.

Goody, Jack. *Capitalism and Modernity: The Great Debate*. Cambridge, UK: Polity Press, 2004.

Groeneveldt, W. P. *De Nederlanders in China, Eerste Deel: De Eerste Bemoeingen om den Handel in China en de Vestiging in de Pescadores (1601–1624)*. The Hague: Nijhoff, 1898.

Guilmartin, John. *Gunpowder and Galleys: Changing Technology and Mediterranean Warfare at Sea in the 16th Century*. Cambridge, UK: Cambridge University Press, 1974.

Guo Rong 郭荣. "Guo xing Zheng Chenggong shi liao tan tao" 國姓鄭成功史料探討. In *Chang gong hai tao lun Yanping: Ji nian Zheng Chenggong qu He fu Tai 340 zhou nian xue shu tao hui wen ji* 長共海濤論延平: 紀念鄭成功驅荷復台340周年學朮研討會論文集, ed. Yang Guozhen 楊国楨, 280–308. Shanghai: Shanghai gu ji chu ban she 上海古籍出版社, 2003.

Hamel, Hendrik. *Verhaal van het vergaan van het Jacht de Sperwer*, ed. B. Hoetink. Middlesex, UK: Echo Library, 2007.

Han Zhenhua 韓振華. "Zai lun Zheng Chenggong yu hai wai mao yi de guan xi" 再論鄭成功與海外貿易的關係. In *Zheng Chenggong yan jiu tao lun wen xuan xu ji* 鄭成功研究論文選續集, 206–220. Fuzhou: Fujian ren min chu ban she 福建人民出版社, 1984.

Hanson, Victor Davis. *Carnage and Culture: Landmark Battles in the Rise of Western Power*. New York: Doubleday, 2001.

Harthouwer, David. Daghregister gehouden bij den coopman David Harthouwer, op zijn reijze als commissaris van Tayouan naar Quelang ende Tamsuij sedert den 28 September 1661 tot den 6 November daaraanvolgende." Dutch East India Company Collection, National Archive of the Netherlands, The Hague, 1235: 935–975.

Helmers, Jan Frederik. "Lofzang op Anthonius Hambroek." In *Nagelaten gedichten van Jan Frederik Helmers*, vol. 2, 101–112. The Hague: Wed. J. Allart en Comp, 1823.

Herport, Albrecht. *Reise nach Java, Formosa, Vorder-Indien und Ceylon, 1659–1668*, vol. 5, ed. S. P. L'Honoré Naber. The Hague: Martinus Nijhoff, 1930.

Het Woordenboek der Nederlandsche Taal. The Hague, Netherlands: Martinus Nijhoff, 1882–.

Ho, Dahpon. "Sealords Live in Vain: Fujian and the Making of a Maritime Frontier in Seventeenth-Century China." PhD dissertation, University of California, San Diego (2011, expected).

Huang, Martin. *Negotiating Masculinities in Late Imperial China*. Honolulu: University of Hawaii Press, 2006.

Huang Yi-long 黃一農. "Hong yi da pao yu Ming Qing zhan zheng: yi huo pao ce zhun ji shu zhi yan bian wei li" 紅夷大砲與明清戰爭—以火砲測準技術之演變為例. *Qinghua xue bao* 清華學報 26, no. 1 (1996): 31–70.

———. "Ou zhou chen chuan yu Ming mo chuan hua de xi yang da pao" 歐洲沉船與明末傳華的西洋大炮. *Zhong yang yan jiu yuan li shi hua yan yan jiu suo ji kan* 中央研究院歷史語言研究所集刊 75, no. 3 (2004): 573–634.

Huang Zongxi 黃宗羲. *Ci xing shi mo* 賜姓始末. *Taiwan wen xian cong kan* 臺灣文獻叢刊. No. 25. Taipei: Taiwan yin hang 臺灣銀行, 1958.

Huber, Johannes. "Chinese Settlers against the Dutch East India Company: The Rebellion Led by Kuo Huai-I on Taiwan in 1652." In *Development and Decline of Fukien Province in the 17th and 18th Centuries*, ed. E. B. Vermeer, 265–296. Leiden, Netherlands: E. J. Brill, 1990.

Hurt, Melchior, and Jacob Clewerk. "Corte aanteijkening van t geene Melchior Hurdt en Jacob Cleweriq naar de vermaarde stadt Hoksieuw doort landt van China is voorgevallen, 16 October 1661 to 3 November 1661." Dutch East India Company Collection, National Archive of the Netherlands, The Hague, 1235: 959–974. In David Harthouwer, Daghregister gehouden bij den coopman David Harthouwer, op zijn reijze als commissaris van Tayouan naar Quelang ende Tamsuij sedert den 28 September 1661 tot den 6 November daaraanvolgende." Dutch East India Company Collection, National Archive of the Netherlands, The Hague, 1235: 935–975.

Imbault-Huart, Camille. *L'île Formose: histoire et description*. Taipei: Cheng wen Publishing Co., 1968. (Originally published in 1893.)

Iwao, Seiichi. "Li Tan, Chief of the Chinese Residents at Hirado, Japan, in the Last Days of the Ming Dynasty." *Memoirs of the Research Department of the Toyo Bunko* 17 (1958): 27–83.

Ji Liuqi 計六奇. *Ming ji nan lüe* 明季南略. *Taiwan wen xian cong kan* 臺灣文獻叢刊. No. 148. Taipei: Taiwan yin hang 臺灣銀行, 1963.

Jiang Risheng 江日昇. *Taiwan wai ji* 臺灣外記. *Taiwan wen xian cong kan* 臺灣文獻叢刊. No. 60. Taipei: Taiwan yin hang 臺灣銀行, 1960.

Jiang Shusheng 江樹生, ed. and trans. *Mei shi ri ji: Helan tudi celiangshi kan Zheng Chenggong* 梅氏日記荷蘭土地測量師看鄭成功. Taipei: Han sheng za zhi she gu fen you xian gong si 漢聲雜誌社股份有限公司, 2003.

Jiang Shusheng 江樹生. "VOC zai Taiwan de zhang gùan gong shu" VOC 在臺灣的長官公署. In *Di guo xiang jie zhi jie: Xi ban ya shi qi Taiwan xiang guan wen xian ji tu xiang lun wen ji* 帝國相接之界—西班牙時期臺灣相關文獻及圖像論文集, ed. Lü Li Zheng 呂理政, 33–55. Taipei: SMC Publishing, Inc., 2003.

Jiang Shusheng 江樹生. *Zheng Chenggong he Helanren zai Taiwan de zui hou yi zhan ji huan wen di he* 鄭成功和荷蘭人在臺灣的最後一戰及換文締和. Taipei: Han sheng za zhi she 漢聲雜誌社, 2003.

Jong, Michiel de. *Staat van Oorlog: Wapenbedrijf en militaire hervorming in de Republiek der Verenigde Nederlanden, 1585–1621*. Hilversum, Netherlands: Uitgeverij Verloren, 2005.

Kalff, Samuel. "De Val van Formosa." *De Gids* 61 (1897): 104–138.

Kawaguchi Choju 川口長孺. *Taiwan ge ju zhi* 臺灣割據志. *Taiwan wen xian cong kan* 臺灣文獻叢刊. No. 1. Taipei: Taiwan yin hang 臺灣銀行, 1957.

———. *Taiwan Teishi ki ji* 臺灣鄭氏紀事. *Taiwan wen xian cong kan* 臺灣文獻叢刊. No. 5. Taipei: Taiwan yin hang 臺灣銀行, 1958.

Keene, Donald. *The Battles of Coxinga*. London: Taylor's Foreign Press, 1951.

Keith, Matthew. "The Logistics of Power: Tokugawa Response to the Shimabara Rebellion and Power Projection in Seventeenth-Century Japan." PhD dissertation, The Ohio State University, 2006.

Keliher, Macabe. *Small Sea Travel Diaries: Yu Yonghe's Records of Taiwan*. Taipei: SMC Publishing, 2004.

"Kort en bondigh verhael, van 't gene op het schoone Eylandt Formosa midtsgaders op het bij gelegen Eijlandt Tyawan en 't Fort Zeelandia, op den vijvden Julij 1661 is voorgevallen, midtsgaeders de overgevingh van 't gemelde fort aen de Chinesen." In *Oost-Indisch Praetgen, voorgevallen in Batavia, tusschen vier Nederlanders den eenen een koopman, d'ander een krijghs-officier, den derden een stuyrman, en den vierden of den laetsten een krankebesoecker*. Batavia, 1663.

Landes, David. "Why Europe and the West? Why Not China?" *The Journal of Economic Perspectives* 20, no. 2 (2006): 3–22.

Le Monnier, A. F. "Eine vergessene holländische Colonie." *Revue coloniale international* 1 (1885): 345–359.

Li Guohong 李國宏. "Xin jin chu xian de Zheng Chenggong shi liao bian xi" 新近出現的鄭成功史料辨析. In *Chang gong hai tao lun Yanping: Ji nian Zheng Chenggong qu He fu Tai 340 zhou nian xue shu tao lun hui wen ji* 長共海濤論延平: 紀念鄭成功驅荷復台340周年學術研討會論文集, ed. Yang Guozhen 楊國楨, 319–333. Shanghai: Shanghai gu ji chu ban she 上海古籍出版社, 2003.

Li Tengyue 李騰嶽, "Zheng Chenggong de si yin kao" 鄭成功的死因攷. *Wen xian zhuan kan* 文獻專刊 1, no. 3 (1950): 35–44.

Liao Hanchen 廖漢臣. "Yan ping wang bei zheng kao ping" 延平王北征考評. In *Taiwan Zheng Chenggong yan jiu lun wen xuan* 臺灣鄭成功研究論文選, 85–108. Fuzhou: Fujian ren min chu ban she 福建人民出版社, 1982.

———. "Yan ping wang bei zheng kao ping" 延平王北征考評. *Taiwan wen xian* 臺灣文獻 12, no. 2 (1964): 47–74.

Lin, Ren-Chuan. "Fukien's Private Sea Trade in the Sixteenth and Seventeenth Centuries." In *Development and Decline of Fukien Province in the Seventeenth and Eighteenth Centuries*, ed. E. B. Vermeer, 163–216. Leiden, Netherlands: E. J. Brill, 1990.

Lin Shidui 林時對. *He cha cong tan* 荷牐叢談. *Taiwan wen xian cong kan* 臺灣文獻叢刊. No. 153. Taipei: Taiwan yin hang 臺灣銀行, 1962.

Liu, James. *The Chinese Knight Errant*. London: Routledge and Paul, 1967.

Liu Xianting 劉獻廷. *Guang yang za ji xuan* 廣陽雜記選. *Taiwan wen xian cong kan* 臺灣文獻叢刊. No. 219. Taipei: Taiwan yin hang 臺灣銀行, 1965.

Liu, Zhen. *Dong guan Han ji* 東觀漢記. Jinan: Qi Lu shu she 齊魯書社, 2000.

Liuqi 計六奇. *Ming ji nan lüe* 明季南略. *Taiwan wen xian cong kan* 臺灣文獻叢刊. No. 148. Taipei: Taiwan yin hang 臺灣銀行, 1963.

Lorge, Peter A. *The Asian Military Revolution: From Gunpowder to the Bomb*. Cambridge, UK: Cambridge University Press, 2008.

Lu Jianrong 盧建榮. *Ru qin Taiwan: feng huo jia guo si bai nian*入侵臺灣 烽火家國四百年. Taipei: Mai tian chu ban she 麥田出版社, 1999.

Lu Qi 陸圻. *Xian yan* 纖言. Shanghai: Shanghai shu dian 上海書店, 1994. Available online at http://zh.wikisource.org/zh-tw/%E7%BA%96%E8%A8%80 (accessed 29 October 2010).

Lü Rongfang 呂榮芳 and Ye Wencheng 葉文程. "Zheng Chenggong zai Xiamen de jun zheng jian she" 鄭成功在廈門的軍政建設. In *Zheng Chenggong yan jiu tao lun wen xuan xu ji* 鄭成功研究論文選續集, 148–160. Fuzhou: Fujian ren min chu ban she 福建人民出版社, 1984.

Lu Ruoteng 盧若騰. *Dao yi shi* 島噫詩. *Taiwan wen xian cong kan* 臺灣文獻叢刊. No. 245. Taipei: Taiwan yin hang 臺灣銀行, 1968.

Lynn, John. *Battle: A History of Combat and Culture*. New York: Basic Books, 2008.

———. "The Trace Italienne and the Growth of Armies: The French Case." In *The Military Revolution Debate*, ed. Clifford J. Rogers, 169–199. Colorado: Westview Press, 1995.

Maddison, Angus. *The World Economy: Historical Statistics*. Paris: Development Centre of the Organization for Economic Cooperation and Development, 2003.

Magisa, Raymundo. *Svcceso raro de tres volcanes, dos de fvego, y vno de agva, qve rebentaron a 4 de Enero deste año de 641 a un mismo tiempo en diferentes partes estruendo por los ayres como de artillería, y mosqueteria*. Manila, 1641 (copy held in the National Library of Spain).

Manthorpe, Jonathan. *Forbidden Nation: A History of Taiwan*. New York: Macmillan, 2008.

Mao Yibo 毛一波. *Nan Ming shi tan* 南明史談. Taipei: Taiwan Shang wu yin shu guan 臺灣商務印館, 1970.

Marks, Robert. "China's Population Size during the Ming and Qing: A Comment on the Mote Revision." Paper delivered at the 2002 Annual Meeting of the Association for Asian Studies, Washington, DC. Available online at http://web.whittier.edu/people/webpages/personalwebpages/rmarks/PDF/Env._panel_remarks.pdf (accessed 29 October 2010).

Marmé, Michael. "Locating Linkages or Painting Bull's-Eyes around Bullet Holes? An East Asian Perspective on the Seventeenth-Century Crisis." *American Historical Review* 113, no. 4 (2008): 1080–1089.

Marshall, P. J. "Western Arms in Maritime Asia in the Early Phases of Expansion." *Modern Asia Studies* 14, no. 1 (1980): 13–28.

McNeill, William H. *The Age of Gunpowder Empires, 1450–1800*. Washington, DC: American Historical Association, 1989.

———. *The Pursuit of Power: Technology, Armed Force, and Society since AD 1000*. Chicago: University of Chicago Press, 1982.

Meij, Philip. "'t Naervolgende sijnde 'tgeene per memorie onthouden van't gepasseerde in't geweldigh overvallen des Chinesen Mandorijns Cocxinja op Formosa en geduijrende ons gevanckenis." Dutch East India Company Collection, National Archive of the Netherlands, The Hague, 1238: 848–914.

Ming shi lu Min hai guan xi shi liao 明實錄閩海關係史料. *Taiwan wen xian cong kan* 臺灣文獻叢刊. No. 296. Taipei: Taiwan yin hang 臺灣銀行, 1971.

Moens, Petronella. "Edele zelfopoffering van Antonius Hambroek." In *Tafereelen uit de Nederlandsche geschiedenis, dichterlijk geschetst voor de jeugd*, ed. Petronella Moens. Haarlem: François Boon, 1823. Available online at http://www.let.leidenuniv.nl/Dutch/Ceneton/HambroekMoens.html (accessed 29 October 2010).

Mokyr, Joel. The *Enlightened Economy: An Economic History of Britain, 1700–1859*. New Haven, CT, and London: Yale University Press, 2009.

Monsterrol van het jacht Broeckerhaven van alle de officieren, matrosen, en soldaten op 20en October 1633 op de custe van China in Erasmus Baij door de vloote van Iquan ondergebracht ende verdistrueert. Dutch East India Company Collection, National Archive of the Netherlands, The Hague, 1113: 769.

Monsterrol van het jacht Sloterdijck van alle de officieren, matrosen, en soldaten op 20en October 1633 op de custe van China in Erasmus Baij door de vloote van Iquan verovert. Dutch East India Company Collection, National Archive of the Netherlands, The Hague, 1113: 768.

Chikamatsu Monzaemon. "The Battles of Koxinga" 國姓爺合戰. In *The Four Major Plays of Chikamatsu,* ed. and trans. Donald Keene, 57–139. New York: Columbia University Press, 1998.

Mostert, Tristan. "Chain of Command: Military System of the Dutch East India Company, 1655–1663." Master's thesis, Leiden University, 2007.

Mote, F. W. "The Transformation of Nanking, 1350–1400." In *The City in Late Imperial China*, ed. G. William Skinner, 101–154. Stanford, CA: Stanford University Press, 1977.

Nan Qi 南棲. "Taiwan Zheng shi wu shang zhi yan jiu" 臺灣鄭氏五商之研究. In *Taiwan Zheng Chenggong yan jiu lun wen xuan* 臺灣鄭成功研究論文選, 194–208. Fuzhou: Fujian ren min chu ban she 福建人民出版社, 1982.

Nederlandsche Oost-Indische Compagnie. *Uytrekening van de Goude en Silvere Munts Waardye, inhout der maten en swaarte de gewigten van Indien*. Middelburg: Johannes Meertens, Drucher van de Ed. Geoctroyeerde Oost-Indische Compagnie, 1691. Dutch East India Company Collection, National Archive of the Netherlands, The Hague, 11207.

Needham, Joseph. *Science and Civilisation in China.* 7 vols. Cambridge, UK: Cambridge University Press, 1954–.

Newitt, Malyn. *A History of Portuguese Overseas Expansion, 1400–1668.* London: Routledge, 2005.

Ng, Chin-Keong. "The South Fukienese Junk Trade at Amoy from the Seventeenth to Early Nineteenth Centuries." In *Development and Decline of Fukien Province in the Seventeenth and Eighteenth Centuries*, ed. E. B. Vermee, 297–316. Leiden: E. K. Brill, 1990.

———. *Trade and Society: The Amoy Network on the China Coast, 1683–1735.* Singapore: Singapore University Press, 1983.

Nomsz, Joannes. *Anthonius Hambroek of de belegering van Formoza, Treurspel.* Amsterdam: Izaak Duim, 1775. Available online at http://

www.let.leidenuniv.nl/Dutch/Ceneton/NomszHambroek1775.html (accessed 29 October 2010).

Ostwald, Jamel. *Vauban under Siege: Engineering Efficiency and Martial Vigor in the War of Spanish Succession.* Leiden, Netherlands, and Boston: Brill, 2007.

Palafox y Mendoza, Juan de. *The History of the Conquest of China by the Tartars.* London: W. Godbid, 1671.

Parker, Geoffrey. "The Artillery Fortress as an Engine of European Overseas Expansion, 1480–1750." In *City Walls: The Urban Enceinte in Global Perspective*, ed. James D. Tracy, 386–416. Cambridge, UK: Cambridge University Press, 2000.

———. *Cambridge Illustrated History of Warfare.* Cambridge, UK: Cambridge University Press, 1995.

———. "Crisis and Catastrophe: The Global Crisis of the Seventeenth Century Reconsidered." *American Historical Review* 113, no. 4 (2008): 1053–1079.

———. *The Global Crisis of the Seventeenth Century.* Draft manuscript being prepared for Yale University Press.

———. *The Military Revolution: Military Innovation and the Rise of the West, 1500–1800.* New York: Cambridge University Press, 1996.

———. "Military Revolutions, Past and Present." In *Recent Themes in Military History: Historians in Conversation*, 11–21. Columbia: University of South Carolina Press, 2008.

Parthesius, Robert. *Dutch Ships in Tropical Waters: The Development of the Dutch East India Company (VOC) Shipping Network in Asia, 1595–1660.* Amsterdam: Amsterdam University Press, 2010.

Pearson, Michael. *The Indian Ocean.* London: Routledge, 2003.

Peng Sunyi 彭孫貽. *Jing hai zhi* 靖海志. *Taiwan wen xian cong kan* 臺灣文獻叢刊. No. 35. Taipei: Taiwan yin hang 臺灣銀行, 1959.

Platt, Brian. "The Chinese Sail." Available at http://www.thecheappages.com/junk/platt/platt_chinese_sail.html (accessed 24 October 2010).

Pomeranz, Kenneth. *The Great Divergence: China, Europe, and the Making of the Modern World Economy.* Princeton, NJ: Princeton University Press, 2000.

Pryor, John H. *Geography, Technology, and War: Studies in the Maritime History of the Mediterranean, 649–1571*. Cambridge, UK: Cambridge University Press, 1988.

Ran Fuli 冉福立 (aka Kees Zandvliet). *Shi qi shi ji Helan ren hui zhi de Taiwan lao di tu* 十七世紀荷蘭人繪製的臺灣老地圖, 2 vols., trans. Jiang Shusheng 江樹生. Taipei: Ying wen Han sheng chu ban you xian gongsi 英文漢聲出版有限公司, 1997.

Resolutions of the Council of Formosa. 11 March to 31 July 1661. "Resolutien des Casteels Zeelandia, sedert 11 Maert tot 31 Julij 1661." Dutch East India Company Collection, National Archive of the Netherlands, The Hague, 1235: 331–416.

———. 1 August 1661 to 14 February 1662. "Tayouanse resolutien, beginnende primo Augustij anno 1661 ende eindigende 14 februarij 1662." Dutch East India Company Collection, National Archive of the Netherlands, The Hague, 1238: 519–621.

Riccio, Victorio. "Hechos de la Orden de Predicadores en el Imperio de China." In *Spaniards in Taiwan*, vol. 2, ed. José Eugenio Borao, 586–627. Taipei: SMC Publishing, Inc., 2002.

Ringrose, David. *Expansion and Global Interaction, 1200–1700*. New York: Longman, 2001.

Roos, M. J. "The Amalgamation of Church and State in a Formula for Colonial Rule: Clergymen in the Dutch Administration of Formosa, 1627–1651." Master's thesis (Doctoraal Scriptie Geschiedenis), Leiden University, 2000.

Rougemont, François de. *Historia Tartaro-Sinica nova*. Lovanii: Typis Martini Hullegaerde, 1673.

Ruan Minxi 阮旻錫. *Hai shang jian wen lu* 海上見聞錄. *Taiwan wen xian cong kan* 臺灣文獻叢刊. No. 24. Taipei: Taiwan yin hang 臺灣銀行, 1958.

Schouten, Wouter. *De Oost-Indische voyagie van Wouter Schouten*, eds. Michael Breet and Marijke Barend-van Haeften. Zutphen, Netherlands: Walburg, 2003.

Seed, Patricia. "Jewish Scientists and the Origin of Modern Navigation," In *The Jews and the Expansion of Europe to the West, 1450 to 1800*, eds. Paolo Bernardini and Norman Fiering. New York: Berghahn Books, 2001.

Senger, Harro von. *The Book of Stratagems: Tactics for Triumph and Survival.* New York: Penguin, 1993.

Shen Yun 沈雲. *Taiwan Zheng shi shi mo* 臺灣鄭氏始末. *Taiwan wen xian cong kan* 臺灣文獻叢刊. No. 15. Taipei: Taiwan yin hang 臺灣銀行, 1958.

Song Zhengyu 宋征輿. "Zheng Chenggong zhuan" 鄭成功傳, from the *Dong cun ji shi* 東村紀事, printed in Chen Zhiping 陳支平, "Zheng shi shi liao ji bu" 鄭氏史料輯補. In *Zheng Chenggong yan jiu guo ji xue shu hui yi lun wen ji* 鄭成功研究國際學術會議論文集, 370–388. Nanchang 南昌市: Jiangxi ren min chu ban she 江西人民出版社, 1989.

Spence, Jonathan. *The Search for Modern China*. New York: Norton, 1999.

Struve, Lynn. *The Southern Ming, 1644–1662*. New Haven. CT: Yale University Press, 1984.

———. *Voices from the Ming-Qing Cataclysm: China in Tigers' Jaws*. New Haven, CT: Yale University Press, 1993.

Su Tongbing 穌同炳. *Taiwan shi yanjiu ji* 臺灣史研究集. Taipei: Guo li bian yi guan Zhong hua cong shu bian shen wei yuan hui 國立編譯館中華叢書編審委員會, 1980.

Subrahmanyam, Sanjay. "Of Imârat and Tijârat: Asian Merchants and State Power in the Western Indian Ocean, 1400 to 1750." *Comparative Studies in Society and History* 37, no. 4 (1995): 750–780.

Subrahmanyam, Sanjay, and Geoffrey Parker. "Arms and the Asian: Revisiting European Firearms and Their Place in Early Modern Asia." *Revista de Cultura* 26 (2008): 12–42.

Sun Laichen. "Military Technology Transfers from Ming China and the Emergence of Northern Mainland Southeast Asia (c. 1390–1527)." *Journal of Southeast Asia Studies* 34, no. 3 (2003): 495–517.

———. "Ming-Southeast Asian Overland Interactions, 1368–1644." PhD dissertation, University of Michigan, 2000.

Sun Zi 孫子. *Sun Tzu's The Art of War Sun Zi Bing fa bai ze* 孫子兵法百則. Hong Kong: Shang wu yin shu guan you xian gong si 商務印書管有限公司, 1994.

Swope, Kenneth. "Crouching Tigers, Secret Weapons: Military Technology Employed during the Sino-Japanese-Korean War, 1592–1598." *The Journal of Military History* 69, no. 1 (2005): 11–41.

———. *A Dragon's Head and a Serpent's Tail: Ming China and the First Great East Asian War, 1592–1598*. Norman: University of Oklahoma Press, 2009.

Taiwan wen xian cong kan 臺灣文獻叢刊. 309 vols. Taipei: Taiwan yin hang, Zhong hua shu ju jing shuo 臺灣銀行, 中華書局經售, 1957–1972.

Tang Jintai 湯錦台. *Kai qi Taiwan di yi ren Zheng Zhilong* 開啟臺灣第一人鄭芝龍. Taipei: Guoshi 果實 Press, 2002.

Tang Yunxuan, 湯韻旋. *Zheng Chenggong shou fu Taiwan* 鄭成功收服臺灣. Fuzhou: Fujian jiao yu chu ban she 福建教育出版社, 2007.

Teng, Emma Jinhua. *Taiwan's Imagined Geography: Chinese Colonial Travel Writing and Pictures, 1683–1895*. Cambridge, MA: Harvard University Press, 2004.

Thornton, John. *Africa and Africans in the Making of the Atlantic World*. Cambridge, UK: Cambridge University Press, 1998.

Tilly, Charles. *Coercion, Capital, and European States, AD 990–1992*. Cambridge, UK: Blackwell, 1992.

Valentijn, François. *Oud en Nieuw Oost-Indiën : vervattende een naaukeurige en uitvoerige verhandelinge van Nederlands mogentheyd in die gewesten, etc.*, vol. 4/A. Franeker, Netherlands: Van Wijnen, 2002. (Originally published in 1724–1726.)

Verburg, Nicholas. "Cort vertooch ende relaas betreffende den stant ende gelegentheijt des eijlants Formosa, hoedanich de generale Nederlantse Oostjndische Comp. het besit vandien met de meeste gerustheijt ende het grootse voordeel gaudeeren can, mitsgaders eenige aenmerckelijcke consideratien over de goede regeeringen desselfs, ende op wat wijse die emportante gouverno wijder in een gewenschte postuijre can werden gebracht ende geconserveert, 10 March 1654." Dutch East India Company Collection, National Archive of the Netherlands, The Hague, 1206: 220–261.

VOC Glossarium: verklaringen van termen, verzameld uit de rijks geschiedkundige publicatiën die betrekking hebben op de Verenigde Oost-indische Compagnie. The Hague: Instituut voor Nederlandse Geschiedenis, 2000.

Vogels, J. L. P. J. "Het nieuwe Tayouan: de Verenigde Oostindische Compagnie op Kelang, 1664–1668." Master's thesis, University of Utrecht, 1988.

Vries, Peer. "Is California the Measure of All Things Global? A Rejoinder to Ricardo Duchesne, 'Peer Vries, the Great Divergence, and the California School: Who's In and Who's Out?'" *World History Connected* 2, no. 2 (2005). Available online at http://worldhistoryconnected.press.illinois.edu/index.html# (accessed 29 October 2010).

Wakeman, Frederick. "Romantics, Stoics, and Martyrs in Seventeenth Century China." *The Journal of Asian Studies* 43, no. 4 (1984): 631–665.

Wan, Margaret. *Green Peony and the Rise of the Chinese Martial Arts Novel*. Albany: SUNY Press, 2009.

Wang Gungwu. "Merchants without Empire: The Hokkien Sojourning Communities." In *The Rise of Merchant Empires: Long-Distance Trade in the Early Modern World, 1350–1750*, ed. James D. Tracy, 400–421. Cambridge, UK: Cambridge University Press, 1990.

Wang Zhongxiao. *Wang zhong xiao gong ji* 王忠孝公集 Nanjing Shi: Jiangsu gu ji chu ban she 江蘇古籍出版社, 2000.

Wills, Jack. *Mountain of Fame: Portraits in Chinese History*. Princeton, NJ: Princeton University Press, 1994.

———. "Relations with Maritime Europeans, 1514–1662." *Cambridge History of China*, vol. 8, part 2, eds. Denis Twitchett and Frederick W. Mote, 333–375. Cambridge, UK, and New York: Cambridge University Press, 1998.

Wills, John E., Jr. "Maritime Asia, 1500–1800: The Interactive Emergence of European Domination." *American Historical Review* 98, no. 1 (1993): 83–105.

———. *Pepper, Guns, and Parleys: The Dutch East India Company and China, 1622–1681*. Cambridge, MA: Harvard University Press, 1974.

———. "Was There a Vasco da Gama Epoch? Recent Historiography." In *Vasco da Gama and the Linking of Europe and Asia*, eds. Anthony Disney and Emily Booth, 350–360. New Delhi: Oxford University Press, 2000.

Wintergerst, Martin. *Reisen auf dem mittelländischen Meere, der Nordsee, nach Ceylon und nach Java, 1688–1710*, 2 parts, vols. 12 and 13 of *Reisebeschreibungen von deutschen Beamte und Kriegsleuten im Dienst der Niederländischen west- und ost-Indischen Kompagnien, 1602–1797*, ed. S. P. L'Honoré Naber, 13 vols. The Hague: Martinus Nijhoff, 1932.

Wong, Edward. "Chinese Military Seeks to Extend Its Naval Power." *New York Times*, 23 April 2010. Available at http://www.nytimes.com/2010/04/24/world/asia/24navy.html (accessed 6 February 2011).

Wong, R. Bin. *China Transformed: Historical Change and the Limits of European Experience*. Ithaca, NY: Cornell University Press, 1997.

Wu Mei 吳玫. "Lun Huang Wu xiang Qing" 論黃梧降清. In *Zheng Chenggong yan jiu guo ji xue shu hui yi lun wen ji* 鄭成功研究國際學術會議論文集, 182–199. Nanchang 南昌市: Jiangxi ren min chu ban she 江西人民出版社, 1989.

Wu Qiyan 吳奇衍 and Huang Wu 黃武. "Lüe shu Zheng shi zai Taiwan de tun ken" 略述鄭氏在臺灣的屯墾. In *Zheng Chenggong yan jiu tao lun wen xuan xu ji* 鄭成功研究論文選續集, 236–250. Fuzhou: Fujian ren min chu ban she 福建人民出版社, 1984.

Wu Weiye 吳偉業. *Lu qiao ji wen* 鹿樵紀聞. *Taiwan wen xian cong kan* 臺灣文獻叢刊. No. 127. Taipei: Taiwan yin hang 臺灣銀行, 1961.

Wu Zhenglong 吳正龍. *Zheng Chenggong yu Qing zheng fu jian de tan pan* 鄭成功與清政府間的談判. Taipei: Wenjin Publishing Company 文津出版社, 2000.

Xia Lin 夏琳. *Hai ji ji yao* 海紀輯要. *Taiwan wen xian cong kan* 臺灣文獻叢刊. No. 22. Taipei: Taiwan yin hang 臺灣銀行, 1958.

———. *Min hai ji yao* 閩海紀要. *Taiwan wen xian cong kan* 臺灣文獻叢刊. No. 11. Taipei: Taiwan yin hang 臺灣銀行, 1958.

Xia Ming 夏明. "Riben faxian Zheng Chenggong shou shu" 日本發現鄭成功手書. *Ke ji wen cui* 科技文萃 6 (1995): 95.

Xiamen University. *Zheng Chenggong shou fu Taiwan shi liao xuan bian* 鄭成功收復臺灣史料選編. Fuzhou: Fujian ren min chu ban she 福建人民出版社, 1982.

Xie Jinluan 謝金鑾. *Xu xiu Taiwan xian zhi* 續修臺灣縣志. *Taiwan wen xian cong kan* 臺灣文獻叢刊. No. 140. Taipei: Taiwan yin hang 臺灣銀行, 1962.

Xin jiao ben Ming shi 新校本明史. *Han ji quan wen zi liao ku* 漢籍全文資料庫 ("Database of the Full Text of the Twenty-five Dynastic Histories"). Taipei: Institute of History and Philology, Academia Sinica 中央研究院歷史語言研究所, 1990–. Available online at http://hanji.sinica.edu.tw/index.html (accessed 29 October 2010).

Xing Hang. "Between Trade and Legitimacy, Maritime and Continent: The Zheng Organization in Seventeenth-Century East Asia." PhD dissertation, University of California Berkeley, 2010.

Yang Jinlin 楊錦麟. "Lun Zheng Chenggong yu nan Ming zong shi de guan xi" 論鄭成功與南明宗室的關係. In *Zheng Chenggong yan jiu tao lun wen xuan xu ji* 鄭成功研究論文選續集, ed. Zheng Chenggong yan jiu xue shu tao lun hui xue shu zu 鄭成功研究學術討論會學術組, 290–302. Fuzhou: Fujian ren min chu ban she 福建人民出版社, 1984.

Yang Xuxian 楊緒賢. "Zheng Zhilong yu Helan zhi guan xi" 鄭芝龍與荷蘭之關係. In *Zheng Chenggong yan jiu guo ji xue shu hui yi lun wen ji* 鄭成功研究國際學術會議論文集, 293–313. Nanchang 南昌市: Jiangxi ren min chu ban she 江西人民出版社, 1989.

Yang Yanjie 楊彥杰. *He ju shi dai Taiwan shi* 荷據時臺灣史. Taipei: Lian jing 聯經 Press, 2000.

———. "Yi liu wu ling zhi yi liu liu er nian Zheng Chenggong hai wai mao yi de mao yi e he li run e gu suan" 一六五〇至一六六二年鄭成功海外貿易的貿易額和利潤額估算. In Taiwan *Zheng Chenggong yan jiu lun wen xuan* 臺灣鄭成功研究論文選, 221–235. Fuzhou: Fujian ren min chu ban she 福建人民出版社, 1982.

Yang Ying 楊英. *Cong zheng shi lu* 從征實錄. *Taiwan wen xian cong kan* 臺灣文獻叢刊. No. 32. Taipei: Taiwan yin hang 臺灣銀行, 1958.

———. *Xianwang shilu* 先王實錄, ed. Chen Bisheng 陳碧笙. Fuzhou: Fujian ren min chu ban she 福建人民出版社, 1981.

Yerxa, Donald A. "The Curious State of Military History." In *Recent Themes in Military History: Historians in Conversation*, ed. Donald Yerxa, 1–7. Columbia: University of South Carolina Press, 2008.

Yim, Lawrence C. H. *The Poet-Historian Qian Qianyi*. London: Routledge, 2009.

Young-tsu Wong. "Security and Warfare on the China Coast: The Taiwan Question in the Seventeenth Century." *Monumenta Serica* 35 (1981–83): 111–196.

Yu Yonghe 郁永河. *Pi hai ji you* 裨海紀遊. *Taiwan wen xian cong kan* 臺灣文獻叢刊. No. 44. Taipei: Taiwan yin hang 臺灣銀行, 1959.

Zandvliet, Kees. "Art and Cartography in the VOC Governor's House in Taiwan." In *Mappae Antiquae: Liber Amicorum Günter Schilder*, eds. Paula van Gestel-van het Schip and Peter van der Krogt,

579–594. ‘t Goy-Houten, Netherlands: Hes & de Graaf Publishers, 1997.

———. “The Contribution of Cartography to the Creation of a Dutch Colony and a Chinese State in Taiwan.” *Cartographica* 35, no. 3/4 (1998): 123–135.

———. *De 250 rijksten van de Gouden Eeuw: Kapitaal, macht, familie en levensstijl*. Amsterdam: Rijksmuseum Press, 2006.

———*Mapping for Money: Maps, Plans, and Topographic Paintings and Their Role in Dutch Overseas Expansion during the 16th and 17th Centuries*. Amsterdam: Batavian Lion International, 1998.

———. “Vestingbouw in de Oost.” In *De Verenigde Oost-Indische Compagnie: Tussen oorlog en diplomatie*, eds. Gerrit Knaap and Ger Teitler, 151–180. Leiden, Netherlands: KITLV Press, 2002.

Zantvliet, Kees, ed. *The Dutch Encounter with Asia: 1600–1950*. Zwolle, Netherlands: Waanders Publishers, 2002.

Zhang Huangyan 張煌言. “Bei zheng de shi ji lüe” 北征得失紀略. In *Zhang Cangshui shi wen ji* 張蒼水詩文集, pp. 1-13. *Taiwan wen xian cong kan* 臺灣文獻叢刊. No. 142. Taipei: Taiwan yin hang 臺灣銀行, 1962.

Zhang Linbai 張遴白. “Ping guo gong Zheng Zhilong zhuan” 平國公鄭芝龍傳. In *Nan you lu* 難游錄, in Chen Zhiping 陳支平, “Zheng shi shi liao ji bu” 鄭氏史料輯補, in *Zheng Chenggong yan jiu guo ji xue shu hui yi lun wen ji* 鄭成功研究國際學術會議論文集, 370–388. Nanchang 南昌市: Jiangxi ren min chu ban she 江西人民出版社, 1989.

Zhang Yun 張云 and Sun Zhaojun 孫兆軍. “Zhongguo chuan tong bing xue yu Zheng Chenggong dong zheng Taiwan zhi yi” 中國傳統兵學與鄭成功東征臺灣之役. In *Junshi lishi yanjiu* 軍事歷史研究 1 (2002): 17–27.

Zhang Zongqia 張宗洽. “Zheng Chenggong jia shi zi liao ‘Zheng shi zong pu’ he ‘Zheng shi jia pu’ de xin fa xian” 鄭成功家世資料’鄭氏宗譜’和’鄭氏家譜’的新發現. In Zhang Zongqia, *Zheng Chenggong cong tan* 鄭成功叢談, 138–149. Xiamen: Xiamen da xue chu ban she 廈門大學出版社, 1993.

———. “Zheng Chenggong shou fu Taiwan ji” 鄭成功收復臺灣記. In Zhang Zongqia, *Zheng Chenggong cong tan* 鄭成功叢談, 15–42. Xiamen: Xiamen da xue chu ban she 廈門大學出版社, 1993.

———. "Zheng Chenggong zai xiamen de shi ji" 鄭成功在廈門的史跡. In Zhang Zongqia, *Zheng Chenggong cong tan* 鄭成功叢談, 175–180. Xiamen: Xiamen da xue chu ban she 廈門大學出版社, 1993.

———. "Zheng shi wen wu shi ji za kao" 鄭氏文物史跡雜考. In Zhang Zongqia, *Zheng Chenggong cong tan* 鄭成功叢談, 206–212. Xiamen: Xiamen da xue chu ban she 廈門大學出版社, 1993.

Zheng Dayu 鄭大鬱. *Jing guo xiong lüe* 經國雄略. Woodblock Print, 1646. Copy in Harvard Yenching Library.

———. *Jing guo xiong lüe* 經國雄略, facsimile edition, *Mei guo Ha fo Da xue Ha fo Yan jing Tu shu guan cang Zhongwen shan ben cong kan* 美國哈佛大學哈佛燕京圖書館藏中文善本叢刊, vols. 19 and 20. Cuilin, China: Guangxi Normal University Press 廣西師範大學出版社, 2009.

Zheng shi shiliao chu bian 鄭氏史料初編. *Taiwan wen xian cong kan* 臺灣文獻叢刊. No. 157. Taipei: Taiwan yin hang 臺灣銀行, 1962.

Zheng Yizou 鄭亦鄒. *Zheng Chenggong zhuan* 鄭成功傳. In *Zheng Chenggong zhuan* 鄭成功傳, 1–40. In *Taiwan wen xian cong kan* 臺灣文獻叢刊. No. 67. Taipei: Taiwan yin hang 臺灣銀行, 1960.

Zheng Zhilong. "Report to Zou Weilian, Chongzhen 6, 9th month, 22nd day (24 October 1633). In Zou Weilian 鄒維璉, "Feng jiao Hong yi jie shu" 奉剿紅夷捷疏. Excerpted in Su Tongbing 穌同炳, *Taiwan shi yanjiu ji* 臺灣史研究集, 34–64. Taipei: Guo li bian yi guan Zhong hua cong shu bian shen wei yuan hui 國立編譯館中華叢書編審委員會, 1980.

Zhou Kai 周凱. *Xiamen zhi* 廈門志. *Taiwan wen xian cong kan* 臺灣文獻叢刊. No. 95. Taipei: Taiwan yin hang 臺灣銀行, 1961.

Zou Weilian 鄒維璉. *Da guan lou ji* 達觀樓集. Jinan: Qi Lu shu she chu ban she 齊魯書社出版社, 1997.

———. "Feng jiao Hong yi jie shu" 奉剿紅夷捷疏. Excerpted in Su Tongbing 穌同炳, *Taiwan shi yanjiu ji* 臺灣史研究集, 34–64. Taipei: Guo li bian yi guan Zhong hua cong shu bian shen wei yuan hui 國立編譯館中華叢書編審委員會, 1980.

Zurndorfer, Harriet. "What Is the Meaning of 'War' in an Age of Cultural Efflorescence? Another Look at the Role of War in Song Dynasty China (960–1279)." In *War in Words: Transformations of War from Antiquity to Clausewitz*, ed. Marco Formisano. Berlin: Gruyter Verlag, 2010.

Index

Note: Page numbers in italic type indicate illustrations.